SOCIAL DOMESTIC

and

PLEASURE

To Ian
with best wishes

Derrick

SOCIAL DOMESTIC

and

PLEASURE

Volume I

Derrick Arnott

Car insurance entrepreneur, Lloyds Name, single parent,
born again Christian, agnostic, unsuccessful sportsman,
failed politician, binge drinker & accidental millionaire.

DIADEM BOOKS

Social Domestic and Pleasure

Published by Diadem Books
Distribution coordination by Spiderwize

For information, please contact:

Diadem Books
16 Lethen View
Tullibody
Alloa
FK10 2GE UK

www.diadembooks.com

ISBN: 978-1-908026-22-4

TABLE OF CONTENTS

Chapter

One

HERE GOES

Whether I shall turn out to be the hero of my own life,
or whether that situation will be held by anybody else,
these pages will show.
Charles Dickens (*David Copperfield*)

THERE COMES A TIME in our lives when we experience a desire to know
more about our ancestors. Our curiosity is often at its most intense, it seems,
when we reach the twilight of our own lives. When we are young we have little time
or desire to listen to the older generations and when we do eventually become
curious about our roots, our grandparents, uncles, aunties and our parents may no
longer be around to be listened to.

One of the reasons for writing this book, therefore, is to record for the benefit of
future generations a little of my life, the lives of members of my family and the times
we lived in. I haven't done extensive research into the family history, but something
is better than nothing. I hope it may be of some interest, at least to my family.
Perhaps even a starting point for further research! It gives me an opportunity, too, to
share some of the happy, sad, serious and frivolous things which have been a part of
my life, to meet again some of the characters who have enriched it – and to get a few
things off my chest.

Back in 1987 my old friend Brian Sutherland was sitting with me in a pub in
Perth – The Turks Head, I think it was – talking about some of the situations and
characters we had encountered in our lives. Brian was an avid Glasgow Rangers fan
and I had supported St Johnstone during my National Service in Perth. The football
match at the McDiarmid Stadium in Perth (the very first of Britain's new family
stadia) afforded opportunities to us both – Brian to see his beloved 'Gers in action,
(Ally McCoist scored what I believe was the two hundredth of his three hundred and
eighty five career goals for them in a one nil victory), me to pay a sentimental visit to
an old stamping ground and both of us to get away for a weekend 'jolly'.

Anyway, as we sat there in the Turks Head drinking and reminiscing, we were both in hysterics as we recalled incidents and people from the past. I remember saying to Brian that if we had set up a microphone at our table there would be enough material for a book. The seed was sown!

After that I started to collect material and scribble down from time to time a few notes – just in case I ever got round to it, which, at that time, seemed highly unlikely since my lifestyle and my business commitments hardly left me time to wipe my backside, let alone indulge myself in such an ambitious, time consuming, but nevertheless exciting project.

Then in 1995 I met an old Newcastle United footballer – Gordon Hughes – who I used to go and watch in the late nineteen-fifties at St James' Park. Gordon had been a pit electrician who turned pro late in his career and who, in those days of short back and sides, was an unusual sight, with his long hair flowing behind him as he tore down the right wing. He always managed to cross the ball at the last second before landing in the crowd. "Open the gates!" the crowd would yell as he set off on one of his runs. Gordon, I learned, had been working in Derby and had just retired.

"How is retirement?" I asked him. "Aren't you bored?"

"No way," he replied. "I used to wake up every morning and think about what I *had* to do that day. Now I wake up and think about what I *want* to do."

At that time I was no longer enjoying the then substantial business which, as a young man, I had started some thirty-five years earlier. It was being taken in a direction I was not comfortable with. I was going to work because I *had* to and not, as before, because I *wanted* to. The secret of true happiness is not just doing what you like to do, but liking what you have to do, and it wasn't happening any more. That night I lay awake thinking about what Gordon had said. By the morning I had resolved to somehow create the circumstances and the time, like Gordon, to do the things I *wanted* to do and not just what *had* to be done.

Two years later I had retired, too, but it was ten years before I finally found myself in a situation where my time, or at least most of it, was my own. By then of course there was more past than future. But it was a past full of memories to be enjoyed and, by recording them, I can share them with you.

I'm not sure whether having a social conscience is a blessing or a curse. Either way I was born with one, and I'm stuck with it. There isn't much time left to make much of an impact in the area of social reform – forty-five years of insurance has seen to that – but who knows, if I write about some of my often radical thoughts they may one day be vicariously taken on board and implemented by others. Not that I don't still have some fire in the old belly myself! There are still some ambitions to be achieved, dreams to fulfil – and a few scores to settle. I may ruffle a few feathers, but only because mine have been ruffled first, or where I see injustice, stupidity and especially intolerance, which is about the only thing I can't tolerate. (For legal reasons some pseudonyms have been used!)

I am looking forward eagerly to the task I am about to embark upon, and I know it won't be easy. I did attempt to learn some writing skills and techniques, by first applying to go on a course in the New Forest by the author Kathryn Hague, but it had to be cancelled when, sadly, she died of cancer. I then tried to join a local writers' club which claimed to encourage new writers. Now there's one thing you would expect a writers' club to do – write! They didn't. I'm still waiting for a reply to my application.

Though I do have some skill with the written word, this is diminishing as I grow older, but I'll do my best and I'll allow myself a bit of literary license. "They" say there's a book in us all.

So here goes…

Post Script

This literary journey was undertaken primarily for my own indulgence and for the benefit of my family. As it developed into something more than that, it was suggested that I should consider the possibility of publication. The ego in me couldn't resist the temptation so, on the advice of New Writing North at Newcastle University, part of an early draft manuscript was sent to The Literary Consultancy and a useful critique was received from author Alan Wilkinson which I found quite encouraging. One of his main observations and, from a publisher's point of view, criticisms, was that I was writing for a variety of readerships.

> *"Books which sell,"* said Alan, *"usually have a narrower and more specific appeal. It may be,"* he suggested, *"that with the material at your disposal, there may be more than one story here."*

The original manuscript turned out to be a lengthy story of over 600 pages and a decision was made to revise it and publish it in two volumes, the first dealing with *social* issues, *domestic* and family life and background and the *pleasure* (and occasionally pain) of human relationships, which inspired the title I chose. This might suggest that this is a story about car insurance. This is not the case since the events leading up to the rise and fall of Arnott Insurance, Lloyds of London and the intrigue and personalities involved are now chronicled in Volume II: *"Accidental Millionaire."*

This manuscript was completed in 2007 but publication was delayed until 2011, the author's seventy sixth year. Certain events and developments relating to its contents occurred during this period and where relevant have been included as addendums to the appropriate Chapters under the heading "UPDATE (date)".

Two

TOMMY ARNOTT

He's as sharp as a button
Chrissarism.

I **SUPPOSE** you could call this book a sort o' autobiography. It is about me, of course, but it is as much, perhaps more, about other people and the way I see them – a collection of mini-biographies. I will start therefore with two people who were very important to me – my father and my mother, both of whom in their own ways were interesting people from whom I inherited conflicting characteristics, making me a person who could be both caring and responsible and at the same time selfish and irresponsible.

They loved me in their own tin pot ways (one of my father's expressions) but if I were to be honest, their input into my own development as an individual was not always helpful. Whatever I have achieved in life has largely been down to my own determination rather than any parental direction. However, I have much to be thankful for. Unlike many parents today, mine stayed together despite having little in common. That's how it was in those days. They were bricks during a particularly difficult time in my life and for that and for many other things I will be eternally grateful. I am not going to be sentimental and drone on about how much I miss them because that would not be entirely honest. I grieved for my loss when they died and came to terms with it. I have fond memories of them both. They played their part in the complex process of my character development as we all do in the lives of those we care for. I believe I can do no greater service to their memory than to record this short observation of their lives.

Tommy, my father, was born on 6th September 1910 in Cambuslang, Glasgow, the middle son of three. His father Richard James was in the building trade and the family left Glasgow when Tommy was a young boy hoping to make a new and prosperous life in Middlesbrough, which at that time was something of a boom town. With the discovery of iron ore in the Cleveland Hills the steel industry was thriving

4

on the back of the industrial revolution. Sadly, tragedy struck when Tommy was twelve years old. His father fell off a ladder and died.

One can only imagine the emotions within that family. There must have been a strong temptation to go back to Glasgow, but Tommy's mother Elizabeth was a dour and determined Scot and she, Tommy and his two brothers, opted to stay on Teesside. The boys were settled in Archibald School, they owned the house, 60 Wicklow Street, where they lived, and it seems that their mother had been provided for. My own kids left the area to explore other parts of the world, but there is still a Clan Arnott presence on Teesside. Tommy's elder brother Jimmy fathered twins Helena and Neville who were inseparable and lived there together all their lives, and Gordon who had a son Colin. Younger brother George McLeod Arnott had two sons, Graham and David, and daughter Judith. David is the father of Jonathan and Lisa, and Judith married Christopher Gorman and produced a daughter, Cheryl, and son, Mark.

My grandmother's maiden name was MacLeod and she would make a point of stressing that she was a MacLeod of MacLeod whose seat was Dungevan Castle on the Isle of Skye and who, unlike the lowland MacLeods who she considered traitors, supported Robert the Bruce. Indeed it was a Skye MacLeod called Roull who, in 1526 it is claimed, saved King Robert's life when he was attacked in the forest of Callendar by a wild bull whose head I believe appears on their Coat of Arms. The event was recorded in a poem by John Leydon in 1801.

> *His arms robust the hardy hunter flung*
> *Around the bending horns, and upward wrung,*
> *With writhing force his neck retorted round,*
> *And rolled the panting monster to the ground.*
> *Crushed, with enormous strength, his bony skull;*
> *And courtiers hailed the man who turned the bull.*

When he left school at fifteen, Tommy, like the vast majority of young men, got a job in the local steelworks, Dorman, Long & Co., but this was short-lived as the effects of the depression in the 1920's and 30's were felt. Shipbuilding in the North East on which the steel industry largely depended declined by 90% and Tommy found himself out of a job as unemployment reached three million in the country's industrial regions. Most working class families found themselves on, and often below the breadline. Ailments like scurvy and rickets caused by malnutrition were prevalent. Men and sometimes women scavenged for coal among the slag heaps. Soup kitchens were set up in some poorer districts. Groups of young men just hung around on street corners but with time on his hands, Tommy soon found a way to occupy himself and, as it turned out, to learn skills which would later assume an influential part in his life. He would hang out in Willie Smith's billiards hall in Wilson Street and soon became a very accomplished player and an adept hustler, which augmented his meagre pocket money. It wasn't long before he ran out of opponents, such was his reputation, and he moved on to pastures new in the shape of the Empire Hotel in Victoria Road, over the road from a little bakers shop. From the upstairs billiard room Tommy could keep watch on the shop and when the manager went out he would go down and charm the young shop assistant into giving him broken biscuits, old cakes and whatever else was going free. They obviously fancied each other but Beatrice couldn't get Tommy to speak to her outside the shop. So, one day, she bought a new completely brown outfit with matching hat and proudly walked towards him in the street. It did the trick because as she walked past Tommy shouted, "Shit hat!" The ice was broken and they were soon going out together. For their first date Tommy asked her to go to the pictures, the Electric Cinema in Newport Road to be exact. Beatrice was thrilled but the wind was knocked out of her sails when Tommy said, "Right, I'll see you inside then." He was a canny Scot at heart. But Beatrice found the charms of this cocky young Cheeky Charley irresistible.

After they were married Tommy didn't change. He wasn't going to allow his new responsibilities to interfere with his lifestyle. I don't really think he considered them his responsibilities at all and his life continued to be centred around his billiards and his buddies. Consequently his financial input into the marriage was minimal, even when after a couple of years he went on to full-time employment back at the Warrenby Steelworks near Redcar where he worked on shifts, 6 till 2 one week, 2 till 10 the next, and nights (10 p.m. till 6 a.m.) the next. Tommy was a popular and likeable character and because of this was able to do the minimum amount of work without creating resentment among his workmates, and in so doing played his part in the decline of the British steel industry and the subsequent industrialisation of Korea.

Whilst he may not have broken sweat often at work, he was reliable in the sense that, except for one brief period of incapacity, I don't think he missed a shift for forty years. Nor did I miss my early morning call when he was on 6 till 2. This consisted of him lighting up a Woodbine, coughing, 'nipping' it, lighting it up again, coughing – a routine which continued until he was out of earshot and on his way to the early morning bus. He did eventually give up smoking but by then the damage was done and the stage set for his lung cancer later. One thing is for sure, though – he would never have died from any stress-related illness!

The "incapacity" which caused Tommy's absence was, I believe, a mild skin irritation due, he claimed, to the heat from the blast furnaces at which he worked. He laid it on thick, of course, and earned himself a three-week sojourn in a posh convalescent home at Scarborough where his fellow residents, most of whom were genuinely incapacitated with mobility problems, paid him well to run errands for them – putting bets on, sneaking in cigarettes, etc. In his own tin pot way perhaps Tommy too possessed some entrepreneurial inclination. Three weeks of luxury and a transfer to a cushier job were not the only benefits Tommy was able to screw out of his employers, as we shall discover in the next Chapter.

There were probably two advantages of working in the blast furnaces and for such unsociable hours. The first was that he was able to avoid being called up when war broke out in 1939 as his firm concentrated on making weapons, and the other was that he could sleep at the drop of a hat anytime – including a few hours every nightshift! He adjusted his social pattern brilliantly around his working and sleeping hours. "If you want to find Tommy," my Auntie Peggy would say, "he'll be at work, in bed, or at the club." He was, I suppose, quite rude. If visitors came to the house he would simply go to bed. Even the King would have received the same treatment. There was a cartoon character in the *Daily Mirror*, Andy Capp, which could have been modelled on Tommy. We used to get the *Daily Mirror* first because it was a left-wing Labour newspaper which suited Beatrice (or 'Beat' as he called her), and secondly, because of Tommy's betting system. He picked the third best in the betting forecast and put sixpence each way on every race. I have always used this method whenever I have been to a race meeting – and with some success.

Tommy may have been a popular figure outside the house but he wasn't so popular with Beatrice. He wasn't exactly generous with the housekeeping money, or with his time. He did take me to the seaside once – an occasion he often mentioned to persuade people what a devoted dad he was! He loved me, of course, and was proud of me. "Is everything all right?" he used to say every time we met. I always reassured him, even in difficult times, knowing that to do otherwise would not have produced any practical help and would only have caused him to worry. He did change for the better later in life and was very supportive when my first marriage broke up. Tommy's irresponsibility is crystallised in a couple of stories told about him.

He was in some trouble domestically, I don't know the details, and was sent out for a bucket of coal. Instead of going back indoors to face the music he called on his brother-in-law – my uncle Edward, who was also a bit of a jack the lad – and they took off to Blackpool, Tommy still with his slippers on. Blackpool FC were at home to 'Boro and after copious amounts of beer they went to the match. Tommy by then had made room in his heart for 'Boro, which it shared with Glasgow Rangers. They thoroughly enjoyed the first half with the score standing at 2-0, and standing in the toilet at half time, exchanged euphoric dialogue about 'Boro's performance. Another nearby 'Boro fan, puzzled at their elation, asked why. "We're winning two-nil, that's why," said Edward. "No we're not," said the stranger, "we're losing two-nil."

They then realised that they had been shouting for the wrong team – the one in shirts that were, vaguely, red, which was Blackpool's colours and similar to 'Boro's home strip. They were so drunk they couldn't tell the difference – or recognise any of the players. 'Boro were playing in their away strip of blue and white. Drinks in, wits out!

During and shortly after the war Tommy and Edward had many trips away – London, Scotland, Wales; Britain was their oyster. None of these trips cost them anything. Dressed in army, navy or air force uniforms borrowed from friends on leave, they managed somehow to fool the ticket collectors. There was some dodge about going into the toilet in two's or three's and pushing one HM Forces travel pass under the toilet door for inspection. Tommy probably got away with his escapades with less severe domestic consequences by roping in Edward, Beat's brother, whom she idolised.

I was in my teens before I found something in common with Tommy. Something on which to build a relationship – a taste for good beer and a capacity to hold a lot of it.

The first night my dad took me to his main club, St Joseph's, sticks in my memory. I had been inside this building many times before as a boy when it was the old Bishop's House. The fact that he was a regular there was in itself strange, bearing in mind his background and his prejudices. St. Joseph's was a Catholic club. I think Tommy rather enjoyed being different. I spent the evening drinking pints of John Smiths 'Magnet', being proudly introduced to dad's friends and listening to the 'turns' which hogged the microphone all night. There were some good old sentimental chestnuts, like 'Too Young' and 'Nellie Dean', but most of the songs of course were Irish and the star 'turn' was Frank O'Connor who was, or appeared to be, reluctant to get up, which apparently was always the case until he had milked the urging and adulation of the audience sufficiently. His coyness disappeared when he did get up, however. You just couldn't get him down again! His final number was always 'I'll take you home again Kathleen', during which you could hear a pin drop. Apparently this was the routine every night, six nights a week (the Sabbath was observed then). So, too, was the highlight of the evening, which was, surprisingly, closing time – or should I say, the closing ceremony. Tommy would go behind the bar accompanied by Frank (another Frank!) the steward on the bell he used to announce closing time – and give a soulful rendition of the old Negro spiritual 'Hear dem bells':

> *We goes to church early in de morning*
> *When de birds am a singin' in de trees*
> *De bible am getting' so hard to read*
> *Wid feet and hands so sore*
> *At night when de moon am shinin' bright*
> *And de clouds hab passed away*

Dem bells keep a ringin' for the gospel fight
Dat will last till de judgement day
Hear dem bells, hear dem bells
Dey's a ringin out de glory ob de Lord
Hear dem bells, hear dem bells…

There were several verses. I sat there fascinated.

National Service interrupted the development of my paternal relationship, but several years later I went back to live with my parents after the break-up of my first marriage and we went for a holiday with my two-year-old daughter Liz to Butlins Holiday Camp at Filey. She was very well behaved. Her granda would threaten to 'fetch' Billy Butlin if she was naughty. Playfully, of course, but Liz was never quite sure! The two weeks we spent there served to strengthen the bond between us and again demonstrated to me what a popular person Tommy was. We hadn't, it seemed, been there five minutes before everyone seemed to know him. I noticed particularly how young men took to him and how he put them at ease. I noticed too how he took advantage of this. He used to send one to put his bets on, another to go and get his paper, another to go and get Liz an ice cream, and so on. Tommy spoke to everyone and took an interest in them and they responded by being happy to do his bidding. There's a lesson to be learned here. Youngsters will respond if treated with respect.

It so happened that while we were there, the Butlins Billiards Championship was being held at Filey and I was destined at last to benefit from Tommy's misspent youth – albeit by default. The entry system worked on the basis that all competitors would put their names down on a list and the first on the list would play against the second, the last on the list against the second last and so on until there were two left in the final. Tommy of course was delighted to have an opportunity to compete and hastened to get his name first on the list. The day before the first round there was still a vacant slot, the final one on the entry sheet and therefore in the bottom half of the draw, and I was persuaded reluctantly to enter. On the big day dad said to me, "Derrick, I've dropped a blob," explaining that all the good players, like him, would have entered early and appear in the top half of the draw which would therefore be tougher than the bottom half. "We'll change names," he suggested. So for a few days I became Tommy Arnott, played the eventual finalist in the first round and lost resoundingly. Meanwhile 'Derrick' sailed through the weaker bottom half of the draw and beat my conqueror in the final. That's how my name appears on the 1967 Butlins Billiards Trophy.

As he grew older Tommy mellowed somewhat, although retirement at sixty-five meant that he could now be found only at the club or in bed! Though he never laboured the point, he had never really approved of Agnes, my first wife. It probably had something to do with her being a Catholic. He was however very fond of Chris, my second wife, who was able to get through to him much more effectively than his own wife had ever been able to. Even his appearance improved under Chris's influence. Under pressure from her, his ever-present green crewneck pullover was washed occasionally and she knitted him a replacement and bought him a new green tie which he wore when he thought she might visit. His favourite greasy old and only other tie, which he wore constantly and always beneath his jumper, summer and winter, was never allowed to be washed and was never ever unknotted. It just looped over his head. He did, however, proudly possess a dickie bow and a cravat which I have kept as a memento. These he wore for special occasions like a rare visit to our house, which he considered to be in a posh area, and also when he went on holiday, which latterly became a feature of his new lifestyle. Not for him your Blackpool or your Scarborough, though. Tommy was, in his own way, a bit of a snob – in the nicest possible way. No one else in his social circle behaved, acted and dressed like Tommy. With his cravat, wavy distinguished hair and carefully cultivated RAF moustache, he wasn't your normal working class bloke. As I say, he was a bit aloof – he would say dignified. The bees' knees. Gentleman Jim, my mother used to call him, and whilst he mixed with some very rough diamonds, he never ever used bad language. He used a six-letter word – "flames" (e.g. what the flames etc.) but that was as bad as it got!

I think he may have been a Tory at heart but since this would have attracted a severe backlash from my mother, who was farther left than Lenin, he used to tell her he'd voted Labour. In fact, I'm quite sure he never bothered to exercise his franchise. Short of a member of the polling booth staff bringing a ballot paper to *him,* nothing as trivial, pointless and inconvenient as going to vote would upset Tommy's routine.

My mother used to tell a story about her 'Gentleman Jim' on holiday – in Cliftonville, of course, a resort more suited to a gentleman of Tommy's social aspirations. Talking to another guest in the hotel he was asked what he did for a living. "I dabble in steel," was the unhesitating reply.

Even though he was an exceptional billiards player, Tommy never won any serious major tournaments, apart from the Father Toner Cup at St Joseph's and, of course, the Butlins Trophy for which he must have really concentrated for my sake and for Liz's and for which I, and not he, received official recognition and a trophy. His problem was nerves – a failing which I seem to have inherited. Strange, because in every other facet of his life he was so calm and unruffled. He was however an excellent coach and devoted his later life to youngsters. He had a way with them. His soothing influence got the best out of many a young scallywag. It was only after he died that I was to learn from his old pupils of the esteem in which he was held. One of them, Mel Pelling, told me of his first encounter with Tommy. Mel, who was about thirteen at the time, was peering through the window of the Steelworks Club watching one of Tommy's teaching sessions and when it was over Tommy came out and walked towards him. Mel, thinking he was going to be told off, was ready to flee when Tommy asked him if he would like to learn billiards. Mel said he hadn't a clue but Tommy promised him he would become a good player if he would try. They went inside and Tommy put a ball on the centre spot, gave Mel a cue and the cue ball and said, "You can go home when you've potted that ball." An hour later, Mel went home and was hooked. He attended Tommy's weekly coaching sessions and became a good player. "If it hadn't been for Tommy giving me an interest in life," Mel told me later, "I would definitely have ended up in gaol."

Tommy also coached the one-time world professional champion, Peter Gilchrist, but his favourite pupil was undoubtedly Geoff Charville. I remember dad talking about Geoff and his cue action and how he was destined for the top. Geoff later admitted to me that he could have indeed become a top pro, but other things had diverted him. When he was under Tommy's wing they went to a top tournament featuring the world's leading players including a very young Steve Davis, who at that time was relatively unknown. "Come on," said Tommy, "let's challenge him to a game of billiards!" – and to Geoff's amazement Steve agreed. They had a very close game and Steve suggested a return match at snooker. Geoff had no chance, and was well beaten. "That young man's going to be world champion," predicted Tommy. Two years later he was.

Though he never said as much, I'm sure my dad was a little disappointed that he was not able to pass on his skills to me, though I do play occasionally and once reached the semi-final of a club competition. I'm sure too that he would have loved his grandson Tim to have gone to some of his coaching lessons. Tim, too, now regrets not doing so.

I suppose most of us eventually have regrets about not spending enough quality time with our loved ones. Certainly that is true in my case and even when I tried to 'catch up' it wasn't to be. As dad's health failed I was too bogged down in other things to devote much time to him. I went with him a few times to another of his clubs, the Civil Defenders, which was only a short walk away. His legs were beginning to fail him by then. I took him down to the Conservative Club, my local watering hole, and I even joined him as a member. How he would have loved it had he joined earlier. Five billiard tables, good cheap beer and people of his own generation to talk to! Alas, he wasn't able to appreciate it. He was tiring. The tablets the doctor was prescribing were not helping despite the dosage being doubled, then trebled. We later found them all pushed down the side of his chair. He hadn't even been taking them. But they were free, and Tommy couldn't resist something for nothing!

The doctor insisted that dad wasn't ill, just getting old, but I wanted to be sure and arranged to take him to the hospital where the doctor there told me he was in the terminal stages of lung cancer and had eight weeks to live. I just went outside, sat in the car and cried and cried. He died precisely eight weeks later on the 12th of August

1993. We decided not to tell him of his illness – why ruin two people's days instead of one – or to involve McMillan nurses. He wouldn't have been able to cope with that – or maybe he would. Who knows? He was confined to bed by then and we tried to make his last days as comfortable as possible. He loved it when Chris visited. He would sing her the songs he sang in the clubs till he drifted off to sleep. Money was important to Tommy and I was sitting by his bedside one day when my mother, obviously a bit jealous of the attention he was getting, tried to get a bit of the sympathy for herself. "Oh, I'm seeing double," she groaned. "Well, count that money in my jacket pocket," was the typically Tommy Arnott retort. He was still good company and our laughter disguised the tears that were always close to the surface.

He died, as I've said, and as predicted, exactly eight weeks after I had taken him for a second opinion. Chris stayed with him and held his hand that night. He would have liked that. I feel so guilty that I wasn't there, particularly, I have to confess, having agreed earlier to the removal of the medical support that was keeping him alive. I couldn't bear to see him suffer any longer. I don't regret that decision and have a great deal of sympathy with people in similar circumstances who are denied such choice.

The funerals of most people who live to a ripe old age are normally sparsely attended, and mostly by old people. Not so Tommy's. Some of his pupils had asked if they could carry his coffin and did so with great dignity and sincerity. People came from clubs and pubs all over the area. It truly was a celebration of Tommy's life. There really was joy and laughter mingled with the sorrow. Clifford Collinson, my new wife Chris's stepfather and an ex-Baptist minister, a wonderful old man, conducted the service beautifully, giving us a potted history of Tommy's life, including the "dabble in steel" story and it evoked more laughter than tears. They all knew what Tommy was like. We had a laugh afterwards too at the 'supper' in the Blue Bell Hotel. Tommy was not renowned for his generosity when it came to buying the drinks and out of the little bit of money he had left, I put, on his behalf, a tab behind the bar for free drinks for all. I announced it saying there's a first time for everything, and that Tommy would probably right then be turning in his grave.

That might have been the end of Tommy but it wasn't the end of the influence he had on so many lives – a situation of which I was quite unaware during his lifetime. Two of the funeral guests, Frank Hagen, whose own father had actually died while playing snooker in the Erimus Club, and Geoff Charville, Tommy's protégé, asked me if they could organise a billiards tournament in his memory and I readily agreed to support this wonderful and touching gesture. The Tommy Arnott Memorial Billiards Tournament has taken place every year since 1993 and has been supported not just by his ex-pupils but by the world's leading players. I was delighted when Geoff himself won the prestigious trophy in 2001 but not, I suspect, as much as Geoff was and, I hope, not as much as Tommy as he looked down, or up, from wherever he is.

His protégé Geoff Charville receiving the Tommy Arnott Memorial Billiards Trophy from me in 2001.

Three

BEATIE GARDNER

*Parents can only give advice or put them on the right path
but the final forming of a person's character lies in their own hands.*
Anne Frank.

IN **1825** the world's first railway was opened—the route was between Darlington and Stockton. The very first steam locomotive was called *Locomotion.* Its more reliable version, *The Rocket,* more affectionately known as *Puffing Billy*, was built in 1829 just in time to replace Locomotion when its boiler exploded, killing the driver. It was designed by George Stephenson and built in Gateshead by his son Robert who went on to build many more railways including the London to Birmingham line and several engineering masterpieces like the Berwick Bridge, the Iron Tubular Bridge over the Menai Straits between Anglesey and Caernarvonshire and the world's oldest sea washed lighthouse at Bell Rock in the North Sea.

On December 3rd 1859 Hannah Stephenson married John Gardner, my great grandfather, at St Johns, Newcastle. One of their ten children, Joseph, married Eliza Hodgson who, before she died very young of tuberculosis, produced two children, John and Jane. Joseph remarried and he and his new wife Margaret Mulcaster produced a further three children. The youngest, my mother Beatrice, was born at Park Lane, Middlesbrough on the 4th June 1914 at the outbreak of the Great War – the war to end all wars, or so it was claimed at the time. If only. Beatrice was christened at St Aiden's Church which had just been erected on the site of the old Middlesbrough FC football ground after the club had relocated to Ayresome Park.

Bringing up a family in those hard times wasn't easy and my grandmother, a gentle timid woman like my mother, had the added burden of two grown-up and at times, resentful step-children to cope with. I know only too well the problems associated with mixed families. My mother's dread of conflict to the point of phobia clearly had its roots in those early childhood days and perhaps also explains how Tommy got away with so much during their years together.

My grandfather was a sign writer by trade but took employment with the River Tees Commissioners to secure a regular income. One of the jobs he was periodically called on to do was to be a member of the crew which painted the giant Transporter Bridge, which spans the River Tees. During the winter he would come home with sores on his hands where the sub-zero temperatures had caused his brush to freeze to his fingers. It would be natural to assume that having spent every working day with a paintbrush in his hand, the last thing he would want to have as a hobby was painting. This was not the case. He was a talented artist and some of his paintings are spread around the family. I remember in particular an oil painting he did of a young man and a young woman setting off in a punt to cross a lake, on the other side of which was a lovely cottage. He had painted this for his new wife to depict the start of their journey through life together. How romantic was that!

Joseph Gardner was also an extremely talented musician. He actually won a prestigious scholarship which gave him the opportunity to study music and develop his talents at a music college in Oxford – an opportunity he had to forego, unfortunately, due to his family commitments. Music was one of the great loves of his life and I can sympathise with the frustrations he must have felt at that time. He did however earn some money from his talent by giving music lessons at home and at the homes of his pupils. More money to supplement his modest income was earned playing in the orchestra pits at the Hippodrome Cinema in Wilson Street (next door to Willie Smith's Billiard Saloon, the scene of my father's misspent youth). This was of course to create atmosphere in the days of the silent movies. Some of the smaller, cheaper, picture houses made do with a solo pianist.

My mother clearly recalled listening spellbound as her father and stepbrother John played her favourite piece, 'Cavalier Rusticana', on violins. I too have memories of my grandfather as a very serious, even stern, old man and of having to wait patiently, sometimes impatiently, for him to finish his piece before I could speak to him. I recall, too, feeling uncomfortable as I sensed his irritation at having his concentration disturbed by my intrusion. He was however a responsible and caring father and grandfather and I wish I had appreciated more fully his good intentions when he occasionally persuaded, cajoled or forced me to accompany him to museums and other places of educational interest – to him, but not, alas, to me at that young age, though I do recall going to an old building with an echo chamber which fascinated me. I would love to go there again but have never been able to find out where it was. It's probably a supermarket or a housing estate now. My grandfather's influence on me did manifest itself, albeit indirectly, since some of his books did come into our possession after he died and after being persuaded by my mother to read *Pickwick Papers* I became at a very early age an avid reader of Charles Dickens

Despite him being rather strict and Victorian, my mother had very fond memories of her father's lighter moments when, for example, he would encourage the children to write and draw pictures on his bald head. Beatrice was intensely proud of her heritage and her family and I regret not listening more attentively when she recalled her family stories, like the pride she felt when her cousin Tom, her Uncle Jack's son, who had emigrated to Australia, was hailed heroically in the press as the first Australian to land in Britain to join the 1914-1918 War. Pride, however, would not adequately describe her feelings for her handsome and talented elder brother. She idolised Edward who, as a young man, became the North East Area amateur ballroom dancing champion at the time when the gramophone was invented and which was unveiled to the world by the Columbia Company with a series of ballroom dancing competitions. The regional one was held at the Oxford Galleries in Newcastle and of course Edward entered and won the first prize. On his triumphant return everyone in the street ran out excitedly to see Edward walking jauntily along carrying his prize – a brand new gramophone! Edward was also a schoolboy champion swimmer and the youngest member of the then very successful Middlesbrough Water Polo Team. The whole neighbourhood again turned out to watch Edward win a swimming race organised in Albert Park Lake. To my amazement I learned that my mother too had some sporting talent and in the 1920's played goalie for the Middlesbrough Ladies Hockey Team.

Edward married Mary Jones and she and Beatrice became good friends, as did Edward and my father. Their son, my cousin Neil, like me, was an only child and we were brought up together which I suspect irritated Neil at times since he was a year older than me.

I very nearly wasn't an only child. Shortly after I was born my mother fell pregnant again. Unfortunately the dread of having to cope with the extra responsibility, coupled with her dire financial situation, drove her to seek an abortion. Apparently these were readily available in those pre-birth control days, although there were rumours within the family of knitting needles being involved which suggests that it may have been a D.I.Y. job. This skeleton was kept securely locked in the family cupboard for many years before I learned about my unborn sister. My mother carried the burden of this guilty secret all her life. She was convinced that all the unhappiness in her life was down to God's punishment for denying life to my sister. For sure, she would have been horrified to find her shame revealed in print, but to quote the famous Irish playwright and socialist, George Bernard Shaw: "If you've got skeletons in your cupboard, you might as well make them dance for you."

My mother's sister, Margaret, Auntie Peggy, was also a very attractive young lady, and as they said in those days, 'did well for herself' marrying a Dutch sea captain, Cornelius (Uncle Cor) Baak. Their two daughters, Marguerite and Janet, lived in a big house in Saltburn by the Sea and we used to visit often – in fact, we lived there briefly, the circumstances of which I will recall later. Marga married Peter Murray who was later given an OBE for his work involving the Yorkshire Sculpture Park where the names of my parents can be found on a pathway known as the Walk of Art.

The famous General Kitchener poster with the pointed finger and caption – 'Your Country Needs You' – must rank as the best and most effective piece of marketing the twentieth century has produced. It stirred up the patriotic spirit in the hearts of young men at the outbreak of World War One and its timing was perfect, since many of the country's young men were unemployed. It certainly worked on Beatrice's stepbrother John who was sent back to his scoutmaster when he tried to join up as a boy in 1915. Another attempt landed him in the Prince of Wales' own Regiment before a transfer to the 2/9 Battalion of the Glasgow Highlanders took him to France in 1917. After being wounded in the leg John (or Jack as he was known) then joined the Highland Light Infantry. He too was a keen amateur artist and apparently had a unique memento of those harrowing days in the form of a sketchbook that depicts the horrors of the war which I have, so far unsuccessfully, tried to locate to include in this book. I do have an old 1918 embroidered card, which John sent home from France. The writing is faint and is just about legible. *"I think this will please Beattie,"* it says. *"The best I can get in the village. Your loving brother John."* He survived the war and lived to a ripe old age, as did Beatie's step-sister Jane who missed out on her one hundredth birthday telegram from the Queen by just a few weeks. Auntie Ginny had been an early activist in the socialist movement as a member of an extreme left wing Fabian style group, though she stopped short of joining the Communist Party.

On the maternal side of my mother's family, I remember her telling me about Aunt Lizzie Mulcaster, who lived on Norton village green and had a high class milliner's shop, and her uncle Jonathan Mulcaster, a member of Middlesbrough Rotary Club and a pioneer of the YMCA. Also, her Uncle Matt Mulcaster, who was one of the few people locally to own a car. The *very* first to own one was the family doctor and my mother recalled what a kind old man he was. Dr Longbotham was one of the old-fashioned school of GP's, a friend of the family to all his patients, always having time to listen to them. After his house calls he would regularly give the curious children a ride round the block in his car. The practice, in Linthorpe Road, Middlesbrough, is still going strong and we are still registered there. Sadly, Uncle Matt Mulcaster and his wife died of typhoid and my mother's cousins Mamie, Ted and Bill went into an orphan's home, Kirkleatham, which was later bequeathed to them and other resident orphans by the benevolent owner. Mamie, too, marred a Dutchman, Tys Kleve, who was Uncle Cor's first officer.

Before going on to relate a little of Beattie's life it may be interesting to look at some aspects of life in general at the time of the two world wars and the intervening depression of the 1930's, as recalled by my mother.

These were times when herrings were sold in the street for "ten a penny", an expression still used today to describe something commonplace and cheap. I can remember when I was a young boy the cries of the herring man as he plied his trade from his wheelbarrow – "Hartlepool herring, kipper herring!" A pound of tripe clippings cost a threepenny bit, but of course there were two hundred and forty pennies in the pound. As well as the threepenny bit, the other coins then in circulation were the sixpence (called the tanner), the shilling (ten pennies – called the bob), the two bob bit (twenty pennies), the half-crown piece (thirty pennies), the ten bob note (a hundred and twenty pennies) and the pound and five-pound notes. Stuff from the shops came without safety caps and hermetic seals because nobody had yet tried to poison a perfect stranger. Tea would be sold in paper bags scooped directly from the tea chests in which it had been imported. These could be borrowed or hired from Hintons the grocers for packing when you moved house which my mother was to do frequently. When the neighbourhood kids were hungry they could fill up with a pennyworth of hot stuff (a mixture of turnips, carrots and potatoes) from the corner shop. To keep the coal bills down fires would be lit only when absolutely necessary, which meant that the adjoining ovens in the old iron ranges couldn't be used, so the womenfolk would prepare their own baking and take it over to Crescent Road Bakery, who would charge a penny for the use of their oven. A rigid domestic routine was observed. Monday was washing day. The ironing was done on Tuesday. The old fireplaces and ovens were blackened on Wednesday and doorsteps were spruced up, according to taste, with Cardinal red polish or Blanco on Thursday. On Friday the house would be cleaned and polished for the weekend and Saturday would be spent baking. Sundays would mean the long mandatory walk, hail, rain or snow, accompanied by parents and grandparents. For some there was the mandatory church service, often two or three times a day. Families fortunate enough to own a mangle (a simple hand operated machine with rollers for wringing out wet clothes) would charge a penny for other families to use it and neighbours used to take turns to buy an *Evening Gazette* and pass it round, then use it as a table cloth or cut it up and use it for toilet paper. "Come in, sit down and read the table cloth," later quipped Bobby Thomson, the northeast comedian. The 'Little Waster', as he was known, later made some recordings and whilst the humour is not so relevant today, some of us who can still remember those hard times still find it hilarious. Here's one of my war time favourites:

> Bobby says *"Hurry up Phyllis the air raid siren's gone."*
> She says *"Hang on Bobby, I'm looking for my teeth."*
> Bobby says *"Howay woman, they're dropping bombs, not pies."*

The phrase 'cap in hand' originated as soldiers returned penniless from the Great War in 1918 and walked around the streets in their uniforms seeking sympathy, in the practical form of pennies in their proffered berets, caps or bonnets, depending on their regiment.

When someone died, the deceased's clothes and possessions were laid out in the street outside their houses for people to buy, thus providing funds for the funeral. What was left over would be the subject of the ancient version of recycling, i.e. collected by the rag and bone men who wandered the streets. There were no toilets in those days, at least not in working class homes. Ashes from the fire were thrown down the middens, as they were called, to contain the smell. These middens were not exactly private and for a laugh, children used to hide and wait patiently for someone to "perform" and then poke them from behind with a stick before running away. String was tied round the trouser legs of the refuse collection officers (dustmen in those days) as protection against rats.

At Christmas you would always get in your stocking an apple and an orange and a threepenny bit. This tradition was carried on into my own childhood but I always got a few extra toys too and always a *Beano, Dandy, Hotspur* or *Wizard Annual* – never the same one as Neil or other close friends, an economical pre-arrangement by our respective parents so that we could later swap. If you were lucky you would be invited into the big houses to sing carols. Uncle Edward, with his sweet singing voice, was a sought after member of the carollers groups. Was there no end to his talents?

Beatrice left Victoria School, Middlesbrough, at the age of fifteen. I don't know whether her schooldays were happy ones. I suspect not, since she never talked about them, though it must have been at school where she gained prowess on the hockey field. Her first job was at Conways Chocolate Shop where, for five shillings a week, she worked from 9 a.m. till 9 p.m. (10 p.m. on Saturday). She left to earn more money at Pybus, the well-known local grocery firm, as a flour packer. Her father, having lost his first wife with TB, was concerned for her health and she was persuaded by him to leave to take up a post as domestic help with a family in Devonshire Road. There, again for five shillings a week, she baked, scrubbed the floors, shopped, cooked and looked after the lady of the house, who suffered from sciatica. Servant, Skivvy or Slave would perhaps have been more adequate job descriptions. Now, Beatrice was the most trustworthy, honest and timid person on earth and when, one day, the master of the house accused her of drinking some of the juice from the lady's breakfast fruit, she plucked up courage and said she was leaving. They begged her to stay, though an apology was never offered, and the mistress said that if she stayed "they would have a peach of a time". Beatrice thought, "Aye, you might, but I certainly won't!" and that was that. By then she was sixteen and her cousin Lily Phillips (her father's sister Annie's daughter) suggested a job with her in service.

To digress for a moment, it is interesting to record that in those days, partly due to shortage of money, undertakers were rarely called out when there was a death in the street, nor were midwives when there was a birth. Every street had an Annie Phillips, who laid out corpses and delivered babies – and maybe terminated the unwanted pregnancies too!

The work suggested by Lily wasn't the kind of service in houses which Beatrice had experienced, but work in hotels. Lily herself, though only a few years older than Beatrice, was by then an experienced waitress with a team of girls and women on call for local functions, a role that Beatrice would eventually take over. So it was that Beatrice became a waitress and went to Scarborough for the 1930 season, to work in the Ramsdale Hotel on South Cliff. Her father was persuaded, reluctantly, to give his permission, partly through guilt that it was he who had been instrumental in placing his daughter on the unemployment register, but largely because their next door neighbour's daughter, Rosie Cassidy, an older girl and also an experienced waitress, would be going with her. This was heady stuff for a sixteen-year-old in those days, living away from home and ten shillings a week in her pocket – plus tips the manager had promised, though the porter always seemed to get his hands on them first and they got no further than *his* pocket.

Tommy and Beat were by then "going out" and so were Tommy and brother Edward.

These two jack the lads now had an excuse to visit Scarborough, which they did together often. After spending the day drinking, and whatever else they got up to, mam told me how, on her first weekend there, they turned up at the Ramsdale and attracted her attention over the wall of the hotel (they weren't allowed inside) and 'borrowed' money for the bus fare back to Middlesbrough. My mother was such a naïve person. It wasn't until many years later that it occurred to her that the bus fare story may have been false, since by the time they had 'borrowed' the money, the last bus was long gone, and they turned up with the same sob story the following day. I can only speculate as to what the lads got up to that night and on their subsequent subsidised outings to the seaside. She obviously found irresistible the charms of this adorable brother and his witty waster of a friend.

Beatrice worked in Scarborough for two more seasons and worked out of season in the aforementioned cake shop and at Aunt Lizzie Mulcaster's shops – first at Miss Bacon's, the milliners, and, when after the death of her husband this closed down, at her general dealer's shop. It wasn't really a shop. Her enterprising aunt Lizzie, realising that there was no shop nearby, used the front room of her house in Junction Road, Norton, to display goods and fancy cakes and the like, bought for resale from Merediths, the local high class bakery. Unfortunately Beatrice's relationship with her Aunt Lizzie deteriorated when her aunt confided in her that she had seen Tommy taking money from her purse, something she refused to believe. Love is blind!

The wedding took place at St Oswald's Church, Grove Hill, on 18th July 1935 and since I was born the following year on 14th April, I'm not sure whether I was premature or there had been a little pre-marital hanky panky – something that in those days, apparently, was taboo and therefore, rare.

My mother claimed that all she wanted was a settled home, yet, during her lifetime, she lived like a nomad. She did tell me she was always trying to better herself by moving, but was often a victim of circumstances. There were I believe twenty homes in all, starting with a flat in Benedict Street, North Ormesby, the first marital home, which proved to be too expensive at twelve shillings and sixpence a week – 12/6p; that's about sixty pence in today's money! Subsequent moves, as far as I can gather, were: 1935 – Gresham Road, a flat above a bakery, 1936 - 60 Wicklow Street (Granma Arnott's house where I was born), and later that year, Laura Street. Then in 1937 - 37a Athol Street from where a £19 life assurance policy was taken out on me for one penny a week through the Liverpool Victoria Friendly Society, whose agents were known as graveyard bookmakers! Then in 1939 when I was three, she managed to rent a tiny one-bedroomed cottage in Marton Road called the Bishop's Lodge where I spent my early childhood days which I will talk about later, as I will about subsequent moves to Marton Grove Road, Lune Street Saltburn, Rockcliffe Road, Southend Lodge, Wicklow Street again, Holy Rood Lodge, the prefab in Roseberry Road, Evesham Road Park End, The Oval Easterside, Marton Road, Deepdale Avenue, Nunthorpe Road Marton, Marton Road again and, finally, Roseleigh Care Home in Lytton Street. When she found herself in difficulties, as she clearly did when it came to finding a settled home, my mother would say, like Micawber in *The Pickwick Papers*, "Something will turn up." It seems she was right. It did – twenty times!

Tom and Beat, it seemed to me, stumbled through their marriage though they did, I'm sure, have some happy times, like when, during one of the early moves, their furniture was transported in an old pram, borrowed for the purpose, and my dad insisted on Beat being tucked up in the pram on the return journeys and stopping to show off his 'baby' on the way. That had obviously 'tickled' her since she mentioned it several times. The main bones of contention in the marriage seem to have centred round money, or the lack of it, and Tommy's lack of interest in the home. There was never any question of Tommy's pay packet being handed over. That was a closely guarded secret. The housekeeping, I suspect, was exceeded considerably by Tommy's spending money. His lifestyle received a boost when he was once awarded some compensation for an industrial "injury". One day Beat was out of cigarettes but dare not take one of Tommy's. Auntie Mary, Edward's wife, a much bolder woman, not that this would take much, told Beat not to be so soft and to get one out of Tommy's pocket. She wouldn't of course, so Mary did. There in Tommy's jacket pocket, she found more than a packet of cigarettes. A bankbook was produced and curiosity overcame Beat's fear. She opened the book to reveal a deposit of £300, presumably the amount of the 'compo', and weekly withdrawals of £3. No wonder Tommy was having a good time! And no wonder Beat was dismayed – £300 was more than enough to buy a decent house then. When he had first received his 'compo', Tommy had generously bought a present for his wife – a new zinc poss tub. Price? Three shillings and eleven pence!

Whilst not wishing to condone my father's meanness and irresponsibility, I have to say, in order to correct any misunderstanding, that he was not by any stretch of the imagination a tyrant. Quite the opposite, in fact. He was easy going, mild mannered and, above all, charming and witty in his own way. His behaviour would certainly not have been tolerated by today's modern woman, but Beat just naturally "accepted her place" as many women did in those days. She had all the responsibility of running the house and paying the bills, which can't have been easy for her, not only because of the financial situation, but also because she was, at best, scatter-brained and, dare I say it, incompetent in these areas. In all the circumstances at that time the termination of her second pregnancy becomes more understandable. Because money was so short, at least in her pocket, Beat supplemented her housekeeping by colouring black and white photographs, a skill at which she was quite adept and for which she was much in demand. This of course was in the days before colour photography. Later, when I was old enough for her to go out to work, she dealt in what she called 'buttons'. These were sort of plastic coins with a value stamped on them and redeemable for goods at certain stores. People who were desperate for money used to buy, for example, a £5 button and pay £10 for it by twenty weekly payments of ten shillings. Immediately they would sell the button for, say, £3 cash – probably to pay off another debt. My mother somehow was able to acquire these buttons, thus getting £5 spending power for £3, or she would sell them on for £3.10s or £4 to make an instant profit. At least in these areas she showed some resourcefulness; born I suppose, out of desperation.

Eventually my mother's lot improved. She was able to achieve some financial relief, first by working as a school dinner lady and when I was old enough to be left – there was never any question of Tommy's lifestyle being upset by staying in to look after me – she resumed her work as a waitress, which she carried on into her seventies.

She worked mostly at the Highfield Hotel, which had at that time the most prestigious dining room in the area and where she waited on many famous personalities. Our pet cat Whiskey however failed to be impressed when one week he was given, as a bribe, the remains of Lord Soper's halibut and Alan Whicker's fillet steak. We had just moved to Marton Road and Whiskey, despite fetching him back several times, could not be persuaded to settle when we moved there from Easterside, where he clearly had a human benefactor or a feline female friend, or both.

Before becoming head function waitress at the Highfield, Beatrice attended many functions at different hotels and venues in the area and took over as head of a team of travelling waitresses when the previous head, Annie Coleman, retired. She spoke fondly of her team who became good friends. There was Olga Smith, who shared her interest in gardens, flowers and artistic things, 'South Bank Hilda', a rough diamond with a heart of gold, of whom she talked a lot, and old Annie Lawson, whose sense of humour gave her many a laugh. Like the time when Annie's son, who became head waiter at London's famous Carlton Club, was driving them back home in his newly acquired fast car and said proudly, "Look mam, we're doing ninety." Unimpressed, Annie's response was, "Well do another bloody ninety, I want to get home."

Beattie, as she was called by her friends, finally found in her work a feeling of independence, and we were able to enjoy the occasional holiday in rented cottages at Swainby and once at Burneston in the Lake District. We even went to Blackpool one year with Auntie Mary and Neil. Later she ventured to Eastbourne with Tommy on a Bee-line bus trip and in 1954 to Italy with Auntie Mary and Auntie Ginny.

She was always a good and inventive cook and she learned through her work in good class establishments, how important it was to present food appetisingly – a skill lost on Tommy who drowned everything in brown HP sauce. Doylies and crystal cruet sets appeared on the kitchen table and she loved it when people came to tea. Mam's culinary skills enabled her to stretch her budget by buying the cheapest food available. Tripe and onions were one of the weekly regulars on the menu, followed by fried tripe the next day. Sunday lunch was invariably Yorkshire puddings and onion gravy for starters, followed by brisket beef, timed to coincide, as far as possible, with Tommy's return from the club – and later, mine. On Sunday night, again after the club, we would have 'crispies', which were pieces of brisket fat (of which there was an abundance) cut up and rendered down in the frying pan until they were crisp. Delicious on their own or as sandwich fillings. The following day or two it would be dripping and bread and thinly sliced brisket and a fry up of Sunday's leftovers. She could sometimes eke out the brisket for a salad the following day if she sliced it finely enough.

But she was at her happiest when she was with children. They felt at ease with her natural warmth and gentleness and she took much pleasure and security in their innocence. Material things were unimportant. Untidiness, muddy shoes and spilled drinks were ignored. As long as the children were happy and relaxed – that's all that mattered. Why then did she not have more children herself? I think part of the answer must be because she loved and worried so intensely, she could not bear to see a child suffer or hear it cry. It was almost impossible to find anything to dislike about Beatie. If she was guilty of anything it was of caring too much. She was, in her own words, "a worrit". She was constantly and deeply concerned about everything from dark nights and cloudy skies to the suffering and injustice she saw in the world.

Beat and Tom were chalk and cheese. Venus and Mars. Yet they stayed together through thick and thin for fifty-seven years with little in common. "They" say that opposites attract and that may well be true, but possibly at the expense of contentment. Not without some justification, my mother constantly complained to me about Tommy all his life and I asked her one day if she could think of any of his good points. "No," was the instant response. "Surely," I said, "there must have been something you liked about him." After a long pause she said, "Well, he came home on time occasionally," and, after another pause, "when he was on two till ten shift." I asked if there was anything else. Another pause, then, "Well, he read the papers when the bombs were dropping so he was a calming influence." Some testimonial, eh?

Despite everything, she missed him badly when he died and I found amongst her belongings a poem she had written on the anniversary of his death.

> *"A year has passed since you left us.*
> *We often talk about the things you did and said.*
> *We have a smile… and then a tear*
> *…and then a wish that you were here."*

I think of him often. Never with sadness. Just with a smile and fond memories of the incorrigible wag that he was. I had a strange and lovely dream about him too. He was a young man and was singing at his own funeral in a sweet angelic voice: "I belong to Glasgow." Weird, or what?

We will say farewell to Beatie in a later Chapter.

Four

AUT DISCE AUT DISCEDE

*Education's purpose should be to replace
an empty mind with an open one.*
Malcolm Forbes.

WHEN I WAS BORN on 14th April 1936 I was too young to appreciate Sunderland being eight points clear leaders of Division One or George Camsell's four goals in Boro's 5-1 victory over Sheffield Wednesday that weekend. Manchester United were top of Division Two.

I have very few memories of early childhood, but when I was barely three years old I vaguely recall the first air raid siren when World War Two broke out, mainly because of the hysteria which followed as my mother and grandmother who was pushing my pram in the countryside, panicked as they rather pointlessly tried to find shelter under a tree. I don't think we posed any threat to the Lutwaffe. There are vague memories too of underground air raid shelters and later, our Anderson shelter, which was a steel box on two levels. I slept on the bottom beneath the thick steel covering and my parents slept on the top, joining me below when they heard an air raid warning siren and returning up top when the all-clear sounded. Thinking about it now, I suppose this was quite a convenient arrangement since the rented lodge cottage where we lived was tiny and only had one small bedroom. I remember my father in his ARP (Air Raid Patrol) helmet and his black overcoat, which was several sizes too big. There was also the incident of the bomb, which dropped very close to us one night when my dad was on duty, causing the soot to cascade down the chimney. The noise and the vibration woke us up and my mother of course panicked, grabbed me out of my bed and ran through to the living room. There was Tommy, who had been sitting next to the fire, covered in black soot. Round his eyes were two white circles where he had obviously blinked and within a few seconds he had taken the heat out of the situation by singing Al Jolson songs and performing the heeby jeebies (a sort of Egyptian dance) provoking uncontrollable laughter from my mother and me. Al Jolson was a famous black impersonator at that time. Tommy was actually on bomb watch at the time as part of his ARP duties but the thought of rushing to the scene of the explosion never crossed his mind. He was enjoying his cabaret performance too much. I couldn't wait the following day to satisfy my curiosity and stood for ages, fascinated and frightened, staring into the huge crater.

Unlike many other wartime children, I was fortunate not to be evacuated to the country to be cared for by foster parents. In fact, I was not particularly aware of any deprivation during this period of severe austerity – probably because I had never experienced anything better. What you've never had you never miss! Rationing meant that our family was entitled to one egg a week, which my dad had. But he would give me the top off it – what a treat that was! Then my mother managed to acquire some day old chicks which were raised in a warm drawer in the cupboard next to the big black range which were then a feature of old houses. Many a new born baby spent its early days in such drawers, me included probably.

For a brief period we had a pet dog, Paddy, an uncontrollable animal with a penchant for chewing furniture and barking at and chasing passing vehicles – but only army ones, never civilian ones. We had, it seems, the country's only pacifist dog! Either that or he was German. Because of the havoc he caused he was quietly disposed of. "He's gone to have his eyes tested," was my dad's explanation when I asked where the dog was! Paddy was replaced by Tibby, the psychic cat. Tibby was able to tell the time. A minute or two before I came into view round the corner from school, he would jump onto the back of the settee until he saw me and then jump down and wait by the door. He had no way of spotting me in advance yet never failed to perform this uncanny ritual. I killed Tibby. Much as I loved the sweet sugary milk, which made up the last few spoonfuls in my cornflakes bowl, I would sacrifice these and gave them every morning to Tibby. He died of worms. Killed with kindness.

Perhaps if my mother had kept her second child she may not have been such an over indulgent fusspot with me, and talking of pots, she made me delay any calls of nature until the rim of my potty was suitably warmed by the fire on to which she would throw a handful of sugar to make it blaze if I was desperate. Until one day, that is, when I suffered second degree burns to my bum! My call of nature was interrupted by a knock at the door which distracted my mother from her routine. When she returned she could see I was poised for action and hastily thrust the potty under my bare bum. Ouch! The rim, having been exposed to the heat of the fire too long was painfully hot.

I took some potty training after that incident. Another, later, example of my mother's irritating solicitude was when I started school. If it was raining or cold she tried to persuade me not to go. "Stay here with me where it's nice and cosy," she would urge. Fortunately for me and my early education I always resisted her entreaties. I couldn't wait to get out. It was a different story in the evenings when I couldn't wait to get indoors before Sand Shoe Sammy got me. I am still not sure whether Sammy was real or an expedient used by my mother - her version of Wee Willie Winkie perhaps!

After we moved into the Bishop's Lodge my childhood became more settled. The chicks grew into hens with plenty of space for them to roam, so fresh free-range eggs were plentiful and the Christmas bird was never a problem. Uncle Edward, Auntie Mary and my cousin Neil lived just across the road from us in Southend Lodge and also kept hens – and a white leghorn cockerel, which I was terrified of. This vicious beast once nearly claimed my young life when it chased me across the road and almost into the path of a passing car. We were fortunate to be able to share with our hens the spacious grounds of the Bishop's House, since we lived in the old gatekeeper's lodge. The house, which was originally the Roman Catholic Bishop of Middlesbrough's manse, was no longer occupied and we acted as unofficial and unpaid caretakers. The house later became St Joseph's Working Men's Club and this and the lovely grounds were eventually flattened. The new Priory Club and an Aldi supermarket now occupy the site. What a shame.

Cousin Neil and I, and later our friends, unofficially I guess, had the freedom of the grounds which included a disused fountain, lawns, a variety of trees, including an orchard, and a circular drive which later became our bike racing circuit. We would pretend to be speedway riders. Our bikes would be converted into motorbikes by putting playing cards in the spokes to simulate the zip of the engines. A square gravel surfaced clearing also provided us with an ideal pitch to kick around the footballs which were ingeniously supplied by our local butcher in the form of inflated pigs' bladders! The church which owned the grounds raised no objections to their harmless use by us, but as we grew older and our circle of friends widened, some of them found the old unoccupied manse irresistible and we managed to find a way inside. To us it was incredibly exciting to have the run of this big beautiful empty house, but there was an inevitable reaction to the abuse of our privileges.

Canon McMullen was a strict and fearsome despot to his own parishioners. We, too, became terrified of him. My friend and golf partner Paul Radigan later told me that his father, then a staunch Catholic, had left the Church after being publicly humiliated by this unpleasant man of the cloth. Neil and I tried to disassociate ourselves with the vandalism of the old house but one day when I was inside with another boy the Canon crept into the house to try to catch us. We knew every inch of that house; every nook and cranny. And we had an escape route planned in advance. But the Canon was cunning, too. After a while, his search in vain, he left, closing and locking the door behind him. From our hiding place under the floorboards where the Canon had walked earlier, mere inches from our noses, we made our way, trembling, to our point of escape at the rear of the building. The other boy was in too much of a rush in his eagerness to escape and scrambled blindly out of the opening, which was our escape exit – straight into the arms of the waiting Canon. I had been more cautious and remained crouched in my cramped hiding place for what seemed like hours, until the coast was clear. All good things come to an end – and another phase of my life now beckoned.

When I was a baby, prior to my granma Gardner dying of cancer, my cot was installed at 18 Marton Grove Road whilst my mother nursed her through her illness. Then when my grandfather fell ill in 1945, again it fell to the willing horse, my mother, to nurse him. The strain of running two homes became too much and a decision was made to vacate the Bishop's Lodge and for us all to move into grandfather's house, where he lived alone. The decision was made with the best of motives but with little thought to the ultimate consequences. Though I missed the advantages of the lodge I soon settled at number eighteen which was very close to my school and I was encouraged by my grandfather to help with his garden, which he had cultivated with pride and with great skill and imagination. His sweet peas in particular were profuse and robust – especially the year we buried Tibby in the plot.

Through Donald Clark, the son of my mother's friend Winnie, I had become interested in pigeons and built a small loft in our new garden. I saved all my pocket money and was lucky enough to buy some pedigree birds with which I had considerable success at local shows. I also bred them successfully and won a prize for 'best bird in show' at the prestigious Durham County Show. The birds were 'show racers'. I found this to be a fascinating and absorbing hobby and my success at Durham County was followed by many more. I later acquired the use of an allotment free, in return for digging and looking after the owner's flower and vegetable beds. But my life was moving on. To the astonishment of my parents I had passed my eleven plus exam and had been accepted for Grammar School.

This was a culture shock for me; a life changing experience. I was to feel out of my depth in my new 'posh' environment and I no longer had a one-minute walk to get to school. I was now in the big world, travelling to school by bus. Though I had spent six years at Marton Grove School – infants and junior - they must have been fairly uneventful since I have no recollection of any major moments there. I do remember though that Brian Clough, the famous footballer and manager, who was in the year above me, couldn't get his game for the school team. He was obviously a late developer. He did have a reputation as a good fighter which he shared with Gordon Lawrence. They never actually fought each other to establish the undisputed title. Cloughie was acknowledged as the best *boxer* and Gordon as the best *wrestler*. I found him to be a bit of a bully, a characteristic which was later to serve him well in his football management days. This trait was evident too when he played for Boro. Ruffled and annoyed by his attitude, most of the other players presented a round robin to the manager objecting to his presence in the team.   Perhaps this was influential in his subsequent transfer to Sunderland.

I looked forward with trepidation to my first day at Grammar School – and my fears proved to be well founded. Horror of horrors! I was the only boy to turn up on the first school day in a blue blazer – and an out of date badge. The school colour was black. My mother had failed to realise that there was a shop in town, which was the official supplier of High School uniforms and had somehow got her hands on a secondhand blazer and badge. I hated her! I wasn't to know that perhaps that was all she could afford. Of course this and the nickname Anna which I was given, made me a target and my treatment in the 'monkey hole' was brutal. The monkey hole was a void at the bottom of the steps leading down to the gym boiler house. It was a tradition at Middlesbrough High School for Boys that fuggies, as first year students were called, would be rounded up and thrown down the monkey hole. The older boys would then form a tunnel by standing side by side, bent over with hands against the wall of the gym. The 'fuggies' would then be ordered to ascend the steps and make their way to safety along the human tunnel as best they could whilst being kicked, punched, knocked to the ground, spat at and, it was said, occasionally be subjected to something even more disgusting—terrifying at the time but all good character building stuff.

My blazer was eventually replaced and I gradually settled in. I realise now how lucky I was to have passed my Eleven Plus exam before the abolition of Grammar Schools. Had I failed and gone to the local Senior School, I am sure like many others who haven't the courage to ignore the bullies, I would have been too timid to do well academically. I just could not have handled being branded a swot by the Mafia element of secondary education and I would have tried hard to be a failure so I could be one of the gang who think it is clever not to be clever.

Whilst situated in the centre of Middlesbrough, the High School was run by the headmaster, Mr Fletcher, on strict public school traditional lines. The first thing, which was impressed upon us, was the school motto "*Aut Disce Aut Discede*" – either learn or leave. The classes themselves were graded in the old traditional fashion starting with the third form (why not the first form was a mystery to me), then the lower fourth, the upper fourth, the lower fifth, the upper fifth and the two sixth forms. Unsurprisingly I found myself in 3C. However, at the end of the first term a re-grading took place and having achieved third in 3C which included firsts in a couple of subjects, I found myself in the A stream for the remainder of my school days. I remember feeling good about it but also a little embarrassed in case I was thought of as elitist, so I altered my first year school report by writing a one before the three to make it appear that I was thirteenth in the class. How stupid was that?

Inevitably the mainstream sports were rugger and cricket, neither of which appealed to me, since I considered myself to be a fairly talented soccer left-winger.

A few of us actually formed our own out of hours soccer team and played a few matches against some senior school teams, but that initiative was quickly squashed when Fletcher found out. I was simply too skinny for rugby and played cricket with little enthusiasm, particularly after my humiliation in a match against Acklam Hall School watched by a contingent of supporters from the girls' school. I was fielding at square leg and the defending batsman snicked a ball off the edge of his bat which bounced before snicking the top of my down-stretched hands and going on to also snick my dangly bits. I fell to the floor like an Italian footballer, writhing in agony to raucous laughter from the girls. I think that was the highlight of the match for them. With the embarrassment of that incident the last vestige of my sporting ambition disappeared and I spent most of the subsequent sports days in the company of Cheeseborough who had perfected a way of avoiding games. We spent much of our time playing bowls in Albert Park and later snooker in the Empire Hotel, always managing to get back in time for roll call. Since we were both disinterested and therefore useless, I suspect the Games Master may have been pleased that we were not around to hinder the progress of his keener and more promising athletes and perhaps turned a blind eye to our truancy.

It was a different matter when it came to school playground activities. I used to like to get to school early for the morning football played in the school playground with a tennis ball. The two earliest arrivals became captains and took turns to pick their players. Matches used to start with maybe three or four on each side increasing to about forty before the bell went for lessons.

Checks, bongies and of course conkers were just a few of the recreational activities we engaged in to pass the time. Checks was a game played solo with small squares or pebbles one of which would be thrown in the air and caught after lodging another between your fingers until you had up to twelve lodged and one in each palm. Not as easy as it sounds. Bongies was the same as alleys but played with ball bearings, usually in the gutter. Your bongie would be thrown along the gutter like a jack in bowls and your opponent would try to hit it with his. If he did he would capture it. If a bongie fell into a drain the thrower would forfeit another one. The skill was to throw your bongie far enough past your opponent's so, if you missed, he wouldn't have a short throw while, at the same time, avoiding the drain thereby bringing it into play for your opponent. Conkers was taken very seriously too. I once had a "hundred and twentier" but some claimed to have "thousanders". The value of your opponent's conker would be added to yours if you succeeded in smashing it. Whoever lost the toss would dangle his conker on a piece of cord at shoulder height and you would attempt to smash it with yours. If you missed then it was your opponent's turn. Cheating by failing to keep the defending conker perfectly still resulted in a free hit – if you managed to win the hotly disputed and lengthy argument that often ensued, and which usually ended in stalemate, a void match and falling out of friends. A re-hit was allowed if the two pieces of string got tangled but only if you shouted "stringer" before your opponent. Similarly if the hit wasn't clean the first to shout "tips" would have the next turn. Huge crowds would gather to watch top contests between high ranking conkers. Many devices were used to create competitive conkers. One year I managed to get my hands on a mature chestnut which wasn't easy since the trees were prematurely denuded, such was the popularity of conkers then. Having acquired the suitable raw material, the next step was to soak it in vinegar and then to keep it in a darkened drawer over the winter. I eagerly awaited the next conker season, regularly checking my potential champion which emerged the following September like concrete. Trouble was, I had forgotten to put a hole through it first and had no way of doing so. It remained a "nonner". Because this innocent pastime, like many others, now seems to have been banned, I decided to include this passage in my book in the hope that some daring youths may go underground and resurrect it.

By far the most popular and dangerous game we played at school was Mona Kitty. Not for the fainthearted, it was played between two teams of minimum four, but ideally up to ten. The defending team's anchor man would stand with his back to the wall with the rest facing him, crouched and braced like a rugby scrum but in a straight line like a Chinese dragon. The attacking team would select what they considered the weakest point in the line and one by one would leapfrog on top of it and then on top of each other. When, and only when, the last man had landed, the defending team would chant "Mona Kitty, Mona Kitty, one two three", repeating it four times while the attackers, by bouncing up and down, or by any means at their disposal, would attempt to collapse the line. If it did, they'd won. If it didn't then victory went to the defenders.

I was fortunate enough to enjoy my schooldays before the SS created our present cotton wool culture by preventing millions of kids from indulging in innocuous activities in case one might suffer a bruise or two. By being denied an outlet to their natural boisterousness, many now turn to anti-social behaviour as an outlet. I went to school when taking drugs meant having your polio injection. When race issue meant who could run the fastest. When having a weapon at school meant being caught with a catapult, a spud gun or a water pistol. When I was old enough to know better, but too young to care. Happy days! SS by the way is short for spoil sports – that small serious minded politically correct group of anonymous people who know what is best for us but lack common sense and foresight and are completely out of touch with reality, yet wield enormous power over us.

Like most adolescents, heroes were important to me. Every Saturday morning we would queue at the Elite or the Gaumont or the Regent cinemas where, for a shilling, we could watch adventure serials in which Roy Rogers, his horse Trigger, the Lone Ranger, Gene Autry and other film stars, chased by the baddies, would plunge over a cliff to what appeared certain death only to discover the following Saturday that they had been saved by grabbing hold of a shrub that wasn't there the week before, thus surviving to continue their crusade against the baddies. Films in those days were about making people happy, not depressed or violent.

Our most credible heroes however were to be found among our peers. Held in reverence would be the best fighter, the loudest farter, the lad with the biggest dick, the one who could piss the highest or, like Tramlines Taylor, spit the furthest. Taylor earned his reputation because he seemed to be constantly suffering from a heavy cold causing two channels of snot to be permanently attached to his upper lip. These, prior to a spit, would be sucked back up his nostrils and prepared in the back of his throat into a deadly missile which could be ejected at enormous force and accuracy at his chosen target – which included you if you had upset him. Taylor who, apart from this attribute, didn't have a lot going for him, was always looking for ways to show off. A crowd of us set off one frosty winter's day when the tramlines were at their most gelatinous, in search of a telegraph pole to ratify Taylor's claim that he could reach the top. He didn't allow for the wind on his first attempt, missed the target and bored with waiting for a suitable re-coagulation of his ammunition to build up, most of us drifted away. He later claimed his mission had been successful of course but with only his best friend as a witness we had our doubts. Porritt was our champion wanker, though it was called tossing off in those days. I didn't qualify for this event because it was held in public and I needed privacy to function successfully in this particular activity. Porritt was unbeatable, on one occasion breaking the ten-second barrier. Surely a world record. Penis Porritt we called him. The appropriately named Carter was our farting idol. His flatulence control was amazing. His longest ever fart, however, never found its way into the record books because it was wind assisted. Carter's piece de resistance however was his ability to produce rectal melodies. We made up a poem in his honour.

> *My best friend's name is Carter*
> *He is a musical farter*
> *He can fart anything*
> *From God Save The King*
> *To Beethoven's Moonlight Sonata.*

When I was in the fourth form the head boy was upper sixth former Peter Robert Robin Pawson Trevor Forrest. With a name like that you have to compensate by being a bit special. I was already in awe of him and on his final day at school he became a celebrity. It was his role at assembly to play the morning hymn on piano and his final performance was memorable. Instead of '*Praise my Soul the King of Heaven',* he played "*Hallelujah I'm a bum",* supported by some of his fellow sixth formers who sang the words. Since this was their final day too, Fletcher was powerless to punish or expel them. Forrest was determined to leave his mark and his other escapade, of which I found out about too late to witness, was to dive off Middlesbrough's famous Transporter Bridge. I was disappointed to learn later that he had only *jumped* off and then only from the vehicle cradle which was supported by pendulum steel hawsers from the sixty-nine metre high structure. I thought he was going to dive from the top, but on reflection I doubt whether anyone has ever dived and survived from a height of sixty-nine metres and his achievement must rank as the most daring and dangerous ever by a pupil of Middlesbrough High School for Boys.

At that age of course we were always hungry and school dinners were eagerly anticipated – and not just for the food. Each table would have a sixth former at its head, flanked by two fifth formers, then two fourth formers and finally by two fuggies. The food would be delivered in tureens to the head of the table where they were plundered by the sixth former, then the fifth former and scraped empty by the fourth formers. The fuggies used to pass the time away watching the girls outside (the dining room was in the girls' school area). The girls would sit on the wall and then jump down so their skirts would billow up, revealing bare thighs and sometimes, a tantalising glimpse of elastic knickers! One of the girls, Titty Foster, was said to be the school bike but gained her reputation I suspect, not for her sexual promiscuity but simply because she happened to be an early developer.

Eventually the call rang out "Seconds" and there was a mad dash for the serving table, led always by the ravenous fuggies. Both before and after dinner the duty master would say prayers: *"Benedictus benedecat, per asum Christum Dominum Nostrum"* to which we were supposed to respond: *"Deo Gratias, Amen."* We used to rehearse each day how we would actually respond. Either "Dear *clarty* arse," or "Dear *farty* arse." You had to make sure that the duty master's eyes were not on you during the response or you may feel the retribution of the Latin master's cane on the hand, Tommy Gough, the Physics master's leather strap, or worst of all, Fletcher's selection of canes on the backside. There was a suggestion that he enjoyed this more, perhaps, than was proper. Minor misdemeanours were dealt with by "lines". We were required to write out anything from ten to a hundred times, depending on the severity of our misconduct, an undertaking not to repeat it. My inability to comply with the pledge *"I must hand in my homework on time"* was actually exacerbated by my requirement to spend a lot of time giving it, in writing, over and over again.

On the whole, I enjoyed my grammar school years and managed to come out with six decent 'O' levels having dropped, in hindsight unadvisedly, music, Latin and history, which I considered irrelevant to my future. Ironically my only failure was English literature, since I really enjoyed reading. I put this down to the English master, a soft touch, who could be, and always was, diverted from the lesson by mentioning one of his favourite topics, rugby or national savings! By 'O' Level time we had barely got half way through *Pride and Prejudice*, a book which many years later I enjoyed reading, though it wasn't my cup of tea at the time. If only it had been *Pickwick Papers* or *Great Expectations* or *Nicholas Nickleby* or *Oliver Twist* that year. I would have sailed through with flying colours.

Not only was I a very shy young boy, I also felt somehow an intruder among the elite, coming from my humble background, and my worst moments at school were when information was sent home by the school and because we had moved, I knew nothing about it. Or when they did an update on our details and I had to give a new address every time. I was so embarrassed and on more than one occasion said nothing and pretended that we hadn't moved again. My grandfather's house was in fact a council house and when he died we were evicted. No thought had been given to this possibility; otherwise we would have presumably either registered ourselves with the Council or retained the tenancy of the lodge. Finding oneself homeless and desperate is not a pleasant experience, so desperate measures were called for and after a brief spell at Laura Street with Mam's friend Winnie Allen, we moved into Rockcliffe Road where, in return for looking after a bedridden arthritic old woman, we had the use of a couple of rooms in her house. This proved to be an unsatisfactory arrangement so we moved to Saltburn-by-the-Sea to live in with Auntie Peggy, which meant I had a lengthy train journey every day to get to school. It was on one of these train journeys that I had a most unpleasant experience, an incident that would have an influence on my views later in life.

Railway carriages in those days were not of the open plan design of today. Each carriage consisted of several isolated compartments. I had been vaguely aware of a man standing on the platform at Middlesbrough Station waiting for the train to Saltburn. There was something about him even then that disturbed me. When I got on to the train and sat in an empty compartment, this man waited until the train was about to set off before getting into my compartment and sitting next to me, too close for comfort. I was too terrified to remember exactly what he was doing or saying but I do recall him asking me, "Does your little feller stand up in bed?" Luckily the next stop, Cargo Fleet, was only a few minutes down the line and I leapt to my feet and even before the train had stopped, flung open the door and jumped out, falling down in my eagerness to escape this vile, evil creature. I got into another compartment further down the train, making sure that there were other passengers in it. Even so, I trembled with apprehension for the rest of the journey. I didn't mention the incident to anyone. Was it fear? Embarrassment? Not wanting to cause a fuss? I don't know. But I do know that this is how paedophiles get away with their ugly behaviour for so long. Although I didn't mind living in Saltburn – Auntie Peggy was my favourite auntie – I was relieved when, for reasons I'm not aware of, we moved back to

Middlesbrough and the reason for my relief was not just the inconvenience. I lived in fear of another encounter with the paedophile.

We still didn't qualify for a council house so we moved in with Auntie Mary where I shared a bed with a not too happy cousin Neil whilst my parents slept on a bed on the landing. This house was on a bus route to school, which should have made getting to school easier, but I was often late. The reason? I was in love. Let me explain. Joan and I had never exchanged a word, but I think she was keen on me too. But perhaps that was wishful thinking. Joan caught her bus to school from the same stop as I did. The problem was that I was hopelessly and incurably shy and was too emotionally uncomfortable to be near her – even on the same bus. I could see the nearby bus stop from the landing window and when the bus approached I would make a mad dash to catch it – if the coast was clear, that is. By which I mean that Joan had either caught an earlier bus or intended to catch a later one. If however she was in the queue or ran for the same bus I had intended to catch, then I would hang back and catch a later one. Consequently I was often late for school and when asked for a reason from my teacher, muttered feebly, "Slept in Sir." How could I tell him the truth? Would he have believed me? Would he have understood? Would anybody? Joan was responsible for me having to write out, usually in copperplate handwriting, *"I must not be late"* several hundred times!

All this upheaval, geographically and emotionally, was not helping my preparations for the forthcoming 'O' level exams, in the middle of which we moved again, back to my birthplace, with Granma Arnott, where I remember trying to do revision whilst the girl next door was loudly practicing her piano keys over and over again. Impossible! I don't think my mother and her mother-in-law were compatible. Surprise, surprise. So our stay in Wicklow Street was brief. We were lucky to find a small house to rent right behind the grounds of the Bishop's House. I was happy there. We had some laughs – like when a bat flew in the window and Tommy was chasing it up and down the stairs with a frying pan, his shirt tails flapping above his spindly legs (he always wore a shirt for bed). Mam and I were ill laughing. Who was chasing who? On another occasion, Christmas day it was, Mam had for convenience bought a tinned Christmas pudding, which as per the instructions on the label she heated for an hour in a boiling pan. As soon as the can opener was inserted, the contents spurted out and deposited themselves on the ceiling. We had about a spoonful each of the dregs for dessert. I think she was supposed to pierce the can *before* placing it in boiling water!

With this latest accommodation came some outhouses, which would have been ideal for pigeons, but I resisted the temptation and instead got some rabbits, mice and an injured jackdaw, which I nursed back to health, at which time I should have released it. Instead I decided to keep it for a bit longer and clipped its wings. This had an unfortunate consequence. Each time it jumped from its perch to feed, it would fall forwards, which eventually caused its beak to cross. Instead of pecking it was forced to put its head on one side and scoop up its food – a comical sight, but a decided hindrance to its survival when I was eventually able to release it. I also lost my mice. Mam had good intentions when she moved their glass-fronted hutch on to a bench outside for some fresh air. She hadn't thought about the sun moving round causing the temperature through the glass to exceed survival level. The mice suffocated. *Oh what chaos we create when man would meddle in nature's state.*

Eventually we amassed enough points to qualify for a Council House and were offered accommodation in Roseberry Road – number 101. It was only a prefab – a basic sectional construction which was intended as a stopgap in the post-war housing shortage and already well past its "Sell By" date. But we accepted it with relief and enthusiasm. We had our own home – at last. We were settled, at least for the time being.

Much was happening in my social life around this time. Next door to the Bishop's Lodge was the Co-op dairy. When we lived there we were disturbed very early every morning by the clanking of the milk churns as they were unloaded full from the milk lorries and re-loaded empty to take back to the dairy farms scattered over the North Yorkshire moors. We never needed an alarm clock, what with this racket, the crowing of the white leghorn cockerel across the road and, on 6 till 2 shift, my dad's Woodbine-induced cough

My cousin Neil and I and our friends were to turn this situation to our advantage. With such lovely and interesting and, at that time, unspoiled countryside on our doorstep, the only problem we had was access to it, so one early morning we plucked up courage and asked one of the lorry drivers if he would give us a lift into the countryside. No problem. This became a regular routine every Sunday during school time and most days at holiday time. We became familiar with the dropping off routine and we were able, from our uncomfortable position on the back of the lorries among the milk churns, to deposit them on the wooden churn stands at the entrance to each farm by matching them with the appropriate identification marks. This way we saved the driver time and earned our lifts. We thus acquired wide access to the North Yorkshire Moors and had many an adventure there.

Our gang, which included Johnny Burton, Dave 'Dabby' Urwin and Brian 'Goopy' Goupelot, often lived rough, sleeping in haystacks or bivouacs made from tree branches and we lived largely off the land from edible berries, mushrooms and vegetables we begged, borrowed or stole from local farms. Goopy was an expert at catching and skinning rabbits. He boasted that he could kill and skin a rabbit so quickly that when he removed its heart it would still be beating. We once challenged him. He insisted that there was a heartbeat but we suspected that some surreptitious hand movement on his part had something to do with it. The result of the challenge was inconclusive. His bloodthirsty attitude worried me but his skill at setting snares in rabbit runs provided us with some interesting meals. I stopped eating rabbits when one day we caught a pregnant doe. The sight of the baby rabbits, revealed as she was skinned and opened up, was too much for me. Goopy later claimed that he had eaten the babies but no one saw him. I suspect there was more bravado than fact in his assertion.

One of our favourite venues was a small lake in Kildale called Fern Deep in a, then, remote area and ideal for camping and swimming. 'Tests of courage' were a feature of our wild young culture. If one of us performed some daring and dangerous act, the others had to follow suit. It could be quite scary at times. I remember once when we were trying to cross a swamp in a forest, Johnny Burton – or was it Goopy? – slipped off the fallen tree trunk we were using as a bridge and fell into the sludge below. He disappeared below the surface and just as we were beginning to worry, much to our relief, his head emerged covered in black slime. His first words were, "Test of Courage!" None of us were prepared to rise to the challenge. The 'rules' were that whatever act was performed it had to be intentional. This we claimed had been an accident, an accusation he strenuously denied. He basked for weeks in the doubtful glory of having performed an unchallenged test.

One Sunday it all went wrong. After being dropped off as usual, this time in Battersby, we set off to go to Farndale. It was spring, and we had heard that Farndale was festooned with daffodils. We walked and walked without a daffodil in sight. The stories we had heard had clearly been exaggerated. Late in the day we realised that we must have walked right through Farndale and well into the North Yorks Moors. We turned tail and began the long walk back to Battersby. We arrived exhausted, hours too late to catch the last bus! It was pitch black. We were stranded and miles from home. We had to somehow contact home, since we knew that by then our parents would be worried. As we set off in search of a public telephone someone unhelpfully mentioned that this was pretty pointless since none of our parents were on the telephone. Speculation followed as to how we could get word back to our parents that we were stranded – but safe. Our search for a public phone box was now not only academic but fruitless. There was no public phone box in Battersby or at least if there was it was well hidden. We still had no idea how we would get a message to our parents who by then, we realised, would be frantic with worry. The situation was bleak. Johnny Burton, I believe it was, who demonstrated his resourcefulness. Noticing a nearby telegraph pole, he reasoned that the line must lead to a telephone. We followed the line to a house and knocked timidly at the door. We had intended somehow to get news back to our parents and sleep rough till we were able to catch a bus the next day, but the local bobby – for it was his house we had been led to – would hear none of it. Transport was duly sent for us and our adventure was over – to the relief of our frantic parents. The following day at school we boasted of our exploits. The day after that we were heroes. The *Evening Gazette*, our local newspaper, was currently featuring a series of local recommended rambles in the area and the Monday edition, under the headline "A Ramble They'll Remember" gave a full report of our exploits and included all our names. We were famous! We all became blood brothers and shared a secret language – one which I was to find very useful when we needed to say something in front of the kids which we didn't want them to hear. It was quite simple really and with a little practice anyone can achieve fluency. Simply add "aig" before the first vowel in every word. Tr(aig)y (aig)it.

Tommy with me (right) and cousin Neil in front of the Bishop's House.

Five

R T & G

Never put off today what you can put on tomorrow.
Chrissarism.

BEFORE ICI built their massive chemical complexes on Teesside, steel was the region's major industry. Dorman Long & Co, who had supplied the steel for the Sydney Harbour Bridge and many other major steel structures throughout the world, and for whom my own father had worked for over forty years, were the region's major employer. I left school in 1952 and whilst my school offered some basic careers guidance, I felt that this was centred on the high fliers and those going on to sixth form, and the only advice I got from my parents was to get a white collar job. So it was that I drifted into an interview and test for a draughtsman's job at Dorman Long, for which there was considerable competition. I failed – probably with flying colours, to borrow a phrase from one of the characters I met in later life.

Much of my leisure time during this period continued to be taken up with travel.

From the limited scope afforded by the milk lorries, our weekend and holiday time countryside destinations had become more widespread as we started to hitchhike. We had joined the Youth Hostels Association and there was much rivalry between us to see how many different stamps we could amass. Each hostel would stamp its name on our membership cards on departure, but they did so only if your behaviour was acceptable, otherwise they would retain your card, thereby depriving you of access to other hostels. My card boasted a wide range of hostel stamps including Acomb, Westerdale, Alston, Ninebanks, Greenhead, Whitby, Scarborough, York, several in the Lake District and Scotland and the quaintly named Once Brewed in Northumberland and Boggle Hole at Runswick Bay in North Yorkshire. The YHA in those days provided a wonderful opportunity for young people to travel cheaply. There was an upper age limit on membership and only hikers and cyclists were able to avail themselves of the accommodation and facilities, thus encouraging young people to exercise. It also instilled into us a spirit of camaraderie, discipline, co-operation and friendship. There was in each hostel a communal kitchen and before leaving we were each allocated by the warden certain duties to perform, ranging from cleaning, washing up and other domestic chores, to painting, repair and general maintenance of the hostel. This and the fact that we had to provide, or hire, our own cotton sleeping bags to avoid laundry bills, kept the price of the accommodation to a very affordable level. Our hitched lifts sometimes dropped us off close to our chosen hostel but many were in remote rural areas so a lot of legwork was involved. I can't describe the buzz I got from simply being a car passenger in those days. People in our circle couldn't afford cars and this was my way to indulge myself in this exciting activity. Of course we would accept lifts in any sort of transport but often one of the latest luxury or sports cars would stop for us. I can almost feel and smell now the soft leather seats of the Ford Zephyr which was my first lift. The exhilaration felt on those occasions sowed the seeds for my love affair with cars which would consume my life a few years later.

Thus it was the name Road Transport & General which attracted me and persuaded me to respond to the job vacancy after being discarded by Dorman Long. I had no idea what the job entailed. All I knew was that it must have something to do with cars – and that was enough. RT&G was, in fact, an insurance company. I had no idea that there was such a thing as car insurance so my interview performance must have left a lot to be desired, what with my total ignorance and abject shyness. They must have been desperate, for I got the job.

I began to lose touch with my old Marton Grove friends when I went to grammar school and later when I started work, and they were gradually being replaced by new ones. Dennis Cass, Terry Cronin, Billy Limbert and Warren Wells, whose unconventional wedding in Aberdeenshire, which included an encounter with a dark planer, we were later to attend.

Allow me to digress for a moment to relate a little tale concerning Billy's girlfriend Marjorie, who was brought up in Canon Street in the slum area of Middlesbrough, from which her family had been re-housed on the Grove Hill Council estate. She started at Marton Grove school mid-term where she was bullied because of her background – not that Grove Hill was exactly Beverley Hills, far from it, though it was much more respectable than it is today. Her bullying was condoned, even encouraged by one of the teachers, Miss W, until one day at summer camp. Madge, as she was known, caught the lovely Miss W in a compromising position with another teacher. From that point Madge's school life improved. Not only did Miss W change her attitude towards Madge but she would come down heavily on anyone who had a go at her. It worked. Madge didn't tell.

I had also fallen in love again several times during this period. There was another Joan, a Nancy (though I think it was her elastic school knickers I was really in love with) and later, Jazz. Then there was Jean at RT&G, and Molly Picknet. I don't know whether any of them were aware of my feelings. I was always too shy to declare them. There was also a girl I met at Butlins but whose name I've forgotten. In the post-war period of the nineteen-forties and fifties Butlins Holiday Camps had sprung up all over the country and had brought holidays within reach of many who could not otherwise afford them. They provided top class entertainment, edible, if not gourmet, food, and clean chalet accommodation, in which many a young virginity was lost. Maybe they were a bit too regimented for some, but when I went with some friends to Filey camp in 1953 we had a great time. I think the fact that a blind eye was turned to underage drinking had something to do with this. Each holidaymaker was allocated a 'House' and each 'House' had its own dining room. There was a team of 'Redcoats' in charge of each House who encouraged us to gain points for the House by entering the various competitions which they organised. I've always been a competitive person and entered into the spirit of things with enthusiasm. Despite my schooldays sporting apathy – and frequent absenteeism – I had performed well on the track and in cross-country running, so I put my name down to represent Cleveland House in the mile race. My preparation for the event was to drink myself into oblivion on the eve of the race, but I nevertheless found myself among the early race leaders. However, the previous night's beer was beginning to filter through my system and I was forced to temporarily abandon the race to visit a trackside toilet, rejoining the race a lap later, now into its final stages, again among the leaders. The energy conserved during my apparently unnoticed break enabled me to produce a sprint finish in which I was narrowly beaten to the tape, producing nevertheless, fifteen points for Cleveland House. Despite protestations from my friends and even the Cleveland House Redcoat, in whom I had confided, I voluntarily disqualified myself. All good fun, though.

Starting a new job, I believe, is one of the most stressful and difficult times in one's young life. You have no skills to offer and feel utterly and embarrassingly useless. So I was mightily relieved when I was given some forms to copy. This was in the days before mechanical photocopiers, which we all now take for granted. These forms, I later learned, were called claim forms and included details of the claimant, the circumstances and a sketch of the accident. There were, I think, only three or four of these forms and when the boss returned to my desk three hours later to find out why this simple task was taking so long, he explained kindly to me that the copies need not be so detailed and so exact. I had taken my task so seriously that I was copying very precisely each claimant's handwriting and producing detailed replicas of their sketches! I can imagine now what thoughts must have been going through the boss's mind at that time. Another, later, example of my innocence, seriousness and naivety (some would say stupidity) was when I had become experienced enough to deal with clients at the counter, and having dealt with one client's problems he offered me two shillings for a packet of cigarettes. "I'm sorry, we don't sell them here," I responded, "but there's a tobacconists just a few doors away." Fortunately they persevered with me. After all, I was only costing them two pounds a week in wages, and I began to tackle my new job, which I was now beginning to find quite interesting, with enthusiasm.

At this point I would like to mention something that I had forgotten but my mother, before she died, reminded me of. I had gone home after my first week at work, she told me, and given her my wages to buy a new purple dress. Purple was her favourite colour. She had apparently cherished this memory all her life.

Fascinated by this new commercial world I found myself in, I decided to make insurance my career and immediately started studying for my professional qualifications. I was appointed to the permanent staff of RT&G on 1st July 1953 at an annual salary of £175 plus a £10 merit bonus for passing the first part of the professional Associateship exam. I passed the second part the following year and was well on the way to completing the third and final part which would have made me one of the youngest, if not the youngest, ACII's ever. National Service put paid to that.

Six

23089563

A shite in knighting armour.
Chrissarism.

Now you mummies darlings get a rift on them boots. Definitely shine 'em
my curly headed lambs, for in our mob, war or no war, you die with clean boots.
Gerald Kersch.

WHENEVER I'VE MET an ex-serviceman I've made a point of asking for his service number. Everyone has, without hesitation, been able to rattle it off. It is one thing in life, it seems, that you never forget.

After the war ended in 1945 the armed forces of the UK were depleted in number. Even many of the regulars had had enough and seizing the opportunity for demobilisation left the services, though some kept on their military connection by signing on as reservists in the Territorial Army (TA) for which they received a gratuity and were given mandatory extra leave by their employers to attend military exercises and training.   This was at a time when Britain's colonial and other worldwide commitments were substantial. Many of these responsibilities relied on military support. So the then Labour government under Clement Attlee introduced, on the 1st January 1949, the first peacetime conscription. This lasted until 1963 when the last National Serviceman, Richard Vaughan of the Royal Army Pay Corps, was demobbed on the 16th May. Very few young men over eighteen were exempt from conscription and insurance exams certainly were not considered by the Ministry of Labour and National Service to be grounds for exemption, or even deferment, so in 1954 I duly received my enlistment notice summoning me to attend the local recruitment office. Bill Robertson, my old boss at RT&G, told me he was well connected in army and air force circles and would 'have a word' on my behalf.

The boys in blue, or Brylcream Boys, as they were called during the war, were always successful with the opposite sex in the films I had seen, so the glamour of the uniform made me plump for the RAF when Mr Robertson asked me for my preferences. I was called up by the army.

Because of my fascination with motorcars I was hoping that my job in the army might have something to do with transport so, again trusting that Mr Robertson's influence might do the trick, I opted for the REME (Royal Electrical & Mechanical Engineers) with the Royal Signals and Royal Engineers as second and third choices. I heard nothing further for quite a few months and in the vain hope that they had forgotten about me I decided to continue my studies for the final part of my ACII exams. These were cut short when the dreaded brown OHMS (On His Majesty's Service) envelope dropped through our letterbox. It contained a British Railways travel warrant and details of where and when I was to report for my basic training. The choices offered by the recruitment officer again proved to be academic and in November 1954 I became 23089563 Gunner Arnott in the Royal Artillery! I was to serve my basic training at Oswestry in Shropshire, the birth place of The Reverend William Archibald Spooner who we shall meet in a later Chapter.

On a cold grey November day I arrived at Oswestry Railway Station where I was rounded up with other new recruits. Our nondescript and bemused bunch was taken in an army truck to the Royal Artillery Barracks where the first step was to get us into uniform. At the Quartermaster's store and after a cursory glance by one of the QM staff my kit was piled on the counter. Since this cursory glance was the closest they got to bespoke tailoring I was lucky, luckier than most, to have been issued with a uniform which (almost) fitted me. I was later to benefit from this good fortune. We carried our kit to the billet, which was to be home for the next three months or so and in which we were allocated a bed and a locker and given some string and brown paper to parcel up and send home our civilian clothes. Once into uniform we were marched to the MO's (Medical Officer's) quarters, ordered to strip naked and take a communal shower. The army made no compromise to individual sensitivities. After putting on our khaki undershorts we were called in one by one by the MO for an examination and interview.

The MO lifted my testicles with a spatula and told me to cough.
Then he stuck the spatula up my backside and said:
"Do you suffer from headaches?"
Then he stuck it in my mouth and said,
"Do you suffer from piles?"
So I said: *"Can you see them from there?"*
"No," he said with some irritation, *"What I mean is, are you constipated?"*
"No sir, Church of England," I replied.
"Look," he said impatiently, *"have you moved your bowels recently?"*
"Wasn't issued with any," I said.
"What I mean," he rasped, *"is have you shit recently?"*
"No sir, I thought it was you."

I passed my medical. Gone was my last hope of escaping.

All young lads of that age are very conscious of their image and many of us sported the fashionable hairstyle of the time, so the next shock to our system was the famous, or infamous, army haircut, or RAO (Regimental All Off) as they called it. Short back and sides was taken to a new dimension as our crowning glory was reduced to almost complete baldness with a few strokes of the barber's shears. Shorn and shivering, we were marched back to our billet where our squad bombardier introduced himself and showed us how to make our beds and blanket roll and how to lay out our kit, stressing that we must follow his instructions precisely and warning us that there would be a kit inspection the following morning. A lecture was then delivered by a subaltern (a lower ranking officer) on how we were expected to behave now that we were in the army – and, more importantly, in the proud and honourable regiment of the Royal Artillery. The regimental motto was, and still is, *Quo Fas et Gloria Ducunt* – Where Honour and Glory Lead. This motto is featured at the bottom of the regimental badge, above which there is a cannon standing on some grass with a crown above. The crown that's never worn. The gun that never fires. The grass that never grows and... something unprintable.

The Geneva Convention provides that if captured, the only thing expected of you by the enemy is your name, rank and number. Your own side's expectations, nay, demands, are much more onerous – smartness, blind obedience, a servile acknowledgment of your status... and much more. 'Other ranks' must always salute commissioned officers and stand to attention before speaking or being spoken to, and must address them as 'Sir'. Similarly they must treat more senior NONCOMS (Non-

Commissioned Officers) in the same way, except 'Sir' must be replaced by the rank of the NONCOM. The lowest rank in the army is Private (Gunner in the RA). Promotion (in the RA) progresses from Gunner to Lance Bombardier (one stripe), Bombardier (two stripes), Sergeant (three stripes), to Staff Sergeant (three stripes plus crown). Officer rankings range from Second Lieutenant, Lieutenant, Captain, Major, Lieutenant Colonel, Colonel, Brigadier, Brigadier General, Major General through to General and Field Marshall. The strict class distinction is relaxed only once – on Christmas Day, when in keeping with tradition the men are served their Christmas dinners by the officers.

After our lecture we were given a short while to settle into our billet, then it was off to the canteen to be fed by the Army Catering Corps, whose credentials for the job obviously did not include personal hygiene. Food was sloshed on to our plates from behind a serving counter by a row of these unkempt individuals who, I can only assume, were excused the army's requirement of smartness. Another example of the army's disregard for hygiene in those days was the nature of the washing up facilities, which consisted of two tanks full of water. You dabbled your knife, fork, spoon, plate and mug in the first, which was lukewarm and which soon took on the consistency of a large bowl of broth and then you rinsed them off in the second tank which was cold and became more like cream of vegetable or consommé! I finished off my washing up in the ablutions back at the billet.

It was amazing that none of us became ill – but on reflection maybe not, bearing in mind the 'procedure.' In the army, if you felt ill you weren't allowed to stay in bed. Your mam was no longer at hand to call out the doctor! Instead you were made to get up, get into your uniform and at 7 a.m. attend 'sick parade' outside the MO's office, missing breakfast in the process. Eventually the MO would give you maybe a couple of minutes consultation before deciding that since you had been able to get up and attend sick parade there mustn't be a great deal wrong with you, so he would send you back to re-join your squad on the parade ground to face a morning's square bashing on an empty stomach.

Day one finally came to an end. Alone and bewildered in our strange beds, none of us took much rocking that night. It had been a long day. We were exhausted. The only intruders in my reverie were the Wainstones and Doris Day until, after what felt like a couple of hours… "HANDS OFF YOUR COCKS AND ON WITH YOUR SOCKS!" – yelled at the top of his voice by our squad bombardier. His words intruded into our senses and woke up those who had not already been disturbed a few seconds earlier by the billet door being almost ripped off its hinges and crashing against the wall as BB made his 6 a.m. entrance. I have forgotten the name of our bombardier so I will call him Bombardier Bastard, or BB for short.

Those of us who did not immediately leap out of bed, which was all of us, were then subjected to the blanket treatment as BB marched round the billet tearing the bedclothes from around us and hurling them on the floor. "STAND BY YOUR BEDS!" was his next command, again screeched at the top of his voice and those who had not complied within sixty seconds were unceremoniously dumped on the floor as BB tipped up their beds. We then had about thirty minutes to accomplish our ablutions, get dressed, make our beds, make up our bed rolls and lay out our kit for inspection which was to take place after breakfast.

None of us that morning escaped without, at best, BB's derision at our efforts to display our kit to his demanding high standards and at worst our kit and bed roll being ripped apart and strewn across the floor – quite soul destroying after so much effort had been put into getting it right. When BB's wrath had subsided and he had finished telling us what a disgrace we were to ourselves, the army and our regiment, there followed another, and final, demonstration of exactly how our kit should be laid out and our bed roll folded – like a triple sandwich of folded blanket, sheet, blanket, sheet, blanket with a blanket wrapped round the bundle. All had to be precisely folded to the required dimensions. To those among us, which was most of us, who had in the past relied on our mams and never had to make a bed in our lives before, this proved to be a formidable task. Our kit had to be painted with a khaki wash (blanco) and the buckles and badges polished till they gleamed. One of the squaddies plucked up the courage to mention to BB that he didn't have any polish or blanco. "Well, go to the bleedin' NAAFI and buy some then, you useless little worm!" was BB's helpful advice. Finally he issued an ominous warning as to what the consequences would be if we failed him in the future – "I'll have you all on jankers!" We didn't then know exactly what jankers was but it was enough to strike terror into our hearts. Not everyone got the message but as soon as I got an opportunity I stocked up with Brasso and blanco from the NAAFI, and made a start on my kit.

Our first daily ritual kit inspection was followed by a mile run in full kit strictly supervised by the PTI (Physical Training Instructor) who expected us to complete this run in something approaching Roger Bannister's recently established world record! Those who didn't come up to scratch were made to repeat the exercise, though it seemed nonsense to me that in a state of exhaustion and having failed at the first attempt, they were expected to succeed at the second. After lunch, which even the fussiest eaters among us devoured ravenously, we were subjected to our first drill training on the barrack square. Square bashing, it was called.

Day three was, in one respect, easier. There was no square bashing or other physical demands on us – but only because this was impossible due to the after-effects of the umpteen jabs we were subjected to. We could hardly lift our arms. We were in agony. From then on it was the same routine. Reveille, ablutions, bed roll and kit layout, breakfast, morning kit inspection, PT, NAAFI break, square bashing, evening meal, bull, lights out. We did later do some rifle practice and artillery training on twenty-five pounders which I found interesting and at which I became quite an adept member of our battery, even on one occasion being chosen to do a flight in one of the light aircraft which were used to locate our targets and pass information back to the battery to enable them to achieve the required direction and elevation on the guns. AOPs (Air Observation Planes) they were called.

BB's preoccupation however was with drill. He was determined that when our basic training was finished ours would be the best performing squad at passing out parade in front of the CO (Commanding Officer) and other bigwigs. To achieve this would be a feather in his cap and, he hoped, an extra stripe on his sleeve. Every day hours and hours were spent square bashing, each session preceded by an inspection of our rifles, boots, uniform and webbing (belt, gaiters and lanyard) and if they were not up to BB's demanding high standard he would react with fury, tearing open tunics with less than gleaming buttons, throwing on to the floor berets not at the correct angle, gouging with his stick webbing not perfectly blancoed or boots that didn't shine like beacons, all of which meant extra hours of 'bull' that night. Only when BB had got off his chest how disgusted he was with our appearance would drill commence. We were required to march (slow and quick), turn (left, right and about), stand to attention, at ease, slope arms, present arms, order arms, eyes right, eyes left, salute, all in unison and in two perfectly symmetrical lines. We would frequently be ordered to halt for one of us to be singled out as a recipient of BB's wrath and abuse – hurled at us from such close proximity that noses occasionally touched. Respond to BB's angry criticism and you could be in trouble. Say nothing and you could be in deeper trouble. Dumb insolence it was called, and was an offence under King's (now Queen's) Regulations. A typical barrack square confrontation would unfold something like this:

BB:	*You are marching like a Pigaldy ponce."* (He couldn't pronounce Piccadilly.)
Me:	Silence.
BB:	*"Well, what have you got to say for yourself you scruffy little moron?* *"What are you?"*
Me:	*"A scruffy moron, sir!"*
BB:	*"Sir? Sir? Are you blind as well as scruffy?"*
Me:	*"No Sir"*
BB:	*"You must be blind – and stupid!"*
Me:	*"Why?"*
BB:	*"Why? Why? – Why **Bombardier!**"*
Me:	Silence.
BB:	(pointing to his stripes) *"What are these? What are these? You skinny Scruffpot!"*
Me:	*"Stripes?"*

BB:	*"So does this make me a bleedin' officer then?*
	"Do I look like a bleedin' officer?"
Me:	*"No."*
BB:	*"What am I then?"*
Me:	*"A Bombardier."*
BB:	*"Yes. A Bombardier. A bloody Bombardier! So what do you call me when you speak to me?"*
Me:	*"A Bombadier."*
BB:	(at the top of his voice) *"A Bombadier **what?**"*
Me:	*"A Bombadier, Bombadier."*
BB:	*"At last! The penny's dropped. Call me Sir once more and I'll have your guts for garters – OK?"*
Me:	*"Yes S-, er, Bombadier."*

A "conversation" with one of the other squaddies went like this:

BB:	*"What are you doing on my parade ground with your beret off your head?"*
Squaddie:	*"I took it off to scratch my head, Bombadier."*
BB:	*"Scratch your head? Scratch your bleedin' head? Would you take your trousers off to scratch your arse?"*
Squaddie:	*"No Bombardier."*
BB:	*"Then put it back on. Get off my parade ground and report to me later for jankers!*

Drill NCO's were not totally devoid of humour.

The survival skills I learned during my boyhood adventures in the countryside were to serve me well during the remaining weeks of basic training. These, coupled with common sense and not a little cunning, were to make my time in khaki not just tolerable but at times enjoyable. I soon learned how important 'bull' was to my captors and how to keep out of trouble. "If it moves, salute it, if it doesn't, polish it!" My kit was always carefully polished and blancoed and well presented. My bedroll was (almost) always beyond reproach and my boots highly buffed. They had a thing about boots. By applying the heat of an iron I was able to remove the pimples from the toecaps. This made them more receptive to spit and polish and using the same iron I was able to carefully burn off some of the heavy serge material from the front of my trousers, which enabled me to give them a sharp crease. By these and other expedients I was always smart and so was my kit. I didn't particularly enjoy these tasks but if it kept them happy then it kept me out of trouble. If you can't beat 'em, join 'em. This wasn't, alas, the case with some of my fellow squaddies who, without their mams around to do the essential menial tasks necessary for survival, found it difficult to cope. Ray Crozier, a pit lad from Wingate who was built like an ox and was hard as nails, used to cry himself to sleep during those early days. I knew because he was in the next bed to me. I also knew why. He just couldn't handle the bull. His kit was always in a mess and BB was always on his back, on a few occasions throwing his kit and bedroll out of the window, so poor Ray had to do it over and over again, even skipping his evening meal so he could spend more time getting it right. I came to Ray's rescue. I think I became his hero. Having quickly mastered the art of 'bull' myself, I had created some spare time in which I was able to help Ray with his kit and make his bedroll in the mornings. This kept him out of further trouble – and just in time too, since Ray was on his final warning from BB and being on 'jankers' would have only compounded Ray's problems by giving himself even less time to accomplish his tasks.

'Jankers', detention and extra duties, could mean anything from peeling spuds in the cookhouse to scraping the 'furry' off the urinals and many other unsavoury and usually pointless tasks, like painting coal or grass white! As I say, Ray was a big hard lad. Nobody gave me any hassle with him as my minder!

We were a motley selection of lads thrown unwillingly together for twenty-four hours a day. It was the army's task to transform us into a well-drilled cohesive fighting unit. BB had quite a task on his hands, particularly with Nigel Clark in our squad. Nigel was a quiet lad from the south. He was intelligent, could handle the 'bull' and was always smartly turned out. His defect was one which simply could not be corrected by shouting, bullying, humiliation or jankers – not that this made any difference to BB to whom picking on the weakest seemed to afford great pleasure. Nigel was a cripple. He had one leg shorter than the other. When the squad marched, Nigel's upper body at every other step would pop out sideways. It would have made for a comical situation had it not been so unfortunate – for Nigel and for BB who didn't ever hide his frustration or anger. Nigel should never have been conscripted; not if marching perfectly is the criteria for becoming an effective artillery gunner.

Andy Wilson was another misfit. We had finally to accept that Andy came from Burning Gum. No amount of elocution lessons from us could get him to convince us he was from Birmingham. Andy was likeable. He was just thick!

Apart from sympathy and encouragement there was simply nothing I could do for Andy or Nigel. It was tough on me and the others but almost unbearably so for these two and for Ray. This trio was picked on unmercifully and it would have surprised none of us if Nigel in particular had been not the first NS man to commit suicide had he chosen that means of escape from his tormentors. But he stuck it out and in the end was able to exact some retribution.

Unsurprisingly, Ray, Nigel and Andy did more than their share of weekly guard duties. The guard consisted of twelve "volunteers" (chosen by BB) and took place during the night and consisted of two hours 'on' (three times) and two hours 'off' (twice). I only did one guard duty and it was, literally, a nightmare. There were no facilities for sleeping other than a few bare benches and on being woken up to do one of my 'on' stints I felt distinctly uncomfortable in the underpants department. I had no time to deal with the problem and spent two hours of extreme discomfort in the cold December air. 'Wet' dreams at the height of a young man's sexual development are not uncommon. The reason I got away with doing only one guard duty was again down to my resourcefulness. Not twelve but thirteen "volunteers" were initially selected and were subjected to a pre-duty inspection. The one who was the smartest was excused duty. I made sure on future parades, that I was the smartest!

Despite the diversity of the characters in our squad a camaraderie gradually developed – an almost inevitable outcome of men being thrown together in adversity. The ingredients existed. There was amongst us a mutual feeling of resentment at having been uprooted from our normal lives. We also had a common goal – to survive basic training – and a common enemy in the form of BB.

After a few weeks we needed a release from the intensity of our existence and eagerly awaited our first twenty-four hour pass, which gave us an opportunity to leave camp and relax together without the burden of a 6 a.m. reveille and daily duties. We made the most of our night out in town. Towards the end of our training we were also given a thirty-six hour pass. Not quite long enough for me to get home and back, but a fellow squaddie, 'Taffy' Thomas, lived only a short journey away and he very kindly invited me to spend the break with him at his home. Some break! Taffy came from the very Welsh town of Blenau Festiniog and his was a very proud and puritan Welsh-speaking family. I could sense that they were not exactly overjoyed at having a visitor, especially an Englishman! His dad barely acknowledged me and refused to converse in English, though his mam was a little less bigoted and I did get fed. The Saturday night out was a bit of a damp squib too. We were expected to be back "not too late" and had to be careful not to display any signs of alcohol. I was actually glad to get back to Oswestry.

As passing out parade approached and with it the end of our basic training, I began to look forward to the next phase of my two-year stint with the RA. Out of the six squads in our intake ours performed the worst on parade day – thanks to Nigel who single-handed, or should I say single legged, thwarted BB's opportunity for promotion.

After passing out I was called before the CO (Commanding Officer) who actually congratulated me on becoming a soldier. I wish I'd been bold enough to tell him I would rather have become an ACII. Nevertheless, having requested a career involving transport, I eagerly awaited news of my fate. Woolwich Garrison for clerical training! I should have known.

Duties at Woolwich, the home of the Royal Horse Artillery, were less onerous. I was able to get home on a couple of forty-eight hour passes and the six weeks there soon passed. I missed my fellow squaddies from Oswestry but soon settled in with my new comrades, among whom was a lad called Alan, an inveterate gambler who helped to pass the time away playing a variety of inventive betting activities for money, the most bizarre of which involved masturbation. Given the match practice I had experienced during my schooldays, I thought I may have been in with a chance, but with his PE problem, Alan was no slouch and had no difficulty winning that one! He knew what he was doing before demanding we put our two bobs into the kitty. No wonder our billet NCO on laundry day would order us to strip our beds and stand the sheets up against the wall!

In the spring of 1955 I emerged from Woolwich Garrison as a fully-fledged Gunner with a trade and a modest increase in pay which I think totalled just under £2. The big moment had arrived – my permanent posting. I was quite excited at the prospect of spending the remainder of my two years in the exotic Far East (first choice), Middle East (second choice) or Germany (third choice). Sitting in the train on my journey to Perth in Scotland I had time to ponder on my ill fortune. Perhaps they were doing this deliberately as part of a strategy of subjugation. Nil Desparandum Carborundum. They wouldn't break my spirit, though.

Squaddies at Oswestry 1954. Gunner Arnott 2308963 (top left) and Bombardier Bastard (top centre).

Seven

TWO INCHES

Ay-ay. Saint Johnston's hunt is up! For the Fair Maid of Perth...
Up, up, every one of you... To the stables. When the horse is gone
the man at arms is useless - lame, maim and stab the horses...
let these proud knights meet us on their feet if they dare.
Walter Scott *(The Fair Maid of Perth).*

IT **WOULD HAVE BEEN NICE** to have seen something of the world at the
expense of HM Government but Perth proved to have more than enough by way
of compensatory factors. I was to quickly overcome my disappointment. Perth is a
lovely city, reputed to be the smallest in the world because it lies between two
inches. It is flanked by two greenfield stretches of land called the North Inch and the
South Inch, which give the city a feeling of space and freedom. It was the home of
General Accident Fire & Life Assurance Company (GAFLAC), of which RT&G was
a subsidiary. Its imposing Head Office, General Buildings, overlooked the River
Tay. I made myself known there and was taken out for tea on a couple of occasions
by two elderly female members of staff. Not quite what I had in mind! Perth is also
a gateway to some stunning countryside with Stirling and the Trossachs only a few
miles to the north and which I later had several opportunities to explore. For a young
man of eighteen, however, it had an even more attractive feature – its population
imbalance. The young men were considerably outnumbered by the young women.
This was because many of Perth's young men left to find work in the larger and
more industrialised towns and cities.

I had been posted to the HQ of the 51st (Highland) Infantry Division of the
Territorial Army based at Highland House. My job was in the admin office of the
Royal Artillery section manned by two other conscripts, Gunner Foster, Lance
Bombardier Rae and a permanent civilian called Reginald Brumfitt. To his immense
relief Rae had just recently been promoted from the rank of Gunner and would spend
the remaining six months of his service no longer the butt of jokes involving a
certain sexually transmitted disease.

The job was easy and could have been a lot easier if Brumfitt and I had not taken an almost instant dislike to each other. A small man with a stereotype pseudo sergeant major moustache, Brumfitt hailed originally from Redcar, only a few miles from my hometown. Perhaps in some perverse way he resented this fact. I don't know. What I did know was that he was pompous and arrogant and clearly enjoyed strutting his power. There was not enough work for us to do so in typical army fashion he would create irrelevant procedures and impose unnecessary tasks on us in order to demonstrate his authority and to justify the existence of his little empire. Although it could never be acknowledged or mentioned openly, he knew that I knew what he was about since I found it difficult to contain or conceal my disdain, not only for him, but for what I at that time considered the whole pointless purpose of two years National Service. As a result, he would try to make life difficult for me in all sorts of snide little ways, like changing the NAAFI break rota to allow the other two to go together first and me last. He would, with I suspect great satisfaction, turn a blind eye if the others returned late, thereby shortening my own break and sometimes depriving me of it altogether. The change in the man from snidey to smarmy when the Brigadier called was sickening to observe. Uriah Heap had nothing on Brumfitt on these occasions.

Working to rule, I just got on with my job and since the duty hours were not onerous, 8 a.m. till 4 p.m., five days a week, it was easily bearable.

Things were different up at Craigie House in Craigie Knowes Road where I shared a room with the other RA lads, Foster, Rae and Sanderson, the Brigadier's driver. Why couldn't I have got Sanderson's job? About twenty HQ lads from other regiments occupied the other rooms and about thirty infantry lads lived in two Nissan huts in the grounds. They somehow managed to persuade a young girl to move in with them. They all shared her. They kept it quiet for a few weeks until they were rumbled after an investigation by the missing persons section of the local police. Though I wasn't involved in the kidnap I had to stand in a seven a.m. identification parade to be eliminated. The Camp Commandant was an easy-going Captain whose career wasn't going anywhere and who was filling in time until his army pension was due. He had long since given up on imposing any meaningful discipline on us; such was the diversity of the soldiers under his command. We had a ball at Craigie House.

Thursday was payday and a night out at the City Hall dance where I enjoyed a good deal of success. There were plenty of fair maids of Perth to choose from. I was particularly pleased when I 'pulled' Kathy McGregor, a stunning lass who was a neighbour of Brumfitt's. I thoroughly enjoyed irritating him by relating to the other lads in the office my exploits with Kathy, making sure that Brumfitt could overhear. This could have backfired on me since I did let slip the fact that when I took her home she would slip into the house and borrow the keys to her father's car so we could have a snog in the comfort of the back seat. Brumfitt had obviously 'snitched' because Kathy was to later find that her father started to take the keys upstairs with him when he went to bed. By then, however, I had moved on to pastures new.

I would always try to save some money for the weekend to enjoy a good drink, black or white pudding suppers from the little chippie on the railway bridge and on Saturday another dance at the City Hall, followed always by the make or break card school back at Craigie House at which, in the early hours, free whisky would appear on the scene for the surviving participants, courtesy of the sergeants' mess. The lads who were on bar duty there had discovered that a two-shilling piece fitted exactly into a whisky measure and as the night wore on and the NCO's powers of observation diminished with drink, the lads would slip first one coin and then more into the measure, by which devious means they would 'win' a bottle of whisky for every three or four sold and, believe me, the NCO's were no slouches when it came to whisky consumption.

One Saturday night on our pub-crawl down to the City Hall we called into the Station Hotel where my pal Dick Shaw from Weston Super Mare had attracted the attention of a seedy little man. Dick had suffered from laryngitis and his voice was high pitched, which had obviously turned this creature on. We were short of money and since he was content to ply us with drinks – nips of whisky and wee heavies (Double Century Strong Ales) – we went along with him. Obviously wanting to be alone with Dick, he gave me a five-pound note, a small fortune to me, to go to the bar and get the drinks in. How tempted I was to disappear with this creep's money, but that meant deserting Dick, and by then the creep was becoming a nuisance. He suggested moving on to another pub where he was evidently well known and where he was asked by one of the locals to get up and give a tune on his harmonica. He was reluctant to leave us – or more accurately, leave Dick – but we were eventually able to persuade him to get up by telling him how much we would appreciate his talent. Halfway through his rendition Dick and I seized the opportunity and left. I will never forget the look in that man's eyes peering at us over his harmonica as they followed us to the door. Powerless in mid-act to stop us, his generosity had been in vain and his designs on my companion frustrated.

The uniform was certainly an attraction to the local girls and I had managed by various means to look less like a 'sprog' and more like a seasoned soldier. My floppy beret had been exchanged for Rae's on his demob. By soaking it in water for two years he had managed to shrink it to half its original size and I thought I was the bees' knees. The days of the RAOs were long gone and I also sported the hairstyle of the day, the Tony Curtis Cut, with the rear quiffed together. This was called a DA because it resembled a duck's arse. This tonsorial creation was kept nicely in place by the thick dandruff I had inherited from Rae's beret, which I blamed for my loss of hair in later life. To further improve my image, and I hoped, my 'pulling' power, I also invested in some fashionable civvy gear – a Donegal tweed jacket, black drainpipe trousers and a pair of crepe soled shoes – 'brothel creepers' as they were known. Though I even now find it hard to believe that they could possibly be in fashion, I later bought some yellow socks and a yellow scarf and gloves – urrgh! How could girls find such poncey gear attractive?   Maybe it had something to do with the 1950's pop song:

> *"Young man in a hot rod car.*
> *Diving like he's mad.*
> *With a pair of yellow gloves.*
> *Borrowed from his dad."*

They don't write 'em like that anymore!

My new image ensured that I continued to have no shortage of girlfriends, all of whom I met at the City Hall dance after tanking up with Dutch courage beforehand. I was still shy when it came to females and the one girl I really fancied didn't go to the dances. Her name, I eventually learned, was Fiona. She dressed stylishly, a little aloof perhaps, but mysterious. I just could not pluck up the courage to approach her. The story of my life? Never mind, there was still plenty going on in other directions to make life exciting and interesting.

Brumfitt was still being a pain. When Rae and Foster, now Lance Bombardier Foster, were demobbed, I was next in line for promotion. The Brigadier, with whom I got on well, was surprised when Brumfitt blocked my promotion. I wasn't! Another example of Brumfitt's bloody mindedness occurred when the Division went on a big TA exercise near Elgin in Morayshire. The weather was glorious and the TA soldiers were a great fun-loving bunch. My duty rota was two hours on and four off, which were spent joking, playing football, swimming and generally enjoying myself with the TA lads – until Brumfitt found out and spitefully changed my rota to two on and two off.

My philosophy during these two years had been to avoid trouble by going along with the system. There was one occasion however when I deliberately courted disaster by going AWOL – absent without leave – which was an extremely serious court martial offence. Not quite as serious as desertion for which in the past, many soldiers were shot, but it carried the risk of a term in the 'glass house', the military equivalent of prison but much, much harsher.

I had travelled home on a seventy-two hour pass, during which the NUR called a national rail strike. All servicemen on leave and due to return to their units were advised on the radio to report to their nearest TA headquarters. Mine was on the Wilderness Road to Stockton where, as instructed, I duly reported on the day I was due to return to Perth. The Captain in charge was taken by surprise when he found maybe a hundred of us waiting for him. He obviously knew nothing of the arrangement. "I suppose you'd better report here tomorrow at the same time," he told us. We did, or at least most of us did. Some had obviously been able to get back to their units. "Report here again tomorrow," we were instructed. This went on for about five days and I found myself eventually the only one to report.

"Where did they post you," said the Captain, "the bloody Hebrides?"

"No Sir," I replied.

"Well, the strike's over now so get back to your unit. I only want to see you again if that's not possible!" he ordered.

Of course by then I had no difficulty in catching a train back to Perth where I was immediately put on a charge and marched between two Military Policemen into the Camp Commandant's Office, where the charge against me was brusquely read out by the Sergeant present:

"Before charging you, do you have anything to say for yourself?" said the Camp Commandant.

"Couldn't disobey the Officer's orders Sir," I replied innocently, standing rigidly to attention and looking into the air.

"What's he talking about, Sergeant?"

"Don't know Sir. What are you talking about, Gunner?"

"Was ordered to report to my nearest TA unit, Sergeant."

"Well, couldn't you get back to your unit?" enquired the Camp Commandant.

"Don't know Sir. The Captain said I had to report back to him."

Having created enough confusion and since, presumably, they couldn't be bothered to check out my story, the charge was dropped. I had beaten them at their own game. Don't think for yourself, obey orders blindly. That was what they expect you to do. So I did – and got five days extra leave for being such a good, obedient soldier! Brumfitt, expecting them to throw the book at me, was furious when I turned up at the office the next day.

There are two other significant memories I have of my time in Perth. One light-hearted and the other tragic. In the 1950's the licensing laws in Scotland were very strict. Pubs closed at 9 p.m. and drink was not available at all on Sundays except in certain rare establishments and then only to bona fide travellers. The White Horse was the only such establishment in Perth and we did try unsuccessfully to bluff our way in once or twice. Noticing a coach parked outside we made some enquiries and discovered that every Sunday this coach was hired by the regulars at the Bridge of Earn Inn only a few miles away, to bring them to Perth for their lunchtime session. By this expedient they became bona fide travellers. Further enquiries revealed that ironically the Bridge of Earn Inn whilst prohibited from serving its own regulars was itself one of the few establishments open to bona fide travellers and in due course another coach was organised to take us there for our Sunday session. The occupants of the two coaches as they passed in opposite directions would exchange friendly waves. What a ridiculous situation! They were heavy sessions. I remember for the first time in my life getting up to sing. My rendition of 'High Noon' went down well and I became thereafter a regular "turn". My dad would have been proud of me.

The other and not so pleasant memory involved motorbikes. I myself had acquired one, a 125 cc James, replaced later by an old Indian Brave. Two of my acquaintances from home, Dennis Cass and Eddie Southern, were into bikes in a big way and owned a 500 cc Triumph Thunderbird and a 500 cc Norton Dominator, the two most powerful bikes of their day. It had been arranged that they would drive up to Perth bringing with them on pillion my two good friends Terry Cronin and Bill Limbert. I had booked B&B for them on the South Inch and was looking forward to showing them what Perth had to offer. Dennis and Terry arrived as planned. Eddie and Bill didn't They had been involved in a serious accident in Castle Eden, only a few minutes after setting off from Middlesbrough. Eddie was killed instantly and Bill was to spend months in a coma, critically ill. The driver of the car involved, a ship's second officer, and his wife played their part in the vigil which was kept by the family during Bill's lengthy coma. They have to be admired for that. Fortunately Bill recovered and later married Madge Stone. I was privileged to be best man.

Life in the fair City of Perth hadn't been too bad at all. With my food and accommodation provided, my pay was pocket money, which I was able to supplement from time to time by taking part-time jobs like erecting and dismantling the circus when it came to town. I was a regular at Muirfield, the then home of Perth's football team, St Johnstone, whose result I always, even now, look for on a Saturday night. The nearby ice rink gave me the opportunity to learn to skate and I played football for our army team. We used to have a kick around most evenings and at weekends in the field next to Cragie House. There were some very good players amongst us and we formed our own team, Craigie Thistle, which we managed to get into the local Wednesday league. Brumfitt of course tried to stop me from playing by refusing to allow me time off duty but I managed to get the Craigie House Camp Commandant, a Captain, to overrule him. Brumfitt was furious. He would have been even more furious if he had realised that when I was not selected I would pretend I was and take the afternoon off anyway to go along and spectate. It was a privilege to play in that Craigie Thistle team which performed very well in the league thanks largely to our bustling centre forward Shaw (not laryngitic friend Dick Shaw) whose reputation soon came to the attention of the local Scottish League pro team Saint Johnstone, for whom he played regularly before his demob. He was always well supported by the large contingent of Craigie House squaddies who went to their home games. Our toughest match in the Wednesday League was always against the team of inmates from Perth prison who were allowed out for the occasion. Many of them had played professionally before being locked up. Does that say something about the game?

I took advantage of another sporting opportunity during my service in Perth. The army had a ski centre in the Cairngorms, Rothiemurchies Hut, and I was able to get away on a couple of ski trips too. I also learned shorthand and typing when the Brigadier decided he wanted to emulate executives in the world of commerce and have a secretary, so I was sent on a course to a Secretarial College which was quite embarrassing, being the only male student among twenty or so giggling young girls. It was worth it though because it meant my army trade status was upgraded to Grade 3 with a substantial raise in pay. I was earning more than a lance bombardier so Brumfitt's block on my promotion became financially irrelevant, much to his annoyance once again. No wonder he hated me.

As the end of my two years approached, I found myself ticking off the days on my demob chart with less enthusiasm. Most of us kept a demob chart, which we religiously updated every day so that we could use the information in the presence of conscripts with longer to serve than us. "Only X days to go," we would gloat. "How long have you got?" I should have been 'demob happy' as they say, but as 'D' day approached I had mixed feelings. Was I becoming institutionalised? Perhaps to a certain extent, yes. It had been an eventful episode in my life. I had experienced much that I would have otherwise missed and had met many interesting characters and made some good, if transient, friendships.

Despite missing out on automatic promotion to Lance Bombardier at Highland House, thanks to my Grade 3 Tradesman's status, signing on as a Regular Soldier at substantially more money, did cross my mind. Unusually, an extra term of one instead of the usual minimum three years was offered to me. There was trouble brewing in the Middle East, which may have afforded the opportunity after all to serve abroad. Colonel Nasser of Egypt had nationalised the Suez Canal and Britain was poised for war, which in the end did not materialise. A combination of Brumfitt (who, for spite, would have probably tried to block an overseas posting), thoughts of home comforts, career prospects and cowardice combined to dispel the notion.

Eight

GEORDIELAND

Let's get the show on the ground.
Chrissarism.

I LEFT PERTH with mixed feelings. Two years is a long time in the life of a teenager. However, seventy-two hour passes were more frequently available in the final year of National Service and I had used these, with one exception, to come home on leave and keep in touch with my old friends. The exception was when I used one pass to go to Aberdeen to see one old friend, Warren Wells, a fellow pigeon fancier from my schooldays, who had done his National Service in the Veterinary Corps and who had then gone to work as a trainee gamekeeper on Lady MacRobert's estate at Tarland in Aberdeenshire. He was in his element. This reluctant 'townie' had escaped from urban life to seek rural contentment and he had found it in his tiny bothy with his two lovely obedient working dogs for friends. Of necessity my visit was a brief one. I spent one night in his bothy and the other in the Salvation Army hostel in Aberdeen. That too was an unforgettable experience – one survived rather than enjoyed. As a young lad dossed down in a dormitory among old down and outs and alcoholics, I was as you can imagine decidedly uneasy and hardly slept. I was lucky enough to find a bed next to a wall which possibly saved me from sexual molestation. I was fortunate too that the bearded old gentleman I had seen downstairs and who stank of stale urine and severe BO did not claim the bed next to mine. My good fortune was short lived since my immediate neighbour's farts were the most pungent I have ever encountered. The rancid cocktail of sweaty male socks, BO, urine and flatulence stayed in my nostrils for several hours on my return journey after forcing down some bland porridge, several slices of bread with homemade plum jam courtesy of the local WI and, once my upper lip had penetrated the oil slick, a mug of hot tea. The hostel's only saving grace was that it was cheap.

I was later to go back up to Tarland with mutual friends Bill Limbert and Terry Cronin for Warren's wedding with Isobel. Much to the dismay of Isobel and her family, Warren, who had never been a churchgoer, considered it hypocritical to marry in church and on principle refused to do so. All credit to the vicar who conducted the wedding ceremony in the bar of the Aberdeen Arms in Tarland! The celebrations, which went on for a few days, got off the mark in the village hall and continued in various homes, one of which was haunted by what they called a Dark Planer, a kind of Highland poltergeist which causes objects to move spontaneously. We were solemnly treated to a demonstration. Our host spoke to the spirit in Gaelic and invited it to reveal itself. *"There,"* he said, pointing to the sideboard where he claimed an ornament had moved. I wasn't impressed. I was so full of whisky the whole bloody room was moving. Warren and his wife now live with their son whom he calls "the mucker" on an estate in Warwickshire.

Whilst I was away serving my Country, Bill and Terry had widened our circle of friends so back at home there was now quite a mixed crowd of people to go walking with in the Cleveland Hills. The Wainstones was our favourite venue and a few of the lads would set off from Great Broughton every Sunday trying to break the record for the ascent to the summit where we were later joined by the girls. The views were stunning and so was Jazz who I fell in love with. Again, I didn't have the confidence to declare my feelings, and although I took her home from the dance a few times and had a few snogs and fumbles on dry land, it didn't go beyond that and another opportunity was lost.

In those days dance halls, sadly to be replaced later by nightclubs, were all the rage. There was an innocence about the old dance halls. Rarely was there any trouble and they were ideal 'boy meets girl' venues. The girls would sit or stand together in one area waiting to be asked up, with the boys at the other side of the dance floor in another cluster. It took a great deal of courage to set out on that long walk across the dance floor which sometimes ended in a refusal, a long and humiliating return journey and the ignominy of taunts from your so-called friends. Our favourite haunt at that time was the Coatham ballroom in Redcar which laid on special buses from and back to Middlesbrough. It was very popular, so much so that tickets would sell out quickly – often before 8 o'clock. This presented a problem. In order to face that long lonely trek across the empty dance floor later, it was essential, at least it was for me, to take on board the necessary volume of Dutch courage in the form of several pints of beer. We managed to get round the problem by going straight inside and after a respectable period we would get "pass outs", then go to the pub, returning later usually the worse for wear. These of course were entirely the wrong tactics since all the good looking girls had been snapped up by the time we returned and as I now realise, too much drink is a sure fire turn off for most females anyway. Such a pity. Self-consciousness is a dreadful affliction and I used to, and still do, love dancing and was no mean jiver. I even won a twist competition a few years later.

My Indian Brave motor bike had died on me and I had abandoned it in Perth, but back in Middlesbrough I managed to buy for £5 an old 1938 Morris 8. This was a potential death trap. There were no MOT tests in those days and with the brakes working only on one wheel, the off-side front, it had an alarming propensity for veering into the path of oncoming traffic. It didn't help either that I had not passed a driving test or even had any lessons. As I mentioned earlier, I left National Service at the time of the crisis in the Suez Canal region and for some reason that I have never been able to fathom, the Government at the time had suspended all driving tests and inexperienced drivers like me were at liberty to drive on the open road untrained, unqualified and unaccompanied. I survived some hairy moments in that old banger especially on the trunk road to Redcar with my cousin Neil on board when the brakes finally deserted the remaining wheel. Shortly afterwards the engine too gave up on me but even after it had spluttered its final cough it continued to come in useful as a snogging haven parked up behind Auntie Mary's house. My appetite for four wheels had been whetted during my hitch-hiking days. Now that I had discovered the versatility of the motor car I was well and truly hooked.

There was little scope for the advancement of my career at the Middlesbrough branch of RT & G so when it was offered, I jumped at the chance of working in their regional office in Market Street, Newcastle. I had completed the final part of my exams and was now a fully-fledged ACII – Associate of the Chartered Insurance Institute – and was keen to advance my career. Moving to a different region was a big step to take in those days and at that tender age and though a little apprehensive, I eagerly looked forward to it.

My first digs were just off Brighton Grove in Newcastle's west end. The only vivid memories of these were the daughter, a real snob, talking constantly of her fiancé who was an army officer, and the other was the length of the ash on the end of the landlady's cigarette which she kept constantly in her mouth while cooking my breakfast. It used to fascinate me by always remaining intact until she was finished cooking. I dreaded it falling into the frying pan amongst my bacon and eggs and never ever spoke to her in case her reply dislodged the precarious stack. Another vivid memory from that time was witnessing the horrific death of a young man on a tramcar as I was returning from town. Some lads in high spirits had got on at the stop before my destination and I came down stairs to see one of them holding the rails on the platform, leaning out backwards and singing his head off. Literally that. As the tram drew in towards the curb before stopping the lad's head came in sickening contact with a roadside tree and he disappeared from sight. I rushed back to help and placed my jacket in support of his head which was bleeding from every orifice. Someone ran across to the General Hospital just across the road but it seemed an age before a porter and a trolley arrived. This incident preyed on my mind for many years. Otherwise I was settling down quite nicely in Geordieland and began to enjoy the excitement of life in the big city although I still at this time spent my weekends on Teesside. I quickly learned the language. I just added "lyek" to the end of every sentence.

I soon made my mark in Market Street and when one of the senior staff left I was put in charge of what they called the 'combined' department which provided in one policy all the various types of insurances needed by traders. The move was supposed to be a stopgap until the old department head was replaced – but he never was. Whilst I was flattered that they considered me at twenty-one-years-old to be capable of running the department, I was disappointed that this 'promotion' wasn't recognised with a salary increase. I plucked up courage to have a word with the branch manager Mr L.R. Burton-Jenkins, a lovely old man who I thought looked out of place there and more suited to strolling round an old manor house with his dogs and a gun slung over his arm. Mr B-J listened to me sympathetically and explained that the company's salary scale was based largely on age which I thought was unfair in the circumstances. He did upgrade me but I was still on a fraction of the salary enjoyed by my predecessor which was a disappointment and unsettling. My ambition was to become what they call in insurance, an inspector – someone who liaises between the agents, policyholders and the office. Syd Twaddle (real name) was our inspector at R T & G and likely to be so for many years to come. So no scope for advancement there – especially at my tender age. I started to read the *Post Magazine and Insurance Monitor*, being careful not to let the chief clerk see me looking at the Situations Vacant. Eventually I found the ad I was hoping for – a junior inspector's job with United British Insurance Co, based in Newcastle, but covering the territory south of the Tyne – which was almost certain to mean the use of a company car. Perfect! I went for the interview and got the job – and joy of joys I was to have the use of a Morris Minor, for two days a week. The car wasn't new and it wasn't pristine, but I had some real wheels at last. Who cared about its condition or about the most unusual dent I have ever seen in a car. Unlike most dents which are concave, this one, on the near side rear, was the opposite and was caused, I was to learn later, by Jimmy Atkinson with whom I shared the car, bracing himself and pushing outwards with his feet as he pushed onwards with another part of his body during love making sessions with his girlfriend on the back seat. Talk about King of the Road! I was in heaven tearing around the County Durham countryside in this dream machine. It wasn't long before the company supplied a new car for Jimmy and I inherited the old one – dent and all.

Shortly after my move to UB a new Branch Manager, Dick Geddes, was appointed. Dick was quite young for a BM and had achieved a meteoric rise to fame as a very successful inspector in Glasgow. He was a human dynamo, a workaholic, and expected us all to be the same. Twenty calls a day he insisted we should make and early each morning he would have the three inspectors, John Taylor, Jimmy and myself in his office to demand from us our list of calls made on the previous day and what we had achieved at each one. This was fine by me, the young and enthusiastic upstart who hadn't known anything different, but less so for Jimmy and even less so for John who for years had enjoyed a cushy number under the old boss. John devised a cunning plan. He started to arrive at the office first instead of last. His purpose? To open the mail and pull out anything that applied to his agents – cheques, proposal forms etc., etc., all of which he would put in his briefcase before going out for a coffee to the nearby Tatler Cinema Cafe and returning to the office later where with a flourish and making sure that Mr Geddes was watching, he would open his briefcase and take out all the documents he had earlier planted in preparation for Mr Geddes' grilling. Amazingly, as far as I know, he got away with this devious charade until Mr Geddes was moved on to greater things in Manchester where twelve months later he suffered a massive heart attack. There's a message in there somewhere.

Meanwhile my social life in Newcastle was flourishing. I had made some good friends, notably Freddie Harrison, FCII, the young manager of Premier Motor Policies in Pilgrim Street. Like me, Freddie was a keen drinker and a keen walker and climber too and we spent some great weekends in the Cheviot Hills with a nice bunch of lads. We planned a holiday to the Pyrenees where we were to climb Los Encantats – the Enchanted Mountains. I saved up my holiday entitlement, we were going for three weeks, and I saved up my money too until I had the grand total of £74. In the end only four of us set off – myself, Freddie, his brother Donald and Jimmy Pearson in whose Austin Princess we were to travel and share the expenses. I can't describe how excited I was to be going all the way to Spain, my first time abroad. What an adventure! I was a little concerned that £74 wouldn't be enough for three weeks' travel, hotels, food, ferry and so on. I needn't have worried. We rapidly drove through France which then was not too expensive but certainly more so than Spain. After two days we crossed the border at Viella and stayed in a lovely hostel for seventeen shillings and sixpence, dinner bed and breakfast – and that was the most expensive accommodation of our entire stay in Spain. So much so, that with only five days left of our holiday I had barely spent half of my money. Let's go to Barcelona," suggested Freddie, "and then drive back via Paris!" Jimmy was reluctant but he was outvoted and he went along with it. I of course, was dead keen to experience the excitement of these wonderful cities which I hitherto could only dream about. And so it came to pass. Billeted in a small pension close to Plaza Real, we strolled down Las Ramblas along with what seemed to be half the population of Barcelona. We sampled the paella in a cheap restaurant and wandered back late at night to the Plaza Real where we sat outside and ordered beers. On the next table there were some young Spanish soldiers with four very attractive senoritas. The soldiers were drinking Campeons – huge three-litre glasses of beer – and were becoming a little worse for wear. They eventually staggered off leaving the four girls alone. Freddie could speak a little Spanish and soon they had joined us at our table. I couldn't believe my luck, particularly as I had heard that in those days Spanish girls were rarely allowed out unchaperoned. Despite the language difficulties we seemed to be getting on quite well. One of the girls in particular made it clear that she fancied me – and the attraction was certainly mutual. She was a little on the plump side but a very pretty girl, even making allowances for the amount I had had to drink. The next thing I knew, a taxi was being hailed and, except for Jimmy, who declined, we all got in and I headed off into the night with a lovely senorita on my knee. I didn't question what was going on. Why should I? I was enjoying myself and was, it seemed, likely to enjoy myself even more later on. It wasn't until I was standing in a queue at the hotel reception, with several other strangers, male and female, that I started to realise that these were not just ordinary senoritas. Too late to get cold feet now! I had no choice but to go through with it. Well, life is about new experiences, I said to myself. It didn't help. It didn't help either when up in the bedroom my senorita took off her clothes to reveal a bump in her belly to which she pointed and said "*Bambino*" and something else which I assume was Spanish for "You must be very careful". Nor did it help when she shouted at me, "*Vass!*" Seeing my puzzled look she repeated, "*Vass! Vass! Vass!*" – eventually leading me over to a sink where she proceeded to scrub me with carbolic soap. Now really, I am quite a romantic at heart and this wasn't proving to be the most warm and tender build up to sex. We did get into bed together but despite her best efforts our relationship was never consummated, and to make matters worse, she started to groan – not with passion I'm afraid. It seems she was having pains in her tummy. I ran to fetch her friend who called for a medico amongst total pandemonium and accusing glares directed at me by her friends and puzzled looks from the two Harrisons.

On the journey to Paris we camped near a vineyard where the local wine harvest had just been completed and bought a bottle of the local *vin rouge nouveau* for a few francs before continuing our journey. A few hours later we stopped for lunch, bread and fromage of course, opened the wine and were sorely tempted to drive back and buy a few dozen more bottles. I don't think I've tasted wine so succulent since. I wasn't happy, though. One of my eyes had become infected and I was convinced I had contracted some awful disease from my escapade in Barcelona. Our route to Paris took us close to Lourdes and we diverted there out of curiosity. I must say that what struck me was not how holy it was but how commercial. I suppose it is inevitable in a place which attracts so many millions of pilgrims. It was nevertheless a fascinating place and whatever your own beliefs, you cannot fail to be impressed by the faith of all those people. It did nothing for my eye. But perhaps that had something to do with my lack of faith.

To digress for a moment and whilst on the subject of Lourdes, I must relate an incident concerning a trip there by a group of people from Sunderland who we insured for the journey. On the return journey through France and despite his visit to Bernadette's shrine, the blessings of several priests and the earnest prayers of his companions, one of the group died. The decision was made to carry on their journey and thanks to the use of a wheelchair, some bluffing and some ventriloquist-like manipulation, they were able fool the authorities and get him through customs, on to the ferry and back home.

Paris was a revelation. My eyes boggled at the hustle and bustle. Seated in a car amongst several lanes of traffic all going the wrong way was a terrifying experience. We found a room in the Rue de Budapest. It fascinated me as I stood on the little balcony with a glass of wine watching the Parisian husbands on the way home from the office with flowers for their wives, popping upstairs with one of the dozens of street ladies and emerging after a few minutes to continue their journey home. I was impressed too with the quality of the Parisian food and the choice offered by the Prix Fixe menus. I vowed to return – and I have, several times.

At a young impressionable age it is most important to get the right advice, guidance and example. My brief time under Dick Geddes' management gave me these which in turn gave me confidence. As a junior inspector it was impossible for me to make twenty calls a day on existing agents since I didn't have that many. "Appoint more agents," was his simple advice. "To do that you must go cold calling." He explained to me what that was and how to go about it. Cold calling was soon to hold no fears for me and it was one of these calls that was eventually to change my life. Before I go on to expand on that, I really must pay tribute to Dick Geddes who, though a hard taskmaster, would always listen to your problems and for me at least he got the balance between carrot and stick encouragement just right. Positive thinking was his strength and was what made him such a super salesman. He could have sold sand to the Arabs! Which reminds me of a story he told me about the two shoe salesmen whose boss had ordered them to go selling in Africa. The first salesmen was dismayed. "But they don't wear shoes in Africa," he complained. The second salesman's reaction was quite the opposite. "What a great opportunity!" he enthused. "Everyone there is a potential customer."

The cold call that was to change my career direction was to a second-hand car sales plot in Monkwearmouth, Sunderland – Tommy Downey Motors. I appointed Tommy as one of my agents and called on him regularly. Shortly afterwards his brother-in-law Jack Reed, who had lost his job at a local engineering firm, joined him to do his bookkeeping and I became friendly with them both. I was persuaded with, I should say, some reluctance, to set up a car insurance business with them, a three-way partnership we called Arnott Reed & Co. The events leading up to this and subsequently are chronicled in detail in Volume II of this story – *"Accidental Millionaire."* Jack somehow squeezed Tommy out of the partnership and a new company was set up with him and me as 50/50 shareholders – Arnott & Reed (Insurance) Ltd – operating from a tiny semi-basement in Frederick Street, Sunderland.

Nine

ECURIE QUELQUECHOSE

This is a close race. It could go right down to the bone.
Chrissarism.

THOUGH I STILL LIVED in Newcastle, having found first new digs with Doris Danby in Two Ball Lonnen, and later a flat in Osborne Road, Jesmond, my social life was now mainly in Sunderland. I was surprised and relieved to find that Tommy Downey did not resent me for squeezing him out of the insurance business. He reserved all his resentment for Jack. With more money in my pocket, I could now keep up with the Tommy Downey and Mort Yuill set. Mort was the son of one of the region's largest builders, C.M.Yuill Ltd – the black sheep of the family due to his riotous lifestyle. Saturday nights would see us race up to Newcastle in their sports cars and then back to the Seaburn Hotel to see the Pino girls. Johnny Pino was the early 1960's in drink and I can still recall the rows of micro mini-skirted lasses sipping their drinks in the Seaburn lounge on a Saturday night. Then it was off to the Seaburn Hall dance to pick up one of them for the inevitable all night party afterwards. One night I danced with a young girl called Agnes who I'd never seen there before. We got on well and I took her outside with the intention of persuading her to come with me to the post dance party. I think I was succeeding until we were interrupted by what I thought was a boyfriend but who turned out to be her brother, who had been charged with the task of keeping an eye on his little sister. She was then barely eighteen and this was the first time she had been allowed to go to the dance. His task was to make sure she didn't fall into the clutches of people like me. So Agnes was peremptorily whisked away – but not before we had been able to arrange a date for the following week.

Apparently, as I later learned, there had been hell at the family home when they learned that their daughter had been fraternising with one of the Downey set and Agnes had been banned from seeing me ever again. However, she had somehow managed to keep our date but only for a few minutes – to explain to me that she couldn't see me again. At least that's what her brother was led to believe. Instead we made a secret rendezvous. Inevitably, under these conditions our relationship blossomed. It was forbidden. It was secret. It was exciting – especially for a young eighteen-year-old to whom it was romantic and risky. I was seven years older and in her eyes I suppose, an experienced man of the world. In fact, this image was more pretence and bravado than reality. Nevertheless, as our relationship developed the time came for me to meet the parents. It wasn't something I wanted or considered necessary but by then we had been rumbled and our secret romance was no longer secret. Brother Jim made sure of that. Perhaps if we had been able to meet openly in the first place our relationship may not have lasted beyond a few dates. After all, we were poles apart in age and in many other respects. My family were anti-Catholic Protestants. That's how it was in those days. Agnes' family were staunch Catholics whose biggest disappointment so far had been their son's decision not to join the priesthood. They were in for a bigger one later.

It was all arranged. I was to call at the house in Station Road, Seaham Harbour, after work one Saturday. I couldn't resist joining Jack and the Palatine Bar Saturday lunchtime crowd first. I needed a couple of pints to wind down after the usual hectic office session and a couple more to give me courage to face my ordeal.

The first time I met Agnes' mother, was with her knickers round her ankles. I knocked at the front door and told Agnes I was desperate for the toilet. The netty was at the bottom of the yard. I rushed out, burst open the door and there she was – the dragon herself. I hastily mumbled something like "sorry sir" and waited uncomfortably until she was finished. Not the best of starts, and it didn't improve much after that. I could sense the resentment towards me. I'm sure they had something different in mind for their daughter. The only people in that family I felt at ease with were Mary, the youngest daughter, in whom I had an ally, and Judy the dog. The three of us used to go for rides in my car when Judy was on heat, followed by scores of excited mongrel dogs until one by one they dropped out of the race from exhaustion. Mary shared my sick sense of humour.

I wouldn't go so far as to say that our feelings for each other were less intense but I think both Agnes and I were now aware of the potential problems that may exist in a permanent relationship between us. Blood is thicker than water and Agnes had been brought up very strictly in the Catholic faith. For my part I resented the closed minded dogma which exists not just in the Catholic religion but in every other religion too. NCTCDS came to the rescue of our relationship. Agnes had qualified for entry to the Northern Counties Training College for Domestic Science in Hexham. She didn't have much interest in cooking or any other form of domestic duty and I suspect she may have been encouraged by the family to go there in order to put some distance between us. However, a few miles drive to me with boundless energy at that age was nothing and I saw Agnes every weekend and often through the week. But there was a new love in my life. I had acquired a Triumph TR2 sports car with, according to Norman Smith, a nipple pink body and a titty white roof. Although the mainstream business of Arnott & Reed (Insurance) Ltd was by then with direct customers, we had kept up our motor traders connection and I still spent some time on the road. I really enjoyed this aspect of the business. It was a change from the office and I enjoyed the contact with the motor trade fraternity like Norman who I always found to be interesting characters. Not rogues exactly but, shall one say, borderline. Norman operated his used car business from a caravan on some wasteland in Coxhoe, County Durham. In the same mould perhaps as Tommy Downey, he was known in the trade as the Kelloe Kid because he lived in the nearby village of Kelloe. I turned up one day to see him and his head popped round the door of his caravan followed by his hand to indicate that I should wait five minutes. When he emerged he walked over to me and said, "I like you, Derrick, so I'm going to do you a favour." I thanked him and he went on, "I've got a woman customer in there," pointing to the caravan, "and I've just knocked her off for ten quid off the price of the car. If you like, I'll knock another tenner off and you can have a go." I politely declined his kind offer and when I got a glimpse of his customer I was glad I had.

I used to eat in the colliery canteens in those days. Nobody ever questioned my presence; the food was wholesome and plentiful and available at a cheap subsidised price. I used to do something similar when I worked in Newcastle, having discovered the British Railway canteen next to Central Station which again was exceptional value until they had to restrict it to rail employees who objected to standing in long queues behind a load of office workers. I'm pretty good at sussing out eating and drinking holes.

"Don't go there," said Norman when I told him where I planned to eat, "I'm going home for me dinner now and our lass will do you something." Having refused his kindness once I couldn't offend him again and found myself sitting down to fish fingers at a table covered by an old army blanket for a tablecloth. That wasn't the problem. Norman hadn't noticed his pet monkey climbing on to the table and shitting right in front of me.

"Do you mind if I don't eat this?" I asked awkwardly.

"Why, what's up with it?" bristled Norman.

"Nothing," I said. "It's just this" – pointing to the brown pile next to my plate.

"You bastard!" yelled Norman, leaping to his feet.

I was shitting *myself* thinking that Norman's anger was directed at *me*. Fortunately for me, but not for the monkey, his fury was directed at the poor animal. He took one swipe and the monkey clattered against the wall and screaming at the top of its voice it fell in a heap on to the floor. Not my most pleasant dining experience, but one I won't forget.

Another of my motor trade customers was George Athey of Linthorpe Motors in Middlesbrough, who owned a Morgan Plus Four sports car in which he was keen to drive competitively, and when I turned up in my Triumph TR2 a bond was created. There was in those days a special camaraderie among the owners of sports cars. They were relatively rare and the drivers when passing would always acknowledge each other with a wave. George was a member of the Darlington and District Motor Club which was the leading club for organised motor sport events in the area and we arranged to go along to the next club night so I too could join. We were joined on the journey in their cars by a few other Middlesbrough enthusiasts, Howard Nolson, Malcolm Sutherland, Tony Wright and his brother Peter. The club was organising a relay race at Dishforth airfield and we decided to enter a team, George in his Morgan, Tony in his Mini, Peter in his chain gang Frazer Nash, Malcolm in his Austin Healey Sprite, and me. Malcolm chose Ecurie Quelquechose as the team name and each car was to sport our emblem, a question mark. The format was that each car must complete a minimum number of laps, not necessarily consecutively, over a two-hour duration. For some reason which I cannot now recall, it was not possible for me to drive my Triumph TR2. I think it failed the mandatory 'scrutineering' (scrutinizing) test to ensure that the cars were race-worthy, which took place early on race day before the practice sessions. I had been looking forward so much to my racing debut and was bitterly disappointed. The company owned an Austin A40 and I mentioned this to the lads. It might be unusual but there was nothing in the rules to prevent a bog standard road car from competing. We dashed back to collect the A40, returning just before the close of 'scrutineering'. It didn't have a laminated shatterproof windscreen and the tyres were unsuitable. Not to be thwarted, I drove to the nearest garage, replaced the tyres and removed the windscreen. My determination must have impressed the scrutineers who, unable to find anything else to fail it on, reluctantly had to give me a certificate. Though the slowest car in the race I completed my mandatory laps. Jack was not at all pleased about the cost of the tyres and I spent weeks removing grit and debris thrown up by the faster cars as they hurtled past me. My face also got in the way of some of this grit and was quite sore for days afterwards. But the exhilaration had been worth it. I was hooked.

I had learned a lot from my Dishforth experience and was determined to repeat it, but next time much better prepared. Clearly the first essential was a competitive car. The British Motor Corporation's Mini was proving to be very competitive due to its unique design and front wheel drive and I managed to persuade Jack to replace the A40 with FSO 779, a green 848 cc Mini on to which I fitted a twin carburettor Downton conversion. I couldn't wait for the 1962 season. During the winter we set up the car for rallying and with Howard Nolson as my navigator we did quite well in our first season. According to Howard our best chance of success was in the Cleveland Rally when, as we waited for our turn to set off, he noticed that all the other cars had turned left. He confidently assured me that they had all got it wrong so reluctantly I turned right. Instead of reaching the first check point some thirty minutes away we found ourselves in the Highfield Hotel having a pint after quickly realising that the other competitors were, after all, right. We've had some laughs about that.

The British Motor Corporation had by then produced their BMC Austin Mini Cooper which made my 848 cc Mini no longer competitive. However, at that point I had located, in Redcar, an old seriously injured Lotus XI Le Mans sports racing car for which the owner wanted £200. Reassured by George Athey's confidence that its banana-shaped chassis could be restored, I scraped together the money and bought it. Working day and night, we did manage to restore the Lotus, not to its former glory but adequately enough for club competitions. During the 1963, '64 and '65 seasons my Lotus XI and I were very busy. We competed at every opportunity in speed hill climbs, sprints and in 1964, with the opening of Croft Autodrome, circuit racing, including the relay race where our team, Ecurie Quelquechose, acquitted itself much better than on its debut at Dishforth. In the GT/Sports Racing class I briefly held the lap record at Croft and competed also at Oulton Park, Rufforth, Castle Combe, Ingliston and my favourite circuit, Cadwell Park in Lincolnshire where I believe my lap record still stands – probably because in 1966 they restricted the circuit to motorcycle racing only.

Motor racing wasn't taken anything like as seriously in those days as it is now. It was down largely to driver skill and courage. It was fun. As more and more sponsored cars appeared on the grid, however, it became harder and harder to compete. I resented being beaten by inferior drivers in superior cars costing ten times what I'd paid for mine. So I put forward the suggestion to the organisers that, similar to horse racing, they should include a selling plate race at some or all of the meetings, split into value categories. The rationale behind my idea was that good drivers could enter their £500 car in the £1,000 or £2,000 category, and if successful would attract buyers who thought it was the car and not the driver who was fast. This would enable the good drivers to buy better cars and continue to compete as privateers with the professional and semi-professional outfits. I thought the idea had merit. The organisers apparently didn't because it was never adopted.

I could go on and on about the thrills and spills of this era. About the two day Scarborough Rally and our nights in the St Nicholas Hotel, for instance. About the new cars we used to hire for overnight rallies when the Mini wasn't up to it. About my narrow escape when I plunged into a concrete ditch at Wallsend Sprint in 1964 – and much more. But Agnes was due to leave college and our relationship had become strained, threatened as it was by my second (or was it first?) love – motor sport. She hadn't been too thrilled at playing second fiddle to a Lotus. There was some patching up to do if we were to have a future together.

The old Lotus XI Le Mans on its way to a lap record at Croft Autodrome 1966.

Ten

THE PALATINE PERIOD

I love cooking with wine. Sometimes I even put it in the food.
Anon.

IN HER FINAL YEAR at NCTDS Agnes and I saw much less of each other. My business made a lot of demands on my time and energy, and in order to relax I had started to join Jack in the Palatine Bar after work, so driving up to Hexham was out of the question. I was involved most weekends in my motor racing activities and Agnes became less inclined to join me. Selfishly, my idea of fun was to be with my mates and their girlfriends and naively I couldn't understand why Agnes said she didn't like them. Cracks appeared in our relationship and a contributory factor perhaps was the opening of Hepples Nightclub in Hexham. Len and Molly Hepple were professional ballroom dancers and decided to use their studio as a club at weekends. Before this opened there were few places in Hexham for young girls to go. Hepples changed all that. It became a regular weekend venue for the NCTDS girls with or without their boyfriends. No longer were they content to sit in the college waiting for letters, phone calls and occasional visits. Letters, no matter how interesting are no substitute for physical presence and I was too stupid, selfish or arrogant to realise that. Nevertheless, after she left college we decided we would get married but this too had its logistical problems. Agnes was under pressure to have a full nuptial mass wedding but this was possible only if I were to convert to Roman Catholicism – something I would never have agreed to. Even to undergo a normal marriage in a Catholic church meant that I was required to accept the rules and demands of the faith. Reluctantly I compromised and agreed to attend instruction sessions with the priest – but only after making it clear to Agnes that I would pay lip service only to his instructions and after we were married the two of us and nobody else would decide how we lived our lives. Her family put a lot of pressure on Agnes not to marry me.

Having conformed to the letter but not the spirit of the church's requirements, the wedding on 1st August 1964 was allowed to take place at St Mary Magdelenes church at Seaham Harbour. Of course, it had to be a showpiece wedding. The Ramside Hall, as the 'in' place for posh weddings, was chosen for the reception and the guest list was a mile long. Perhaps with all the undercurrents, doubts and resentments, we should have stepped back and given things a little more time but, for better or for worse, the deed was done. We bought a nice house – 23 Cairnside, East Herrington, and I suppose we were happy enough there – for a while.

Obviously the three years domestic training at Hexham had not inspired Agnes enough to become a devoted housewife and she got a teaching job at Camden Road School in Seaham – too close to her family's influence for my liking. Business was doing really well and expanding. I bought her a Triumph Spitfire sports car. However, this wasn't happening accidentally and I was working long hours and often at weekends. It didn't help either that I was finding the Palatine Bar very convivial and a good place to wind down after work.

Agnes became pregnant immediately and our lovely daughter, Elizabeth Jane, named after my paternal grandmother and an old girlfriend from Amble (Agnes was unaware of this when we were choosing names), was born on the 14th May 1965. We were both thrilled but I just felt that perhaps I was more so than Agnes who couldn't wait to get back to work despite her new daughter, house, sports car, friends – and me. So – enter Mrs Willis who was to be EJ's nanny.

Maybe I am old-fashioned but I thought the woman's place (certainly a new mother's place) should be in the home. This was how I had been brought up and new age fathers had not been invented then! I'm not saying Agnes didn't love EJ but I had this awful feeling that something wasn't right. My own mother spent half her life nursing me – and any other kid she could get her hands on. Agnes wasn't like that. She didn't breast feed of course – not good for the figure. I think she had designs on becoming a mannequin after once appearing on TV. Even bottle-feeding was a case of laying EJ down and propping the bottle up against a pillow. Our daughter it appeared was an intrusion on her flighty ambitions. This wasn't what I thought it was going to be like and I dare say it wasn't Agnes's idea of married bliss either and we had our first serious row when I came in from work to discover from Mrs Willis that behind my back my daughter had been christened with full ceremony and guests. Can you imagine it? Not being invited to your own daughter's christening! Not even being told it was taking place! At that point we should have gone to marriage guidance. Instead, we polarised, blaming each other for everything. But there was no question of not sticking with it – not in my mind, at least. We had a daughter and she was more important than our own feelings. The situation was clearly having an effect on her and I became concerned that she was exhibiting signs of distress, particularly when she had been out with Agnes in the car. I am sure she was trying to tell me something. I just hoped that somehow it would all work out given enough time and I kept my head down. I had my work and my motor racing to take my mind off marital problems.

Agnes dealt with them in another way. I began to feel uneasy at her behaviour with some of our male friends – but the thought of adultery never crossed my mind. To me marriage vows and any other vows are sacred – not always easy to keep but never lightly broken either. Not with so much responsibility or with so much at stake and surely not by a staunch Catholic girl who, it would appear from past events, took her religion so very seriously. It came as a devastating bombshell when one day she told me she was having an affair and intended to leave me. I suppose I was too hurt and too proud to object or to reason. She left that night.

Only those of us who have gone through the painful experience of a marriage breakdown in these particular circumstances will appreciate what a devastating effect it has on the deceived partner – the powerful emotions of rejection, humiliation, despair and loneliness. I felt wretched. I was taken to hospital with severe chest pains convinced I was having a heart attack. The pains were, fortunately, just the symptoms of severe stress.

Having inherited my mother's naïve and trusting nature, I hadn't been able even to contemplate this turn of events. I suppose I was hoping that given time things could be worked out between us. That Agnes, even if she did not take her domestic responsibilities seriously, would at least remain faithful to her religious principles. That our daughter would enjoy her birthright – her parents accepting their responsibilities and staying together for her sake. Was I too old-fashioned?

I was not free from blame myself and must share some of the responsibility. Throughout my life I have always, it seems, needed to escape from pressures and reality into my comfort zone – the pub or the club. I am my father's son in that respect. In the past, before Jack Reed came on the scene, the last hour or two before closing time would be my drinking time. Jack introduced me to the delights and the dangers of early hours drinking. He was usually the first into the bar at opening time and invariably bought the first round of drinks. During his many years' experience as a bar fly he had become familiar with the etiquette of his pass time. Whilst he had beer in his glass it was his round and he would buy the drinks for anyone joining the company. Then the round would pass to the second person joining the company and so on. As the company grew there would be many who would escape their round, so an unwritten code of conduct was introduced. We started to drink in half pints in order to catch the latecomers. This tactic got rid of a few of the opportunists and hangers on – those who would deliberately join the company late, have a few pints on other people's rounds and then leave before it was their turn.

Invariably I had to stay behind at the office to catch up with paperwork but Jack would never work a minute after opening time. This meant that Eva our typist had to stay behind too so that she could take down my letters in shorthand, before the introduction of that wonderful piece of technology, the dictating machine. Consequently I was among the late arrivals into the Palatine company and was at first able to have three or four halves before driving home. Gradually I was put under pressure to stay longer. "You can't go home yet. You haven't bought a round," was what they said. "OK, I'll buy the next round," I offered. "You can't. It's not your turn," they countered. So, weak-willed as I was – and still am in this area – I would stay for a few more until it came to my round and I could escape with honour. As the atmosphere at the bar became more convivial and the atmosphere at Cairnside deteriorated, the temptation became more and more difficult to resist. "Stay and have another," they would urge. "Might as well be hung for a sheep as a lamb," they would say persuasively. "All you'll get for your tea at home is hot tongue and cold shoulder!" When these facetious remarks became reality I took little persuading.

The early doors Palatine crowd – a cosmopolitan bunch ranging from burglars to barristers – was compulsive company. I learned a lot of street wisdom there. A select few of the regulars, fourteen to be exact, formed our own little society, the Fourteen Club, with our own inscribed tankards. We met every Thursday evening in a hired room in the Hotel where we drank, smoked, told jokes and stories and had supper which invariably included pigs' trotters supplied by John Eltringham, a member of the club and local butcher. On Saturday afternoons they would have a gambling session which I managed to attend occasionally. John would bring along a dozen or so of his best steaks and Bill, the Chef, would cook them to perfection, dice them into bite-size pieces and present them on an enormous platter accompanied by crisp fresh French bread, a delicious accompaniment to the main activity which was watching the horse racing on two TV channels that provided us with a race every fifteen minutes. We would all put a half-crown into a kitty and take turns having first choice in selecting our horses. The system gave us all a fair chance over the afternoon. We cut out the bookie's profit and the winner would scoop the kitty with the exception of one half-crown for Bill the chef. I suspect the hotel picked up the bill for the steaks.

You could buy all sorts of things in the Palatine and one evening I landed home with some fresh lobsters from a local fisherman by way of a peace offering, which was of course rejected. I would have my lobster supper alone then – or so I thought. I put them in a pan of water, placed it on the gas ring and went off to watch TV. I vaguely heard some strange noises but at first took no notice until it suddenly dawned on me that my lobsters, instead of being humanely stunned by plunging them into boiling water, had suffered a slow and agonising death. I couldn't bring myself to eat them. They were thrown in the bin and I've never eaten lobster since. As if my conscience wasn't giving me enough hell I was informed the next day that the lobsters I had bought were "nancies" which, Jack explained, were undersize and therefore illegal and should have been thrown back into the sea. Child murderer, that's what I was. Many years later, on the 15th September 2007, in fact, I watched on TV a food programme by the Irish celebrity chef Rachel Allen in which she said that the correct way to humanely prepare lobster was, like I had done, to boil them from cold. So I could have been enjoying lobster all these years. Mind you, I really don't know, unless she can speak lobster language, how Ms Allen can be certain what the poor creatures are feeling.

In the Palatine, Agnes had another rival for my affections. It may have saved my sanity, but it undoubtedly contributed to the breakdown of my marriage.

Eleven

LIMBO

It's neither nowt nor ornament.
Chrissarism.

A FEW DAYS AFTER Agnes left I tried to go back to work because it was such a busy and difficult time there. It was a waste of time. I couldn't concentrate. My mind was in pieces. For my daughter's sake I had to pull myself together. She must be protected from the trauma at all costs and thanks to Mrs Willis and my mother at weekends we were able to keep Liz in her familiar routine and environment. I was so grateful for the support I received also at that time from people at work and my friends at that time – Joe Applegarth, Pete Stonor, David Taylor and others. One of them confided in me that Agnes had come on to him too – an approach he had firmly rejected. I admired his honesty and his integrity.

Finding myself single once again was a strange experience but at least these friends were all unattached too. I wasn't entirely free of responsibilities though, and finding a new woman was going to be a problem in the limited free time I had at my disposal. Dating agencies and other similar facilities are commonplace nowadays, but the first one in this country had just been formed. I suggested to Dave Taylor and Joe Applegarth that we should give it a go. Being a little apprehensive and worried in case we may get stuck for the evening with an unattractive or unsuitable date, we devised a cunning plan. We would all arrange to meet our dates at the same time on the same day and at the same place, usually a pub. We would not acknowledge each other, pretending to be complete strangers and by pre-arranged codes and signals followed by a toilet meeting we would decide whether we should go on ignoring each other (if we were happy with our dates) or whether we should suddenly 'recognise' each other (if we weren't) and take the pressure off by joining each other's company. Actually, I did meet a really nice girl, Sarah, and there was certainly a mutual attraction between us. I'm sure this could have developed in different circumstances but I had to tell her that I wasn't entirely a free agent and

78

after that the relationship wasn't the same and fizzled out. Very frustrating. One of Joe's dates was a student at Newcastle University and she invited him and Sarah and I to a fancy dress ball at the Students' Union. She was a really posh prim and proper well-spoken girl away from home for the first time in her life and playing at being the rebel. I remember her saying to Joe in order, I suppose, to shock: "I'm living in a house with six men." Joe, one of the bluntest people I've ever met, brought her down to earth with his response: "Are they all shagging you?" he asked. She was deeply affronted. Certainly Joe wouldn't be scoring that night. There were many stories and incidents involving Joe who was at that time one of the oddest and funniest men I'd met. Like the time in a nightclub when the female singer during her rendition of 'These Boots Are Made For Walking' held the microphone to Joe to finish off the line "One of these days these boots are gonna"... "KICK YOU UP THE FLUE!" was Joe's spontaneous response, accompanied by a not particularly subtle lunge at her private parts. Not quite what the artiste had bargained for. We were, not very politely, asked to leave the establishment. Joe's repertoire of rugby songs was incredibly entertaining – all delivered with the rude words (and actions) of course. His rendition of 'Swing Low Sweet Chariot' was a classic. We were members of North Durham RUFC at that time. Joe was a very accomplished racing driver too and at the wheel of his Lotus VII had many good wins to his credit, the most notable of which was at Ingliston, near Edinburgh, in 1987 when in the rain he demolished the opposition all of whom were driving much superior cars. He was later to buy Joachin Rindt's Formula 2 Brabham and I had a go in it once at Croft Autodrome. Apart from my crash into the ditch at Wallsend I experienced my most hairy moments in this beast. Normally a fearless driver in those days, I confess to experiencing moments of sheer terror behind the wheel of Joe's recent acquisition. Thrilling, though. He eventually married, calmed down and settled down and my second wife and I became Godparents to his daughter. We lost touch during my troubled time. I would love to see him again.

It wasn't easy trying to hide from Liz the upset and emotions of that period but we succeeded. For a while she did of course sometimes ask where her mammy was and we gave her low key reassuring explanations which she readily accepted. She was actually much calmer and, seemingly, happier after Agnes had left thanks to all the hard work we put in to shield her from the reality of the situation which, at her tender age (she was not yet two) she would not have been able to understand. My mother used to say that one day when the time was right she will find out the truth and hopefully be old enough to handle it. We had in mind her teens or twenties. Mrs Willis was a brick at that time too. We worked it between the three of us. I was able to get Liz into the Gateway Nursery School where she quickly settled. I dropped her off at 8.30 a.m. and picked her up at lunchtime. On Fridays we went down to my mother's in Middlesbrough, driving back up to Sunderland on Monday mornings. It was hard. Very hard. Jack wasn't very happy that I was taking so much time off work and I felt uneasy about that. However, my most important job was to ensure that Liz was catered for. She was my priority. My social life was restricted to nights out at the weekends after Liz had been settled.

I had filed for divorce and a hearing was arranged in July 1967 and was to include the issue of custody. My lawyer explained to me that I was unlikely to be given custody though in the circumstances I could expect generous access. This I accepted. It is extremely rare, and understandably so, that fathers are awarded custody, particularly of very young children. I consoled myself with the thought that the transition would, hopefully, be carried out sensibly and undramatically and that, in the meantime, I had given Liz some stability during the early traumatic days of her parents' break up. *A few weeks before the hearing, I received a letter from my solicitor which I have kept and which informed me that Agnes did not want custody.* We were astounded. My divorce went through unopposed and I was granted a decree nisi on July 27th.

It then dawned on me that we now had on our hands, not just a temporary situation but a lifetime commitment. My mother and I talked at length about the situation and how best we could handle it. "What kind of woman could give up her child like that?" she asked rhetorically. There was much conjecture. Obviously, for Agnes it was convenient not to have the responsibility. She could carry on working without having to worry about having Elizabeth looked after. She had the freedom to devote to her new relationship. In contrast, I was having to struggle to fit in work and other aspects of my life – and so was my mother. We had no help from Agnes who seemed content not to see Elizabeth, which we both found then and later on to be incomprehensible. Had Willie, Agnes' lover, put his foot down? He too would obviously prefer not to have the inconvenience and responsibility of someone else's child to interfere with his cosy relationship. What kind of man would be so thoughtless? Perhaps the kind of man who has affairs with young married mothers and breaks up marriages. My mother and I shared all these and other thoughts, wondering whether we would ever discover the answers to our questions. Certainly my mother won't. She died a disillusioned old woman.

Writing about this episode of my life and things that happened subsequently involving Agnes stirs up all the old feelings of frustration, anger and injustice. I haven't slept well during this part of my book and I have questioned the advisability of rattling old skeletons. But to write a book about my life and to exclude one of the major issues in it would be quite pointless. I vowed to write, warts and all. So be it. The whole object of autobiographic writing is not to let sleeping dogs lie but to wake them up!

About a year later Mrs Willis dropped the bombshell. Her daughter had given birth to a little girl and there were problems. We took Liz to see the baby and were shocked at her deep blue colouring. Mrs Willis was needed by her own family. She gave me plenty of notice for which I am indebted to her. Sadly her granddaughter died a couple of years later. It made me count my blessings.

The business was still growing and demanded more time than I was able to devote to it. After much deliberation I decided to see if I could find a permanent live-in nanny by advertising in the local newspapers – I hadn't at that time heard of the *Lady Magazine* which specialises in domestic vacancies. The response was overwhelming (though the quality didn't always match the quantity) and I made a short list of ten. After the ninth interview I was worried. There were some nice girls, but I wasn't easy in my mind with any of them. I had arranged to interview number ten in her home at Wolsingham, over an hour's drive away, and her application looked promising – on paper, at least. The weather was foul and I considered cancelling, but I was getting desperate and it was vitally important for me and for Liz that we solved the problem. I drove through a snowstorm and arrived at Angate Street, Wolsingham at about 8 p.m. on that cold February night in 1967.

The first moment I set eyes on Christine Marshall I knew she was the one. Not in the sense that I found her immediately sexually attractive. She wasn't my usual type. Seated on a stool in front of the fire with her hair up wearing a tight but not too tight maroon dress, she was a vision of lovely serenity. There was an aura about her. Very, very nice, I thought to myself. She had just returned home from Capenwray Bible School to look after her mother who was actually in bed with a bad back in the same downstairs room in which the interview was conducted. . Am I fated always to meet my future mothers-in-law in unusual circumstances? One thought did cross my mind: at least they're not Catholics!

The interview was academic. I arranged to call again and take Miss Marshall to Cairnside to meet Liz before she decided to accept my job offer. One potential stumbling block was George, Chris's father, who objected strongly on the grounds that I was too young and there was no wife involved. This only made her more convinced that she should accept. The very fact that there was not a mother involved was to her an attractive aspect of the job. Another important aspect was the fact that the job was only for five days a week. In her previous Nanny's post with the Lewin family in Hamsterley Forest, she had been lucky to get one day off a week. The Lewins had provided a glowing reference and I felt totally comfortable with my choice – and more importantly, I knew that Liz did too.

I agreed to let Chris, as she preferred to be called, take Liz up to Wolsingham over the Easter holidays and, she told me later, Liz went straight to her mother Vera and sat on her lap. She was clearly used to older people like Mrs Willis and my mother.

Twelve

COCOA, MR ARNOTT?

Love is staying up all night with a sick child – or a healthy adult.
Sir David Aradine Frost.

LIZ'S NEW NANNY officially took up her post immediately after the Easter of 1967. She was, and still is, a natural with children and I was well satisfied with how things were working out. We all settled down into a nice routine. We would drop Liz off at the Gateway Nursery School, then Chris would drop me off at work, then pick up Liz at lunchtime which enabled me to devote more quality time to work, much to Jack's relief – and mine. At home the new nanny was working wonders. A birthday party was organised for Liz and the boys from next door were invited. I was beginning to get a glimpse of what family life should be about. On Fridays Chris would pick up Liz from Gateway and take her to Middlesbrough on the train, drop her off at my mother's, then continue her journey home to Wolsingham, a round trip involving three buses. I am ashamed to admit that it never crossed my mind to reimburse Chris' travelling expenses which she paid out of her own pocket. I began to rely more and more on the new Nanny and I am afraid I took her for granted. She was more than a nanny. She washed, ironed, cooked, made the beds and, after we had decided to get rid of the cleaner, she did those chores too. I forgot to pay her the cleaner's wages as we had agreed. It's just as well I didn't run my business in the same thoughtless way. This arrangement was working very well – for me, for Liz and except for what appeared to her as my meanness, for Chris too. I even used to forget to reimburse her for the groceries she bought. She was too shy to remind me.

Our new nanny was twenty-one on the 30th April, just a few weeks after she took up her post and was then able to drive my new Ford Cortina for which we bought a baby seat which was secured to the rear seat. On her very first journey, a trip to Wolsingham to take Liz to meet her parents, Chris took it into her head to stop and transfer the baby seat into the front. Shortly after that she stopped at a road junction

82

and a lorry crashed into the back of the car. Fortunately, thanks to what can only be put down to a premonition, Liz was unhurt. Spooky, or what? The lorry driver, full of apologies, bought Liz a lolly from a nearby shop before the police arrived to take statements and Chris later had to go to court as a witness – the first of three court appearances she was to endure during our relationship. She was terrified that I would be angry when I saw the damage to my brand new car. She didn't know me very well then.

I was still involved in motor sport and used to go up to the Northumbrian Motor Club in Newcastle after Liz had gone to bed. Chris was bored. She asked me whether I would be going out one particular night because she would like that night off. When I found out that an old friend of hers, Harry Wealands, was calling for her, I experienced a pang of jealousy! What was happening? I didn't object of course but I waited up for her coming in. After that, I started to stay in more often. We would talk, play monopoly and I would drink sherry. Chris, who was a non-smoking, non-drinking Christian, could not at first be persuaded to join me. At bedtime she always made me a nightcap. "Cocoa, Mr Arnott?" Our relationship at that time was still quite a formal boss and nanny one.

Things changed in the November. It was the night of the Newcastle Insurance Institute Dinner and I came downstairs in my dinner suit and black tie. Embarrassed, I opened the living room door, kicked my leg in the air a la Frankie Vaughan (a sixties pop star) and started to sing, "Give me the moonlight. Give me the girl, and leave the rest to me!" It was this incident, Chris told me later, that first stirred in her a spark of physical attraction. By then I too was starting to have feelings for her, feelings I suppose I had suppressed because I didn't want to prejudice the cosy situation that existed. But something was happening to us both and it felt good. It felt right, too.

Winter was on its way and several days after my cabaret Chris complained of being cold in bed and asked me for some extra blankets. "It would save money if we shared a bed," I offered, hastily adding, "Only joking!" But I wasn't and that night I suggested playing monopoly for stakes – if I win Chris would have to share my bed and if I lost I would give her the money to buy blankets. For the first time she joined me in a glass of sherry. I lost at Monopoly but somehow we finished up in bed together after Chris had brought me my cocoa. I got more than cocoa that night. It was wonderful. The memory of our first kiss particularly sticks in my mind – so warm and tender. I'd never experienced anything like it before. For months Chris had been going home every weekend and making unflattering remarks about me to her parents. The weekend after that first kiss she said nothing. "Oh, oh!" observed her father intuitively, "What's going on?" Chris couldn't disguise her feelings. It was an exciting time and things were fine for a while. But our contentment was not allowed to continue. Agnes got wind of the situation and set out once more to disrupt my life.

Since I wasn't going out so much as I had previously, I used occasionally to invite some of my motor racing friends to the house – Joe Applegarth, David Taylor and several others, who were all convinced that Chris and I were having it off even before we were. My guests one evening included John and Bruce Blanckley whose brother Willie was the one with whom Agnes was then living and with whom she had recently had a baby, Simon. Until then there had been no sign of Agnes; then one day our next door neighbour Moira spotted her red Triumph Spitfire driving up and down Durham Road outside the house. Word had obviously got back to Agnes and out of the blue Chris received a telephone call from her, saying, "I am Elizabeth's mother and I am coming round to take her out for the day" – which of course she was entitled to do. Chris didn't even know what Agnes looked like and it wasn't possible for me to be there so she waited patiently at the window with Liz. Agnes eventually arrived, late of course, pressed her finger on the doorbell and removed it only when the door was opened. "Are you ready Elizabeth?" she said without looking at Chris, and off they went. Two hours later she brought Liz back. This happened two more times and then nothing.

Events after that are not too clear in my mind. I think Agnes contacted me to talk about Liz's future and before I knew what was happening she was back on the scene. She landed at Cairnside with Simon and moved in. My mind was in shreds. I had allowed this to happen because in my mind I thought that for Liz's sake maybe she deserved to have her mammy and daddy together after all the trauma she had been through. But it didn't take long for me to have doubts about the wisdom of allowing Agnes back into my life. It didn't work out. Looking back now, I realise that it never could. Any real feelings I had for Agnes had been damaged irrevocably. We tried to make it work but maybe neither of our hearts were in it. I don't know. All I did know was that I had lost Chris. She had gone back to Wolsingham. Her father was ill and there seemed no future any more for her in Sunderland. I wasn't able to clearly articulate my thoughts and feelings at that time. I wanted things to be right for Liz and Agnes' return offered a quick fix. I was vulnerable but as the practical reality of the situation started to sink in, my reservations intensified. I was expected to take on the responsibility of another child. I quite liked the little feller – and after all it wasn't his fault. But my trust in Agnes, as a mother and as a wife had been destroyed. I doubted her motives and her commitment. Even straightforward relationships have their times of stress and polarisation and this one was far from straightforward. Would Agnes then rush back into Willy's arms at the first sign of trouble? I wondered too whether Agnes' return may have been motivated by pressure from her family. In their view she was still married to me in the eyes of God, and if we were to get back together again she would be able to confess, have her sins forgiven, take communion and everything would be all right. She would go to heaven! But what about the rest of us whose lives had been fucked up? We weren't Catholics – so no heaven for us – except perhaps Liz who, thanks to her clandestine christening may have been saved. So, Liz, just in case I'm wrong and they are right, when you get to heaven put in a good word for me, pet! This may be a simplistic view, but it does, I think, crystallise the absurdity of what I believe religion, fundamentally, is all about.

In hindsight and in the light of my now considerable experience of the devious ingenuity of the female psyche, was this simply an attempt by Agnes to break up my relationship with Chris, and hers with Liz, thereby ensuring that I would be deprived of the practical means of caring for Liz on a daily basis? Or am I being over cynical? You decide.

I was missing Chris too. During our brief relationship there had been a closeness and warmth that I hadn't experienced with Agnes. On the physical side I had sex with them both but with Chris there was a difference. She wanted me to make love to her – and I hadn't yet learned how to do this properly. Anyway, Agnes went back to Willy and I had no choice but for her to take Liz with her. At least Simon escaped the damage associated with broken homes. It fell to Liz to experience the confusion, insecurity, resentment and other problems and as it later turned out, for Chris to be the fall guy. The wicked stepmother. Life can be unfair.

Agnes and I made an arrangement that I would have Liz every weekend and holidays and I would pick her up after school on Fridays and take her back on Monday mornings. I sold the house and moved into an apartment in Planet House in Sunderland town centre only a few minutes' walk from the office. I kept in touch with Chris but, understandably, her feelings for me had cooled. She had been badly hurt. She telephoned me one day to say she had met someone else and they planned to go to Seattle in the USA, and could I give her a reference? My heart sank. In desperation I suppose I told her that I would only give her a reference if she came to see me personally. I wanted an opportunity to talk to her. When we did talk there were certain aspects of her new relationship that made me feel uneasy. Before giving her the reference I made her promise that if things didn't work out, she would get in touch and I said I would pay her airfare back home.

How strange the way things work out. Chris found out that her new friend was married and again had to endure a broken relationship and the emotional heartache that goes with it. Chris, who was very close to her mother, was able to share with her the emotional turmoil she was experiencing, and Vera suggested that she should contact me even though I too had been guilty of causing her daughter so much heartache. I responded immediately and drove up to Wolsingham. The first step in the rebuilding of our relationship was taken. But there had been much damage done and it would take a long time for bridges to be built. Chris had been offered another nanny's job, this time in Reading with the Fuller's Brewery family. Naturally I readily gave Chris a glowing reference when Mrs Fuller telephoned me.   In September 1970 I drove Chris down to Reading and a few weeks later, when the family had gone on holiday, I went down and stayed in the nanny flat with Chris. It says a lot for the confidence the Fullers placed in her that they felt comfortable enough to go away and leave her solely in charge of their two children, Camilla and William, so soon after her appointment. We talked long and hard about the situation we had got ourselves into – or more accurately, the situation I had got us into.

I asked Chris if she would marry me. She accepted my proposal. I didn't deserve it. I was a very happy man as I drove back up North on the Friday to pick up Liz, at least in one aspect of my life. I was deeply concerned about Liz. She had been asking for Chris and I was now able to tell her she would soon see her again. She was not the happy little girl of a year or so ago and was exhibiting signs of severe stress. I could sense the relief on her face every Friday afternoon. I found it almost unbearable when she had to go back on the Monday crying and pleading for me not to take her back to school. She would sit on her potty throughout the journey and fill it by the time we got to the school gates.

Thirteen

OLD FRIENDS

The devil you don't know is better than the devil you do.
Chrissarism.

ONCE I BECAME heavily involved in motor sport I saw less of those friends like Terry Cronin and Bill Limbert, who were not themselves enthusiasts and I began to spend a lot of time with the Darlington Motor Club crowd. George Athey faded from the scene and I spent most of my time with the Ecurie Quelquechose team members. Howard Nolson, my rally navigator, had met and married Dinah and had the sense to devote himself to his new life, producing no less than six daughters. Out of all the 'gang' at that time and in hindsight, Howard was the one I really liked the best.

Edward 'Ned' South was probably the most interesting. Ned was a pilot in the RAF and flew the latest fighter planes. His wife Glyth was a really nice girl and they had a daughter to whom they were devoted – Glyth more so than Ned as it turned out. He was a very intelligent and knowledgeable lad with a degree in law before joining the RAF, but he was, like many RAF pilots, wild and irresponsible, hence his attraction to the dangers of motor sport. He once confided in me many years later when talking deeply about what went wrong in his life, that whilst not preventing him from enjoying a full sexual life, his penis was slightly deformed. His obvious hang-up in this area led to his downfall. Despite being happily married he could not resist the temptation to prove his manhood by having an affair with a member of the WRAF (Women's Royal Air Force). This turned out to be disastrous on two counts. Firstly, when Glyth discovered his infidelity she left him and went back with their daughter to live with her mother in Gloucestershire. Secondly, it led to his dismissal from the RAF. It wasn't simply the extramarital sex that was frowned upon by the RAF hierarchy, which happens all the time. The problem was that he had chosen for the object of his lust a non-commissioned WRAF girl. Had he knocked off a senior WRAF officer then his job would not have been threatened. There are some strange, but perhaps understandable, rules in the forces. Ned did later get a job as a training officer in the Sultan of Aman's Air force until he crashed and wrote off £1 million worth of Lightening Jet Fighter. After that he desperately tried to patch things up with Glyth, but she had been hurt too deeply and there was no way back. His life took yet another turn for the worse when on his way down to Ross-on-Wye to see his daughter, he wrapped his car round a tree and suffered severe injuries. I visited him in Oxford General Hospital and was shocked to see him with his skull held together by a helmet-like contraption. He never really fully recovered. Indeed he would not have recovered at all had he not, because of the intense pain, taken matters into his own hands and during the night dismantled his 'helmet' and 'escaped' from the hospital. They found him the next day, unconscious. They also found where one of the screws had been inserted into his skull, what would have turned out to be a fatal infection. Had Ned not done what he did he would most certainly not have survived. He was never the same again. We used to see him every Christmas until I loaned him some money. I've always found this to be an effective way of getting rid of friends. Ned was always the worse for drink when he called and being such an oddball, the children were, they confessed later, frightened of him. I must locate his whereabouts and make an effort to see him and find out how he is doing.

Peter Wright was a nice enough lad though, I felt, always in the shadow of his elder brother Tony. When I first met Tony he was married to George Athey's sister, a really nice girl. Beverley, I think they called her. Shortly afterwards they were divorced.

With Tony then single and Agnes away at college in Hexham, we were footloose and fancy-free. Before going on to a nightclub the rest of us would enjoy going for a drink – usually a perfect pint of John Smith's Magnet Ale in The Broadway Bar – but Tony didn't join us until much later and would turn up at the nightclub fresh and sober so that his chances to 'score' would be improved. To the rest of us that wasn't the priority. I think I have always, until recently, preferred men's company. Tony eventually succeeded in seriously 'scoring' and married Marion – a bit of a madam. Tony's father George was a longstanding Freemason and Tony had followed in his footsteps. I nearly joined myself in 1972, but Chris was and still is very much anti, so only a week away from 'going through', I backed off, realising that I already had enough commitments, in addition to which I was at that time involved in a Christian Fellowship which had concerns about some moral and ethical aspects of Freemasonry. Anyway, the reason I mentioned this now was to say something about Marion, Tony's new wife, and why Chris didn't like her. We had been invited to Tony's Masonic Lodge Ladies Night and Chris was not too comfortable. She doesn't like formal functions and is a nervous wreck when it comes to meeting new people. After dinner, quite innocently, she lit up a cigarette and madam Marion made her feel wretched, telling her loudly and pompously that she wasn't allowed to smoke until after the loyal toast. Chris could have crawled into a hole in the ground. Later,

Madam Marion's bitchy behaviour manifested itself when, again for all to hear, she remarked to Chris, "Should you be drinking when you are on medication?" Not very nice. A doctor in the company, Bhupinda Chaudrey, gallantly came to Chris' rescue by announcing that her drinking was not a problem. This may not have been strictly true, but it was a nice gentlemanly gesture, contrasting starkly with Marion's malice.

Many years later, on the 17th March 2000 to be exact, I did join the Masonic Peace Lodge, so called because it was established on D-Day 1945. Nothing I said was able to convince my mother and my wife that it was a quite innocuous, quaint and harmless men's gang. Their minds were closed as many are which consider Freemasonry to be a sinister organisation comparable to the Ku Klux Klan. One evening when my mother was round for dinner her estimation of Chris soared when the subject cropped up and Chris left the room, reappearing a minute later with my Masonic tie which she ceremoniously cut in half with the kitchen scissors. But I never succumb to what I consider unreasoned argument or intimidation, and it wasn't this that led me to drift away from the Craft where I had been raised to the rank of Steward. I gradually stopped going to the meetings because I found the ritual, though quite harmless, to be longwinded and boring. I had joined mainly for two reasons – curiosity and fellowship – and I had satisfied the first and I was getting more than enough of the second from my other activities. Besides which, most of the Masonic fellowship takes place at the after meeting meal, and this occurs too late for me. I can't sleep if I eat late.

The other member of the Ecurie Quelquechose team, Malcolm Sutherland, was an enigmatic character. Quiet and a bit of a loner, I never really knew what he was thinking. He did have a short-lived relationship with a girl but I didn't think it would last, and it didn't. He moved out of town to a little village called Chop Gate (pronounced Yat) where he lived with his cat. Malcolm had an extremely rare disease of the respiratory system and was fortunate enough to have in a local hospital one of the few world specialists in that particular ailment, on whom he was free to call night and day whenever he had an attack. He had been told by this specialist that if he wished to survive beyond forty he should remove himself from the industrial climate of the North East and find one more suitable. On medical advice he moved to South Africa where the plateau of Johannesburg with its rarefied altitude would, he hoped, ensure his longevity. It didn't. We used to correspond regularly until a year later when he died because he did not have the same ready access to treatment and advice that he had enjoyed in England. I received a letter from him posted before, but received after his death, in which he told me he was about to die. I felt sad of course but it was only when I later discovered that he had offered his body for medical research that I broke down and sobbed violently. They had declined his offer. Poor Malcolm, not much use to anyone alive and now they had rejected him in death.

Before moving to Chop 'Yat', Malcolm lived in Harrogate Crescent, Middlesbrough, with his mother Agnes and stepsisters, twins Irene and Janice. Twice widowed, Agnes was a typical down to earth broad Glaswegian who enjoyed a bit of fun and her whisky. She couldn't really quite fathom out how Malcolm and I were friends since we were so different in nature. "You would really get on with oor Brian," she used to often say. Then one day when I called at the house there he was. He had fled his beloved Glasgow, the reasons for which were never fully revealed, and had moved in with his mother, twin sisters and Malcolm. Brian's father, Agnes' second husband, had died in his early forties with a heart attack and Brian, anticipating a similar fate, instead of looking after himself by following a moderate lifestyle, was intent on living life, while it lasted, to the full.

Once Brian appeared on the scene I began to see more of him and less of Tony, Peter, Malcolm, Howard and Ned. Not that I hadn't enjoyed their company. I just found them rather dull compared to Brian. In fact, I can recall some good times with Team Ecurie Quelquechose tearing round the countryside in our cars with frequent 'refreshment' stops. The introduction of the breathalyser law in 1968, however, curtailed our activities somewhat. At that time I had a Mark II Jaguar Saloon and I suggested that we should take turns at having a duty driver on our nights out so that the rest of us could still drink. I acquired from somewhere a peaked chauffeur's cap and the driver for the night was required to wear this – and a dark suit and tie – and to open the doors for us when we got out and in, accompanied of course by a polite salute. The new law was life changing in its implications and we were all paranoid since driving meant so much to us all. We expected to see police cars lurking in every side road. This fear was resoundingly dispelled on the 5th November 1968. I had bought two large boxes of fireworks for Liz and as soon as dusk arrived we went out into the back garden of my mother's house (we were staying there at the time) and I placed a rocket in a bottle and lit the blue touch paper. Instead of soaring into the dark sky it decided to arc backwards and crash into an upstairs window. My mother, being of a nervous disposition, screamed and fled with Liz back into the house. No amount of reassurances and entreaties would persuade them to venture out again and this left me with an entire firework display untouched, save for the errant rocket. When Liz had gone to sleep I called on the lads and suggested a pub crawl. On the way back from Fatfield in County Durham, for it was there we had crawled to, and in high spirits, we decided to let off some fireworks (which I had put back in the car) and propel them from the rear windows as we hurtled along on our return journey. We were dead ringers to be pulled over, particularly at that time of night – but there wasn't a police car in sight. I became a little more blasé about drinking and driving after that.

Maybe it was my attraction to complex and 'different' characters that was to cause me to pal up with Malcolm's stepbrother Brian in preference to these old friends. Our friendship has endured. Brian's mother was spot on. We did immediately become kindred spirits and our wives were to become very good friends too. My friendship with Tony Wright, on the other hand, I would come to regret.

Fourteen

PLANET HOUSE

Sometimes too much to drink isn't enough.
Anon.

W E HAD FIXED the date for our wedding – the 2nd January 1971 – and had decided we would live in Middlesbrough, even though this meant a long drive for me every day to Sunderland. The plan was to make a new start away from the scene of so many traumatic experiences for me and for Chris, who I suspect may have been just a little bit anxious to avoid any opportunity for Agnes to exert any further influence on me. She need not have worried on that score.

The few months leading up to the big day were to be busy and eventful. There were so many things going on. When I moved into Planet House, I hadn't thrown a flat warming party so I decided to throw a flat cooling party before vacating. Chris, wisely as it turned out, decided not to attend. She knew what it would be like. This was intended to be my final Sunderland 'fling'. I don't know how many guests turned up that night but I've been in smaller crowds in the Clock Stand at Roker Park where I was then a season ticket holder. Following the transfer of Brian Clough from Boro to Sunderland I started to attend their home games more frequently and after being almost decapitated in the Roker end during a local derby match against Newcastle, I willingly paid for a season ticket with only half a season left. When grounds were full in those days the crowd became a sort of living organism in which you were crushed and pushed in whatever direction the surges of the crowd destined. Such was the situation at that particular match. Powerless to resist, I found myself pushed down the terraces until I was pressed against a barrier hardly able to breathe. With arms aching from the backward pressure I was exerting in order to avoid my ribs being crushed I somehow managed to summon up enough reserves of strength to push backwards and in the few seconds before the crowd once again bore down on me I fell on my haunches and was thrust under the barrier among the legs of the people in front of it. I felt the bottom of the barrier brush the hair on the top of my

91

head (I had some then) and the thought crossed my mind that had I dropped an inch less than I did, my skull would have been torn open, such was the force from behind. A familiar sight in those days was the waving of white handkerchiefs to attract the attention of the St Johns Ambulance people when someone in the crowd had fainted or been hurt, which was frequent. The unfortunate fan would then be passed down by the crowd over their heads like a bucket chain at a fire. There was a Heysell disaster waiting to happen and when it did, with the advent of all seater stadiums, the danger was removed from football spectating. But so too was much of the fun and excitement. We need a bit of danger in our lives.

Although by then I had become a Sunderland supporter I did not abandon my boyhood team, Boro. Like my dad who had found a place in his heart for Boro, so too did I find one in mine for the Black Cats. The two clubs at that time played at home on alternate Saturdays and I was able to get my football "fix" weekly instead of fortnightly.

The Clock Stand at Roker Park was to my knowledge the only football stand in the country where you did actually stand. Normally you sit in the stands and stand in the terraces. So why do they call them stands and not sits? Having been used to being crammed in the terraces like a sardine I was then able to watch my football without risking my life. I remember later in that season there was an FA Cup tie against Manchester United which drew a more than capacity crowd of nearly 60,000 people, many of whom had gained entry when a wall collapsed. Sadly there were many seriously injured. It was with some relief that I looked down at the mayhem from my civilised vantage point. Money well spent, I decided.

Anyway, back at my party in Planet House, I had a problem. A few people had complained to me that the gin wasn't very strong. I told them to just pour themselves bigger measures since I had made sure I was well stocked with booze – and particularly with spirits which we had bought through the company ostensibly for gifts for clients and which I had collected from the office on the morning of the party. Eventually I was persuaded by Lynne Brannan (now Sutherland) to taste the gin and, sure enough, it was pure water! My guess is that our office cleaner had a good Christmas that year, although she of course denied tampering with the bottles as they laid in pre-Christmas storage. Anyway, a trip to the off-licence soon redressed the deficiency and I think I am right in saying that Lynne's relationship with Brian Sutherland was consummated that night. I wish water had had that effect on some of the girls I had taken out.

As I have said earlier, parties were pretty wild in those days and full of incidents, and the one that sticks in my mind on this occasion was when the doorbell rang at about 3 a.m. Being a penthouse flat there were stairs leading down to the door and I eventually responded to the persistent ringing of the bell. As I got to the top of the stairs I saw one of my neighbours standing in the doorway asking Johnny Johnson if we wouldn't mind keeping the noise down because he had an early start that day at work. Johnny had somehow got to his feet after falling down the stairs earlier where we had left him to sleep it off. He was slouched against the door post attempting to talk to the neighbour – "Ssschwoor werraman jursharer unshush," he said with one hand on the neighbour's shoulder. The neighbour's reply was a classic. "Tell you what," he said, "just forget it. If they've sent *you* to the door, what bloody state must the rest of them be in!" – then turned and went back to bed. I laugh every time I recall that incident which I suppose only I, who witnessed it and who knew Johnny, can appreciate fully. I do admire the literary skills of authors who can successfully create characters and situations in the minds and imaginations of their readers which enable them to fully share moments like this.

Whilst on the subject of parties, let me tell you about the turkey. Our company's office party, always one of the most popular on the 'circuit', was held, as then used to be the norm, on Christmas Eve – not the most sensible arrangement for those with families – and I of course still had Liz with me at weekends and school holidays. Having established the tradition, however, there was no way we could change it. The Arnott and Reed party was eagerly awaited by our customers and friends and was one occasion when I left my car at home. I had resolved to put in an appearance and escape at the earliest opportunity. The road to Hell is paved with good intentions! Several hours later and well pissed, I staggered to the station where, amazingly, I had the presence of mind to remember Christmas Dinner. We had bought through the business some Christmas fayre from John Eltringham, our butcher friend, and for the first time in my life we had a turkey to look forward to – except I had left it on a wall in the yard behind our office to keep cool. I had to go back for it, missing my train in the process. When I arrived at the office I was greeted by Miss Duckett who lived alone in the small second floor flat above the office. "Oh, thank you very, very much for being so kind, Mr Arnott!" she gushed. "You've made my Christmas!" Not having a clue what she was on about, I just replied magnanimously, "Don't mention it, Miss Duckett. You have a lovely Christmas." I had that warm festive glow you get when you do good things for people. Until, that is, the awful thought dawned on me. "Bloody Hell! She thinks I've left the turkey in the yard for her!" Brought well and truly down to earth I pondered on my dilemma. Too late to go and buy another bird, and we faced, instead of our first Christmas with a turkey, our first Christmas with no bird at all!

What was I to do? I could already hear my mother's recriminations. Not only was I to be home very late, I was birdless. Thinking it was pointless, I nevertheless opened the back door into the yard and was surprised to see the John Eltringham High Class Butchers carrier bag where I had left it earlier. I now had a big decision to make. If I made off with the bag there was only one person who would be disappointed – Miss Duckett – and she would probably already have bought something for dinner anyway. Anyway, it was a bit stupid of her to leave it outside on the wall instead of taking it inside, but maybe she had the same idea as me and left it there to keep cool. But our need was greater than hers. I would make it up to her after the holidays. By these unconvincing arguments I persuaded myself that I was perfectly justified in hurriedly snatching the bag, locking up and leaving the office before she had a chance to confront me. Throughout the train journey back the turkey was clutched close to my bosom lest it might escape again.

Liz was still awake awaiting my return and my guilt was complete as I drunkenly fell over on her bed trying to show her the turkey. I wonder if she remembers this. Needless to say the turkey next day stuck in my throat and my festive mood was haunted by recriminations.

♣

The week after my miserable Christmas, Chris and I were married at Wolsingham Baptist Church where Chris's father was a Deacon. It was a massive emotional occasion for Chris who had refused to put on her wedding dress until she was sure I had arrived with Liz who was to be bridesmaid, such was her feeling of insecurity at that time. She was shaking so much when she walked down the aisle on her proud father's arm that there were no petals left on her bouquet by the time she reached the alter. George suffered from MS and was quite poorly that day. He had made a big effort to be there to give away his only daughter. It was a nice simple affair without the pomp and ceremony of my previous wedding. The Minister George Lindo took the service and I noticed Liz listening intently to the words and the vows. In the car on the way to the reception at The Duke of York in Fir Tree near Bishop Auckland, Chris and I received a long lecture from Liz on what we were and were not allowed to do now that we were married. Lynne was Maid of Honour and Brian performed his duties as Best Man impeccably. One of those duties was to shower with pennies the dozens of children waiting outside the church when the bride and groom appeared – a quaint and lovely local custom.

I had booked a table at The Billingham Arms Hotel dinner dance for the evening and invited a few friends. Brian and Lynne of course, Peter and Tony Wright and their wives Iris and Marion, Ned South and his wife Glyth and Brian's stepbrother Malcolm Sutherland. Chris was congratulated by them all – except Marion.

Looking back now I wonder what my new in-laws were feeling as their daughter was whisked away on her wedding night to face an evening of 'celebration' which didn't include any of her family, only a few of my friends, most of whom Chris didn't know very well and some of whom she did not particularly like. Vera and George must have experienced grave misgivings over their young daughter's future as she started her new life in an unknown and (almost) friendless environment with an unreliable divorcee husband and the immediate responsibility of a ready-made family. To their eternal credit, they didn't interfere or show any outward signs of concern and were quietly supportive. It can't have been easy for them. I later learned that Vera had said to George at the time, "We don't know him; we'll just have to learn to love him." Many years later when she and Chris were reminiscing, she added, "…and it was easy."

After the dance the newlyweds spent what was left of the night at the hotel and that was our honeymoon. My mother was looking after Liz and we had to be back early the next day. Not the most romantic of starts for my young twenty-three-year-old bride who was to discover later what an onerous commitment she had let herself in for.

After Chris and I were married we lived with my parents in Middlesbrough at 331 Marton Road until the conveyancing was processed for our new house at 11 Westwood Avenue, only a mile or so away, which meant that Liz would see a lot of my mother who had been one of the few consistent factors in her young life. Chris was relieved to be away from Sunderland – and Agnes – and was looking forward eagerly to our new start together. Although it meant a long day for me, I enjoyed driving, so the two-hour round trip to my Sunderland office was an acceptable downside given the other benefits of living in Middlesbrough – and I wouldn't have the Palatine to tempt me. I did call in briefly from time to time but now I had an excuse not to stop late. Besides, Middlesbrough was not short of a pub or club or two! Chris was to make friends too and this was very important. She had first met Lynne when I had arranged a night out at Grey's Club in Newcastle with her and Brian. Until then, apart from me, she had never ever in her life met anyone who had been divorced, that's how naïve she was in those days. Both Brian and Lynne had been married before. They too were married in 1971. I was Best Man and a heavily pregnant Chris, Maid of Honour.

♣

I needn't have worried about the Christmas turkey. As soon as I got back to work after my honeymoon I went to see Miss Duckett to apologise and face the music. No wonder she looked puzzled. Jack, without my knowledge, had given her a chicken as a Christmas gift!

Fifteen

NEW FRIENDS

My mother used to say there are no strangers. Only friends you haven't met yet.
She is now in a maximum security home in Australia.
Dame Edna Everage.

MY **MOTHER** had become head waitress at the Highfield Hotel in its glory days when its cuisine was renowned throughout the area. The hotel played a brief but eventful part in my life, too. By then, alas, it was one of the many steak houses which had become fashionable in the late sixties and early seventies. Camerons, the old Hartlepool brewers, had sold the hotel to a national chain, Chef and Brewer, and had installed a young ambitious manager called Dave. Brian and I were to make the most of Dave's hospitality.

When marriages break up one and sometimes both partners often react by going through a period of irrational behaviour. That's why police officers in these situations are often temporarily suspended on full pay or given desk jobs. They are considered, certainly by the Glasgow force, to be unreliable and vulnerable while they were having their 'fling'. I had resisted this temptation. Because of my commitment to my daughter I had little choice. This responsibility had been removed to a certain extent when Liz went to live with her mother for four nights each week during school time. During that period and for a while after I married Chris, I was able to release some of the urges created by the irresponsible genes I had inherited from my father and which had been stimulated by my frustrations. I experienced a delayed reaction to my rejection. I started to drink more heavily. This was possible because Planet House was but a few minutes' walk from the Palatine Bar and the Highfield was even closer to my parents' house where I stayed after moving back to Middlesbrough. In Brian I had a willing accomplice. Agnes had been right – not ex-wife Agnes, Brian's mother Agnes. I did get on with 'oor' Brian whose company I found in comparison with my other friends much more interesting and adventurous. He too at that time was escaping from a domestic situation in

96

Glasgow and we had much in common. We became soul mates. Naturally being a Glaswegian he liked his drink too. I decided we should become beer brothers. Teesside was renowned in those days for the quality and strength of its beer and anyone who drank shorts was considered suspect. I would introduce Brian to proper beer and Camerons Strongarm was the Highfield beer on tap and an excellent pint it was. Brian would love it, surely. With my encouragement he forced down a couple of pints but then insisted that I too should be willing to accept a challenge, and challenged me to have a couple of 'halves'. I was at first puzzled since I always drank pints, but he was of course referring to halves of whisky! Finding that English measures were smaller than those north of the border, he ordered doubles. We had met at opening time for a few pre-match drinks – Celtic were due to play their famous European Cup Final, which we planned to watch in the residents' lounge on TV. I was told afterwards that they had won – the first British team having achieved top honours in Europe – but the match itself I found very confusing. There were forty-four players on the field and they played with two balls! I crawled home in the early hours and I'm ashamed to say, my father had to put me to bed. I've been wary of the amber nectar ever since.

Nothing establishes a relationship better than getting totally pissed together. Bonds are formed. True selves revealed. Feelings of camaraderie are awakened and mutual trust is established. I used to mistrust anyone who wasn't prepared to reveal themselves, warts and all, by drinking till the death. Brian and I have had many black boozing sessions together and we were to lead each other astray on many future occasions. I think we both have found, in drink, an escape from life's often brutal realities. The Highfield became our regular watering hole and in Dave we had a very accommodating 'mein host'. We vied for position at the bar with another party of regulars who at first used to irritate us because of their two massive Labrador dogs over and around whose bodies we had to negotiate to get to the bar. We grumbled about this inconvenience to Dave but he told us he couldn't stop people bringing in pets. "Yes," he said when we asked him if that included us. He changed his attitude a few days later when Brian and I arrived with a goat we had borrowed for the occasion. It was all taken in good humour and the ice was broken with our hitherto rivals for bar space with whom we subsequently had some good fun sessions. The Highfield was my new Palatine, without the discipline of closing time. This was, on one memorable occasion, to prove a distinct hindrance to Brian's athletic aspirations. Having been a successful car salesman in Glasgow, he had taken a similar job with Blue Bell Garages in Middlesbrough where he had quickly achieved the post of Sales Manager. It was at Blue Bell he first met Lynne who was the receptionist there. He and the General Manager John Snaith didn't always see eye to eye and a sort of civilised but nevertheless serious rivalry had developed between them. A challenge had been thrown down by John whose lifestyle by comparison was rather less punishing than Brian's, whose pride refused to allow him to do the utterly sensible thing and duck the challenge.

So it came to pass that on the eve of their race round the track at the Co-op Athletic Club sports ground, Brian and I met after work for a quiet drink on the pretext of discussing tactics for the race which was to take place at seven o'clock the following morning. I was to be Brian's second and it was really serious stuff. There had been a lot of ribald exchanges between the contestants and bets had been placed. It was quite a lengthy tactic talk, which had to be continued in the residents' lounge after closing time. Panic set in when Brian looked at his watch and realised it was 4.30 a.m. He dashed home to make what he called 'final preparations' which, I think, was to pick up his plimsolls. Alas, despite all the planning and preparation, or perhaps because of it, Brian lost his bet. After barely fifty yards he collapsed by the trackside and threw up.

You can take the Scot out of Scotland but you can't take Scotland out of the Scot. Brian finally settled on the Sassenach side of Hadrian's Wall but it took over thirty years. Passionate about his country and his football team, he used to drive every Saturday all the way to Carlisle, a good two-hour journey, so that he could tune into Radio Clyde and sit in his car listening to the commentary on the Rangers matches, after which he would drive all the way back again. Whenever he went up to Glasgow to visit relations nobody, including wife Lynne, would hear from him for a week. With one exception he spent every Hogmanay north of the border – much, I might add, to my relief. On the one and only occasion he did celebrate "the bells" in Middlesbrough I spent most of the night in the A&E unit of the General Hospital. The normally benevolent, affable Brian, fuelled with sufficient whisky, can change into a homicidal hothead if something upsets him, as his dear wife did that night. The skirmish which involved Lynne brandishing a firearm and Brian punching a window resulted in severe lacerations to his arm. He eventually received treatment at 9.30 a.m. on New Year's Day. I complained about the delay but only once, after a nurse had explained the nature of the other casualties, some of whom were fighting for their lives. One, the nurse told me, was on life support after he had for a bet downed a litre bottle of whisky in one go. It was certainly a different and interesting way to spend New Year's Eve but not one I wish to repeat. The duty staff have at these times a lot to put up with and I take my hat off to them.

That particular festive season may have ended in disaster but it had started off on the right note – with a laugh. I had bought ostensibly for the kids (but I do confess it was more for me) a Santa Claus outfit – the full works. I had in my mind a cunning plan to indulge my weird sense of humour and Brian was the perfect accomplice. We arranged to meet in the Blue Bell pub at opening time on Christmas Eve with me arriving first in full Santa gear. My entry prompted some odd glances from the people at the bar, many of whom I knew but in my disguise I was not recognised. I greeted them with a "Good evenin'", ordered a pint and stood at the bar humming 'Jingle Bells'. They thought I was some kind of crank and I suppose they were right. They ignored me. When Brian walked in I greeted him in the same way but, as planned, he responded with a "Hello there, Santa! Didn't expect to see you in here tonight. Thought you'd be too busy!" I explained that one of my reindeers had shed a shoe and was down at the blacksmiths so I was killing time. "Mind you," I said with an empty glass in my hand, "wouldn't you have thought that one of these miserable bastards" (pointing to the other customers) "would have bought Santa a pint tonight of all nights?" Brian ordered a pint for me and we got into a bizarre conversation in which I promised him that his family would receive extra special presents that night – "Unlike these tight arses. They'll get nowt," I said, glaring again at the other customers who by then began to suspect it may be Derrick in disguise. The Christmas spirit prevailed after that and more pints were ordered. Mrs Claus was not at all amused that night when Santa returned to the North Pole where the atmosphere was decidedly icy. "What a load of bullcock!" was her response when he attempted to explain why he had been delayed.

Brian and I were undoubtedly bad influences on each other. The Santa incident is but one of many such escapades during the early days of our friendship. After James was born I made an effort to curtail my drinking. There was one particular Saturday night I had promised Chris that I would stay in and had every intention of doing so when a pair of eyes peeping over the windowsill made contact with mine. A hand then beckoned. I went out on the pretext of popping to the shop for a *Sports Gazette* and Brian (for they had been his eyes and hand) persuaded me to join him in the club. The reason for his clandestine behaviour, he explained, was that he too had promised to be a good boy, not to drink and to prepare a cosy dinner for Lynne who was at our house visiting. Their meal had been arranged for eight o'clock and he had fancied a couple of aperitifs and had no-one to play with! Our quick drink of course was followed by a few more, but we didn't fall entirely by the wayside. Brian went home to prepare dinner and wait for Lynne and I returned home full of contrition of course. Chris was bathing James who was only a few months old and in order to earn some brownie points I asked her if I could do anything to help. She told me to carry the baby bath outside and throw the water on the lawn. The absurdity of the request should have registered with me since it had been pouring down for hours and the last thing the lawn needed was a bathful of soapy water. Chris opened the French doors for me and as I staggered through them I felt a foot on my backside which sent me and the baby bath sprawling. Soaked to the skin and covered in mud, my entreaties to be allowed back inside were ignored. I eventually gave up and with nowhere else to go in my bedraggled state I decided to seek refuge at Brian's house. As I walked into his living room Brian was crouched at the hearth trying to coax some flames from the recently laid fire in preparation for his wife's return. Without looking up he spoke in an uncharacteristically meek and ingratiating tone.

"Hello pet," he said.

"Don't you bloody pet me," I replied. "Look what a bloody mess you've got me into!"

Startled, he turned round and just howled with laughter.

Like me, Brian enjoyed the company of oddball characters and on occasions when we happened to be in Glasgow at the same time, I was introduced to several of his acquaintances, some of whom became Arnott clients, including a builder called Jack Stewart. Jack had a luxury apartment in Bearsden and I enjoyed his hospitality there on a few occasions. On entering Jack's apartment his guests would be given three darts and before being allowed into the living area, were required to throw the darts at a dart board in the hall. Pinned to the dartboard was a picture of his estranged wife. They were divorced, then re-married and divorced again. I don't know their current marital status but I sometimes wonder whether the dartboard is up or down!

Yes, I had found in Brian a friend who was on a wavelength with me. We had enough in common to create an affinity and sufficient disparity in our temperaments to maintain it. It was because we were such different characters in so many ways that we found each other interesting and were able to help and support each other over so many years. One major common denominator in our ongoing relationship was our wives who, again whilst such opposites in so many ways, became friends too. They had something in common of course – irresponsible husbands. There was rarely a dull moment when we were together.

Our holidays together started with Brian and Lynne joining us on our Easter break with Liz at a Scarborough hotel where the guests were treated to a bit of fun by Liz's performance in the dining room on our first night.. We played "I spy" and for her turn Liz chose something beginning with 'ch'. After twenty minutes and umpteen wrong answers by us and most of the other guests who had joined in, we gave up. I don't think Liz realised why her answer – 'tulips' provoked so much amusement and applause – but she enjoyed her moment of fame and revelled in her ensuing celebrity status during the rest of our stay there. This turned out to be brief. The weather on the East coast was foul and, in contrast to the West coast, continued rain was forecast so we decided to check out and drive to Blackpool where it was dry and sunny. The hotel we had often stayed in with Liz and my parents, the Bourne, was full so we booked into the Warwick. Chris, despite our concerted attempts to convince her otherwise, had got it firmly into her head that it was called the Warrington. We gave up and joined in Chris' dyslexic dilemma by adding 'ington' to the end of everything we said. After a day on the beachington I would order pints of beerington in the barington and Brian drank lageringtons while the girls had gin and toningtons after which we would take a tramington into townington and go for a chineseington. You've got the idearington.   This was just one example of a special means of communication which the four of us developed over the years – like 'profiteroles'. We would say this about anything that appeared a bit suspect and came in handy when we wanted to warn each other without revealing to an outsider what we were doing. By nature Chris is extremely suspicious, excessively and often irrationally so in my opinion.   I refer specifically to the occasion at Ninos by the Sea, an Italian restaurant at Saltburn by the Sea where the four of us were dining one evening and where the waiter had recommended for dessert the chef's special – profiteroles. "Don't have them," Chris whispered to me out of the side of her mouth so, despite really fancying them, I didn't, assuming that she must have some very good reason for her advice. "They're trying to get rid of them before they go off," was her rationale. Thus was created in the English language, at least among the four of us, a new meaning for the word profiteroles – BEWARE.

"No," said Chris many years later when a young man asked her for her ticket on the Tranvia – a tram service in Santa Cruz, Tenerife, which is operated on trust by inserting a pre-paid Bono ticket in the ticket machines on board. The young man again asked Chris for her ticket. She wasn't going to give in to this Charley Cheeky (Chrissarism) trying to sponge a free ride at her expense and responded with a more emphatic, *"No!"*

One of the other passengers then gently pointed out that the young man didn't want to use her ticket, he just wanted to inspect it!   She didn't expect ticket inspectors to be dressed in cool casual uniforms.

The Sutherland union was blessed in 1972 with the birth of their daughter and our ward, Kirsten and many joint family holidays followed which included a week at Blackpool with one of Lynne's five sisters Sharon who, though a little older than Liz, made a good companion for her. Sharon was a lovely girl with a generous nature, a characteristic which resulted in her death several years later when she was brutally murdered by a drug addict who she had taken under her wing and tried to help.

I have fond memories of Blackpool. With its working class brashness it isn't posh enough for some snobby people and isn't therefore everybody's cup of tea. Indeed, it wouldn't be mine now, but it served its purpose at the time. With its unpretentious façade of fun it was a quick, cheap escape into a world of phoney make-believe which made no demands on you other than to part with your money by conning the kids. All the old legendary comedians like Ken Dodd, Harry Worth and Les Dawson played the theatres during the summer and illumination seasons. I don't think Chris was too impressed but my mam, the kids and I enjoyed them. They say the best things in life are free and the Uncle Peter Webster children's talent show on Central

Pier was a source of some wonderful entertainment – especially the year when the little lad from Burnley won. He sang 'Three Wheels on My Wagon' completely off key and Uncle Peter's attempts to shut him up were ignored (and deftly dodged when they became physical) until every verse had been droned. The winner was judged on applause volume. Winning this particular competition carried with it a great deal of prestige and for many youngsters opened the door into the entertainment profession. Could entertainment score over talent? Surely the little lad from Burnley who had resoundingly won through his heat wouldn't stand a chance in the Grand Final held in the South Pier Theatre. To the obvious chagrin of the rest of the very talented acts, he brought the house down. The judges simply couldn't ignore the level of tumultuous applause this scruffy little lad from Burnley received from the packed audience with tears of laughter and emotion inspired by pity, rolling down their cheeks.

In 1974, instead of staying at the Warwick – or was it the Warrington? – we chose not to book but to take pot luck. We were there only for a long weekend and on this occasion Brian wasn't with us. He and Lynne were going through a sticky patch and had split up, so we looked for somewhere cheaper to stay. Boro were playing Carlisle and I had arranged to meet Brian there. By the time we had found some digs it was late, so I dropped the families and the luggage off at the Avon Court Guest House reception before hurriedly driving off to Carlisle. There was something about the place that made me feel a little uneasy and I was feeling guilty too about leaving – but not guilty enough to stay. I couldn't let my mate down and besides, I was informed by the proprietor that it was party night and I would be missing a treat which was all I needed to confirm that my decision not to be there was a good one. On my return in the early hours of the morning the door was opened by a heavily made up mein host dressed in a frock with a corn plaster peeping through his open toed sandals. "Ooh, you've missed all the fun," he announced, "your wife's been raped three times." I think it was his idea of a joke. I certainly hoped it was. Ignoring him I went upstairs to our room where Chris explained to me that she and Lynne had been forced to join in some quite bizarre party games but had managed to survive with her honour intact. Every word of our conversation was being listened to. The baby listening system behind reception was far too sophisticated for that purpose alone and I am convinced had been installed to enable the man in the frock to indulge in some verbal voyeurism. Kirsten, fortunately, was sick during the night and gave us an excuse to leave that day. That was our last visit to Blackpool.

Gangsters and Molls at Wynyard Gold Club 1998.
Lynne, Chris and first prize winner Brian.

Sixteen

THE GINGER LURKER

My toughest fight was with my first wife.
Muhammad Ali.

WHAT AN IMMENSE feeling of relief it was when during the Christmas holidays of 1970 I decided to keep Liz with us and send her to school in Middlesbrough. I would no longer have to face the awful task of persuading, even forcing, Liz to go back to Agnes and her school in Newbottle, County Durham. The decision wasn't taken lightly. I was conscious of the fact that Chris would have to take on the added responsibility of a ready-made family. She readily accepted the situation for my sake and for the sake of Liz who she had grown to love and whose love was clearly reciprocated. Liz herself jumped at the chance of staying with us. So no more stressful Monday morning journeys in the car for Liz or me, either. Wonderful.

I was of course fully entitled to take whatever steps I felt necessary to protect Liz's welfare and ensure her happiness and security. I was her legal custodian as well as her father and it was clear to me that she was not happy with the existing arrangement. I didn't know the reasons for her unhappiness. She was reticent to share these with me. Consequently all manner of conjecture and speculation was flying around in my head – not the least of which, in the light of Agnes' previous desire not to take on the responsibility, was the possibility that she and Willy were finding Liz to be a burden. I just couldn't bear the thought that she was unwanted. What I did know was that she was calm and happy when she was with Chris and me and with my mother close by I decided that this would be a better environment for Liz to be in. She immediately settled into Green Lane School and soon made friends there and with other children in the neighbourhood. There had been no immediate reaction or response from Agnes when I informed her of my decision, nor was there any immediate contact from her wanting to see Liz, although from past experience this wasn't unusual, nor was it to be unusual in the future when months, even years, would pass without contact.

A huge birthday card from Agnes arrived for Liz's sixth birthday in May, followed by an official notification that she was to apply for custody. My initial reaction of surprise and disappointment was, after reflection, followed by not exactly relief, but at least some comfort from the thought that if Agnes' bid failed then my decision to keep Liz would be vindicated by an independent ruling, and if it succeeded then the responsibility for Liz's future would rest with the appropriate and 'expert' authorities, having satisfied themselves that such a decision would be in her best interests. Either way we would just have to get on with it and do whatever we could to ensure that, for the sake of Liz's happiness, we made the best of a bad job. Visits by social workers followed, presumably also to Agnes' home. Reports would no doubt be sent to the court for consideration. This was a comfort.

On the day of the hearing Agnes, dressed in a long white leather coat with a fur collar, tried to blacken my name by revealing that I had once told her that I had watched a blue movie at my Tankard Club in the Palatine. Although I didn't understand its relevance, she told the court that Liz and her brother Simon should be brought up together – an argument I was able to counter by announcing that my new wife was in fact pregnant and that we too would soon be able to provide Liz with a brother or sister. I don't know, having no access to their contents, what bearing the social workers' reports had on the court's decision, but I suspect the biggest single factor may have been Agnes' earlier reluctance to seek custody. "Why," she was asked by the court, "have you waited so long to challenge the earlier decision on custody which was made in favour of the father?" Her reply I think spoke volumes: "I didn't mind when Mrs Willis was looking after her [Liz], but I object to her [glaring at Chris] looking after her." The court could find no reason to overturn the previous decision and I was awarded custody with Agnes given access every other weekend and an annual holiday. Chris was relieved when this, her second ordeal in court, was over. She had been innocently caught in the crossfire of an unnecessarily bitter battle. "Let's hope," said my mother afterwards, "we can all now get on with our lives and make the best of it for Elizabeth's sake."

Had the decision gone the other way I would of course have been disappointed, but having said that, I would have co-operated with Agnes and her husband to do everything possible to make the transition as smooth as possible. This was about a child's welfare, not surely about personal vendettas or feelings. My mother and I and later Chris, had been very careful, often in the face of severe temptation, never to say bad things about Agnes or her husband. We made a vow never to do so. Hopefully Liz would one day, when the time was right, find out for herself and be able to form her own opinions uninfluenced by others.

Agnes exercised her custody option infrequently. When she called she totally ignored Chris which made it difficult for some kind of dialogue to be established. I tried to be in when she called in the hope that we could establish some civilised arrangement. It didn't help that Agnes' visits were invariably at short notice and, as usual, commitments in other areas were to frustrate me. V & G crisis (see Volume II) had come at an inconvenient time and again I found myself being pulled in different directions by the demands of home and business. True to form, Agnes' visits suddenly stopped and we looked forward to a period of normality in which to settle into our new home. Then one day out of the blue the police arrived at the front door demanding to search the house and interrogate Chris who was several months pregnant at the time. She was terrified.

A few weeks earlier a woman had been sexually assaulted and strangled whilst walking on the nearby Eston Hills. Many years later I was able to find out more about the case from Detective Superintendent Tom Stoddart of Cleveland Constabulary and the details are worth recording here.

There were two people, an elderly man and a younger woman, who had seen a man hurrying from the scene of the incident. Both gave quite different descriptions of the man. The woman described the suspect as having red hair and wearing overalls, but according to the elderly man he had dark hair. Whilst not totally discounting the man's evidence, the police decided that the young woman's description was more dependable and they progressed their investigation accordingly. The press were quick to ascribe a name to the murderer. 'The Ginger Lurker' was emblazoned in the headlines of local and national newspapers.

Despite the graphic description given of the killer, the police made little progress with their investigation and were to pounce on the lead given to them in an anonymous phone call from a female purporting to have seen the suspect getting into a car with a woman called Christine. Her description of the woman and her car matched that of Chris and her car.

Chris was alone when she was disturbed by the doorbell followed by a purposeful and heavy knocking at the door. The police unceremoniously virtually invited themselves inside. They grilled her for hours. Since she was several months pregnant at the time of the alleged sighting and was resting at home, she didn't have an alibi. Afterwards the police questioned the neighbours and later returned to interview me, probing to find whether I suspected that Chris may be having an affair. Chris was visibly shaken by the incident and I was quite annoyed that she had been put through such an ordeal, particularly in her condition. Anyway, the police must have been satisfied that we were not involved because, thankfully, after one final visit they didn't return. The identity of the anonymous caller was never established, but I know who my number one suspect is.

It was almost a year later that the police, having made no headway, began to wind down their investigation, when out of the blue they got the vital breakthrough that was to solve the case. A particularly nasty rape had occurred in Leeds in which the victim's hands had been taped by her assailant and the police there were able to trace the origin of the tape to the British Steel plant at Lackenby on Teesside. In progressing this line of enquiry they liaised with Cleveland Police who had taken the unusual step of photographing every person interviewed during the Eston investigation. The photographs were shown to the Leeds victim and she was instantly able to identify her attacker. The police moved quickly, calling at the suspect's house in Dormanstown and taking him into custody whilst, at the same time, breaking into his locker at the Lackenby plant where he worked. There they found some tape and his diary in which he had written on the day of the murder, "Today I did a terrible thing." He was convicted of both crimes and sentenced to life imprisonment. He died a few months after his release many years later.

Did the young woman witness in the Eston case make a terrible mistake, or did she deliberately try to mislead the police? The murderer wasn't ginger at all. He was dark haired and fitted exactly the description given by the elderly man.

After the Ginger Lurker incident the anonymous nuisance telephone calls we had been receiving night and day subsided and there was a period of relative domestic normality at 11 Westwood Avenue. Agnes telephoned a couple of times to arrange to pick up Liz but didn't turn up. Our first son was born on 18th October and was christened James Marshall (Chris' family name) Arnott, and I was actually invited to the christening this time! And he wasn't ginger! We were all thrilled of course but no-one more so than Chris who, after years of loving and caring for other people's children, finally had one of her own – and a son too. She would proudly push him in his pram when she took Liz every morning to Green Lane School and then again in the afternoon when she picked her up. It was on one such afternoon that out of the blue Liz called Chris "mammy". This gave Chris a warm glow and I suppose confirmed how close they had become and how Liz had settled into our family. Liz obviously wanted to be like all the other children and with no regular contact with Agnes and the likelihood that, as in the past, she may choose not to be a part of Liz's life, we saw no reason to destroy Liz's quite innocent desire to be normal, so we didn't correct her. Why destroy a child's desire to seek security? There would be a proper time in the future to explain the situation to her – a time when she would be able to understand and accept. This was a mistake. It should not have been, but as events a few months hence would show, this quite innocent and natural development would have deep and lasting consequences.

Before staying out of Liz's life for another lengthy period Agnes made one final appearance. She did on this occasion, actually, for the first and only time in her life, speak to Chris. "Isn't he ugly?" she remarked, glancing at James in his pram. After spending time with Agnes, Liz invariably came back agitated but we were always quickly able to settle her down. This wasn't so easy when this time Liz returned particularly distressed. "Children should be with their own mammy and daddy," she said angrily and accusingly to Chris. "You aren't my proper mammy. You are not even my real auntie Chris. You are just a stepmother." Agnes had clearly filled Liz's head with these brutal truths and had succeeded in undermining, if not destroying, the security in Liz's mind which had been so carefully and painstakingly built up. A lot of damage was done. A little girl's dreams and peace of mind had been destroyed.

I was furious. Surely, if you truly love a child, then you do everything possible to protect her from the brutal reality of our imperfect adult world. We must all face up to reality at some time in our lives, but a caring parent's duty is to delay disillusionment as long as possible, certainly until a child is mature enough to understand and handle it. In this duty Agnes failed with flying colours. Annoyed, dismayed and hurt as we were, we decided not to join in this game of emotional football with a six-year-old child as the ball to be vindictively kicked around. It wasn't easy.

Had we not truly cared for Liz, then I could have quite easily and, unlike Agnes, justifiably reacted to her provocation by causing more damage and distress by filling Liz's head with comments like "We used to be a family but Willy stole your mammy from us and that's why you can't be with your real mammy and daddy," or "Your mammy didn't want you because she didn't love you enough," or "Me and Chris and Grandma love you and that's why we want you to be in our family," or "Your mammy wants to be with Simon and Caroline because she loves them more than you" (Simon and Caroline are Agnes' other children) and, "Oh, by the way, there's no such thing as fairies and there's no Father Christmas either." Yes, we too could have indulged in a bit of disillusioning and sowed some seeds of hatred. Instead, we never ever said a bad word about Agnes. Not until now.

Seventeen

THE ENDEAVOUR

Birds of a feather flock together - until you clip their wings.
D.A.

IT WAS NO SURPRISE, given the lifestyle we were leading, that Brian's relationship with his wife reached breaking point and had finally broken down after barely eighteen months. What was also surprising was that mine hadn't too. Brian went to live in a small flat above Tudor Garage in Marton on the outskirts of Middlesbrough. The garage and petrol station had been acquired by Brian when he left his job as sales manager at Bluebell Garages. We talked about going into partnership together in the new venture but I had second thoughts and pulled out. At first sight the location had seemed ideal. More and more people were moving out of Middlesbrough to live in the rapidly expanding towns and villages to the south in the beautiful North Yorks Moors and the garage was located at a busy crossroads on the main commuter route into town. The trouble was that the access was difficult, particularly during peak periods. This was perhaps why so many previous tenants had failed to make a go of it and why Texaco were offering such an attractive deal.

If anyone could make a go of it then Brian was the man and I am certain that he would have done so if he and Lynne had stayed together. As I knew from my own experience, focusing on one's business is difficult after a marriage split up and is often followed by a period when one or both partners go off the rails, and since Brian even before the split hadn't exactly been on them, a crash was perhaps inevitable. At first the business flourished. Brian was a first-class car salesman and he made a lot of changes to the site to encourage fuel sales. To attract attention, he first bought a goat which he tethered on a small grassy patch in front of the forecourt, but goats have voracious appetites and the grass quickly disappeared. Before he left Lynne and moved into the flat above the garage Brian took the goat home every night and kept it in the garden where it would devour every bit of vegetation within the circumference of its tethering rope, the position of which had to be changed frequently until the garden was completely plantless. Nellie's rope then became an item on her menu and after that the gardens of both neighbours. She had to go.

Nellie made way for David but the small grassy patch which had been Nellie's first territory was not suitable for a donkey either, so David was kept at the side of the garage where he could be seen only from traffic travelling in one direction and therefore not as effective a marketing icon as Nellie. He proved to be an adventurous creature too and escaped on more than one occasion to cause serious disruption to traffic before being rounded up by the police. David too moved on to pastures new.

Perhaps Brian's greatest and most infamous achievement during his brief interest in zoology and ornithology is one that I doubt has ever been matched by anyone else throughout the ages. He drowned a flock of ducks. What better to attract the interest of children and get their parents to stop and fill up at Tudor Garage than a duck pond? Charley Vere, a friend of my dad's, dug a big hole, lined it with a huge sheet of plastic and filled it with water. To make sure the recently acquired replacements for Nellie and Dave settled in and didn't fly away, their wings were clipped. In their attempts to get out of the 'pond' they had exhausted themselves on its steep and slippery banks. They were discovered the following morning floating – and dead. It wasn't just the ducks that died off – the trade did too. After a couple of years the business collapsed.

During the Tudor Period of Brian's history I saw very little of him. I curtailed my early drinking and went out only for the last hour before closing time. I steered clear of the local clubs – Acklam Park and the Cons – choosing to frequent the nearby Endeavour pub, named after Middlesbrough's most famous son Captain James Cook's ship in which he discovered Australia. Except when we were away on holiday I only missed my nightcap in the Endeavour once and that was the night that Brian Clough predicted a resounding victory for England in their World Cup Qualifier and referred to Poland's goalkeeper as a clown. I stayed in that Wednesday night and watched the match on TV. Tomaszewski the clown played a blinder to deny England qualification. I went out the following night and the Friday and the Saturday and the Sunday and Monday and Tuesday which had been my unquestioned routine for over a year. When, on the Wednesday as I put on my coat, Chris asked me where I was going, it threw me. I looked at her incredulously and said the obvious – "The Endeavour, of course. Why do you ask?" Her reply typifies not just her attitude towards these situations but that of many women: "You don't usually go out on a Wednesday," she said.

This reminds me of the hermit story. One episode of BBC's 'Meet the People' programme took Judith Chalmers, the interviewer, to a remote Scottish island on which there lived a hermit called Hamish. She visited his remote dwelling high on a brae overlooking the village and small harbour. In reply to Ms Chalmer's question,

"Why do you live alone like this and why do they shun you and why do they call you that awful name?" Hamish explained:

"Well miss, ye see the wee boats bobbin' aroond in the harbour yonder? I built them a'. But do they call me Hamish the Boat Builder? Oh no, they dinnae.

"And ye see the bonnie cottages beside the harbour? Well, I built them too. But do they call me Hamish the Hoose Builder? Oh no!

"And the wee kirk on the brae there? I built that too, but they dinnae call me Hamish the Church Builder.

"Ye shag one lousy sheep!"

If you can't beat 'em join 'em. Chris eventually got a babysitter and began to join me at the Endeavour bar. She enjoyed the company. A really nice bunch of regulars frequented the place in those days, the early 1970's. We had some good laughs together, especially in Arenal. With money regularly contributed by us all to the 1973 Christmas kitty, we decided that instead of the usual meal and night out, we would have a weekend in Majorca. It was touch and go whether we would make it because Teesside Airport was covered in a blanket of snow, but we eventually took off and such was the jollification during the flight that Chris who was heavily pregnant with our second son Tim and well over the recommended 'safe time' for flying, was in danger of giving birth. "Put the kettle on!" Ray Porter would shout every time Chris's laughter reached danger level – which of course made her laugh all the more. Fortunately Tim did manage to hang on in there till we got back home.

The hotel was okay considering how little we had paid for it and the service was fine except at breakfast on the second day when every member of staff downed tools and ran outside. It had actually started to snow there too and this was the first time in their lives that most of them had seen real snow!

Eighteen

SPINNING PLATES

There's hope at the end of the tunnel.
Chrissarism.

I WAS QUITE EXCITED about the family's move in 1975 to Wolviston, a pleasant village on the fringe of the sprawling industrial and residential urbanisation of North Tees. The village is a bit of an oasis really, with its duck pond, a small school overlooking the village green, its two village pubs and its ideal location just minutes away from the main A19 Middlesbrough to Sunderland road which would save me up to an hour in travelling time every day – time I was determined to devote to family now that I was to distance myself from the temptations of The Endeavour, Middlesbrough Rugby & Cricket Club, the Highfield, the Broadway and various other licensed establishments and their convivial customers. We would have a new five-bedroom house backing on to a farm, a large garden which I would landscape and in which I could have the shed I had just constructed in sections for easy relocation. I could also have my own fertile and productive vegetable patch on the site of an old pig farm – and plenty of room for Liz's pet Dutch rabbits. Actually Liz took only a passing interest in these 'pets' and I'm sure she was encouraged to have them to indulge me in reliving a bit of my childhood when I was a keen breeder and exhibitor of livestock. Looking back I realise now that though I was to persuade her to enter them in the fur and feather sections of local agricultural shows, she showed little enthusiasm. At the Cleveland Show 'we' won two first prizes but Liz was bored and left early. I stayed to collect her trophies but these, I sensed, were presented grudgingly. Her rabbits had been entered in the junior classes and the judges, not, I now realise, without some justification, suspected that they were in fact my rabbits and I was guilty of 'pot hunting'. Embarrassed, we were never to show them again.

While the new house was being built I drove over to Wolviston one Sunday morning to build hutches for the rabbits. I didn't have my watch but my stomach was telling me it was time for Sunday dinner, which traditionally had to be preceded by a couple, sometimes more than a couple, of pints and, concerned that I might not have time to get back to the Rugby Club before closing time, I called at one of the two village pubs. I walked up to the bar in the Ship Inn and ordered a drink, only to be told by the barmaid that time had been called and I was too late. Disaster! Was I to be denied my traditional pre-Sunday dinner pint? Luckily not. I was called back and served. The boss had overheard his barmaid, shrewdly sensing perhaps that I could be a potential new regular, and so it proved to be the case. Alf Stephenson, who I was to get to know quite well during my subsequent frequent visits and stoppy backs at the Ship, kept a superb pint of Camerons Strongarm, a beer brewed in Hartlepool that varied in its quality from house to house. In one it could be vinegar, in another, nectar and I later asked Alf why this should be the case. He was a connoisseur and he too had suffered from Strongarm's unreliability. Such was his frustration that he had sold his successful haulage business in Hartlepool to buy the Ship, determined that his beer would be the best in the area. Beer must be poured with the sparkler set properly and from clean pipes, of course, but the real key to a perfect pint, Alf explained, was to let the barrel settle after delivery and only draw the beer at its peak, some forty-eight hours after delivery, making sure that it was all sold within three days, after which the quality would deteriorate. This meant judging customer consumption and re-ordering twice and if necessary three or four times a week, something which most landlords are too lazy to do. The ale quality and the conviviality of the Ship Inn were often too much of a temptation to me and were to cause many a tense atmosphere at Number Twenty The Poplars, Wolviston. So much for my good intentions. Would that leprechaun ever get off my shoulder? Those rabbits have got a lot to answer for!

Chris didn't entirely share my positive attitude to the move. She didn't like the idea of living on a posh new housing estate, preferring older houses with character in more anonymous communities. Because of her shyness she was anxious about meeting new neighbours and having to keep up with the Jones's. These fears however were put to the back of her mind as she involved herself in choosing kitchen units, curtains, furniture and carpets, her choice of the latter being predominantly brown in colour, proving to be not very practical with a toddler in the house not yet potty trained. Tim, our balcony baby, was only eighteen months old when we moved in. Apparently potty training is a highly skilled operation requiring a great deal of patience and is the cause of much pride and rejoicing when accomplished, like the time when James first performed at his Gran Marshall's and a delighted Chris rushed off to fetch her mother from the shop to show off her son's first potty 'biggies'. They returned to find that it had disappeared. The mystery was solved when after a few flabbergasted minutes they noticed Buddy the family dog sheepishly licking his lips in a corner. Much time was spent at Wolviston hunting the 'biggies' camouflaged by the brown carpet.

Biggies. Now there's a rare word for you. It has its origins in Hamsterley Forest where Chris used to work as a nanny several years earlier. Why isn't there a universal *nice* word for shit? Because shit is generally regarded as a swear word and not therefore to be used in front of the children, this deficiency in the English language has led to the spawning of some amusing and often bizarre substitutes, individually invented by hundreds, maybe thousands, of families up and down the country. Gems like 'Bobos', 'Pappy', 'Joby', 'Ackies', 'Ba Ba', 'Poo'and 'Cackie.' When I get time I'm going to do some research into this quaint subject and maybe involve the local radio station to do a phone in with a prize for the most unusual, original and acceptable name which I will submit for inclusion in the Oxford Dictionary!

Soon after moving in to our new house, Chris, as she had feared, was put under pressure by our immediate neighbours. One of them furiously confronted her complaining that James had uprooted her newly planted conifer trees. Perhaps he had done so with some foresight since they could eventually block out our afternoon sun! We offered to pay for them of course but by then James, at the tender age of four, had established a reputation as a vandal. Following this incident notices appeared round next door's property exhorting (presumably) children too young to read, to keep off the grass and forbidding entry into her garage, the floor of which was regularly red leaded and polished. I was beginning to realise why Chris had been so apprehensive about the move. Then another neighbour, hands on hips, angrily challenged Chris with "I know boys will be boys, but your James has just weed over our Melanie!" Didn't she realise that, at that age, this may have been a sign of affection? The neighbours' children, having seen ours for the very first time during construction completely covered from head to toe in mud after rolling round in what was to become the garden, were convinced they were naughty children to be avoided. These goody two-shoes kids were later quick to 'sprag' on ours and blame them for later misdemeanours – accusations which were readily believed by their parents until, several months later and to support Chris, who was fed up with our kids being blamed for everything, I decided to tackle one of them after she had upset my mother with yet another complaint while we were out at a school consultation evening. I painstakingly gathered evidence from other youngsters on the estate and armed with this I told her that in fact it was her own daughter and not James who had perpetrated that particular indiscretion. She refused to believe me of course so I challenged her to allow me to confront her daughter and, looking her straight in the eye, was able to extract from her a full confession. Petty I know, but it made her mother think twice before sounding off after that.

Chris could be quite assertive with family and people close to her. In fact she could be a real aggressive bossy boots at times but it was a different story when it came to dealing with other people. In this area she was totally lacking in confidence. As a result she began to display signs of stress. She was not happy in her new home and the situation wasn't helped when she fell pregnant again not long after the move to Wolviston. In fact it happened on the eve of our first Christmas there. It beats me how females can pinpoint a particular occasion but Chris has been uncannily accurate in her perception in this respect. John Jacob Edward, our tinsel tot, was born on the 11th September the following year, 1976. It was a difficult pregnancy complicated by a hernia, which had to be operated on before the birth. This was her third operation – her appendix and an ovary having been previously removed – and there were over a dozen more in the pipeline, many during our time at Wolviston. Little wonder she has few fond memories of our time there. After the birth she was quite depressed, a state which worsened into clinical PND (post natal depression), culminating later in a nervous breakdown and then, at the tender age of thirty, a hysterectomy. She also managed to fit in during this period an operation to replace a disc in her spine and another, though slightly less serious, breakdown.

With my wife either gaga under the surgeon's scalpel or convalescing, I was close to breaking point myself. Running a business is one thing. So is running a family. Trying to run both is something else again. As the father and at times sole operational parent to four active children and also the Chief Executive of what was becoming a substantial Company, I was acutely aware that the bottom line was mine and I sensed too that some of those who had been left in charge of the business could not be trusted to maintain the high standards I had set, or to support the business philosophy I had introduced. The staff relied on me. If I didn't get it right they wouldn't be able to pay their mortgages. This deep sense of responsibility I felt for others added to the pressure I was already under due to my own personal circumstances. That kind of stress can be dangerous.

Looking back I thank God for the support I received during that difficult episode in my life. Unlike the couple in the floods in Chapter Twenty-Four, I did not reject my fire engine, boat or helicopter! My mother and father with whom Tim and of course Liz had a great affinity helped out. I am grateful also to Barbara Davies our child-minder who stepped in to become full-time nanny and to Josephine Glombik our Austrian home help at Middlesbrough who had agreed to travel to Wolviston twice a week. Josephine had become almost one of the family. I was especially grateful to my mother-in-law Vera's help in bringing up Jacob as a baby and toddler, and also for looking after James to enable Chris and I to escape with Liz on our first sunshine holiday.

All these problems could hardly have arisen at a worse time for me with the business in a critical stage of development. It was down to me to do the shopping, most of the cooking, the nursery school run and much more, as well as looking after Chris in and out of hospital. I was spinning more and more plates and they were in grave danger of crashing down, so I made the decision to work from home however unsatisfactory that might be.

In my absence a power struggle developed among the senior management. The growth in turnover ground to a halt and went into decline. At that time some major companies were seeking acquisitions and paying good money for them. I was very tempted. I went to my room and prayed.

It is said that God works in mysterious ways and you can imagine my astonishment when the following month's figures showed a healthy reversal of the recent trend. Was He telling me something? I prayed about it and decided then to soldier on but I would do so with peace of mind, calmly and confidently in the sure knowledge that there would be light at the end of the tunnel because of the direction God had given me. I know this may sound weird, supernatural and even cranky, but there was absolutely no reason for the inexplicable turnaround in the business figures. Indeed, there was every expectation that they would deteriorate further rather than improve.

Though at that time not a fully committed Christian, I fairly regularly attended a fellowship in Middlesbrough held at St Aidens Church where my mother was christened and where, as a girl, she went to dances. At first my attendance there was simply to please Chris whose faith had been rekindled during her coffee mornings at the Hintons. Patrick and Jane Hinton of the well-known local grocery family were neighbours before we moved to Wolviston and Chris continued to visit them whenever she was able. The St Aidens congregation included many young people with problems who had been helped, counselled and "saved" by this very special couple. Gradually I began to feel a little more comfortable with the Christian fellowship scene though I disagreed strongly with much of the doctrine. It was clear however that the members of the fellowship had a deep and real relationship with God and without question this had an influence on me.

I like to think that our eight years at The Poplars wasn't a complete disaster. We had managed to get away on some nice holidays. We had acquired a caravan to which we were able to escape regularly at weekends and during school holidays and whilst being perhaps unlucky with our immediate neighbours, there were many who were friendly and with whom we got on very well, like the Darleys, the Stewarts, the Summers, the Bexleys, the Macdonalds, the Mahoneys, the Waltons, the Harkers and especially the Peytons, whose close friendship has endured. They have a son Jonathan who is Downs though thanks to the love and input they have devoted to him he is as normal as one can expect, is good company and a credit to his parents. Whenever we meet, even thirty years on, he always wants to talk about Scottie, a boy a couple of years older than James who also lived on The Poplars and constantly bullied Jonathan. James put a stop to this by plucking up the courage to stick up for him. There was a confrontation which led to a challenge being thrown down and a fight witnessed by most of the kids on the estate, from which James, conceding age, weight and height, emerged victorious. This dramatic event obviously had a big and lasting impression on Jonathan.

The Magic of Vienna at **Billingham Forum Theatre, January 1989. Sponsored by Arnott Insurance - Richard Baker with host and hostess.**

Nineteen

BRIAN FORGIVES THE DAGOS

When in Spain do as the Romans do.
Chrissarism.

PERHAPS BECAUSE when I first went into business I didn't take any for seven years, holidays had become for me an essential escape from the stresses of work and, paradoxically, from domestic pressures. I say this because of course we took the children with us. At home they were a handful. On holiday they were a pleasure and it was good to spend some quality time with them with no work or pub or other selfish alternatives to distract me. Chris was more relaxed too and perhaps the good times we had on these escapes from reality did much to save our marriage. The kids were a boisterous bunch and I realised how important it was to plan our holidays with that in mind. In choosing a venue one single factor above all others influenced me. Would the kids be happy? If they were and had plenty to occupy them, then we could relax too, Chris I have to say more than me, which, since she had them twenty-four hours a day, was fair enough. At home I used to envy couples with only one or two children and often those with none! On holiday those feelings of envy evaporated. The pleasure more than made up for the grief. As my mother used to say, "If you have none to grieve you, then you have none to please you."

Our 1971 summer holiday at Blackpool had been a washout and instead of spending time on the beach, the free sandy one, we were spending it, and lots of money too, at the other 'beach' for which Blackpool is famous, The Pleasure Beach, a sprawling amusement park crammed with rides and other attractions designed to relieve you of your holiday money. When I counted the cost later I said to Chris, "We could have gone abroad for that!" So we did.

For our first sunshine holiday we chose Ibiza where we stayed on a package deal at the small Copacabana Hotel in the resort of Figueretes. It was May – the bucket and spade season, they called it, because children went free. The sun shone every day, there was a nice swimming pool, there was a beach nearby and it was strawberry season. The local fresas con nata were plentiful, cheap, juicily large and delicious. The service in this small two-star hotel then was as good if not better than that which we now experience in five-star establishments, yet it was all very laid back and friendly. One night the hotel proprietor even took us out to dinner to a superb restaurant up in the hills, accompanied, I might add, by one of the very pretty waitresses. I think we were his 'cover'. On this holiday we only had seven-year-old Liz with us, having left our new baby James at home with Vera, his Gran. I took with me my newly acquired manual wind-up eight millimetre cine camera to record the holiday action. When we later watched the movie films I had taken, Chris queried why she rarely featured in them. The reason I explained was quite simple. She had rarely moved. She spent most of her days prostrate on a sun bed.

It was a different story at night. Thanks to the "Little T Club", a children's activity programme provided by the holiday company, which included a reliable babysitting service, we were able to get out and sample the local bars where we were treated as guests rather than customers. Optics were unheard of. After a couple of generous Cuba Libres the bottle of Bacardi would be left on our table for us to help ourselves. We were trusted to afterwards pay whatever *we* and not the bar owner thought was a fair price. On one occasion he refused to accept what we offered him and gave us half of it back! There was in those early days, unspoiled by commercialism and British lager louts, such a relaxed attitude and such a spirit of fun. Everyone would join in the improvised Spanish music which would spontaneously break out. Occasionally there may be a guitar but the locals could produce some amazing rhythm using only glasses, coins, tables, whatever came to hand – or feet. Symphonies were created with an amazing concerto of hand clapping techniques. We had some wonderful late boozy nights but it didn't matter. An early morning glass of Fernet Branca or Hierbas soon revived us.

We went home bronzed and relaxed. In fact, I had felt relaxed as soon as the aeroplane had taken off from the UK when I realised that whatever catastrophe occurred at home or at work there was nothing I could do about it for two weeks. Liz had a great time too. She had discarded her arm bands and in a fortnight had become an accomplished swimmer. Many years later she put together a compilation of my old 8 mm films, entitled it "The Arnott Family" and gave it to us for a Christmas present. Great to watch when we feel a bit of nostalgia coming on!

The following year, with James this time, we went back to Ibiza and stayed at the huge Mare Nostrum Hotel. But another Balearic island beckoned. Majorca was a favourite destination for the Brits and with flights available from local airports, apart from 1976, our next three sunshine holidays were spent there. By then our numbers had increased to five with our second son Timothy who had been conceived on an Ibizan balcony.

On our second Majorcan holiday I said to Linda our holiday rep that she was puzzling me because I couldn't figure out whether her star sign was Aries or Taurus. I asked her not to tell me because I wanted to work it out for myself. "I'm a famous mystic and astrologer," I lied to her. During the next few days I kept looking at her which I'm sure she found a little disturbing, until eventually to her amazement I announced that she was a very late Aries. I later told her the reason I knew her birthday was on 20th April (the last day of the Aries sign and the day before Taurus). She had been our rep for our previous year's holiday and I had remembered her celebrating her birthday then. My sense of humour is occasionally unorthodox.

In 1976, the year we didn't go to the Balearics, we became more adventurous and went to the Greek island of Corfu. This time we invited Josephine to come with us, partly as a thank you for her devotion to us and more selfishly to look after the children. Josephine was our home help. She was Austrian and cleaned the house with Teutonic efficiency. Jacob came with us, too, or rather came with his mother. He was no trouble at all. He was still in the embryo stage. Chris and I took the opportunity one day to have a break and visit Corfu town on our own. We took the local bus in the morning expecting it to bring us back after lunch. We didn't take into account the bus strike which was planned for that day and of which we were completely unaware. Corfu town was at the opposite end of the island to our resort so it would have to be an expensive taxi ride – except the taxi drivers had decided to come out in sympathy and to compound our problem there wasn't a hire car to be had for love or money. Even the motorcycles had been snapped up – except one. When we pointed hopefully to the battered old scooter in the corner of the garage the proprietor told us that it wasn't roadworthy or reliable and therefore not available for hire. After a few drachmas had exchanged hands, however, he reluctantly agreed to let us take it and we chugged off up the road with the proprietor waving goodbye and shaking his head. The journey over the mountains was painstaking and perilous. Chris, who was heavily pregnant with Jacob, had to get off and walk up the steeper banks, but we eventually made it. The expression of astonishment on James' face when he saw his mam and dad riding towards him along the beach was unforgettable. At first he ran to greet us, then fear took over as the noisy smoky jalopy coughed and spluttered towards him and he fled in tears. Apart from that it had been good fun and thereafter we regularly hired motorbikes on our holidays and so did the boys when they were older.

When our friends Brian and Lynne were reconciled we waxed lyrical about our sunshine holidays in the hope that they, or more specifically Brian, might be persuaded to join us. "It's bad enough having to put up with the English, never mind the bloody dagos," was his opinion on the subject. Brian was nothing if not dogmatic in his views, which of course made it difficult for him to acknowledge that he just possibly could be wrong. However under pressure from Lynne and daughter Kirsten he was finally persuaded and in 1978 both families booked package deal holidays to Alcudia in Majorca at the same hotel as we had stayed in the previous year. We arrived in the early hours with Brian in a grumpy mood, seemingly determined to find something wrong so he could say "I told you so". That all changed a few hours later. We had deliberately slept late and missed breakfast in the hotel, but I assured Brian that this wouldn't be a problem. We all went across the road to a nearby Spanish bar and enjoyed a first-class breakfast at a cost of only a few Pesetas. Brian couldn't decide what to have to drink with his meal and not thinking he would take me seriously so early in the day I said, "Have a lager." He had three. The fact that he could do this at ten o'clock in the morning was sufficient for him completely to revise his opinion of Dagos from greasy sinister Latinos to the most hospitable and civilised race in the world – after the Scots, of course.

We had a great holiday together. We hired a car and drove down to Palma where I introduced him to our friend Manuel and to one of my most favourite eating houses in the whole world – El Celar Sa Prensa, where the cocinillo (roast suckling pig) is to die for. I don't know how we managed to cram so much into a fortnight. We were young of course. We had flair and lots of energy. We booked up for all the trips. We rode on dinkeys (that's what it said in the brochure), sailed in boats, went on sightseeing excursions and had some fabulous meals – two in one evening at El Globo, a restaurant close to our hotel which served such delicious fish we couldn't resist returning there for 'seconds', having already dined there earlier. Organised barbecues were very popular in those days so we went to one of course. Set in a massive ranch house we pigged out to our hearts' content. To take the edge off our appetites they came round with poros (wine dispensers with a spout) and attempted to pour as much cheap wine down our throats as we were prepared to take. I had warned Brian and Lynne and unlike many who were sick afterwards we took it easy and joined in just long enough for them to take the compulsory photographs which you were expected to buy later when you were too drunk to say no. We got more than our fair share of the decent wine that night despite the efforts of the organisers to bring proceedings to an early close before the atmosphere which was building up between the Germans and the Brits boiled over into World War Three. While we were up on the dance floor I noticed that they were closing the bar and the staff were hurriedly collecting all the wine bottles from the tables. They wanted us to leave. We had a crisis on our hands. Not the impending clash between the warring factions. That didn't bother us. The night was young. We were in the mood for more vino.

I had a solution. I joined the staff in collecting the wine bottles from the tables, making sure that a few were stashed away beneath our table. Chris, Brian and Lynn found it hilarious so I carried on collecting the bottles and taking them into the kitchen like the rest of the staff. I was able to get away with my charade because I was wearing a red shirt identical to the waiters. I got really into my part. At one point

I received a bollocking from the boss for going into his kitchen through the wrong door. Among the torrent of abuse he hurled at me I caught the words, *"Este dispede."* I think this means I got the sack. Great fun.

We had many other holidays together. They didn't all go as smoothly as Alcudia where Brian was on his best behaviour. He could be a bit cussed at times and over the years we have had our differences. There was the "Fall out in Florida", the "San Lorenzo Sulks", a "Fracas in Americas", his "Pet lip in Puerto Banus", a "Cob on in Cala Honda" and he was "Moody in Majorca" on my fiftieth birthday golf trip.

Brian became a proper Spanophile (if that's the word) and actually bought a property there several years later. He couldn't wait to book up for Majorca the following year when he and I were to become the Valparaiso tennis champions.

Brian Sutherland before the fags and booze took their toll.

Twenty

JIMMY DUNCAN

It was so quiet you could hear a bomb drop.
Chrissarism.

IN THE 1970'S, in the basement below our office at 55 Frederick Street, Sunderland, a lad called Dave Donneky had set up a boutique, the first of its kind in the North East, selling young trendy fashion wear. We became friendly with him and his wife Audrey and through them met Geoff Rowell. Geoff had a younger sister Jenny, who had gone on holiday to Majorca with their parents and, like many young girls at that time, she fell in love with a Spanish waiter. His name was Manuel (not the one from Barcelona!) and when the time came for Jenny to fly back to England with her parents she went AWOL. I'm not sure exactly what happened, but she refused to return home and stayed in Majorca. She had just turned sixteen and her parents could do little about it. Anyway, Jenny fell pregnant and unfortunately lost the baby, due, she insisted, to the inadequacy of the, then, basic Spanish health-care system. The story, however, had a happy ending. She married Manuel and they had another child who Manuel insisted on calling Jenny too. She and Manuel came back to England for the birth but they were both happy together in Majorca and they settled in Palma. We were able a few years later to visit them on a few occasions and became quite friendly. We even considered setting up a business together. Manuel used to rave about the English bacon he had enjoyed so much on his visits there. In actual fact the bacon was Danish but we didn't tell him that. We used to bring him a few packs in our suitcases. Our plan was to open a small bar specialising in traditional British breakfasts. This was before there was one on every calle corner. I made enquiries with the Board of Trade regarding the importing of bacon from the UK to Spain and was amazed to discover that whatever I paid for it over here, thirty per cent would be refunded to me by the government. What a strange and complicated system exists in this area of trade between nations. My bewilderment at the "system" was empathized in a letter sent by Tom Benyon as follows:

Dear Secretary of State

My friend who is in farming at the moment, recently received a cheque for £3,000 from the Rural Payments Agency for not rearing pigs... I would like to join the "not rearing pigs" business.

In your opinion, what is the best kind of farm not to rear pigs on, and which is the best kind of pigs not to rear? I want to be sure I approach this endeavour in keeping with all government policies, as dictated by the EU in the Common Agricultural Policy.

I would prefer not to rear bacon pigs, but if that is not the type you do not want rearing, I will just as gladly not rear porkers. Are there any advantages in not rearing rare breeds such as Saddlebacks or Gloucester Old Spots, or are there too many people already not rearing these?

As I see it, the hardest part of this programme will be keeping an accurate record of how many pigs I haven't reared. Are there any Government or Local Authority courses on this?

My friend is very satisfied with this business. He has been rearing pigs for forty years or so and the best he ever made on them was £1,422 in 1968. That is until this year, when he received a cheque for not rearing any. If I get a cheque for £3,000 for not rearing 50 pigs, will I get £6000 for not rearing 100? I plan to operate on a small scale at first, holding myself down to about 4,000 pigs not raised, which will mean about £240,000 in the first year. As I become more expert on not rearing pigs, I plan to be more ambitious, perhaps increasing to, say, 40,000 pigs not reared in the second year for which I would expect about £2.4 million from your department. Incidentally, I wonder whether I would be eligible to receive tradable carbon credits for all these pigs not producing harmful and polluting methane gases?

Another point: these pigs that I plan not to rear will not eat 2,000 tonnes of cereals. I understand that you also pay farmers for not growing crops. Will I qualify for not growing cereals not to feed the pigs that I don't rear?

I am also considering the "not milking cows" business, so please send me any information you have on that too. Please could you also include the current DEFRA advice on set aside fields? Can this be done on an e commerce basis with virtual fields (of which I appear to have several thousand hectares)?

In view of the above you will realise that I will be totally unemployed and will therefore qualify for unemployment benefits. I shall of course be voting for your party at the next general election.

Mr Benyon, an ex-Lloyds Name like myself, is a founder and director of ZANE, a Zimbabwean charity providing urgent support for old people there, for which he was awarded the OBE.

Manuel and I didn't progress the café bar idea and he secured a good job as deputy head receptionist at the Valparaiso Palace, a five-star hotel in Palma. The hotel had been built by an ordinary working man using money he had won on the Spanish lottery and he occupied a magnificent suite on the top floor of the hotel, which one day Manuel was able to give us a brief glimpse of in the owner's absence.

In 1979, Geoff and his wife Anne were staying in the hotel with Dave and Audrey, at the same time as we were holidaying in Majorca on a cheap package deal with the kids and our good friends Brian and Lynne Sutherland and their daughter Kirsten. Chris and I were invited by Dave and Audrey to have lunch with them at their posh hotel. Quite an experience for us after what we had been used to – buffet meals in the two-star Alcudia Sol. We were able to leave the kids with Brian and Lynne and were free to enjoy the day, which I looked forward to with excitement and Chris with some trepidation, since she had not met Geoff and Anne. She need not have worried – we had a wonderful day with them. I had asked Dave how the hell he could stay at such an expensive hotel and told him I was going to pack in the insurance business and open a few boutiques, since they were clearly more profitable. He explained that Manuel had been able to arrange it for them at a greatly reduced rate and that if we were interested he would ask Geoff to arrange through Manuel a similar deal for us. The following year we took advantage of this offer. It was during this holiday that we met Jimmy Duncan. Before relating the Jimmy Duncan story, however, it may be worth recording the tale of the Valparaiso Champions Tennis Tournament.

After our splendid meal with Dave, Audrey, Geoff and Anne, which seemed to last forever and consisted of several delicious courses, we swam and relaxed round one of the several pools in the hotel grounds and enjoyed the luxurious sun beds and instant service from the attentive staff at the snap of a finger – Dave and Geoff's, not mine. It just wasn't in my nature to treat waiters as servants, probably due partly to the fact that my mother was a waitress but mainly down to a lack of self-confidence and humility in that area.

As we made ready to tear ourselves away from this Utopia to return to earth in the shape of the Alcudia Sol and four kids, Dave and Geoff decided they would play tennis. Now, I had actually brought my old racquet on holiday with me as there was a tennis court of sorts at our hotel, so I suggested to Dave and Geoff that they should come and have a game with us there.

"Better still," said Dave, "why don't you come back over here to play?"

"What about our friends and the kids?" I said.

"Bring them along," replied Dave.

And so the challenge was made for the Valparaiso Championship. The bet was that losers pay for the meal afterwards and with eight adults and five kids to feed at five-star prices, the stakes were high.

As the big day approached, Brian and I prepared for battle. He went out and bought a cheap child's wooden racquet and I repaired mine with some Mr Men plasters. Of course we didn't have any tennis gear with us so we would have to play in our swimming shorts and beach shoes. We spurned the wives' entreaties that we should spend a fortune on proper clothing. We couldn't justify that just for one match. We would just have to show them and ourselves up!

On the appointed day we duly met at the Valparaiso Palace, had coffee and made our way to the tennis court while Dave and Geoff went up to their rooms to change and collect their gear. When they returned, the contrast was vivid – Brian and I with our cheap racquets reinforced with the Mr Men plasters, sand shoes and baggy swim shorts and our opponents with designer shirts and shorts, proper tennis shoes and not one but *two* state of the art tennis racquets each. Our wives muttered something about having told us so, being a disgrace, etc., refused to watch us and returned to the poolside. So, here we were – playing away from home, deserted by our only supporters and facing two apparently experienced and seasoned tennis pros. We felt we were there just to make up the numbers, defeated before a ball was served. No wonder we lost the first set. But – not by the wide margin we had anticipated. A team talk at the break was called for.

"Actually Brian, they're not as good as they look."

"You're right, Derrick. We threw away that set."

"If we lose the next set it's going to cost us a bloody fortune. How much money have you brought with you?"

"Not enough – unless we treat them to chicken and chips at the bar down the road."

"I think the bet was to pay for a five-star dinner here."

"Shit."

"We'll just have to go for it. We can do it."

"Bloody right," responded Brian with clenched fist.

We took the second set – narrowly.

The scene was set for a fiercely fought third and final set but Brian and I were fired up now. We had wrested the initiative from our illustrious opponents. We had the bit between our teeth. We noticed as the second set slipped away from them, that Dave and Geoff had started to niggle at each other when they lost a point. As we got into the final set they were openly arguing with each other. We knew then we had them. And so, Brian and I became self-appointed 1977 Valparaiso Palace Tennis Champions. Did we enjoy that meal – or did we enjoy it!

The following year, courtesy of a substantial discount arranged by Manuel, Chris and I returned, minus kids, to the Valparaiso Palace for a week of sheer luxury and indulgence. The package was fully inclusive. Breakfast served on the balcony of our room which was more like a luxury apartment, lunch in one of the various pool bars and restaurants and after nibbles and aperitifs listening to lovely piano music in the lounge, a six-course dinner in the dining room overlooking the bay of Palma with the lights of the luxury yachts twinkling on the water. As if this wasn't enough, we were serenaded between courses by songs, guitar and violin at our table. Perfect. Though, to be honest, the saying "you can have too much of a good thing" after a few days became relevant and we went out a couple of times for simple meals at local eating places, including my favourite one in the whole world, The Cellar Sa Prensa.

We hadn't spoken to any of our fellow guests, who were wealthy and daunting people and mostly non-Brits. However, after a few days we noticed some new arrivals. It was difficult *not* to notice them. They were definitely less daunting, definitely British, definitely Scottish and obviously Glaswegian. They were also definitely very wealthy. Every time a waiter came near them he was given a five hundred peseta note for a tip. We were relaxing in one of the indoor pools when they came in, Jimmy with that loud self-assurance which is a characteristic of the Glasgow male – even those who have little going for them other than simply being Glaswegian. His two daughters, who he addressed as "ladies", were his double. His wife gave us a warm smile. I called across the pool: "There's no mistaking that accent!"

That was it. The ice was broken. It became clear that they, like us, felt there was something missing from this luxuriously overpowering lifestyle – a friendly and familiar voice. You could sense the relief as he introduced himself and his family. "Aye, we're fae Glasgow. I'm Jimmy Duncan, this is my wife Elspeth and these are my two ladies." I can't recall their names. Jimmy, we learned, owned an obviously very successful engineering company and they lived in a large house with its own helipad. We spent quite a lot of time with them over the next few days. They too were finding the constant attention just a little too much and when I mentioned the Cellar Sa Prensa he was keen to try it. We invited them for lunch there the following day, which was to be the last of their short break.

Having got to know Jimmy quite well during our brief time together we were only mildly surprised when we found he had arranged a luxury limousine and chauffeur to take us to the restaurant. Now the Cellar Sa Prensa is more your cheap and cheerful local eatery than your high class dining experience and is situated in a not very prestigious area of Palma. I doubt whether customers had ever before been delivered there in a limo. It raised a few eyebrows. I hoped Jimmy wouldn't think it too basic for his lavish way of life. On the contrary, he was most impressed, as I thought he would be, with the simplicity and quality of the place. The menu was indeed simple but extensive and I recommended their speciality, roast suckling pig.

He would have been even more impressed if I had told him how little the meal had cost. It became my ambition to return some day to that wonderful value for money, spacious bistro with its bare wooden tables and super-efficient service from an army of waiters in their white aprons. His appreciation of the experience was shown in typically Jimmy Duncan style when a bottle of vintage champagne was delivered to our room after their departure. I guess we could have eaten at the Cellar Sa Prensa every day for a week for less than that bubbly cost! I did meet up with Jimmy once again, a few months later when we had lunch in the RSAC (Royal Scottish Automobile Club) in Blythswood Square, Glasgow, where we were both members. Yes, Jimmy was an interesting character, but the reason I have included him as one of my biographical characters, is down to a true story which he related to us and which in many ways typifies Glasgow and which can, I believe, only be truly appreciated by Glaswegians, though it ranks among my very favourites.

Jimmy and Elspeth, when they married, had a big and expensive wedding of course. The reception was held at a newly opened exclusive French restaurant in Glasgow, the name of which I have forgotten. All the relations from every branch of the family had been invited, including Auntie Meg dressed in her C&A dress and stiletto heels. Meg had taken full advantage of the free bar tab provided by her hosts and had reached the incoherent and staggering stage – way beyond the twilight zone. Every family has at least one auntie Meg, doesn't it? Anyway, in attempting to totter her way to the ladies, which was situated down a stairway, the combination of Auntie Meg's lack of coordination and slender four-inch stiletto heels resulted in her tumbling down the stairs where she lay at the bottom, motionless in a crumpled heap. The attentive patron of the establishment rushed to her aid, knelt down beside her and gently raised her head. Monsieur the Patron snapped his fingers and barked an order to a nearby waiter: *"Garcon. Vite, vite.* A brandy for madame!" – at which point Auntie Meg slowly raised her head and opened her eyes – and her mouth. "No, no," she slurred, "I'm on the whisky and lemonade."

Twenty One

GYPSIES

He was so close he was breathing right down my throat.
Chrissarism.

ON THE WAY BACK from a weekend in the Lake District with the family in the summer of 1978, we called at the Whitbarrow Hall Caravan Park at Greystoke near Penrith to visit Chris' brother Paul who had a small caravan there. It had just stopped raining. We knocked at the door and were taken aback by the pandemonium that followed. What seemed to be a never-ending exodus of bodies bursting with excitement tumbled from the tiny structure which must have been bursting at the seams. First to emerge were two dogs with Paul making a futile attempt to restrain them. Then his son Andrew, daughter Leigh, his adopted son Mark, his new wife Linda carrying their baby son Joe, and two black children who they were fostering at the time. I wondered how it was possible that so many people, out of choice, could live in such cramped confines – and to make matters worse some of them were suffering from some sort of bug. Sensitive to the feelings of the foster kids, I determined that they would not be excluded from the general greetings and I picked one up, the girl, who repaid my affection by plucking out my chest hairs – a sure-fire sympathy killer!

Then the sun came out and the nine older children ran off to amuse themselves, leaving the grownups alone to talk. It came as no surprise when Paul announced that he was getting rid of the small caravan and buying a larger static model. Out of curiosity and for something to say I asked him how much he wanted for his little box. He was willing to sell for only £200 but at that time we entertained no thoughts of becoming caravanners, particularly with the memories of our disastrous Whitby experience in our minds.

Ten years earlier Brian and his fellow car salesman at Blue Bell Garage, Colin Brewster, had invested in a caravan at Whitby, the purpose of which was primarily to entertain lady friends. The subject cropped up in conversation one night and Brian

129

mentioned that since meeting Lynne he was not now getting sufficient use out of the van and perhaps I might be interested in taking a third share in it. The idea appealed and the price of fifty pounds did, too. We could spend time there with Liz. She liked Whitby. We decided to go and view the caravan the following weekend. After collecting the key from Brian, accompanied by Liz and her friend Stephen Colligan, the son of a neighbour of my mother's, we set off with excited anticipation which intensified as we drove on to the very impressive site and found our destination, pitch number twenty-seven. We were pleasantly surprised when we found the caravan to be a quite modern static model with plumbing, a flush toilet and a shower, a picnic table and chairs and numerous other accessories including a supply of toys for the children to play with. I couldn't wait to get back and give Brian his fifty quid.

I had gone into Whitby for fish and chips and as we sat round the picnic table enjoying lunch, our bonhomie was interrupted when a car pulled up and out jumped a stroppy man in a tee shirt.

"Who the fxxx are you?" he yelled.

Stung by his attitude the tone of my response was also a little aggressive.

"I'm a friend of Brian's," I countered. "Who are you?"

He wasn't impressed. "Only the guy who owns this caravan," he hissed through clenched teeth. "Who the hell is Brian and how did you get into my caravan?" he demanded.

A niggling doubt crossed my mind and my response was a little less assured. "Brian gave me the key. I'm thinking of buying a share in it."

The angry man demanded to see the key and I offered to demonstrate its bona fides. Sod's law, of course. It refused to turn in the lock this time. By then I was having grave misgivings. It did seem odd that Brian and Colin would keep toys in their caravan – unless perhaps one of them was shagging a married woman with children and the toys had been acquired to keep them amused while their mother was occupied in the bedroom. Highly unlikely. Highly unlikely, too, I now began to realise, was the price I was being asked to pay for a third share in what was obviously a valuable caravan. How easy it is for the mind to persuade us to believe, despite all the evidence, something we want to believe.

Back at the site office with fire being breathed down my neck by the man who, we then realised, was in fact the genuine owner, I telephoned Brian to try and clarify the situation. "What site are you on?" enquired Brian. Having sought confirmation from the site manager, I told Brian we were on Spout Farm Park. Fearing severe physical damage from the muscular tattooed arms visible beneath the sleeves of the owner's tee shirt, it took a massive effort to suppress my urge to join in Brian's laughter on the other end of the phone, but with profound apologies and an offer of compensation, which was declined, the situation was eventually diffused and we drove half a mile down the road to the correct site and found the proper number twenty-seven.

What a hovel! I wouldn't give fifty pence for a share in it. Chris and I saw the funny side of it and so did four-year-olds Liz and Stephen. We all stood and laughed until our ribs ached. Looking back, I suppose the owner's appearance at Spout Farm saved us from paying £50 for a grotbox. Brian and Colin did eventually manage to sell the van. Unfortunately, in transporting it back to Middlesbrough, it became detached from the tow bar. After paying for the tractor to retrieve it from the farmer's field and for the cost of repairs to the hedge, their net proceeds were the princely sum of £12 – £6 each!

We gave in to children power and were pestered into forking out £200 to buy Paul's caravan when he moved into his new one. They had really enjoyed the few hours they had spent there the previous summer. Angela Peyton made new curtains and covers and we quickly made it into a cosy little pad. We enjoyed some nice weekends there except when the weather was bad and we were forced to stay indoors, so when a three-bedroom static came up for sale on the site we splashed out £1200 and bought it. We had happy times there as a family and it also served as a base for some memorable lads' golf trips after I had joined the nearby Penrith Golf Club in 1980. It proved an ideal place, too, for working on business projects and other matters which required solitude for maximum concentration. All in all, it had been a good move.

Our contentment wasn't to last. In 1983 the caravan park was sold. Before the arrival of the Hopkinsons the site was run in an easy-going relaxed manner and there was never any trouble, but for some reason, probably because he was unemployable elsewhere, the new owners' son was appointed as a site superintendent, a role which was irrelevant and quite unnecessary and for which he was totally unsuited. There were no rules in existence at that time so Hopkinson junior made them up as he went along, constantly following the children round the site "to keep an eye on them". He wasn't the brightest of lads and the children reacted by making fun of him. They gave him the nickname 'Hippy Hitler' which very appropriately reflected his appearance and his attitude. The small children, some as young as four, would put their tongues out at him and the older ones, with left forefingers across their upper lips, would click heels and give the Nazi salute every time they saw him, the bolder ones doing it openly to his face. War was declared between Hippy Hitler and the children.

One Saturday afternoon around five p.m., halfway through the 1984 holiday season, Hopkinson arrived at our caravan escorted by a policeman "to keep the peace", and told us to get off the site within two hours. The Anderson and Duffy families received similar treatment. I was prepared to stand my ground but Chris didn't want any trouble so we packed what we could and left. Chris' cousin David, his wife Jean, her two children, their nephew Brian and their dog were staying in Paul's caravan which he had vacated when he bought a cottage in the nearby Village of Threlkeld, and they too were evicted.

Caravan sites were and still are strongholds of unfair and restrictive practices. It's a closed shop. Site owners would only allow the siting of static caravans which had been bought through them, thereby creaming off handsome commissions. This meant that a caravan without a pitch had little value and because we had to sell on the open market we received only a fraction of the market price. By the time we had paid the cost of removing the caravans from the site we had very little left over from their sale. I felt a court case coming on. Having assessed our losses which included a disruption factor and loss of holiday enjoyment, the claim was over the limit for County Court which meant that we had to be prepared to take action in the Crown Court with its substantial costs were it to fail. Undeterred, I decided to press on, and so did the Duffy family.

Before actions can be heard in Crown Court it is necessary for a procedure called 'Disclosure' to be followed where "Further and Better Particulars" are exchanged between the parties. This is to identify spurious or weak cases or defences, encourage out of court settlements and save the court's time. I will now quote and comment on some of the justification put forward by Hopkinson for his defence:

"The Plaintiffs were handed a copy of the Rules on commencement of their seasonal license." UNTRUE – NO RULES ACTUALLY EXISTED.

"The Plaintiff's children climbed a high wall and damaged a lavatory block which was under construction." THE EASILY ACCESSED PARTIALLY CONSTRUCTED BLOCK HAD BEEN IN THE SAME DELAPIDATED STATE FOR YEARS.

"On four nights in July the children were playing noisily as late as 11 p.m." HOPKINSON COULDN'T IDENTIFY THE CHILDREN.

"The Duffy children rode bicycles recklessly, once nearly knocking an old lady down and also blocking traffic on the road." HOPKINSON COULDN'T REMEMBER THE NAME OF THE OLD LADY DESPITE HER BEING A RESIDENT ON THE SITE. THE "ROAD" WAS A QUIET COUNTRY LANE CARRYING MAYBE ONE CAR AN HOUR.

"In an attempt to mitigate the danger the Defendants banned the use of cycles after 8 p.m. With the Plaintiff's knowledge the children refused to comply." WHEN I HEARD OF THIS RULE I TOLD HOPKINSON IT WAS RIDICULOUS AND HE AGREED TO EXTEND THE DEADLINE TO 9 P.M. AND I TOLD THE CHILDREN. HIPPY HITLER CONTINUED TO HARRASS THEM AFTER 8 P.M. THEY TOLD HIM THAT MR ARNOTT HAD SAID IT WAS OK. HH RETORTED, "MR ARNOTT DOESN'T COUNT FOR SHIT ON THIS SITE."

LATER I AGAIN CONFRONTED HOPKINSON WHO SAID, "IT'S MY SON WHO MAKES THE RULES NOW."

"The Plaintiff's children attempted to provoke and ridicule the Defendants and their son by putting their tongues out at them." THAT WAS BECAUSE THEY WERE PROVOCATIVE AND RIDICULOUS PEOPLE.

Hopkinson's case was not a strong one but he was stubborn and the case proceeded at Carlisle Crown Court before a learned judge whose name I cannot unfortunately recall but whose sense of humour I'll never forget. In appearance, mannerisms and speech, he was the stereotype of an English judge you would expect to see in a 'Carry On' film or TV comedy sketch. He had that nasal public school accent that is almost buffoon-like but, as we were to soon discover, this man was no fool. Extremely sharp witted and very funny, there were times in court when my sides were aching trying to suppress my laughter. Things of course always seem funnier in sombre and serious environments – like courtrooms.

The case opened with presentations by our barrister and theirs, who was interrupted by the judge. "Umph," he grunted. Everything he said started with an "Umph". "Tell me counsel, is this caravan place residential or does it comprise of holiday homes?" Having been enlightened on that point, "Umph... So it's a place where families go with children to have fun and perhaps laugh and even be a little noisy from time to time?" There followed a silence, another "Umph" and then, "I think counsel should meet me in chambers. Come along." I knew then we had won and this was confirmed by our barrister who told us that the judge had recommended that Hopkinson should be urged by his counsel to make an offer to us in settlement. The Hopkinsons had declined to heed this advice. Mrs Hopkinson in particular wanted her day in court. In fact, she got two since the case wasn't completed on the day and we had to return next morning. It hadn't been the most sensible decision to ignore his worship's advice. It didn't enamour him to the Hopkinson cause. Mrs Hopkinson would not enjoy her day in court.

Day two's proceedings opened with the judge asking some searching questions about the site rules to which defending counsel was unable to give satisfactory replies. His body language displayed signs of discomfort in the face of the judge's now visibly hostile attitude which was evident to me but not apparently to the Hopkinsons who again rejected an opportunity to settle when the judge for the second time interrupted proceedings to talk to the two counsels in his chambers. We would now all be subjected to the ordeal of appearing in the witness box to give evidence. Chris was called first. So nervous was she that when asked her name gave her maiden name of Marshall instead of Arnott. Recognising her plight, the judge spared her a lengthy cross-examination and told her to step down. He was a kindly old soul. He wouldn't be so kind with Mrs Hopkinson. Next to be called was Mrs

Duffy whose son Ian was the eldest of the children on site and who was generally thought to be the ringleader by Hippy Hitler. His protective mother was determined to tell the court what a good lad he really was and embarked on a lengthy character reference on behalf of her son. As the judge stifled a yawn, Mrs Duffy, with her head on one side and eyes down, coyly announced, "Everybody loves our Ian." The judge's reaction was a classic, which I will remember always. He stirred from his reverie, lifted his head, peered over his glasses and said, "Mm, well not quite everybody, Mrs Duffy. Otherwise we wouldn't be here today, would we? Umph." He occasionally reserved his *umphs* till the end. My appearance served mainly to explain that the so-called toilet block under construction was in fact a derelict site and had been for several years. The judge was later to use this information to put in his judicial boot when he had the Hopkinsons in the stand.

If our case needed strengthening, then the appearance of Hippy Hitler in the box would undoubtedly have done the trick. He bottled out. Instead, Hopkinson senior was put through the mill. Had construction of the toilet block been completed yet? Why not? Wouldn't its existence naturally attract inquisitive children? Was it not his responsibility to secure it adequately etc. etc.? Before dismissing him from the stand the judge said sternly to Hopkinson: "You have led me to believe, quite erroneously I now find, that as fast as the builders were laying tiles on the roof, a gang of young hooligans were tearing them off." Hopkinson's attempt at a response was cut short.

Mrs Hopkinson was the target for some caustic comments from his worship and, too thick to recognise what was going on, she allowed herself to be led on, coming out with more and more ridiculous statements the more rattled she became. Let me quote a few examples:

Mrs H: "The Arnott children were well behaved when they were sat in the bar with their parents. It was afterwards they were noisy."

Judge: "Umph. Yes, Mrs Hopkinson, but if one has a licensed bar then one must expect the customers to become a little boisterous when they leave. Even grownups can be noisy in such situations."

Mrs H: "But they played some game called Hare and Hounds, like Hide and Seek, round the caravans."

Judge: "Umph. Oh dear. Enjoying themselves at your holiday camp, were they?"

Mrs H: "Well, all I know is when they left the site things were a lot quieter."

Judge: "Umph. Yes, yes, I can understand that, Mrs Hopkinson. That course of action was very effective during World War II when the Nazis occupied Norway. Shoot a few civilians. That'll keep the rest of 'em quiet."

We were awarded our damages, but more satisfying to me was that the judge awarded all the costs of the two-day Crown Court hearing against the Hopkinsons. A sum well into five figures was the price they paid for their arrogance and stupidity.

I missed the caravan and the wonderful feeling of tranquillity that always came over me the instant I caught a glimpse of Saddleback Mountain as we made the descent towards Greystoke in the final stage of our journeys there. We had found caravan life to be such a relaxing escape from the stresses of business and home and had it not been for a certain amphibian creature we would have had an alternative holiday home in which to spend the remainder of our 1984 summer holidays, which had been so peremptorily cut short by Hopkinson. Earlier in that year I had once again been offered, this time by John Shaw, a share in a caravan. This one was located in the south of France, a prospect which had appealed to me greatly. We had driven down to view it in the early spring of 1984, taking the opportunity to have a short touring holiday and to "run in" my new Rover car. It would be educational too.

Leaving the boys in the care of our mothers, Chris and I set off on our long journey with Liz who was fifteen at the time and who would soon be taking her O-level in French and for whom we thought the trip may be a useful exercise. The object of our interest was sited on the Mediterranean coast close to the lovely university city of Montpelier and the journey, broken with overnight stops in some interesting Michelin Guide recommended Logis, was a most pleasurable experience. We did of course make absolutely sure that we knew exactly which site we were going to this time. The inspection of the Chalet Mobil, as it was attractively called, took no more than two minutes before it was given a resounding thumbs down by Chris, who had lifted the toilet seat to reveal, wallowing in the toilet bowl, a massive toad. (Yes I am spelling this correctly.)

Over lunch in Montpelier we decided, now that we were so close, to take in the French Riviera and we drove through Nice to Menton, a small ancient (and very expensive) delight on the Italian border. Having paid the equivalent of around £5 for a coffee on our arrival there and having sussed out and rejected a few restaurant menus, we booked into our small hotel and decided to go for a pizza. This was when a pizza was a novelty and before there was a pizzeria on every street corner. In fact, I had never even tasted one before. Menton, being a bastion of Haute Cuisine Francais, was a pizza-free zone, so where better to get one than Italy? We changed some francs into millions of lira at the border and headed for the first Italian town which, a surprisingly long journey away, was San Remo. Our pizzas El Pais washed down with some local red wine were perfect. We drove back home with some good memories, but caravan-less.

After being kicked off Whitbarrow Hall we were worried in case our reputation might go before us and that we may have been blackballed and have difficulty finding another site, but in fact we were up and running by the following season at a nice site near Appleby in the Cumbrian Eden valley, which meant a much shorter journey time for us. Our hopes of having a peaceful, trouble-free sojourn there, however, were quickly dashed. Our children, particularly the youngest who was then only eight, had proved themselves to be quite skilful in the games room on the site and we were not unduly concerned when from time to time they landed back at the caravan with a pocketful of coins. Not, that is, until we once again found a policeman at our caravan door. We later discovered that the system they had been using to beat the gaming machines was not down entirely to the boys' expertise but had involved a screwdriver and silver paper! Fortunately they escaped with only a severe admonishment and a warning, on condition that the proceeds of their illegal 'racket' were returned to the site owners – a pretty harrowing and embarrassing experience for us all. We hadn't got off to the best of starts at the Wild Rose Caravan Park.

The park was owned by two brothers, Martin and David Stephenson, and we did spend many happy years there until the boys grew up. Martin Stephenson in particular did not like teenagers, especially ours, and we began to get more and more earache from him. Our boys were just normal adventurous teenagers and whilst no angels, they carried the stigma of their earlier games room indiscretions and were picked out among all the other equally culpable teenagers on the site, as the objects of Martin's wrath. I sometimes wonder how his own young sons turned out. Even on hot summers' days they were dressed in suits, collars and ties. Obviously dominated by their strict father, they were too well behaved for their own good and I will be surprised if this suppression didn't do them a lot of harm, made them rebellious and caused themselves and their parents problems in later life. Martin eventually made it quite clear that he wanted rid of us and offered us a high price for our caravan if we agreed to leave. We accepted his offer for our two-year-old caravan, which was more than enough to buy a new one, and we moved on. Liz was by this time away at university and James and Tim were reaching the age where they didn't want to spend weekends and holidays with their mam and dad, but I felt sorry for Jacob who had made some very good and lasting friendships at the Wild Rose, as indeed the others had.

With our cheque from the Wild Rose in the bank, we went caravan shopping to the annual Camping and Caravan Show at Earls Court in London. There were scores of exotic and elaborately furnished models on display but our favourite was the fairly basic, but spacious and comfortable, Cosalt Rimini Super 35. When we next visited the East Landings Caravan Site at Barnard Castle, which we had earlier earmarked as our next location, we were astounded to find the only caravan they had for sale on site was a Cosalt Rimini Super 35. We were lucky enough to get on to what perhaps is the best pitch on the site backing on to a horses' field and quite private. We had the small garden landscaped and a large balcony constructed and, since the ninos have flown the nest, have enjoyed many peaceful and trouble-free years since moving there in 1994. Barnard Castle is a quiet market town only a ten-minute walk to its centre from our caravan, which in turn is only a short forty-five minutes' drive from home. I don't think, caravan-wise, we will be making any more moves, enforced or otherwise, unless of course the grandchildren follow in the mischievous footsteps of their parents and upset the site owners!

Twenty-Two

BORN AGAIN

I would rather live my life as if there is a God and die to find out there isn't,
than to live my life as if there isn't and die to find out there is.
Albert Camus.

WHEN I WAS A VERY YOUNG CHILD I used to lie in bed and try to figure out what was in the sky and whatever it was, what was beyond that, and so on and on and on. I should have counted sheep like my mother told me to. This would have sent me to sleep. Instead, I would lay awake for ages worried, frustrated and frightened – the fear of the unknown (I'm sure there is a word for this but I can't bring it to mind). I was in good company. Many scientists and astrologists, much wiser and learned than a six-year-old boy, had throughout the ages failed to come up with a satisfactory explanation of infinity, nor have the world's religions, that expect us to accept the existence of "heaven" – a vague and unsatisfactory answer which they hope will satisfy our curiosity. Each religion has its own concept of heaven, or at least of how to get there. So which one are we to believe, or indeed are we to believe any of them? They do at least all agree on an afterlife and on the existence of a supreme being, usually called God. But where did God come from? And who made God? There I go again. I would torture myself too by speculating on other hypothetical theories about the nature of life. Could Earth be merely an atom and its inhabitants molecules which make up, with all the other planets in the universe, another huge living creature which itself is a molecule within an atom which is a part of another huge planet whose inhabitants are molecules… and on and on. Could our own bodies in turn be galaxies and our cells planets within that galaxy inhabited by tiny creatures invisible even to the most powerful microscope? To my mind these could well be the meaning of life and are no less plausible theories than the idea of earthly humans being chosen by God to go to Heaven. Is it because our intellect, at its present infant level of development, is incapable of grasping or even considering such inexplicable possibilities as I have

138

described, that we humans have invented our own versions of "God" and "Heaven" instead?

During those difficult years of the late seventies when both my domestic and business lives were in turmoil and rapidly reaching a state of chaos, I found, as I had done as a child, and as many do at times of despair, some peace of mind in prayer and though my visits to St Aidens were not always undertaken with a great deal of enthusiasm, there were times when they provided some comfort. In particular I remember one of the songs we used to sing, not from one of the old traditional mournful hymnbooks, since St Aidens was an evangelical church, but from a book called *Songs of Triumph* – number twenty-eight. The particular verse that grabbed me and said something to me, went like this:

> *Let my peace rule within your hearts*
> *Do not strive, do not strive, do not strive (repeat)*
> *For mine is the power and the glory*
> *For ever and ever the same*
> *Let my peace rule within your hearts*
> *Do not strive, do not strive.*

The men sang lines one, three and four and the women the chorus. Quite beautiful. But then I've always been up for a singsong. The message was clear. There are lots of people out there worse off than you. If you trust in God he won't allow your yoke to become too heavy to bear. Worrying and becoming stressed out won't solve anything. Do your best and what will be will be.

I found St Aidens to be less formidable than mainstream Protestant churches because although the services (or 'meetings' as they preferred to call them) were conducted in a traditional church building, there were no robes, incense, sceptres or fire and brimstone sermons designed to put the fear of God's wrath into the congregations, were they ever to fall foul of the dogma preached from the pulpit even more fervently than the Catholic churches. At least in these you could confess your sins and the priest would forgive you, whereas judgement for many Protestants was left to puritanical heads of households. Many young girls who became pregnant out of wedlock were told by their puritanically brainwashed and unenlightened parents "Never to darken this doorstep again" or "You've made your bed, now you must lie on it" and were cast out of their homes.

There were at the time of my involvement in St Aidens, and presumably there still are, rallies and gatherings at which the various evangelical fellowships from all over the country join together. In 1977 we spent a week under canvas at the Dales Bible Week near Harrogate and again the following year at the Stafford Festival at which four-year-old son Tim asked me why Jesus was no-one. "I thought he was important," he said. I explained that to many people Jesus was very important. "Why do you ask?" I enquired. "Because it says so on the banners," replied Tim. Puzzled, I asked him to show me these banners and, sure enough, there it was: "JESUS IS No 1." I explained that No was short for number!

At these gatherings I was exposed to the influence of practical Christian lifestyle at a time when I was in a fairly vulnerable and receptive state of mind. I wouldn't say we were pressured, but we *were* encouraged to attend the sessions of mass worship which I must confess I didn't enjoy. I felt it was too intense, too hysterically spiritual and a bit competitive. If you didn't wave your arms in the air and, like some of them did, speak in tongues (a kind of gibberish for those in a high state of spirituality who found their minds transported to such an extent that they couldn't articulate in English), you felt somehow that you didn't belong or that you were a second class Christian. However there *were* positive aspects of these jamborees which I found interesting and I was particularly impressed with the practical workshops which dealt with various aspects of day-to-day living and which were held each morning. With my parenting skills less than perfect, I was able to pick up some useful tips from the parenthood sessions. With the mother out of action for much of the time, successfully bringing up four young children was, to say the least, a difficult and daunting task, and with limited time to devote to this very important role I needed all the help I could get. I wasn't cut out for full-time parenting. It didn't come naturally to me but it became obvious that before anything else could be accomplished some degree of domestic order and discipline had to be established. I had put in place already my Children's Charter, a move which met with scepticism on Chris' part, but I had learned from running my business how to solve problems and this was my way of dealing with this particular problem in a business-like way. She would have done things quite differently I'm sure, because she was good at it. I wasn't. I had to make up for my deficiencies the best I could and the Charter was a practical substitute for my lack of hands on parenting skills. I believe it worked rather well and had it not been dismantled by Chris on her return to duty I think it would have continued to do so. But nanny knew best. It was quite simple, really. Their pocket money was split into twenty units so Liz's units as the eldest on £10 a week were worth 50p and Jacob's as the youngest on £2 a week were 10p. The others were somewhere in between. Jobs and different types of good and bad behaviour were allocated a unit value on a sliding scale according to their value and importance and would be added or deducted during the week. A large chart was devised and pinned up on the kitchen wall. Siblings are notoriously competitive and this created a desire in them to end up with more units than their sister or brothers come pocket money day. Of course it also caused disputes when, in their opinions, points were unfairly deducted (and sometimes insufficiently added) but since prolonged arguing carried further penalty points these objections were usually quickly subdued. Friday, pocket money day, was a good one for getting jobs done as there would often be an eleventh hour scramble to top up, particularly if they'd had a naughty week. Before the introduction of my Charter nobody would willingly do the washing up. Afterwards they would fight each other to get to the kitchen sink first.

So much for the carrot, but not being a violent man the stick aspect of parenting was the one I struggled with most until, that is, I attended the Parenthood Workshops at the Dales and bought the audiotapes. I didn't agree with the spare the rod and spoil the child school of thought but children sometimes need to be chastised and this, as a last resort or as a punishment for very naughty behaviour, needs to be physical. The secret I learned was never to administer the punishment in anger or as an immediate reaction, or in front of siblings or anyone else for that matter. Nor should it be administered by hand. The hand is the instrument of love and comfort. A wooden spoon was recommended and I recall one occasion involving middle bulb Tim, which probably serves as a good example of the effectiveness of this method. Though I cannot recall the exact details, he must have been seriously naughty because I had in mind five whacks on the bottom with the wooden spoon. I took him to his room where we calmly discussed the matter. I explained why I considered the punishment to be necessary, giving him every opportunity to explain and defend his actions which he did, I must say, quite eloquently and effectively, causing me to spare him one of the whacks. I explained as per the audiotapes that though I was disappointed with his behaviour I loved him very much and wasn't looking forward to smacking him. A glimmer of hope flashed across his face. "Well, don't then," he suggested hopefully. This earned him a further reduction in his punishment. My resolve was weakening. In answer to my next question, he did agree that he had to be punished, but since he promised faithfully never to do it again thought one whack would be enough. We settled for two, shook hands and I let him off with one and a stern warning followed by a hug. The little conman! The point is, that we had spent almost an hour of quality time together, reached agreement, created mutual respect for each other and consolidated our relationship, which is stronger than ever today. I think I can say the same for Liz, James and Jacob.

There is a very influential element within our society which would brand my behaviour as criminal. These people are pressing for a law to ban smacking of children and what is so worrying is that they are likely to succeed. What gives them the right to interfere in my family in this way? Are they so perfect as parents that they can dictate how the rest of us should bring up our kids? Let them show me their perfect children as examples. Let them demonstrate how to keep order and discipline within a large family. They probably only have one or two themselves – and maybe none at all! I wish the law had existed when I smacked Tim. It would have given me the opportunity to be a martyr by going down to the police station, confessing to my crime, being charged, refusing to accept my punishment and being sent to prison. Far better for Tim to have his dad in gaol than giving him a smack on the backside. Is this really what the lawmakers are saying? By all means issue guidelines to parents and punish those whose excesses warrant it, but sadly the dogmatic people who wield the power are capable only of seeing things as black and white. Their ears are deaf to balanced and reasonable views, or to compromise, so zealous are they to impose their opinions upon us. A bit like Hitler. They must be crushed before they too become even more megalomaniacal than they are now.

After Jacob was born and after spending the first seven years of our marriage struggling with the contraception issue (we found condoms unsatisfactory because they inhibited the spontaneity of lovemaking, and the pill was invented too late for us and in any case medically unsuitable for Chris), I had a vasectomy in 1978. (Needlessly, as it turned out, because Chris had a hysterectomy in 1979.) Unless we see a bright star in the east and three blokes riding camels down the A19 we can safely assume that our loins will no longer feature in the procreation of the human race.

It took a long time for Chris to recover from her hysterectomy but after my vasectomy I just had to ignore the pain and discomfort and get on with it. (I only put this in for a reaction from female readers.) To help Chris recuperate we booked a holiday with Brian and Lynne to Ibiza. It was a bargain package in the hotel's final week of the season before closing down for the winter. The staff were in wind-down mode and the service was poor. Our room was just about adequate and the weather was bad – 'sowling down', we were informed by a woman from Nottingham where, I expect, that expression is commonplace. I came away stressed out with the pressures of work and of once again trying to manage the domestic situation with an inactive wife. Her mouth on the other hand was extremely active, constantly instructing me what to do, how to do it and, when I'd finished, telling me how inadequately I had done it. In short, I was not a happy bunny and was desperate for Chris to use the holiday to take it easy and get well. But she had other ideas. After being unwell and out of action for so long, she was going to have a ball and on the evening of the 28th October 1979, after too much drink, she decided to climb from our fifth floor balcony onto the one next door where Brian and Lynne had gone for a siesta – that's what they call it in Spain! I pleaded with her not to be so stupid. It was a highly dangerous, almost impossible manoeuvre, but Chris' foolhardiness was more than matched by her stubbornness and with me standing by helpless and distraught she managed with difficulty and, I suspect at one stage, some doubts and second thoughts, to somehow achieve her objective. It was touch and go at times. When drinks are in wits are out!

I was awake half that night worrying and speculating about the possible consequences of the previous evening's events and the little sleep I did have was an opportunity for unpleasant dreams to trouble my subconscious. I desperately wanted

Chris back at the domestic helm at home, not lying on some cold mortuary slab in the Balearics.

I was at a very low ebb when I got up at daybreak and went for a long walk along the deserted beach. After a while I paused, stood on a rocky promontory and gazing out to sea, in desperation I prayed for God to give me peace. Back at the hotel I needed to talk to Chris and sort things out so, alone, we went into Ibiza town and chose for lunch a very basic non-touristy semi-basement restaurant just off the square and frequented by the locals (always a sign of good food and good value). I don't know how adequately to describe the events that followed. I had just finished my potage (a cross between soup and stew) when my whole being was engulfed in a surreal feeling of joy and ecstasy, which I knew instantly, was a spiritual response to my earlier prayer. I had in the past looked on others who claimed to have been born again as a little cranky so I guess in the eyes of others I'm now a crank. I'm not going to say I don't care, because what people think about me is important and this is why I didn't make a big deal of it to others, even those within the St Aiden's Christian Fellowship. The sceptics wouldn't understand and the people in the Fellowship would have made a big embarrassing issue of it and probably expected me to get baptised or something. I telephoned Vera, my mother in law, because I knew she would understand, but I confess to being a little disappointed at Chris' matter-of-fact reaction, but then nobody could get within a million miles of the height of euphoria I was feeling at that time. But what mattered was that I knew in my heart and head how real the experience was. What I wasn't sure about was why, if I was chosen by God to have it, what He subsequently expected of me. Perhaps I was meant to share my feelings and thoughts with others. Perhaps I am meant to write about my beliefs.

I was on a high and at peace for a long time. There was a conviction in my heart and mind that my troubles were over. Not, that is to say, I wasn't going to have any more problems, but that I had been given the inner strength to deal with them – not always to solve them but more importantly to live with and tolerate them. Some earlier proverbial words of wisdom from Vera, "In acceptance lies peace," became for me at that time, profoundly relevant.

Out of curiosity we went the following day to find the scene of my wonderful experience. It wasn't there! Puzzled, we unsuccessfully searched and double searched the area in the unlikely case we had mistaken the location. Spooky, or what?

After I arrived home from our Ibiza holiday I began to take St Aidens Christian Fellowship more seriously. I read the Bible and attended the meetings with more enthusiasm, thinking that God may perhaps want me to become part of the Christian movement in which St Aidens was involved. However, I had no aspirations in that direction. Some of their ideas and beliefs were a little pie in the sky for my liking. The fact that I was now part of God's Army whose Christian troops were on course to convert the country and then the world were just a little unrealistic for my logical mind to accept. No doubt about the sincerity of their beliefs, but clearly too hopelessly ambitious, a fact that twenty odd years on they now accept, or at least Pete and Jess Gilgan do. Pete, then a young man some twenty or so years my junior, nevertheless held the position of an elder of the church. A talented musician, he had formed a rock band, Giant Killer (named after David the slayer of Goliath) which played at festivals and churches all over the country as a witness to the fact that God was relevant to young people and that church wasn't all organ music and doleful hymns. Our boys and theirs, Joe and Dan, became good friends and still are today. We met up with Pete and Jess again in 2004. During a bar meal earlier in the Redwell Inn at Barnard Castle, Chris and I read a leaflet announcing the appearance there the following week of the popular rock group Giant Killer. Could it be *the* Giant Killer? We went along, had a great night with them and renewed our friendship. Pete and Jess both agreed that the objectives of the Christian churches all those years ago had perhaps been just a little over the top and not perhaps God's will at that time after all.

Though St Aidens was a pretty liberal Christian group, there was to my mind too much emphasis by some of the members on the old-fashioned intellectual dogma of the Christian faith and on the irrelevant aspects of the scriptures – majoring on the minors, I call it – and when one day at home I answered the door to two Jehovah's Witnesses, instead of turning them away, I couldn't resist the opportunity to try and make my point. Thinking that at last they had a prospect, they launched enthusiastically into their spiel. As soon as I had the opportunity I interrupted to ask provocatively if they were the cult that didn't believe in blood transfusions. "Yes," was the reply, "and we count among our followers a number of eminent surgeons." The thought ran through my mind that if that were true, I hoped they weren't employed by our local NHS Trust, the North Tees Health Authority, in case I ever needed surgery. Without giving me a chance to verbalise my thoughts they went straight back into their well-rehearsed presentation, which I interrupted again with the simple question, "Why?" They waffled uncomfortably and impatiently for a while, obviously keen to press on. "Is it in the Bible?" I asked, "Because I've read the Bible" (a little white lie) "and I haven't seen anything about it." Anxious to keep the dialogue on safe ground they gave me a brief assurance that it was scriptural and resumed where they had left off when I had interrupted. But terrier-like, I persisted. "Show me it then," I challenged. Conveniently perhaps, they hadn't brought a Bible with them. "I've got one," I offered, then produced it so that they could demonstrate the scriptural authority that outlawed blood transfusions. Diverted from their mainstream purpose and with, I sensed some reluctance, they identified a text in the Old Testament – Leviticus Chapter 17 – which deals with pagan sacrifice of lamb, goat and ox (v3) and goes on to say in Verse 12, "No one among you shall take (*eat* in some versions) blood. Nor shall any stranger among you take (eat) blood" – which to me is more a justification for vegetarianism than their interpretation and I told them so. "Would God punish me if I had a blood transfusion?" was my next question. I suggested to them that, on the contrary, He would punish me if I refused a transfusion, since according to them suicide is a sin. They were relieved when I showed them to the door but before they left I asked them to ignore for a few minutes what had been indoctrinated into them by their leaders and to go home, pray alone with an open mind and ask God to reveal to them the *true* meaning of this text. I promised them that I would do the same and if after that God told me to share their interpretation I would join their church the following Sunday. He didn't and I didn't. I don't know whether they did. I doubt it.

Despite my misgivings on some issues, St Aidens on the whole was a good Fellowship, well run by the elders, Pete Gilgan, who I have mentioned, Dave Tomlinson, Derek Fields and Ken Whiteway, a down-to-earth scouser with a twinkle in his eye and a great sense of humour. Ken, I believe, is still the leader of the Fellowship. So I was delighted to be of some help when my particular talents were called on. Many people in Middlesbrough will remember a café in Devonshire Road in the Linthorpe suburb called the Old Butchers with as its centrepiece an old butcher's bike with advertising panel, handlebar wickerwork carrier bag and all. This popular café was leased by St Aidens and run by members of the Fellowship, but despite its popularity was running at a loss. I was invited by Ken to become involved. By then its name had been changed to Centrepeace and as a side-line was selling crafts supplied by Traidcraft, an international organisation set up to find markets for crafts made by the poor in third-world countries. To support this worthy venture a large stock had been purchased and this had put a strain on the cashflow, as did the monthly payments for the sophisticated and expensive cash register more appropriate for a large department store or busy pub than a small coffee shop. What was the point of having in an establishment run by Christians, a machine designed primarily to prevent pilfering by staff? I managed to find somebody who was prepared to take it off our hands and take over the five-year commitment which had been entered into. My next task was to address the problem of the wooden elephants. Everyone who, probably out of sympathy to the cause, had wanted a wooden elephant had already bought one and the shelves on which they were displayed could I felt be put to better use. The café, whilst being located just off the main Linthorpe Road, had two large shop windows which, if we could find a way to reduce the condensation from the kitchen, were ideal for display. As well as attracting passing trade there was a steady stream of regular visitors to the café, all of whom were potential craft customers. We needed to take advantage of these features and to expand the range of stock. Chris suggested that to start with we introduce a range of greetings cards, which proved to be a very profitable decision. But with no retail experience the next step proved more difficult. I suggested that as a starting point we should suss out the competition and we visited various craft and gift shops in the area, none of which particularly impressed us. It was only when we widened the net and explored outside the area that we got the breakthrough we were seeking. We came across a shop in Leeds, which carried a wide and attractive range of good quality stock tastefully displayed. "Bingo!" announced Chris. "That's the sort of thing we need to introduce into Centrepeace." But where did the shopkeeper get the stock from? We needed an introduction to a wholesaler. I plucked up courage and, tongue in cheek, bluntly asked the shopkeeper the question, explaining that we were not in competition and that we were engaged in research on behalf of a Christian charity shop in Middlesbrough. At first we thought our blunt up-front approach had failed because our request was rejected, but as we were leaving after making some purchases a couple of cards were given to us. "Try them," said the shopkeeper. He had given us details of two of his suppliers, Cha Cha Dum Dum in Kensington and Prismatic in Brighton which we later learned was owned by the son of a local Linthorpe florist, Barbara Thompson.

The following day we telephoned Prismatic to place an order though we had no idea what we wanted or what the reaction would be. "Why don't you come and see us in Harrogate next week?" was the response. An invitation was sent to us for the Harrogate Trade Fair. We were elated. We were in! We couldn't believe our eyes when the following week in Harrogate the big mystery of retail trading was revealed to us. The selection of potential stock was huge, too much to do justice to in one day, so we booked into a hotel and continued our shopping the next day. We bought extravagantly all at amazing wholesale prices and we set up a number of trade accounts on behalf of Centrepeace. That was the first of many trips to trade fairs and to our suppliers in London, Brighton and elsewhere. Ken Whiteway very kindly offered to reimburse our expenses but we declined. We were enjoying what we were doing, it was for a good cause and we didn't want to restrict ourselves to an expenses budget, preferring to indulge ourselves, using the opportunity to stay in nice hotels and eat in nice restaurants. There was however one trip which, due to overindulgence in the wine department, turned out to be not so enjoyable – when cooperation was replaced by confrontation. We were staying in a quiet guesthouse in one of the many green belt areas in Harrogate and after an exhausting day went for a meal in a nearby Italian restaurant. I don't know how it started – probably something trivial that usually triggers off arguments between the sexes. Chris stormed out of the restaurant leaving me completely embarrassed and seething, to pay the bill. Chris was in our room when I returned after stopping off for a pint to cool down, but our argument flared up again with renewed ferocity. I tried to stay calm but failed. Our dispute became noisy and then took a violent turn. I suggested to Chris that if she wanted to fight then we should go outside and do so in a civilised manner where we wouldn't disturb the other guests – if indeed there is a civilised way for a man and woman to fight. Chris rose to this challenge in true Marshall fashion, so there we were on God's business outside on the grass trading punches. What fine examples we were.

In the retail trade the secret of good selling is good buying and Chris certainly had flair in that area. Back at Devonshire Road our stock was selling like hot cakes, or should I say hot bananas. One of our best lines was inflatable bananas. I think every household in Linthorpe must have bought one. But Chris' choice was not always to everyone's liking or taste. At one of the staff meetings I had introduced at Centrepeace her toy rubber snakes were criticised as being a symbol of the devil, and the bananas were accused of being phallic symbols. These are examples of the narrow thinking that exists in the minds of too many religious people and which alienates people against the church and was later to do so in my case. Chris, who had chosen the offending items, quite innocently was at that time quite naïve, and when the meeting had ended and the staff had dispersed, she turned to Ken in all seriousness and asked him what a "frolic" symbol was. After we had recovered from our bout of laughter we gently explained to her what Margaret had meant.

Yes, Centrepeace was buzzing. It always had a good reputation for its food and had appeared in a number of good food guides, but then with the successful retail side encroaching on the limited space it wasn't always easy to get a table. It was popular with all sorts of people and boasted among its customers local celebrities, footballers and even Eugene McCoy who dropped in from time to time with his family. This, as Chris observed, Spooner like, was quite a feather in our *bow!* Eugene ran the prestigious Cleveland Tontine restaurant, a winner of Britain's top restaurant award.

Alas, the Centrepeace success story came to an end in 1985 when their lawyer cocked up the renewal of the lease, an oversight which was pounced upon by the owners of the property who had recently opened their own Italian restaurant, Pyrgi, in another part of the building. Compensation was paid by the lawyer's professional indemnity insurers but an era had come to an end. It was a sad day for me and for Chris, Ken and his wife Liz and, of course, the wonderful staff, Margaret Pearson, Maria Thomas, Heather Godwin and all those who had given their time and help – but most of all their shining examples of Christian faith. Below is the press release on 13th December 1985, later printed in the *Evening Gazette*.

HOME FROM HOME TO CLOSE

Centrepeace in Devonshire Road Middlesbrough is to close after nine years. The popular café which also sells crafts and gifts has been described as a home from home and oasis in Linthorpe Village and has enjoyed good write-ups in the Gazette's Just a Bite *and in food columns of several other publications.*

Run by members of St Aidens Church, it has provided a peaceful refuge from the hurly burly world.

Once called the Old Butcher's when it was started by Jane Hinton nine years ago, the shop was part of the old Co-op building which was recently sold to an Italian restaurateur who has refused to renew the lease.

It is a sad Christmas for the staff of six who will be jobless and for the customers who loved the shop and all it stood for and for whom it had become part of their life.

On hearing the news customers were stunned, some were in tears and one says she is leaving the area as a result. All proceeds from the shop went to charity.

There are no immediate plans to re-open.

I have occasionally looked back and wondered how interesting it might have been if I had sold my Company when its value was at its peak, and embarked on another career in the Wholesale, Retail, Import and Export business. I think I would have enjoyed that.   And I think we could have made a success of it.   Chris undoubtedly had the buying skills and I had the business experience. Apart from our brawl in Harrogate we worked well as a team and I would have had from the sale of Arnott Insurance substantial capital with which to establish the venture.

During the Centrepeace era I was still enjoying my time in the club with my mates, my golf and my football and other secular activities, which are sometimes frowned upon by certain religious bigots and without Centrepeace to keep my involvement interesting I gradually drifted back into secular life full time. I suppose I became in the eyes of the church what they call a "backslider". I did apply once for re-admission and was told that I had to do a penance. Three months without sex. After only three days I had to go back and confess my failure to the elders.

"When I saw my wife stretching up to pick a tin of beans off the shelf I couldn't control myself and I had to have her there and then," I told them.

"You can't come back in then," said the elders.

Crestfallen, I replied ruefully, "They won't let me back in Tesco either."

Twenty-Three

HEAVEN

*I disapprove of what you say, but I will fight
to the death for your right to say it.*
Voltaire.

FOR THE FREEDOM to write this chapter I have to thank Prime Minister
Tony Blair and his Chief Whip Hilary Armstrong – Mr Blair for failing to turn
up to vote on his controversial Religious Hatred Bill on Tuesday 31st January 2006,
and Ms Armstrong for cocking up her job of mustering enough yes men and women
MPs to ensure that it became law. The motion was defeated by a tiny majority of ten.
Had the bill become law I would not have been free to comment on certain aspects of
religion in case my comments, instead of mere rational observations, were
interpreted as religious "hatred" just because a minority of narrow-minded people
might find them offensive as I am sure they will. In effect, the Bill would have
reintroduced the crime of heresy, a feature of the dark ages. This should have no
place in an enlightened twenty-first century. The Government's role in a free and
democratic society is not to morally instruct its citizens by making it illegal to hold
certain views and opinions. They should be there essentially to maintain the
functional administrative aspects of a nation. How ridiculous is it that, just like they
did centuries ago, I could have faced imprisonment for expressing a politically
incorrect personal view, and how worrying that freedom of speech and opinion are
under attack like this. Mind you, prison may have been the safest place to be
because I could be the subject of a Fatwah (an Islamic death sentence) for
questioning the credibility of some of their beliefs.

Had the Bill become law I wonder how diligently it would have been enforced?
Soft targets like comedians would have been criminalised for light-heartedly and
innocently poking fun at poms, paddies, jocks and frogs and others we are not
allowed to mention, but I wonder whether the authorities would have dared to enter
places of worship to arrest those guilty of anti-Semitic and other intolerant rhetoric.

Hatred is of course a very dangerous emotion and I would love to see it eliminated from the repertoire of human feelings, but passing such a Bill would simply curtail moderate comment and have absolutely no effect on the extremists it was presumably intended to curb. Instead of trying to gag me and others who believe in free speech, the law should be enforced on religious leaders who preach intolerance and incitement to violence. Religion is and always has been a breeding ground for hatred. This will change and progress can be made only by questioning old-fashioned views. Not by stifling curiosity, criticism and comment. Could I remind Mr Blair too that he and his Party in fact depend on hatred to maintain their position of power? A substantial part of the Labour Party ethos which they encourage and on which they depend for support, is an indiscriminate and irrational hatred of the Tories and the upper classes which is a bit out-dated and quite unfair since the Tories and the upper classes don't hate working class people. There has been no attempt by the Labour party to condemn this type of hatred. So, we are not discouraged from hating people in a different social class (or for that matter, anyone who talks posh) most of whom are perfectly nice people, yet we are expected to "love" members of a religious sect, for example, many of whom regard the indigenous British people as infidels and their enemies. Isn't there just a hint of double standards here? Those MPs who voted in favour of the Bill would do well to read Matthew 7:1-5 –

> *Judge not that ye be judged. Why do you criticise the spec in your brother's eye but do not see the plank in your own? How can you say let me remove the spec from my brother's eye? Hypocrite. First remove the plank from your own eye and then you will see clearly to remove the speck from your brother's eye."*

We would be better off with a political hatred bill!

When I told my daughter Liz about my 'born again' experience, my involvement with St Aidens and my intended commitment there, she observed that this may be not the end of a journey of discovery and revelation, but merely the start. That I would move on. Words of wisdom indeed from one so young, aware no doubt that as an individual thinker it wasn't my nature easily to conform to a rigid set of religious rules. I prefer to have a mind open to doubt than one closed by belief. It was daughter Liz's opinion that I would evolve from that point in my spiritual development and so it was to be. I remain convinced of the existence of 'God' but I don't know what form of being He is. Only that there exists either now or in the future a superior intellect to even the most intelligent person on earth. That isn't really important. What is important is what is expected of me as a human being and what worries me is that because of my selfishness I fall way short of these expectations. In simple terms, am I doing enough to go to heaven? Matthew 19 verses 21, 23 and 25 tells us:

*"If you want to be perfect, go, sell what you have and give to the poor...
and you will receive riches in heaven... I say to you it is hard for a rich
man to enter the Kingdom of God... for what profit is it to a man if he
gains the whole world and loses his own soul?"*

"There's no peace for the wicked," says the old adage. Could heaven be simply complete peace of mind here on earth? Peace which comes only from having a clear conscience?

The simple solution for most people is either to dismiss the whole Heaven thing as pie in the sky and just get on with life, or to be a member of a religion and pass on the responsibility for our afterlife to the religious leaders who will tell us what we need to do to get there. But I can do neither because God has chosen to remind me of His existence and because I don't trust religions' introvert leaders, mere men doing a job, to interpret God's will for me. Professing to speak for God, they say, "Submit to my authority and you will go to heaven. Question it and you go to hell." God makes sure that we are born with a mind and with free will. Do not let any man take away that birth right. That is what those who would control us try to do.

It may appear that, perhaps unfairly, I have chosen Jehovah's Witnesses as an example of religious absurdities, but I hasten to explain that I mean no offence to them. It is not the individual people I have a problem with, it's their leaders who fill their heads with such nonsense. If their God is offended by what I say then He will punish me! That's his job. So why should people get angry if their religious beliefs are questioned? If such people find it necessary personally to punish their critics they cannot have much faith in their God's ability to do so. I have an open mind. I am willing to be persuaded to change my views. So should they. If I am to be accused of having an inquisitive mind and relying on my own intellect and God, not men, to interpret what I read, then I plead guilty, and if this causes people to be offended, then I am sorry – for them, not me. I hope they will forgive me. But I am not bothered if they don't. They are not God.

There is no way of proving it of course, but I am sure there are as many, if not more, good non-religious ordinary people out there as there are among "believers", with as much chance, and more, of going to heaven. This has certainly been my experience. And those good ordinary people are capable of having a much more balanced view of things, unlike many smug devout "believers". The Jews for example think they are God's chosen race. Well, if you are, I would say to them, what exactly did God choose you for? To be killed in your millions during World War Two? Why didn't your God choose to save you then?

God and religion are often incompatible and uncomfortable bedfellows. I would love to find a spiritual home, a church, a mosque, or a temple in which I felt at ease and at peace with like-minded fellows, but until they have a wholesale purge of antiquated irrelevant doctrine and ceremony I think me and God will quietly go it alone. There are however many people who do find comfort, support and security within a group and religion has practical benefits too – like having somewhere to get married and buried! These are enough for many people and who can blame them? These functional aspects of religion are fine – as long as you don't take the others too seriously. Some of the things that religions would have us believe – indeed insist that we do – are frankly an insult to our intelligence. None of us have the answers to the meaning of life, death, the mysteries of the universe, infinity or eternity, and if it were left to religious leaders, we would never ever find the answers, so closed are their minds to any reasoned or scientific alternatives to their dogma. Mind you, there are some who reject the notion of a Supreme Being or intellect and are dogmatic in their opinions that science will eventually provide answers to all the mysteries of life. To them I would say, "Perhaps, but open your minds too to the spiritual dimension of the human psyche." How can there be a scientific explanation to *my* personal experience described earlier?

A little knowledge can be dangerous. Why do people who profess to have it rarely say, "I don't know"? Instead they invent vague explanations and tell us that these are facts of science or the word of God. What credentials do they have for making such extravagant claims? People who are prepared to confess that they don't have answers to our questions deserve far more respect than those who cling to opinions which they cannot substantiate. People may *believe* there is a God and a heaven and hell but nobody actually *knows*. The trouble is that man has invented answers, convinced subsequent generations that these answers are fact and many followers believe them with a fanaticism which is dangerous.

I am all for religious people promoting God. What I don't like is them detracting from God's will by filling people's heads with religious dogma which causes them to behave irrationally. God's real purpose for us is all too often hidden in a smokescreen of myths of doubtful origin or ceremonial mumbo-jumbo which has its roots in fear, superstition and ignorance. To illustrate my point, I'm sorry to have to pick on Jehovah's Witnesses again but please, if only you would ditch your blood transfusion nonsense you would gain so much more credibility. Their followers are expected to, and blindly do, accept their leaders' interpretation of Leviticus 17 as a matter of fact and they refuse their children or relatives a blood transfusion even if their lives are threatened. In 2007 Emma Gough, a Jehovah's Witness from Telford, was allowed to die after refusing a blood transfusion following the birth of her twins. Really, can anyone of free will and (God-given) intellect believe that those Leviticus scriptures related to human blood and not pagan sacrificial animal blood? That God intended those poor kids to be raised without their mother? What a heartless brute *their* God must be!

Like other sects and religions they are anxious to convert people to their beliefs and to this end must surely realise that the unbelievable blood transfusion dogma is a huge obstacle. Is that why they offer no explanation and make no mention of it in *Watch Tower*, the booklet they hand out on the streets? I dare say their modern leaders would love to ditch it, but don't have the courage to admit to the orphan Gough twins that they may have got it wrong. In failing to do so more lives will be unnecessarily sacrificed.

I don't know how many other people have been denied a blood transfusion and have died but, to be fair to Jehovah's Witnesses, these examples are quite innocuous compared to some atrocities carried out by followers of many other religions in the name of God. There have been, and still are, many scriptural (mis) interpretations by other religions which have led to much more widespread, serious and tragic consequences and have even caused nations to go to war against each other. How can it be possible to have a "Holy" war in which God wants us to kill each other?

Jehovah's Witnesses are not by any means alone in interpreting the scriptures in a way which, in my view, may be inaccurate, misleading and in some cases downright dishonest. Adolph Hitler during World War Two, conveniently ignored Commandment Number One – "*Thou shalt not kill*" – and used scripture to persuade the citizens of occupied territories to accept and submit to the authority of Nazi rule – "*Render unto Caesar the things that are Caesar's*" – (Mark 12:17) – and Hitler isn't the only one to have used scripture selectively to achieve his own will and not God's.

Because in a typical Bible there are some eight hundred and thirty-four pages of ancient and often contradictory text there is a lot of scope for 'cheating' by which I mean people and religions selecting a particular text and, to suit their own purposes, claiming that it means something that it doesn't. Contained within those pages there is much scope for the intellectuals and theologians to indulge themselves and then confuse us with their theories, but how can ordinary laymen like me discover the real truth – if indeed it lies, as Christians claim, within the Bible and according to Muslims within the Koran or indeed within other religious books, all of which were written by men and not God?

Very few of us have the time, inclination or even the ability to read religious scripture and due to this apathy allow ourselves to be intellectually dominated by the 'experts'. We put our trust in men – and that is a risky business however sincere they may be and however holy they profess to be. I am a sceptic. I don't easily accept things at face value and I am certainly very wary of being given directions by men – especially when it involves something as important as going to heaven! I was busy spinning plates at the time of my spiritual experience and had little time then to study the Bible but I did read it when I could and it seemed sensible to me that since I was at that time attending a Christian church and therefore involved in a religion which started with Christ, I should ignore the Bible's six hundred and forty nine pre-Jesus pages and concentrate on the one hundred and eighty five pages of the New Testament. Within these I found only the equivalent of about a dozen which actually recorded the words of Jesus, most of which seemed to be concentrated on discrediting the outdated, mostly pagan, laws and customs written about in the Old Testament and which are still nevertheless widely practised within the Christian religion today. So, faced with something of a credibility crisis, I decided to do some research and came up with some interesting information, very little of which did anything to enhance my faith in religion. There exists little early evidence about the life of Jesus and as far as I know, no contemporary written record. The Gospels of Matthew, Mark, Luke and John were not written until thirty years after his death and, apart from the Bethlehem Manger story, there is little or no mention of his life before he was thirty years old. What we know about Jesus was handed down by word of mouth and no non-Christian versions exist of events associated with his life. The Gospel writers were not biographers. Their purpose was to convert unbelievers. Might it not be possible therefore that, in their enthusiasm to win over what, we should remember, were fairly primitive and impressionable pagans, and their desire to promote their new church, some dramatic stories may have been invented and/or exaggerated simply to impress and persuade? Like an overzealous salesman may over embellish the quality and performance of the product he is trying to sell. Sincere in their beliefs as they might well have been, the Gospel writers were in fact the early leaders of an infant church and like all human pioneers would have been ambitious to see their baby grow, perhaps thinking that the means (the exaggerations) justified the end. But what was the end? Salvation of mankind or a big powerful church? Don't get me wrong. There is much truth and wisdom in the Bible and in the Koran and I'm sure in other religions' scriptural equivalents. So by questioning, even discrediting, certain biblical or other holy book content I'm not throwing the baby out with the bathwater. I'm just saying there's an awful lot of bathwater and this has almost succeeded in drowning the baby.

As we become better educated and if we are not discouraged from thinking for ourselves then surely, in the light of almost irrefutable scientific evidence, religions will find it increasingly difficult to sustain their credibility, particularly in the West where freedom of speech and openness exist. In the past, religious leaders have relied for their power on fear, obedience, blind faith and simple-minded people. Things are changing. A century ago, I would have been branded a heretic, now I barely qualify as merely idiosyncratic, such is the growing rejection of religion, as we know it. And I am not the only one to doubt the authenticity of the scriptures – or should I say more accurately, the interpretation which has been put on them. I'm sure (ex) Father James Kennedy won't mind if I quote from his book *Fat God Thin God* in which he says:

> *"Obedience in spite of this rubbish thing about it being one of the big three virtues of religious life, is just a controlling mechanism. It has the same purpose within the Church as in the army, only it is more subtly administered. The trick is to see the person of Christ in one's superior and by obeying Christ in him or her you obey the superior. Isn't that some sleight of mind? I've always seen a need to respond to honest and competent leadership without any of this crap. I have also served diligently under a superior or two in whom I couldn't see Jesus – in a fit."*

Mr Kennedy was a Catholic priest who became a missionary in the Philippines and left the priesthood when he could not reconcile his own Christian ethics with those of the Vatican and its hierarchy.

The power and influence of the Church will continue to diminish unless it indulges in a lot of introspection, has a long hard look at the dogma and doctrine it has been steeped in for centuries and has the courage to make some radical changes, and until it stops insisting that as a pre-requisite for eternal life we must believe in all sorts of unacceptable things. Like Papal infallibility and like having to be a Catholic to go to heaven, dogma flimsily based on a convenient interpretation by the Catholic Church of Matthew 16 verse 18: "On this rock (Peter) I will build my church." Come on Vatican, you can't get away with that for much longer. And why do you call your priests Fathers when Jesus said in chapter 23 verse 9: "Do not call anyone on earth Father for only one is Father – He who is in Heaven."

See what I mean about interpreting scripture to suit your own ends – and ignoring it when it doesn't? And, your Holiness, which scripture says your priests must remain celibate, a dogma which causes them to desert their calling in droves? And how's this for hypocrisy? In some dioceses, particularly overseas, Bishops are turning a blind eye to the carnal practices of their priests while in others priests are stripped of their ordinance for having it off, while yet again some priests can abuse altar boys, or anyone else they can get their hands on (like Paul Ryan, a friend of mine who told me of his own experiences as an altar boy) and being 'punished' by being transferred to a different diocese – and a whole fresh supply of altar boys! And from where, your Holiness, do you get your authority to forbid couples to practice birth control? I suspect the reason, though you won't admit it, is to ensure an increase in the Catholic population to maintain the power of the Church. At least the Hindu leaders are honest about it by telling their people to multiply in case the Muslims overtake them numerically. And finally, why do you have all those magnificent buildings and billions of pounds worth of land when there are people in the world dying of starvation? What did Jesus say about church buildings?

> *"Pull them down...not one stone shall be left here...that shall not be thrown down."*

But the people would have nowhere to go and pray, you may say. Well, I say, tell the people to follow Jesus' advice in Matthew 6:5-8 and

> *"When you pray don't be like the hypocrites, for they love to pray standing in the synagogues (churches)....that they may be seen by men... But you, when you pray, go into your room... shut the door, pray to your Father in secret... do not be like them. For your Father knows what is in your heart before you ask him."*

Praying is good for the soul. Through prayer you can reach your inner self, your conscience. Prayer is, or should be, time set aside for meditation. Your private and personal time together with God or, if you like, your conscience. Not for repeating some words learned from religious leaders. Jesus has told us that we don't need a church for this. God is merely a convenient medium through whom we can direct our meditation. We all know what is right and wrong, but all too often we avoid having to face up to our wrongdoings and instead allow them to prey on our subconscious minds. This makes us unhappy, even though we may try to ignore this truth. Far better to at least acknowledge our shortcomings privately by sharing them with "God". The act of doing so makes us feel better, even if we do nothing about them. I know little about Buddhism despite its huge following, but its philosophy of seeking wisdom and well-being through individual meditation rather than collective obedience of intransigent dogma, its tradition of peace and forgiveness rather than conflict and its purpose of fulfilment in our lifetime rather than rewards in Heaven and punishment in Hell, do seem to be a more abiding approach to spirituality than other religions.

I believe it was Abraham Lincoln who said: "When I do good I feel good. When I do bad I feel bad. That's my religion." It's a pity some of the Holy Joes don't have this attitude. In a Christian Fellowship I once attended there was a fine example of fanciful rather than practical devoutness. An ex-C of E vicar, he prayed with great eloquence and spoke fluently "in tongues". His arms spent a great deal of time raised aloft in praise of the Lord. He was not just a good Christian spiritually for he did good works too. He and his wife adopted and fostered unwanted children. I heard later that he had buggered off with another woman!

And how credible is the Immaculate Conception and even the resurrection? I know these are fundamentals of the Christian religion but I don't think they are the fundamentals of Christianity, which should be the actual teachings of Jesus which, incredibly, are ignored. This is where the Churches are going wrong – majoring on the minors. If Churches spent more time on true Christianity instead of religion, they may just enjoy a resurrection of their own!

OK, a few timid steps have been taken in the right direction. The "infallible" Vatican has now cancelled Limbo where dead people were sent if they hadn't been good enough to go to Heaven or bad enough to go to Hell, which includes millions of innocent babies who died before they were christened and whose poor Catholic mothers were denied the comfort of believing they would be reunited in Heaven. This has given God a real dilemma. As if he didn't have enough to do, the poor old chap has now got to decide for himself where to relocate these millions of refugee souls. Throughout the ages religion has made people believe some pretty unbelievable things, some of which are finally being acknowledged by the Vatican which has also decreed that we need not now believe in some of its other hitherto compulsory dogma – The Genesis version of the creation of Earth, Noah's Ark and Jonah and the Whale for example. Too little – and too late for those "sinners" who didn't believe this claptrap before the rules were relaxed. If we are expected to accept the credibility of the Christian Church, we must ask the question, "Why for centuries have they told people that they are condemned to Hell for refusing to believe that a man called Jonah lived inside a whale?" Are these "sinners" now going to be allowed out of Hell and go to Heaven? Come on! God hasn't changed His rules and never will, so there's a lot of catching up to do! Let's hope that having just opened the lid of a Pandora's box full of myth, superstition and dogma, all the nasty goblins are allowed to fly out and perish on the altar of truth and scrutiny and let's hope that other religions follow suit.

Religion has a lot to answer for – and a lot of blood on its hands. Some Muslim clerics justified the suicide bombers by claiming that they acted on the will of Allah. President Bush of the USA claimed to be guided by God when he invaded Iraq. What chance has peace got when these people make such idiotic claims?

"Those who can make you believe absurdities can make you commit atrocities," said Voltaire, the French philosopher, with remarkable perception.

After the Tsunami tidal wave on Boxing Day 2004 thousands of homes were destroyed but some mosques were left standing – "Because of their peculiar method of construction," said the engineers. "No," said the clerics, "it was because Allah spared them because of his approval of Islam." Again when Hurricane Katrina wiped out most of New Orleans killing hundreds of people there was smug rejoicing in some Muslin quarters because it proved that God was taking revenge on America. There was a tight-lipped silence from that direction when a few weeks later an earthquake claimed the lives of thousands of Muslims in Pakistan. It terrifies me that these people who expound such nonsense are in powerful positions of influence over the uneducated minds of some of their followers.

Having had a go at Jews, Jehovah's Witnesses, Evangelicals, Protestants and Catholics, it is only right, in the interests of fairness, that I should include Islam in my credibility exercise. But there is a problem. There shouldn't be, but there is.

In an early draft of my book I did indeed do such an exercise but some followers of Islam may have considered what I had to say punishable by death and there are some hot heads capable of carrying out such a threat – indeed have already done so. In addition there are some equally obdurate people who would have me prosecuted for being racist or Islamaphobic. I therefore reluctantly on this occasion decided not to publish my opinions on the subject. Half a century ago I would have felt safe to do so, but not now. Since I am personally inhibited from doing so may I recommend to you a book by Irshad Manji, herself a Muslim – or a Muslim *"refusenik"* as she calls herself. The book is called *The Trouble with Islam Today.*

What has happened to my Country which was once the bastion of freedom of speech and expression?

I fear that in Britain as the Christian Churches become more moderate, Islam will seize on this 'weakness' and become the new Catholics for whom, until fairly recently, marriage and even fraternising with other faiths was discouraged and even forbidden just like the Muslims of today. But, as I look out of my window right now I see children of various colours and creeds playing happily and innocently together. I see hope too. These children in their more enlightened contemporary world will, I'm sure, question and reject the unsustainable dogma of their parents and religious leaders. I only hope that the future generations of Muslims seek alternative enlightenment outside their mosques and away from their fanatical Mullahs because whilst they are under their bigoted and often evil influences they present a danger to freedom and world peace. If I had one wish, I would make it compulsory for every Muslim to read the book already mentioned by Irshad Manji – *The Trouble With Islam Today.* But I am told that they dare not read it because it has been forbidden.

I confess that I have not studied the Koran but I'm sure that, like the Bible, it also allows religious leaders and others to interpret the scriptures to suit their own ends in the name of Allah. A month before suicide bombers destroyed the Twin Towers in New York, a recruiter for the extreme Islam group Hamas told CBS TV that he dangles the vision of seventy virgins in front of candidates. *"Those who can make you believe absurdities can make you commit atrocities!"* I am told that the Koran is strong on martyrdom and contains the words: *"Know that the gardens of paradise are waiting for you in all their beauty, and the women of paradise are waiting, calling out, come hither friend of God."* It also includes something about martyrs sitting at God's right hand and having the 'use' of seventy virgins. It doesn't appear to be very considerate to the feelings of women. Well, after all, *"Women are your fields. Go into them whenever you wish."*

That doesn't leave much to the imagination, does it?

Let's imagine a young simple-minded Muslim boy with not a lot going for him in the looks and sexual attraction department. Not able to find an outlet for his urges here on earth he falls into the clutches of one of these fanatical and persuasive Mullahs who tells him that to get his leg over whenever he wants it, with the choice of seventy beautiful virgins to boot, all he has to do is to blow up a few infidels and, of course, himself. How can he refuse such an opportunity?

I did speculate about what rewards the Creator of the Earth and the Planets may have for the dutiful Muslim women but was advised against publishing these hypotheses.

Despite all I've had to say about religion I have to say in its defence that it does provide an alternative to the irresponsible and undisciplined behaviour we are experiencing in the West today, and I also understand only too well why Muslims, by which I mean Muslim men, are resistant to change and are so desperate to protect their status quo. Had I learned about Islam myself years ago I may well have been tempted to join and got myself an obedient submissive wife, or maybe two or three, who, if they wanted to go to heaven, would have to let me "enter the fields" whenever I chose – and no headaches allowed!

Twenty Four

CHRISTINE MARSHALL
READING COMICS

You've got more energy than me put together.
Chrissarism.

THIRTY-EIGHT YEARS ON, Chris and I were reminiscing over a glass (or was it a bottle?) of wine in our tiny studio in Paris. Well, it isn't *our* studio, we just rent it from time to time when the urge comes over us to have another Francophile fix. I fell in love with France in general and Paris in particular all those years ago when, as a young man, I stayed in Rue de Budapest on the way back from my trip to Los Encantats in the Pyrenees. Situated in the narrow bustling Rue St Dominique close to the Eiffel Tower, the tiny studio is accessed by one of those huge imposing doorways which are a feature of the city. This opens into a passageway that leads into the heart of the block and to the ground floor studio overlooking a small courtyard. You become instantly conscious of the silence which follows the clunk of the closing street door, in vivid contrast to the sounds of the city outside from which the studio offers a perfect and tranquil escape.

Apart from indulging in this wonderful city's obvious attractions, its architecture, the spacious well planned layout of its infrastructure, its cleanliness, its culinary excellence and, in stark contrast to our cities, the genteel politeness of its inhabitants, our visit to Paris on this occasion had another purpose for each of us – me to write and Chris to visit the sprawling and fascinating Clignancourt Market to re-stock with raw materials with which, for a hobby, she made jewellery and other items which she gave to local charity shops. As the wine flowed and we laughed at the Chrissarisms I had just written (next Chapter) and which I read out to her, we talked about the situations in which they had been spawned – and much more. Chris opened up and revealed more about her past – post and pre-me – and I suggested that she too should include in my book some of her thoughts and feelings about our life together and her life in general – a woman's angle. At first she wouldn't hear of it. *She didn't want*

160

everyone to know her business. This is one of our private aphorisms and goes back to a conversation she had many years ago with Lynne in which she said something to her about having a ninety-nine. "What on earth is a ninety-nine?" enquired Lynne. Chris, assuming that Lynne was simply naïve, started to explain to her the details of this particular sexual manoeuvre. Lynne laughed. "You mean a sixty-nine, don't you?" she said. Chris thought for a moment before coming out with another of her gems. "I don't want everyone to know my business." Such was the repertoire of silly anecdotes and sayings shared between the four of us, Brian, Lynne, Chris and I, that our conversations would often attract puzzled looks from ear wigging strangers.

Though refusing to provide a written contribution, Chris did agree to me doing a potted history of her life and to reveal some of her feelings. But first some background of a family situation quite different to my own. Her father George who she adored was, during World War II, a sergeant in the Royal Horse Artillery. With as far as we know, no horsey background, it isn't clear how he found himself employed as a riding instructor, but this doesn't surprise me, being only too familiar with the army's reputation for deploying square pegs in round holes and, pardon the pun, not horses for courses. In 1942, after serving in the Middle East, George was posted to Newry in Northern Ireland as part of the guard for Italian prisoners of war, and from there to Frosterley a few miles up the River Wear dale from Wolsingham where, one fateful Saturday night, he went to the village dance. As he walked into the dancehall his eyes caught those of a young Wolsingham lass. They danced together all night. It was love at first sight and Vera was to ignore her father's parting words as she left the house that night – "If I see you with a soldier, I'll break your back." A few months later George Thomas Marshall and Alice Vera Tennick, with her back intact, walked down the aisle together – with her father's blessing.

George's childhood hadn't been easy. His mother died when he was a young boy and his father was left to bring up him, his two brothers and a sister who also died a couple of years later. She was only eleven years old. What a tragic time that must have been for 'pop' Marshall, losing both a wife and daughter in such a short space of time. He himself died when only fifty-seven.

Before contracting MS which too led to his early death, also at the age of fifty-seven, George had been a keen and accomplished sportsman. As well as his equestrian exploits, he boxed and played football for the army, and in 1939 was presented to His Excellency the Viceroy of India before helping his team to victory in the prestigious Vizianagram football tournament in Delhi, the final being broadcast on AIR – the Indian Radio Service. After the war he continued his sporting activities as a regular member of the successful Wolsingham cricket and football teams. His prowess with the latter led to him being 'spotted' by Bishop Auckland, the most successful English amateur soccer team of that era, for whom he signed in 1948.

On the Tennick side of the family, Vera's father Herbert, a mild-mannered man despite his threat on the night of the dance, worked at Wolsingham Steelworks, as did most able-bodied men of that small village. The founder of the works was one Thomas Atwood and the reason for their Wolsingham location was the proximity in Weardale of a special iron ore that had the properties necessary for shipping accessories such as anchors, chains, etc. What Chris remembers most about her grandfather Tennick is his skill at carpentry, his hobby, and the doll's pram and other toys including a milking stool, which he made for her. Herbert's brother, Chris's great uncle Jimmy, had a farm in Weardale where she recalls being taught how to milk cows – seated on Herbert's stool of course. When he retired from the steelworks Herbert was able to fulfil his dream of becoming a farmer like his brother – a dream, alas, that was to be short-lived. He died only four months after renting a small remote farm at Mickleton – Hannah Hawkswell country. Chris was eight years old when Herbert died and it fell to her mother to look after Nanna Tennick, who suffered from epilepsy and had to be closely and constantly watched to thwart her repeated attempts to wander off. With a young family to look after too, Vera found it very hard, until after twelve years the family GP, Dr Thomson, persuaded her to agree to Nanna Tenwick being taken into Sedgefield Hospital where she and Chris became regular visitors. All credit to Vera during those difficult twelve years, for 'normalising' her mother's frequent fits and removing the fear and mystery which her children may have otherwise felt. When Nanna had a fit Chris used to actually enjoy it, her mother having pretended it was a game in which she would sit on her Nanna until the fit subsided whereupon she would invariably break into song!

Several years after they married, George formed a second partnership with Vera. They set up a draper's shop in Wolsingham together, using part of their house in Angate Street, which had, I believe, previously been a butcher's shop. From there George travelled around the county selling clothes on tick while Vera looked after the shop. A stock of overalls and uniforms was bought to supply chemists and other shops on his travels – this at a time when it was not the norm for shop assistants to wear uniforms. Commendably enterprising, I thought. Unfortunately George's health deteriorated before he could get the business properly established and though Chris briefly carried on her dad's round, that aspect of the business was abandoned. Vera continued to run the shop but she was far too soft hearted to be a businesswoman, giving clothes away to the needy and letting people off with their payments when faced with the weakest of sob stories. When George died in 1972 she closed the shop.

Soon afterwards Vera moved to South Shields after marrying again. She met Clifford Collinson when, as a visiting preacher, he took a service at Wolsingham Baptist Church, where Vera, a devout Christian, was a leading member and where George had been for many years a Deacon and whose Bible in his memory is used in the pulpit to this day. At first there was strong opposition to the relationship from

Chris and her brothers who presumably felt that it was too soon after their father's death and that their decision to marry was perhaps taken too hastily. But Vera, who was barely fifty and Clifford, a widower whose wife Lillian had also recently died, found in each other first solace and, very quickly, love. The family's fears proved unnecessary and they soon learned to accept and love Clifford. He and Vera had nearly thirty years of happy marriage until Vera died of breast cancer in 2000, on 26th April, the same date as her father and her grandfather! The length of their marriage whilst not in itself unique was unusual, since both had celebrated silver weddings with different partners, a fact that came to the attention of the local newspaper, the *Shields Gazette*, who prominently featured this lovely story on 19th May 1999.

I loved them both dearly. They were both shining examples of true Christian grace but not at all stuffy. In particular, I used to thoroughly enjoy Vera's company, her jollity and her sharp sense of humour with which I was on a complete wavelength. I used to quip that I got on with my mother-in-law better than I got on with my wife, and there was more than an element of truth in that. Vera's generosity of spirit (she put money into every collection box or beggar's hand she encountered) caused her and Clifford to live very frugally, an example of which was experienced many years later when Chris managed to persuade them to accept her offer of a week in the sun at our apartment in Tenerife to celebrate Clifford's ninetieth birthday. In a restaurant Clifford, on his birthday, chose the cheapest meal on the menu but Chris instead ordered lamb chops for him. He could not believe his eyes when his meal arrived and there were six chops on his plate, a fact that he repeated over and over again until Chris asked him for heaven's sake how many chops he got at home. "None!" was the blunt reply at which they were creased with laughter. Vera was always laughing.

We tried to help them financially but despite their own altruism, pride prevented them from accepting what they considered charity from their children. Unlike today's, Vera's era was one in which austerity was considered a virtue. Vera and Clifford had a very strong faith in God which, while commendable in some respects, does I feel often go hand in hand with a narrow and blinkered view on life. To illustrate this let me relate the tale of the floods, which swept the Norfolk Broads in the nineteen-fifties.

One couple refused to budge from their house despite warnings from the authorities, relying instead on their faith in God to keep them safe. But the water level continued to rise and a fire engine was sent to rescue them. They refused, again claiming that, as believers in God, He would save them. As the floods intensified and they were forced upstairs a boat was sent for them, which again they turned away. A few hours later, the rising water had forced them to climb onto the roof at which point a helicopter arrived to haul them to safety. Again they refused this help, adamantly insisting that their strong faith and belief in God would save them. Alas, the floods engulfed their house and they drowned. Arriving at the Pearly Gates they were furious. They insisted on speaking personally to God and demanded an explanation from him as to why He had done nothing to prevent them from drowning. "What are you talking about?" said God, "I sent you a fire engine, a boat and a helicopter, didn't I?"

As the philosopher Hippocrates said, "Prayer is indeed good, but while calling on the gods, man should himself lend a hand."

The means by which Vera's life could have been made easier did exist. I believe God gives us all opportunities to help others. Call it Fate if you like, but whatever it is and whenever it happens, we should be sure we respond. We should be sure too to recognise when someone is willing to offer us help and provided the help is genuinely and altruistically available, we should not allow pride or blind faith to deny us from enjoying its benefits. But if pride is a sin, then it is one easily forgiven if it doesn't harm others.

The second product of the Marshall/Tennick union, Vera Christine, was born in Wolsingham on 30th April 1947. Chris's elder brother (George) Paul was the brainy one in the family, who went to the local grammar school, then university, and afterwards had a career as a university lecturer. Although they married young, Paul and his future wife Angela started "going out" when they were at Wolsingham Grammar School together. They became parents to Andrew, Leigh and adopted son Mark before Angela died at the age of thirty. Paul remarried and has two sons, Joe and Tommy, from his second marriage to Linda, which unfortunately ended in divorce. He is now on his hat trick and seemingly enjoying his third marriage to Jean, a professor at the University of Edinburgh where they now live, Paul having retired to become a kept man!

Philip, Chris' younger brother, joined the Army. A well-built lad who could handle himself and who later became a part-time night club bouncer, he got into a scrap with a fellow soldier in his billet, as a result of which he was summoned before the Commanding Officer whose manner was surprisingly affable. "So you enjoy a bit of a scrap, do you, Private Marshall?" the CO good-humouredly enquired. "I suppose so, sir," was Philip's reply. A few weeks later the CO posted him to Belfast in Northern Ireland at the height of and in the midst of the troubles there and he narrowly escaped with his life when one day on patrol, he felt an unfriendly bullet ricochet between his legs, leaving a hole in his trousers – not, fortunately, in his groin, but too close for comfort. He learned his lesson the hard way. Now married to Kath, they have two lovely daughters, Natalie and Rebecca, and after a spell running his own car hire company, he achieved every boy's dream and became an engine driver.

Until she met me, Chris' life had been fairly plain sailing. Born into a loving Christian family, she spent a carefree childhood in the safe and secure environment that characterises village life, where everyone knows everyone else and where strangers are viewed, if not with suspicion, then certainly with wariness and curiosity. In such circumstances parents can allow their children more freedom and at a much earlier age than their town and city counterparts. Sunday in those days was still observed and on that day Chris' freedom was curtailed with mandatory attendance at church and Sunday school at which her mother was a teacher, assisted some years later by Chris herself. She obviously hadn't however been paying attention at Sunday school when it came to the bit about the ten commandments and in particular commandment eight, because she wasn't above nicking sweets from the corner shop. She was as Uncle Jack, Vera's brother, used to say, "A bit of a sport." Fortunately her progress from petty theft into big-time crime was thwarted when a tube of lipstick was found in her bedroom. Under interrogation from her father she broke down and confessed and was marched down to the shop by George who presented his sheepish daughter to the owner and announced: "Christine has something to say to you, haven't you, Christine?" She was spared her anguish only when her mumbled confession and apology had been repeated until it was loud and clear. This proved to be a very effective cure for kleptomania then, and again twenty years later when we applied it to one of our boys.

Chris was never happier than when she was pushing a pram and when she was old enough, which wasn't very old, she progressed from dolls' prams to real ones. She would knock at doors and ask to take the baby for a walk or simply walk off with a pram left outside, which was then a common and acceptable practice. Children and particularly babies were her fascination and with no birth control in those days there was always plenty of material in the neighbourhood for her to indulge her passion. Rosie next door had four and the Sampsons a few doors away had nine. Rosie would come into the shop for a fag and a gossip until it was time to do some baking, once famously remarking, "I'll have to get back now Vera to make some bread and get these nails clean." Ugh! The nine Sampsons were all born within a period of nine years. Mrs Sampson only missed one year, then had two the following year to make up for it! Chris spent a lot of time with the Sampsons and was a welcome help to the harassed mother. She was only thirteen when she stayed there for a weekend to look after this houseful of kids to give the parents the only break of their married life, a weekend in Scotland together, during which no doubt, another conception occurred.

As I remarked earlier the Marshall and Tennick academic genes were not fairly or evenly distributed and Chris' school years were spent less on learning than larking about and she regularly felt the sting of Mrs Metcalfe's slipper on her bottom or headmistress Miss Walsh's ruler administered on the painful, and in those unenlightened days dangerous, inside part of the arm opposite the elbow. When she was eleven, full of confidence, she skipped happily home from school on the day of her eleven plus exam. "I was first to finish. It was easy!" she announced brightly. She failed. Chris left school at fifteen with few qualifications, at the time when her elder brother was accepted for university. Feeling a tad threatened and perhaps a little jealous of Paul's academic achievements, she once remarked grumpily, "Paul Marshall reading economics. Christine Marshall reading comics."

Her ambition was to work with children and after brief periods working as a ledger clerk at Howards in Bishop Auckland and then nearer home at Mr Black's chemist shop, she responded to an advertisement for a nanny at The Grove in nearby Hamsterley Forest. She remembers vividly her interview with Mrs Lewin in that grand old country house, the living room tastefully and expensively furnished and the grand piano almost dwarfed, such was the size of the room, which adjoined a conservatory leading through French doors into the garden. She was most impressed but unfortunately Mrs Lewin apparently wasn't. She didn't get the job, though this came as less of a surprise than the fact that she had actually got an interview, since the post was for a girl aged twenty-one plus. She was in for a pleasant surprise though. A few days later Mr Ernest Lewin called at the house in Angate Street, explained that the reason for Chris not getting the job was her age, which at fifteen was only a year older than his eldest daughter Caroline though the post was actually as nanny to Debbie, his three-year-old youngest daughter. The new nanny had left after only a few days and the job was offered to Chris, who readily accepted. Full of confidence as she was then, and not in the least overawed, she arrived to take up her new post at the Grove. The house was divided into three sections and occupied by various branches of the family of German Jews who had fled to England to escape the Nazi regime, minus Ernest's cousin who was caught and shot dead. There were several servants at the Grove and the post of nanny was one of privilege within the domestic hierarchy of the household. Chris lived in the main house and ate with the family and was discouraged by Mrs Lewin from fraternising with the other domestic staff who lived in separate outbuildings. She nevertheless settled in well, taking to her new role like a duck to water. Ernest would introduce her as Debbie's nanny, "...but she is more like my eldest daughter," he would add. She was soon to become almost a part of the family in more ways than one.

Stuck out in the country, discouraged from contact with the other staff and with only one weekend off a month, Chris became lonely and I suppose it wasn't surprising that an attraction developed between her and seventeen-year-old Charles Schlam, a young member of the family whose parents lived in Johannesburg and who had sent him under the Lewin's guardianship to be educated at boarding school in England. Charles lived in the house when he had free weekends and during vacations. Chris, then sixteen, and Charles became unofficially engaged. What a commotion this caused! His parents flew over from Johannesburg hoping to break up the relationship. They failed.

When Debbie started school, however, many of Chris' duties became redundant; she became bored and she felt it was time to move on. The family had become very fond of her and tried to persuade her to stay on, but she wanted to look after young children. She went to live back at home while she looked for another job, working in the meantime as a receptionist at Fosters Builders Merchants in Bishop Auckland. Away from the Hamsterley Forest environment, her feelings for Charles cooled and she broke off her engagement.

Around that time there was an international Christian mission involving the Baptist churches and when it came to Wolsingham the leaders were invited to tea by Vera. Among the guests was one of the leader's sons, a young man called Harvey who was being trained for the ministry. A romance developed between he and Chris and marriage was talked about. It was suggested that it may be appropriate for Chris to receive some training if she were to become the wife of a minister, and an anonymous donation was received through the letterbox to fund a course at Capenwray Bible College near Lancaster, a six-month sabbatical, normally taken in preparation for university. Chris enjoyed the experience and made some good friends there but unfortunately, or was it fortunately, her course was cut short when her help was needed at home after her mother had suffered a slipped disc and was confined to her bed. It was at this bedside that I was to first make Vera's acquaintance when I interviewed her daughter in 1967. By then the idea of being a minister's wife had become less attractive to Chris and whilst she and Harvey were to remain friends, she made it clear that marriage was out of the question. She still nurtured the urge to be with children and applied for three advertised posts and was accepted for them all. Her reference from the Grove was of course impeccable. She turned down Lord and Lady Lambton and the opportunity to live in Lambton Castle. She also turned down Lord and Lady Barnard.

So what was it that I had and the aristocracy didn't? The fact is that I personally didn't even enter the equation. Chris thought that I was a bit scruffy and not at all her type. The five-day week helped, but what attracted her most was the fact that there was a little girl who needed loving and caring for and crucially, there was no mother involved. This was Chris' perception at the time since there was no mention made of a mother either by me or by my mother or indeed by Liz herself and Chris was too shy to enquire. This illusion was to be well and truly shattered in the light of subsequent events.

Before her relationship with me, Chris had always been in control of her love life. She had never been short of admirers and boyfriends, all of whom were keener on her than she was on them, and all of whom were ditched when she grew tired of them. For the very first time in her life she was on the receiving end when Agnes and I briefly got back together. The biter bit, you might say. Hurt and her confidence dented, she tried to pick up the pieces of her life again. She got a job as an auxiliary nurse at Wolsingham Hospital, had a brief fling on the rebound with a lad she met until she discovered he was married and she had a call from Charles, her old fiancé.

Chris was flattered of course but was not interested in renewing a romantic relationship in that particular direction.

When Chris and I eventually tied the knot her dream of married domestic bliss wasn't matched by the reality. She wasn't comfortable being married to a workaholic businessman with a full social life. With one or two exceptions, she didn't like the people I associated with and resented my efforts to force her into socialising with them. In turn I, unfairly, resented her reluctance to do so. It was the socialising, which caused lots of problems in our marriage – and many arguments. She accepted the need for me to socialise for business reasons and occasionally even accompanied me despite her shyness, but always under protest.

One occasion that sticks in my mind is having dinner at the Five Bridges (now the Swallow) Hotel in Gateshead with Ken Gregory, one of our Lloyds Brokers. The occasion was to introduce his new regional manager, Peter Leggett, and it was touch and go who was the most nervous – Peter or Chris. We arrived early so that Chris could slug back a couple of G & T's for Dutch courage and Ken and I did our best to relax the situation by talking incessantly. Peter eventually plucked up courage and asked Chris how her cats were. Puzzled, Chris asked him what cats he was talking about and Peter, then feeling decidedly uncomfortable, hesitantly suggested that the cats he was referring to were the ones she bred and exhibited at top cat shows up and down the country, to which Chris responded by saying she hated cats, following which Ken, no longer able to contain himself, burst out laughing. He had wound Peter up earlier, advising him that if there was a lull in the conversation he should impress Mrs Arnott by introducing the subject of cats. The ice was broken and we had an enjoyable and almost relaxed dinner together. Ken of course knew of Chris' aversion to cats. The subject must have cropped up on the only previous occasion when he and she had met, which was after I had been out for the day with Ken and Ted King, the underwriter for Hermes Motor Policies at Lloyds, and we had called at our home in Wolviston where Ken had taken over from Chris and fed Jacob his boiled egg and soldiers. This and Ken's general affability had endeared him to Chris and was the reason why on that later occasion I had been able to persuade her to accept his dinner invitation.

I said our dinner at the Five Bridges with Ken and Peter was *almost* relaxed because Chris was never comfortable in company unless she knew the people well or they were close family. She would become totally screwed up in such situations and this made it difficult for me to feel confident and at ease. I couldn't relax fully because I was conscious of how uncomfortable she was feeling. I considered it important for my wife to be a part of my business (and other) socialising activities and arrogantly expected her dutifully to "perform" in such situations. This and many other incompatibilities resulted in our marriage being a quite tempestuous affair – a love-hate relationship. Though, because of our strong wills, never less than passionate, our relationship must have been fundamentally sound since we have, notwithstanding, stayed together through some very difficult times, often out of a sense of loyalty which we both also share in abundance. I suppose most couples with spirit must fight too. Fortunately the way God has constructed us helps us to enjoy the making up process and prevents permanent polarisation.

Like many young men with high libido, sex for me was about quantity, not quality. With four lively young children around, privacy was at a premium and creating time for relaxed lovemaking was difficult. Unfulfilled needs would lead to frustration and tension. I like the Billy Connolly story about the Vaseline salesman seeking feedback from his old customers. He asked Billy what he had used the product for and Billy claimed that it had enhanced his sex life no end – by smearing it on the bedroom doorknob so the kids couldn't turn it and get in!

We did have sex very frequently in those days, but rarely made love. Chris taught me how to do that and I am grateful to her for patiently waiting for me to learn the distinction between loving and fucking. As we get older most men become more patient, considerate and less demanding – three important essentials for lovemaking to become truly fulfilling for both partners. Like electric light bulbs, men are quickly and easily switched on. Females are electric irons. They take a little longer to warm up. It took us a long time to establish the closeness, trust and security so vital for a female to experience her sexual potential and I discovered late in life the importance of what I once heard described as the "cuddle button". Perhaps this is what George Bernard Shaw may have had in mind when he said that youth was wasted on the young.

So, getting old can have compensations other than free bus and cheap rail travel. Women however are less philosophical than men during the ageing process, worry more about their looks and seek constant reassurance on that score. We men don't always give them it. Standing naked in front of the mirror one day, Chris bemoaned the grey hairs, the flabby belly, the wrinkles and the droopy tits. "Can you tell me *anything* good about my body?" she demanded hopefully. "Yes," I replied, "your eyesight."

Pam Ayres had the right attitude when she wrote:

> Will I have to be sexy at sixty?
> Will I have to keep trying so hard?
> Well I'm just going to slump
> With my dowager's hump
> And watch myself turn into lard.
>
> I'm not going to keep exercising
> I'm not going to take HRT
> If a toy boy enquires
> I'll say "hah, hard luck squire"
> Where were you in '73?
>
> I'm not going to shave my moustaches
> I'm going to let them all sprout
> My chins'l be double
> All covered in stubble
> I'm going to become an old trout.
>
> My beauty all gone and forgotten
> Vanished with never a quibble
> I'll sit here and just
> Kind of gnaw on a crust
> And squint at the telly and dribble.
>
> As my marbles get steadily fewer,
> Must I struggle to keep my allure?
> Have I still got to pout
> Now my teeth have come out
> And my husband has found pastures newer?
>
> Farewell to the fad and the fashion.
> Farewell to the young and the free!
> My passion's expired!
> At bed time... I'm tired!
> Sexy and sixty? Not me!

Wedding celebration at Morton House. Wife and daughter.

Twenty-Five

CHRISSARISMS

You know where you are if you want me.
Chrissarism.

IT **DOESN'T FOLLOW** that people who are confused are necessarily thick. William Archibald Spooner's affliction made him famous and Spoonerisms, as his verbal slips were known, caused much amusement during his lifetime and continue to do so today. These usually occurred when he became agitated or angry.

Born in 1844 at Oswestry where I did my basic army training, Spooner was ordained as a priest in the Anglican Church and one of his early slips of the tongue was when announcing in church the hymn for the day – "Kinkering Kongs [Conquering Kings] Their Titles Take." Far from being a hindrance to the Reverend Spooner's career, his verbal slips and phonetic transpositions seem to have helped. He was a scholar and academic and later became Dean and Warden of New College Oxford where he taught history, philosophy and divinity. The attention of his students was assured as they eagerly anticipated his next "tip of the slung". A forthright disciplinarian, the admonishments of his students had the sting taken out of them when they came out as "Spoonerisms". Here are some examples:

"Stop nicking your pose."
"Which one of you is guilty of fighting a liar in the quadrangle?"
"That, sir, is a lack of pies."
"With your poor attendance at lectures you've tasted two worms."
"Know your blows, boy."
"I demand an explanation for hissing my mystery lesson."

Before he was promoted to the post himself he once told one of his students who demanded to see the main man, "I'm sorry, the Bean is dizzy." At dinner one

172

evening he proposed a toast to "Victoria, our queer Dean", and visiting a friend at his cottage in the country said to his host, "You've got a nosey cook here."

Since his death there have been many more examples of Spoonerisms published, some attributed to the Reverend gentleman and many to those who have had fun inventing them. Here is a small selection:

"It's roaring with pain."
"Chipping the flannel." (On TV)
"Cuss and kiddle."
"A blushing crow."

But I believe the best humour of this kind is spontaneous and what the Rev Spooner's grammatical dyslexia did to words, my wife often does to proverbs and everyday sayings. If she could deliberately think up some of the funny things she has unwittingly said, maybe she could turn pro like Stanley Unwin who some older readers may remember. Chris reminds me of Gracie Allen whose black and white TV show with George Burns was, for me, in the fifties, a must watch. To my knowledge it has never been repeated. What a pity. Like Chris, you knew what Gracie meant but it was never said in the correct and conventional way. Chris's "tips of the slung" usually came out when she was angry, or tired, or drunk, or all three. Let me relate a few episodes of what I mean.

Like when we were having a male versus female argument and I'd referred to Venus and Mars to illustrate our incompatibility:

"It's got nothing to do with Mars and Penis."
Then, when I'd stopped laughing:
"What's wrong with that?"
And after telling her it was wrong:
"What is it then, Venus and Penis?"

Then there was the time on the beach in Gran Canaria when she couldn't get rid of a local male pest despite telling him repeatedly to "vamos", which of course is Spanish for "come on".
…and sitting near a gobby German woman in a bar in La Gomera:
"She could talk for England, that one."
…and a café in New York:
"It's good in here isn't it? They come round and tip up your coffee."
…and speculating on our prospects of having grandchildren:

"Knowing my luck if I have a grandson it'll be a girl."
...and to an Australian friend:
"Have you ever done bungle jumping?"
...and giving directions to a stranger:
"It's about two miles as the fly crows."
...and in Central Station Glasgow waiting for a train after a hectic Davis Cup weekend when she decided to go to the toilet, then turned back and said:
"The train's at the platform now so I'll wait and go on the bus."
...and one particularly expressive gem which we have adopted and use frequently in our alternative language. A German man who tried to claim her sunbed beat a hasty retreat when he was told to:
"Mickey Neinen Offen."
...and her opinion of one of our dodgy acquaintances:
"I can't stand that bloody black sheep of Calcutta."
...and in Ireland once she informed me that:
"Guinness puts iron in your pencil."
...and once when driving back from a restaurant, probably over the limit, I was ordered to:
"Pull over on to that cold shoulder – now." (She later apologised for being *"a back street driver".)*
...and at the Stella Artois Tennis Championship:
"If I could sum up Pete Sampras in one word it would be that shot."
...and describing to a friend a night at the theatre in the West End:
"We went for a pre-dinner meal."
...and speaking of meals, we've had a few that were only good in parts –
"Like the parson's nose!"
...and concerned about my waist line:
"This is the third meal we've had and you've had a dessert both times."
...and discussing the timing of Easter one year she asked me:
"Which month comes in like a March hare and goes out like a lamb?"
...and after she had sunk a few McEwans Export ales one night:
"I've lost count of the number of McEwans I've exported tonight."
...and when she was offered another:
"No thanks. I'm not very good at drinking when I've been drinking."
...and not in the mood for lovemaking one night, offered:
"To lay back and look like England."

...and the songs:
Roast nuts chesting on an open fire.
...and

Whose that team they call the Arnotts
Who are the lads that I adore
They're full of shxxx, but they're full of dynamite
That's why I love them all the more.
…followed by:
"Stick that in your book and smoke it."

So I did.

…and those frustrating conversations:

"Where would you like to go tonight?"
"Anywhere".
"OK, we'll go to the—."
"I don't like it there."
"Where do you want to go then?"
"Anywhere."
"Right, we'll go to the—"
"It's too far."
"Well, where do you want to go—" etc. etc. etc. ad nauseam.

…and finally a recent classic from Paris:

"What kind of men go and watch girls pole vaulting?"
"Athletics fans?"
"No, I've got it wrong, haven't I. You need a horse for pole vaulting."
"No, you're thinking of polo."
"I'm not. You're thinking of gymkhanas where they jump over hurdles."
"I give up."
She was referring originally to pole dancing – I think!

Chris rarely got them right but nevertheless persisted in coming out with proverbs and sayings. I've used some other of her words of wisdom as Chapter sub headings.

While on the subject of Spoonerisms I must mention the Sportsman's dinner I attended many years ago. The object was to raise funds for Hartlepool United Football Club. The star turn of the evening was a young lady from Seaton Carew appropriately billed as Susie the Seaton Stripper. She made her entrance dressed in a full Hartlepool strip, plus hat and scarf, stood on a table and offered her clothing for auction – first the hat, then the scarf, followed by boots, socks, top and shorts leaving only her knickers intact, at which point she made a swift exit leaving behind a roomful of disappointed males, followed by catcalls and boos. I admired her courage – and of course her other attributes. For the benefit of her football club Susie raised a lot of money (and a lot of other things) that night. I wonder how much she would have got for her knickers!

But for me Susie was upstaged by the comedian for the night whose name I cannot recall, He related, Spooner like, the fairy tale Cinderella. I wish I could repeat his delivery verbatim but I was too busy laughing to take in much of the detail. Instead, using a combination of the two 'isms' – Spooner and Chrissa – I have invented my own version. I hope you can interpret it and enjoy reading it as much as I have enjoyed writing it.

PRINDARELLA

Once upon a time in an olden day's city there lived a gritty pearl called Cinderella. City Prindarella lived in a bosh pig house with her father Mr Potter, her wicked and stepful spite mother and her two sisty uglers Chictoria and Varlotte. The sisty uglers were not sisterlogical buyers. They were in fact cyst steppers. You see, Mr Potter had lost his worst fife – Motherella's cinder – and remarried. The new pisses Mee was jealous. She felt threatened by her husband's relationship with his cinder Daughterella. She thought he biked her letter. So, when he was out jerking at his wob she cindered Ressarella in drags and made her do all the chasty nores – like dishing the washers, flopping the mores and fleaning out the choir.

Each year there was a Royal Ball in the Kince's prassel and this year Cindarella and the two sisty uglers had invited receivitations. But on the day of the ball Sanderella was sid because her stepful spite mother had given her extra chasty nores to do because she knew that the presence of her beautiful step daughter at the ball would chinder the hances of her own gugly earls in handing the win of the pransome hince in marriage.

However the rescindful Sourcerella worked her bingers to the phone to finish chewing the doors in time. But alas, it seemed that her cream was to be dushed. The stepful spitemther had made sure that all Frinderella's socks had been cocked up in a lubbard so she only had her rags to wear.. Cheers tickled down her treeks. Was she destined never to preet the mince?

Suddenly there was a light brash of flight and there fronting in stand of her was a grand old lady, *"Don't be afraid,"* said the land old grady. *"My name is Felena and I am your hairy godmother. I am able to wish you a grant."*

The now cindy Happerella smiled and told the old lady that if she were wished a grant, then it would be to go to the ball.

"Your grant will be wished," said the hairy Godmother.

However, the old lady was deceptive and sensed that Sanderella was still sid. *"But,"* explained Sanderella sidly, *"my best cocks are frocked up in a lubbard and I have nothing to wear."*

"Don't worry," said the hairy Godmother and with a hap of her clands Dinderella was pressed in a gowniful beaut. Not only that but when she looked down she let out a gloop of wee when she saw the slip glasses on her feet. It wasn't that she needed slip glasses because she suffered from sort shite. These were the sort of slip glasses that were fawn on the wheat.

Then, with a few wagic merds, a pellow yumpkin appeared at the step door. Another wagic merd and pray hesto it changed into a colden goach with a team of white stairs and mallions and a diver to take her to the brawl at the Kinces prassel.

As soon as the pransome hince eyed claps on her his start hopped and when she hanked her dropperchief he roomed across the rush to acquaint her makeance. They took to the flance door and the night pissed quackly in each other's arms.

The sisty uglers were potally tuzzled. Who was this gritty pearl prancing with the dince? They didn't cinderise Recognella in her gowniful beaut and slip glasses. They didn't chance a stand.

Everything was nearly rice until the strock cluck twelve and Cinderella remembered the winal ferds of the hairy Godmother. Before the spell wore off and her rock turned into frags and the colden goach turned back into a yumpkin, she bled from the fall. In her haste she slipped off her kickers.

The disaprinted poince had forgotten to ask his would be nincess her prame and next day set out and tied all over trown to find the slut of the girl the gas fitter slipped. But the sinning custy uglers told the part broken hince that they were the only ones who lived in the bosh pig house. Prestfallen the kince was about to horse his mount and ride away when he sinded Spoterella through a wide sindow.

As you all know of course, the fit slippered Finderalla's soot, the mince asked her to parry him, they had a wig bedding and the story had an endy happening.

The Morning After.

The Night Before in Brigsby's Bar, Florida.

Twenty-Six

BACK TO BORO

Doing a twilight flip.
Chrissarism.

I RESISTED THE PRESSURE on me from Chris to move from Wolviston for as long as I could. I was settled there and so were the kids. New housing estates attract young couples of breeding age so there were plenty of young friends for Liz, James, Tim and Jacob to play with and our house was at the end of a cul-de-sac, so it was perfectly safe for them to play outside even when they were quite young. It was nice to get them out from under our feet. "Go outside and play with the traffic," I used to quip to them. It was hard work with four boisterous children.

Chris was never happy on the Poplars Estate. She had too many unpleasant experiences there and if the woman of the house isn't happy then the home can never be a truly happy one and, having tried everything to persuade her to stay, including an extension which gave us an extra two bedrooms, a study and a quiet reading/music room, I could delay the inevitable no longer. When Liz left Northfields, the local comprehensive school and went to university I ran out of arguments for not moving. We sold up and in 1983 moved back to Middlesbrough.

Westlands in Roman Road was an imposing old house with five bedrooms and a granny flat, only a short distance from our previous house in Westwood Avenue, so Chris was able to renew her acquaintance with old friends and neighbours which was nice for her. What wasn't so nice for her was me renewing my contact with my old barfly buddies at Acklam Park Rugby Club and other nearby hostelries. The kids soon settled in. The house had belonged to Dennis Maxwell, a local bookie, who had left behind a few legacies – including a fancy drinks bar with its own optics in the huge lounge, which I later learned had been the scene of some extravagant and wild parties. The property also boasted a purpose-built detached centrally heated snooker room – minus table unfortunately. This made an ideal playroom for the kids with several one-armed bandits complete with hundreds of sixpences, another of Mr

180

Maxwell's legacies. I acquired a table tennis table and needless to say the kids acquired lots of friends attracted by such idyllic facilities. The downside from our point of view was that the kids took most of their meals in the games room and instead of catering for three we often found ourselves catering for a dozen or more. Chris and I also spent a lot of time in there, inviting friends round for table tennis teas. She became quite proficient and played in one of the Teesside TT leagues for a spell. She played equally proficiently with her left hand when she sprained her right one. The boys also became good players, particularly Jacob. I encouraged them by giving them at first eighteen start out of twenty-one so that I would have to play my hardest to beat them. If they beat me I would reward them with extra pocket money and a reduction in their handicap. In the end Jacob was giving me start and we had some fiercely contested matches together. He and I joined the local Ormesby TT Club, which was a hotbed of local talent due to the high standards of coaching available there. At that time it was perhaps the leading club in the country having, only a few years earlier in 1972, won the TT European Cup, the only English club ever to have done so.

My own game improved during this period and when I had failed to persuade Jacob to enter a tournament when we were on an activity holiday at a hotel and sports complex in Ibiza, I had to set an example so I entered it myself and was beaten – no, crushed – in the final. We were there for two weeks, so undeterred and hoping that my opponent Gerd's holiday was over and he had gone back to Germany, I entered again the following week, reaching the final once more. As I entered the sports hall on the big day I was dismayed to find that Gerd was once again my opponent. I raised my hands in mock surrender, shrugged my shoulders and walked out. I returned of course and went through the motions. We shook hands and talked after my humiliation was over but since the only German I knew was 'Heil Hitler' and his command of my language wasn't much better, the conversation didn't last long – but long enough for me to gather that he played in the German TT Bundesliga and was one of their top ten players. No disgrace there then.

The move to Westlands meant a change of school for the boys. When James was due to leave Wolviston Village School a year earlier we had thought long and hard about the prospect of him following Liz into Northfield. She had done quite well there thanks to her friends Joanne Taylor and Deb Lindsley who were bright girls, and after a shaky start, Liz was eventually influenced by their attitude and began to take her schoolwork seriously. Not all children at comprehensive schools are as fortunate and James displayed a tendency to always gravitate towards the more irresponsible types in his age group, as indeed did Tim and to a lesser extent, Jacob. Image is all-important to boys of this age and I think to girls too. They must at all costs avoid being branded as a swot and it didn't take much to gain this reputation. Handing in homework on time was often sufficient to earn it! Being a lefty at heart it went against the grain to consider private education, although I had earlier tried, unsuccessfully, to persuade Liz to consider it. However, I knew deep down that the Labour Government's sweeping and indiscriminate destruction of our old education system and its replacement by the comprehensive system was an ill-conceived policy which New Labour tried later to reverse by reintroducing grammar schools but called them academies so we wouldn't notice! Political parties would gain so much more credibility if they occasionally admit they got it wrong.

A decision was taken to send the boys to Red House Private School in nearby Norton. A year later the decision to remove them was in effect taken for us. On a school skiing trip one of the boys and a few of his friends nicked some kinder eggs from the shop at the centre where they were staying in the Swiss Alps. The reaction from the school was, to put it mildly, OTT. For what amounted to no more than boyish pranks by ten-year-olds, the school decided to suspend the 'criminals' for two weeks. Now in my book, the object of punishment is primarily to prevent a repetition of the offence. Rewarding these boys with an extra two weeks holiday was to my mind nonsense. Not only that, but I had paid a lot of money for my boys to receive a full term's education, not a term minus two weeks. I confronted the headmaster who referred me to one of the Governors. I think they expected me to humbly apologise and beg them to lift the suspension. Instead I made it clear that the punishment was both inappropriate and disproportionate to the offence. The school's response was intransigence. My first reaction was to go public and involve the press. They would I'm sure have loved it, particularly those of a left wing and anti-private education persuasion. *"Private School in Suspension Shame."* *"Kinder Crime at Public School."* I could just imagine the headlines. For the sake of the children, however, to whom this notoriety may have been embarrassing, I didn't do what I should have done. I withdrew the summons I had prepared to claim the value of the two weeks' fees when the school refused to give me a refund. The boys were removed from Red House School and when we moved to Middlesbrough went to local schools there, James to Boynton Comprehensive and Tim and Jacob to Green Lane, Liz's old school. They tried to conceal the fact that they had come from a private school but it leaked out. A cowardly gang of lads at Green Lane who didn't have the bottle themselves coerced a lad called David Rankin to have a fight with Tim one evening after school. Almost all the school turned out to watch. It was a sell-out. A passer-by attracted by the commotion found out what was going on and called at the house to tell me. As usual when there are domestic crises, I was away. Tim won the fight and he and David who confessed that he had always been a reluctant combatant, became good friends.

Being uprooted from Wolviston and the sudden end to their private education was less traumatic for the two younger boys who transferred to primary school, than for James. Because of his background, he was given a hard time by the other boys there. In an effort to fit in he began to talk rough and behave even rougher. The fact that James lived in a big house, came from a well-to-do family and that the Arnott name was so well known made matters worse. He would crouch down in the back of my car and always entered the house by the back door to escape being seen and identified. Liz who had by then gone to university was fortunately not affected by the upheaval.

I was working hard and was now faced with a much longer journey when I travelled to Sunderland and beyond. I used this as an excuse to resume my 'early doors' drinking routine. I justified this in my mind when Chris complained, by blaming her for 'forcing' me to move from Wolviston. Some of the five o'clock crowd were drifting away from Acklam Park, one of the reasons being that the beer wasn't always up to scratch. It was OK when Jack Atkin the regular steward was on duty but in his absence the bar was run by a relief steward who used to boast about how he fiddled his customers in one of his previous jobs. One of his tricks had been to put short measures of spirits into the glasses and top them up with chasers. To fool the customers he would first dip the rims of the glasses into special trays of spirit, which he kept to one side. This would make the customers, as they lifted the glasses, experience a strong smell of the spirit and assume that they had been given good measures. I suspect the relief steward was up to his old tricks.

Somebody should write a book about clubs and particularly workingmen's clubs. They abound with characters and there is a wealth of material there. Before I continue I just want to mention something that John Wilder told me. John was the steward at the Longbeck Club and made no secret of the fact that he watered down the beer, and he made no attempt to disguise the fact. He even boasted that his BMW car was paid for by the Northumbrian Water Board. "I water down their beer and they still fight each other," he said. "If I didn't, the buggers would kill each other – and I wouldn't want that on my conscience!"

In spite of my early political indoctrination I was becoming aware of the broader picture and beginning to realise that politics was a cause and not a solution So it was with few pangs of conscience that I decided to join the local Conservative Club where many of my drinking partners were now quenching their thirsts. When challenged by my despairing mother and others still immersed in out-dated left-wing prejudice, I explained to them that if the Raving Monster Looney Party Club was only three minutes' walk from home, boasted five snooker tables, served a perfect pint of eighty bob beer and provided good company, then I would have joined that too. Mavis the steward knew exactly what every customer drank and by the time they reached the bar their drinks, in my case a perfect pint of beer with an old-fashioned creamy head on it, would be waiting for them. Mavis ruled the roost. She was discreet, turned a blind eye to the odd expletive and wouldn't tolerate any nonsense or petty interference by committeemen. The perfect steward. When she retired several years later she was the longest serving club steward in Britain, after which it is I think, fair to say, that the club went downhill. It needn't have done. There was an ideal successor. But the committee knew better!

I didn't realise it that time but as I spent more time on social, domestic and pleasure and less on business, I had an historical counterpart – the Emperor Nero of Rome.

After the hiccup in the progress of my business when I was spinning plates in the nineteen-seventies, I had managed to get it back on course and it was growing rapidly once again. But I was enjoying myself socially too and wanted more time to play billiards and snooker with friends in the club, to travel, to spend holidays with the family and to reduce my golf handicap. I was financially comfortable and was beginning to question the purpose of expanding my business and giving myself the extra responsibility. But I couldn't relax. I had already experienced what problems could arise without me at the helm.

You don't, or you shouldn't, make the same mistake twice. You just make different ones.

I met Brooks Mileson when his construction company Edwin Davis (Cleveland) Ltd won the contract to develop some properties I had bought, the first floor of which was to be new offices for our successful Middlesbrough branch. In Volume II I describe in detail how I came to appoint him as Arnott's managing director in 1985, how, with his help and support, I was persuaded to embark on an ambitious expansion programme in order to achieve plc status, how we acquired an old manor house, Morton House, in County Durham, for our executive offices, how I gave shares in one of our subsidiary companies to an old friend and why I came to regret it, how my partners in my car repair business let me down, how my disastrous decision to become an underwriting "Name" at Lloyds of London almost bankrupted me, how this allowed Brooks to achieve a position of power and control within the Arnott organisation, how he almost destroyed it, how I decided to cut my losses and sell out, how Brooks later, after boasting how wealthy he was, became the Chairman of little Gretna FC and took them into Europe, then into liquidation and how he later died in mysterious circumstances, before being posthumously declared bankrupt – and how fortunate I was to survive these setbacks.

Twenty-Seven

PATSY

Q. What does a woman do with her arsehole before making love?
A. Drops him off at the club.
D.A.

FOR ME THE GREATEST INVENTION since the wheel and sliced bread was undoubtedly the mobile phone but not for the obvious reasons, though these did make a big difference. The forerunner of the truly mobile cord-free model was the car phone and I had one fitted to my first new Jaguar. It gave me something useful to do while I was driving. I'm not one for listening to music in the car, preferring when I do, to sit quietly on my own at home and concentrate totally with only a glass of something to distract me. Not to be recommended whilst driving, though. With my new phone I could be contacted easily, which was very handy since I spent a lot of time behind the wheel. The Jaguar clocked up over 100,000 miles. I could also make calls which would normally have had to wait until I reached my destination, thus utilising a lot of what I considered wasted time in transit. These benefits were outweighed however by one which I doubt was envisaged by the inventor – the ability to have an extra hour's drinking time. I usually phoned home to say that I was leaving the office, an hour's journey away. With my new invention I could do so, not from the office, but from the club car park.

So what made the club, first Acklam Park Rugby and Cricket Club and then the Cons Club, seemingly so much more attractive than home? I suppose, apart from the need to wind down after work, the answer was good adult male company (the Cons was men only) and as I have mentioned earlier, I found the early drinking crowd so much more interesting than the 'last hour' people. Every evening at the bar or seated in the Cons Club round our square table I could rely on a regular minimum turn out of half a dozen characters, all with a tale and a joke to tell – and sometimes a trouble to share. Brian inevitably was an ever present, as were John "Hodgy" (and later "Podgy") Hodgson who ate nothing all day, swam twenty lengths every morning and sank as many pints of lager at night before going home at closing time to eat his only meal of the day; Dave Smith, Chris Manson, the best butcher in the universe, as nominated by Brian; "Penina" Pete Hardisty, whose nickname will be explained in a later chapter, his business partner Mick Coppinger, with a razor sharp wit; Graham "The Duff" Duffield, who was to later become Chairman of the club; John "Basher" Westwood, the scrap man, in more than one sense of the word and whose side you would rather be on in a fight; Riki "Builder" Birch, who carried out major structural surgery on our house in Linthorpe; Ray "Rainbow" King-Lane, the paint sprayer, known also as "Ray the Spray"; Peter "The Carpet" Horsefield, carpet fitter to the millionaires; Alan "The Gallon" Godson; John McCart, the stockbroker who was to become my main sponsor at the 2005 General Election and Solicitor John "Tatey" Tate and last but by no means least, Patsy, all of whom defected from Acklam Park to the Cons. The squad there was strengthened by the periodic guest appearances of some of the Acklam Park diehards and other characters like John Shaw, his business partner (later to briefly become mine) Keith McGuinness, Trevor Hirst, Norman Craggs, the Quinns – Michael, senior and junior, and later some young blood in the form of Graeme Craggs, Paul Radigan and my son Tim before he emigrated. Another old 'tabler' Stevie Lowe re-married and moved to Aberdeen. We missed his funny jokes – Stevie Joe Lokes, as Chris called them. Invariably corny you could always tell them to the kids. Here's an example: "Can you name six fish beginning with 'H'?" (Answer at the end of the Chapter.)

Among those who stayed loyal to Acklam Park were Ian Sanderson, Paul Adams, John Tate's brother Adrian, an individual I nicknamed Shep and Sandy Shaw who later returned to his native Glasgow to run Arnott's financial services operation there. Adrian, in his year of captaincy at Teesside Golf Club, sadly contracted a rare disease of the blood and died leaving a widow, Christine, and three children.

One of the reasons that we evolved into a quasi-exclusive group of drinkers was that we found each other's company to be constantly stimulating and interesting. There were however certain people who would join the company purely to talk about themselves or about a subject which may be of interest to them, but rarely to anyone else and who lack the sensitivity to realise it and refrain. These individuals were skilled intruders who had developed strategies to infiltrate and bore us. The individual I have in mind would maintain his position in the circle of the company at the bar until he was able to seize an opportunity to isolate the person standing next to him which, because I am more polite than most, was all too often me. He would edge his way in between his prey and the rest of the company until he was in a one-to-one situation, whereupon he could pounce and then monopolise the conversation. On the occasions I was targeted I felt like a sheep separated from the flock by a well-trained collie, hence the name I gave to these human sheepdogs. Those of you who have been singled out in this way or in other similar situations will I am sure, identify with me and will recognise your own particular "Sheps". There are quite a few of them out there. I wasn't the only one of course to be singled out to be the subject of tedious discourses. Brian was also occasionally shepherded but he was not as patient and long suffering as me. I remember him on one such occasion in Acklam Park becoming increasingly irritated and itching to get back to the general company. Unable to contain his exasperation any longer he told his tormentor quite bluntly that he was boring him, which of course Shep totally ignored. "Look," said Brian eventually, "will you just fuck off." We shouldn't have been surprised by Shep's response. "Ok," he said, "but before I do can I just tell you about…!" Undeterred he continued until Brian turned his back and walked away.

At Acklam Park we always drank whilst standing at the bar and whilst this may be a very sociable practice, it does make the company vulnerable to anyone who feels like butting in to the conversation. Whilst "butters in" often have amusing and interesting things to say and are welcome, some don't and are not. From our table at the Cons Club we could assess the credentials of those we may wish to invite to join us. We didn't have a specific corporate policy in this respect, it just became an unwritten and unspoken convention. I suppose we were perceived as a quite arrogant unsociable clique really. A club within a club, one older member called us. I knew what he meant and it made me feel uncomfortable. It was, after all, a social club. Occasionally I stayed at the bar and had a chat only to be greeted on my return to 'our' table with remarks like, "Tired of your new friends are we?" I was made to feel like a traitor. Our vague selection process however ensured that the conversation at our table was always stimulating, relaxed and uninhibited. An escape from reality. Men go out for a drink to socialise and forget their troubles. Women, it is said, do so to talk about theirs. That isn't to say that we didn't share problems with each other or support and help each other, often in a meaningful and practical way. Chris Manson for example had a small flat above his butcher's shop and a few of the company whose marriages broke down were given accommodation there by Chris. The flat became known as Heartbreak Hotel. The club was undoubtedly influential in marital disharmony among some of its members. I honestly believe that our wives or partners would have preferred us to have mistresses. At least they would have seen more of us – it takes a lot longer to drink several pints of beer than to have sex – and they would have enjoyed the bonus of receiving regular bunches of philanderers' flowers. My own wife is not alone in hating the club with an intensity that most two-timed wives reserve for their human rivals.

If you can't beat 'em, join 'em, is usually sound advice, but no way will Chris set foot in the club, even when it became the victim of the greatest sacrilege of all and opened its doors to females. I don't really have a big problem with that in these days of economic survival. Working men's clubs have for years been aware of the extra revenue potential and have welcomed women. The difference is that most of them still retain a room or rooms in which men can enjoy each other's company uninhibited by the presence of women. What for heaven's sake is wrong with that, as so many women seem to think? Men don't want to infiltrate the WI or gate-crash on Tupperware parties. We wouldn't object if women too had their own havens and it's not our fault if they don't want them. There was a ladies' bar in the centre of Newcastle in the 1960's which folded due to lack of custom and the room at Brancepeth Golf Club reserved for ladies lasted less than twelve months because the ladies preferred mixed company to their own. I'm afraid that some women can cause trouble and disharmony where none existed before. Like they did at Newcastle Golf Club when it decided to accept lady members in the nineteen-sixties. It didn't take long for complaints to be made to the committee by the lady members who took tea on the veranda overlooking the eighteenth green and who took exception to the occasional bad language by the men on the green. The problem was solved by a triumph for common sense – the ladies were banned from the veranda!

I enjoy the company of women. It's just that I prefer where and when this pleasure occurs. I'm sure most women must feel the same way. Why then did the committee of the Cons Club have to destroy its tradition entirely? Was there some female influence at work behind the scenes? My pleas for a separate men's room were ignored despite its obvious commercial benefits. Such a room could have been easily and inexpensively created while the necessary alterations (to provide female facilities) were being carried out. 'Our' table, no longer an oasis for close male companionship, was invaded by 'outsiders' who joined it usually when the rest of us were 'well on' and our tongues loose – a fertile forum for scandal and an opportunity to gather material for potential gossip. On these occasions I found it difficult to relax, became irritable and left. The club was no longer the attraction for me that it once was, although looking on the bright side I didn't then drink as much and my health improved! Men and women are in many respects different species. But as Maurice Chevalier once said, "*Vive la difference!*"

To illustrate "*la difference*" and how females usually get their own way, I can remember an exasperated Patsy coming into the club one day gasping for a pint. He and his wife had been out shopping to choose some wallpaper. Patsy's suggestion that he had complete faith in his wife's taste and that, therefore, she should perform this task on her own resulted in an angry "You never take any interest in the house" – and his guilty capitulation. Once inside the decorating department of B&Q Patsy, in an effort to appear interested, picked up a couple of rolls which he thought were OK and sensibly priced, only for his wife to make some scathing remarks about his aesthetical inadequacy in this area. Eventually a choice was made. Patsy didn't particularly like it but was diplomatic enough to keep quiet. In fact, he exhibited feigned enthusiasm for Doreen's choice. Her tactics had been a complete success. Her objectives had been achieved. These were, first to get Patsy's approval for buying the most expensive wallpaper in the store, and secondly, by being able to blame Patsy if it didn't look right when it was hung. "You said you liked it in the shop. That's why we bought it!"

Doreen was a formidable adversary when it came to the battle of the sexes. She phoned Patsy at the club one day asking if it would be all right if they swapped cars, an unusual request which puzzled him but which, in order not to lose brownie points, he readily agreed to without question. Influenced by her surprisingly pleasant and mellow manner, he arranged for her to drive down to the club and exchange keys. All very civilised, Patsy thought, bearing in mind that when he left the house earlier he hadn't exactly done so with a kiss and a "Have a nice time pet" – far from it. After handing over the keys his wife's parting shot was: "Oh by the way, your daughter's in the baby seat. I'm going shopping. Goodbye."

Another example of Doreen's revenge was when one day she got annoyed with him because he was drunk but insisted on driving the car. Irritated by her criticism of his driving Patsy challenged her with: "You bloody drive if you think you can do any better!" He stopped the car, got out and walked round to the passenger side. As he did so his wife slid across into the driver's seat and drove off leaving Patsy standing with no coat on in the freezing rain.

Patsy's was not the only wife to exact retribution for her husband's irresponsibility. My own had her moments too. Whenever she hears music by the Irish group The Waterboys it reminds her of barbecues – and one in particular. It was a warm sunny summer evening and we had invited the Sutherlands round for the two families to enjoy some time together. I was watering the plants when they arrived and was easily persuaded by Brian to abandon this task in favour of an aperitif in Acklam Park Club, promising to return soon. I can't remember how many aperitifs we considered necessary but with our good intentions in tatters my telephone call to "explain" was received with some hostility. Deciding that we might as well be hung for sheep as lambs we stayed for another drink and returned home much the worse for this defiant decision. What made matters even worse was that the bonhomie which is a by-product of too many aperitifs resulted in the hospitable, but not particularly sensible gesture of inviting Hodgy to share our table at the BBQ. Chris was livid (in hindsight perfectly justifiably so) and to the tune of the Waterboys hit 'Fisherman's Blues' and much to the delight and amusement of the kids, she turned the garden hose on us and didn't stop until we were thoroughly soaked to the skin and Hodgy, with his best suit ruined, took the hint and fled!

Until he was eventually stopped and breathalysed, Patsy had carried on driving, quite oblivious to the drink driving laws. He had a good run for his money, however, which was surprising since he often left the club in some well advanced states of inebriation, ignoring all advice and pleas for him to leave his car. He always turned down offers of lifts because he needed his car for work the following day. He came into the club one night and related to us a really weird experience he had had the previous night in the car park. He had got into his car, started the engine and was convinced he was hallucinating when the cars at each side of him, with no drivers in them, started to drive away from him. Not only that, but the car behind him, again minus driver, had crashed into the back of him! Even this bizarre experience didn't stop him from driving home – minus rear lights. As you may have guessed, the stupid bugger had engaged reverse gear instead of first.

Patsy was convinced that there was a God of Drink who watched over and protected him and as living proof of His existence, revealed Himself in a miracle one Sunday lunchtime in Acklam Park Club. We were drinking in the men's room when Patsy's wife appeared in the doorway and shouted to him that his dinner was ready. He told her he wouldn't be long and then ordered another pint. Observing this act of defiance, his wife strode over and confronted him menacingly. "I'm coming now," said a then not so defiant Patsy. "So you won't need this then," said Mrs Patsy, picking up his full pint and with a flourish, dropped it on the floor, turned away and flounced out. She couldn't resist turning round to see what had caused all the cheering and laughter. Unbelievably, the glass had landed squarely on the floor where it stood intact without one drop of its contents displaced. Patsy, now convinced he was the chosen one, picked up his pint and drank it.

Needless to say, Patsy was a candidate for Heartbreak Hotel and became a guest there when he was thrown out by his longsuffering wife, who was really a nice caring girl – perhaps more towards animals than humans. Patsy had strongly advised her against adopting an Orang Utang through some animal protection charity. "I told you so," he said smugly when she received a £5000 vet's bill when the creature suffered a series of maladies, including ingrowing toenails, all of which were carefully detailed in the invoice from the vet. Patsy had access to some pretty sophisticated printing equipment at work!

Patsy's dad too would often beguile us with some wonderful accounts of his experiences. A devout Catholic, he swore like a trooper. On returning from a trip to the Holy Land which had been his lifelong ambition, he was full of it and related his experience to us enthusiastically and earnestly as follows: "I actually walked in the same fxxxxxg footsteps as Jesus and stood on the same ground as the cxxt did all those years ago." These days I assume that the Catholic doctrine no longer condemns its followers to eternal damnation for blasphemy or using the Lord's name in vain! A veteran of Tobruk and El Alemein during Field Marshall Montgomery's desert campaign in World War Two, he insists that the first German he ever saw was Bert Trauttman playing in goal for Manchester City at Ayresome Park in 1947. Alas, father time caught up with him and it was sad to witness the inevitable deterioration of such a vibrant character as he tried to match the sharpness of the repartee around the table and keep up with the younger ones. We humoured him of course and he was always welcome at the table by everyone except Patsy, to whom he had become an irritant. When his father collapsed in the club one day Patsy told us all to ignore his plight. "He's just attention seeking," said Patsy. Poor old chap. I suppose we'll all be there one day.

Patsy himself was an enigma. His lifestyle was lavish. We often wondered whether he had a money tree growing in his garden. The mystery was gradually unravelled after his arrest. He had embezzled a substantial sum of money for which he was convicted and sentenced to five years imprisonment. We all thought this was harsh – and so did Patsy of course. Our penal system is so inconsistent. He hadn't harmed anyone physically. He would have been better off feeding his extravagant lifestyle by mugging defenceless old ladies for which sentences are much more lenient than the one Patsy received. We missed his company in the club and even when he was released, after having his sentence reduced on appeal to two years, we didn't see him for several months because he had been tagged, which meant his movements were severely restricted. If you can see the logic in this, then please let me know. He had lost his job. There was no way he could re-offend. So what's with the tagging? Fine if he was violent and had to be kept off the streets because he was a danger to the public, but in Patsy's particular circumstances completely senseless. During his incarceration I regularly sent him magazines and letters but I doubt whether he enjoyed reading them as much as I did reading his replies. Patsy is both eloquent and articulate and with his permission I wouldn't mind trying to get his experiences and letters from inside published. Here are a few excerpts:

March 2004

"Pentonville Prison was the worst place I have been in my life. I was locked up twenty-three and a half hours a day without a TV, newspaper or books. Fortunately I had my radio with me and so was able to listen to the ball by ball commentary of England in the West Indies. Of course England ruined this by winning two days early. Typical England. They don't win a test match there for years and when I need them they let me down."

November 2003

"I have finally got a decent room in the posh wing. I was formerly in the Bronx and I'm now in Hotel California. Everything in here is referred to in slang. I'm beginning to think that I would get more meaningful and understandable conversation if I had been jailed in Bangkok."

March 2003

"I am having to learn a new modern language in here. It's a mixture of prison slang and undecipherable Geordie riddles. I will give you an example by reference to a conversation at dinner last night.

"We and wor tea bitch were snuggled when this cross threader burgled the family seat. It was a premier league pad spin. As luck would have it we hadn't drawn the boiler. The scag was posted well plastered. I was cradled thinking about giving it twist and shout on wor lass's smiley. Mind you I think Harold was putting the hat on and off the dolly. Didn't matter we were both in solitary and tarpaulined any road. I'd just chanted the beautiful noise and it was anthrax when he slipped the cat flap. It was the Russian Judge who'd pulled me for diluting yesterday. Fucking Pinnocchio. I had a gallon aboard but I was rattling for the yall. The car's used to a full tank on a night time. You know what I mean. Anyhow he started dismantling the scaffy around the pad but couldn't get a result. It was well interred. In the end Harold just told him to finish himself off and rolled over with a headache. Left him gagging for it. He was looking for love and he got two pushes and a squirt. Fucked off screaming for a divorce. It was funny as he ended up fucking the nest of fairies on S wing. Serves them right. Week-end banger-jockies! These screws should leave the Bronx lads alone and get over to Hotel California! Do you know what I mean?"

Using the Glossary, why not practice your skills at prison language in case you are ever locked up? Have a go at translating the dinner conversation. (Answer at the end of the Chapter.)

GLOSSARY OF PRISON TERMS

WE (me)
WOR (my/our)
TEA-BITCH (cell mate)
SNUGGLED (in our beds)
CROSS THREADER (bad prison officer/screw)
BURGLED (room inspection)
FAMILY SEAT (cell)
PAD-SPIN (search of cell - for drugs)
DRAWING THE BOILER (lighting a cannabis cig)
SCAG (cannabis block)
DOOR POSTED (hidden behind door frame)
PLASTERED (dug deep in wall)
CRADLED (in bed)
TWIST AND SHOUT (oral sex)

SMILEY (short for smiling face/female sex organ)
HAROLD (cell mate has a beard and looks like Dr Harold Shipman)
PUTTING THE HAT ON AND OFF THE DOLLY (masturbating)
SOLITARY AND TARPAULING (in our beds)
CHANTING THE BEAUTIFUL NOISE (farting)
ANTHRAX (smelling of fart)
SLIPPING THE CAT-FLAP (opening the door)
RUSSIAN JUDGE (unfair prison officer)
DILUTING (replacing part of one's urine sample with tap water)
PINNOCCHIO (an inordinate liar)
RATTLING (experiencing withdrawal symptoms)
THE YALL (beer)
DISMANTLING THE SCAFFY (taking the place apart. Scaffy = scaffolding)
PAD (cell)
INTERRED (buried in plaster)
FINISH HIMSELF OFF (proceed to a solitary orgasm)
GAGGING FOR IT (frustrated at failing to orgasm)
TWO PUSHES AND A SQUIRT (unsatisfactory result)
NEST OF FAIRIES (two homosexuals in next cell)
WEEK-END BANGER JOCKEY (bisexual)
THE BRONX (North wing and South wing)
HOTEL CALIFORNIA (K & L wing)

================

During Patsy's absence from the club big changes were taking place. Her son Stuart briefly reigned as club steward after Mavis retired. He was the ideal successor and the quality of the beer was maintained at the very high standard set by his predecessor. We all welcomed the continuity. Well, not quite all of us. The Secretary and he didn't hit it off. Stuart was his own man. He knew the job inside out. He should have been well looked after and left alone to get on with it. I knew only too well how important it was, having got valuable and reliable staff, to encourage and look after them, recognise how important they are to an organisation and to keep them sweet. Club committee men in my experience are rarely so sensible. Having achieved a position of power and authority, probably for the first time in their lives and usually with no man management skills, they want to assert themselves. Their attitude is often condescending and Victorian. Stuart may have been a server but he certainly wasn't a servant (in the Victorian sense) and he didn't take kindly to being treated like one. He left. Our loss was Great Ayton Cons Club's gain. His replacement, recommended and appointed by the Secretary, was a nice enough lad. I got on with him fine but I couldn't get on with his beer and had to drink Newcastle Brown Ale, aka "the amber nectar" and "journey into space". A copious supply of bottles was kept on the shelf for me. I drank it at room temperature as I had done many years ago before pubs got refrigerators. Newky Brown gained its reputation in the pre-fridge days so why does the label on the bottle say "Serve Chilled"? It's not the same smooth drink when it's cold.

It took a couple of years for the committee to realise that things weren't as they should be. Ignoring, it seems, all the statutory procedures, the new steward was summarily dismissed before a full investigation had been carried out and proper evidence established, leaving the club vulnerable to a charge of wrongful dismissal. I'm not sure of the final cost to the club of this fiasco but I am sure that it would have certainly exceeded by a long way the small increment in Stuart's salary which may have been enough to secure his loyalty and his services indefinitely.

The senior barmaid Rose was sensibly appointed as steward by the competent replacement Secretary, Richard Ward, and she, with the help of her sister Val, Rosemary, Joyce and Barbara, the lovely widow of the Acklam Park steward, Jack Atkin, restored the beer and the club to something approaching its former glory. Sadly Mavis passed away in 2006 and her funeral must have led to some speculation among those not familiar with her background. Among the mourners were over a hundred old men on their own. Few women of her age can have been remembered in this way by so many male admirers.

When Patsy was transferred to an open prison near the remote Yorkshire village of Wealston we were able to visit him occasionally. Naturally his family were given priority over us in the precious and not over-generous visiting quotas. Before my first visit I asked him in one of my letters how to get there. "Simple," he replied, "you just embezzle a load of money."

As his sentence dragged on a deterioration in his spirits could be detected and the tone of his letters lost much of their humour and optimism. Of course there must be a degree of punishment in our penal system and custodial sentences are very necessary, but surely their purpose should be primarily to protect the public and to rehabilitate the offender. In Patsy's case it served neither. When he was released Patsy was fortunate to have his Cons Club friends to support him although his wife didn't see it that way. I suppose she hoped that he would reform and curtail his drinking habits. He didn't and was once more banished to Heartbreak Hotel and only at Christmas was he conditionally welcomed back into the marital home. Now there's something different – being allowed IN on parole!

Considering his irresponsible behaviour and other exploits which we will hear more about later, it is not surprising that Patsy's marriage wasn't idyllic. There but for the grace of God go those remaining few members of the square table whose marriages are still intact.

At this point I would like to explain that Patsy exists only as a quasi "factional" entity. An eclectic version of us all. The stories attributed to him in this book are all true but actually relate to some of the other characters mentioned earlier whose names have been concealed for reasons of confidentiality. Some books and newspapers change the names of their characters to protect the innocent. Patsy is here to protect the guilty and to avoid embarrassment or offence. I hope readers will take into consideration Patsy's background of deprivation and find it in their hearts to forgive him. When explaining to me one day how poor his family were, he said if he didn't wake up on Christmas Day with an erection he would have nothing to play with!

===================

ANSWER TO STEVIE JOE RIDDLE

HERRING, HUSS, HADDOCK, HAKE, HALIBUT and HALIFAX. Well, Halifax is a PLA(I)CE isn't it?

===================

TRANSLATION OF DINNER CONVERSATION

"My cell mate and I were in our beds when a prison officer entered with the intention of searching our room for illicit drugs. It was a thorough investigative search. Luckily we were not indulging at the time and our supply of cannabis resin was securely secreted behind the door post. I was comforting myself with romantic thoughts of my beloved spouse with a particular and specific emphasis on the physical pleasures in our relationship. I had a vague suspicion that my cell mate was touching himself impurely in private. In any event we were both covered up in our own respective beds.

Regretfully I had recently broken wind and there was an unpleasant smell in the air when the door opened unexpectedly. It was the same prison officer who had conducted a voluntary urine test upon me earlier in the day. I suspect he is less than honest. It is true I had ingested eight pints of water but this was a reaction to the craving for liquid induced by alcohol deprivation. I am used to taking several pints of liquid on an evening. I'm sure you'll understand.

Do you know, without permission he started to conduct a thorough search involving a structural investigation of the walls. His efforts proved to be fruitless. In the end my cell mate told him his quest would remain unfulfilled and he should desist accordingly. My cell mate refused to discuss the matter further and suggested he continue his pointless task on his own. This obviously left him unrequited and unfulfilled and he left the cell abruptly in loud and offensive protest.

He went to the cell next door, which is inhabited by two homosexual inmates. I have little sympathy with these two as they are both married on the outside and only seek a relationship with another male when physically deprived of female company.

I really do wish that the prison officers would cease these searches of North and South Wing and adopt a fairer and more democratic use of their time. It seems they never search the better cells in K and L Wings."

Twenty Eight

HOULDER SHY HIGH

Sometimes you've just got to suffer your pride.
Chrissarism.

THEY SAY OPPOSITES ATTRACT and despite being different in so many ways my friendship with Brian has endured. I suppose he became the brother I never had. We do of course have much in common. We are, or were, both piss artists, we are keen golfers, we love our football and we both 'came out' on the same day when we met up with my old pal Ned South for a drink. His fall from grace as a lawyer and later RAF pilot meant that Ned had to take work wherever he could get it. The Zetland Hotel opposite Middlesbrough Railway Station was suggested by him as a venue because it was close to the site of the Cannon Park redevelopment where he was night watchman. He frequently deserted his post to drink at the Zetland and was obviously well known by the regulars. We were the only straights in the place but after a couple of drinks joined in the spirit of the proceedings. When in Spain do as the Romans do, remember? Things got a bit heavy when a couple of beefy transvestites arrived on the scene, invited us to a party and wouldn't take no for an answer. Having come out only a few hours earlier we quickly went back in again and then went out – making our escape via the toilet.

Our final family holiday with the Sutherlands which was to include an image-changing experience for me, took place in 1988. After finding a really cheap fly-drive deal for my family, the Suthies decided only at the last minute to join us in Florida. We had also rented earlier a condominium at Indian Wells on the Gulf Coast. Why do they call them condominiums in Florida and apartments everywhere else in America? The plan was that they would stay in our condo for a few days until they found a place of their own. The condo was quite spacious, more than adequate for the five Arnotts (Liz was by then at University), but when Brian showed no inclination to move out, the stresses of two families living under the same roof for three weeks began to get to me. There was no privacy. What would I have given for a call from Billy Connolly's Vaseline salesman! To make matters worse, though we were both entitled to a hire car Brian insisted that instead we should upgrade to only one – a people carrier to accommodate the eight of us and since he had been drinking steadily for ten hours during the flight, there was no way he would be dissuaded. So there was no escape for me, having recently given up smoking, and I had constantly to put up with three heavy smokers.

Things were fine at first. Brian and my youngest boy Jacob converted the open plan kitchen into BRIGSBY'S BAR, so named by a compilation of their two names, Brian and Riggs, one of Jacob's many nicknames, as I will explain later. Every time we needed a drink or snack from the kitchen we would be charged a few cents and Jacob thought it was great fun. So did we all apart from just a little filial jealousy.

I was only away for three weeks but by the time I returned to the UK my appearance had totally changed. I had been gradually losing my hair and, as we vain males do, I tried to disguise the fact by moving my parting closer and closer to my left ear and combing the wisps over the bare patch. Don't men who do that look stupid? But it's never easy for us to make the change. One day Kirsten and I conspired to give the others a laugh. In the style of the well-known singer of the time, Phil Collins, I slicked back my hair, put on some heavy shades and stood on our balcony which overlooked the pool area where the others were relaxing in the Jacuzzi. Kirsten hid behind a curtain and sang a song to which I mimed. The puzzled expressions on the faces of my audience were replaced by astonishment and then, when they recognised me, by admiration. "You look really cool!" enthused the boys and the others agreed. I replaced my Bobby Charlton hairstyle with my new cool one. It felt good.

However solid friendships may be, a sustained 24/7 involvement, particularly in a confined space inevitably put a strain on relationships and cracks began to appear. Tempers, already frayed, eventually erupted when Brian accused me of ignoring him in the British Pub at the Epcot Centre. I simply hadn't seen him. Oddly enough this didn't happen on the Gulf Coast where we had been on top of each other in the condo, but while we were staying in separate accommodation in Tampa where we had booked in for a few days while we did the Disneyland experience. The air was soon cleared and harmony restored however.

With Spain in danger of pricing itself out of the market, Florida, a golfers' paradise, offered perhaps the best value for money golf in the world. Brian and I had some memorable games, none more so than at a course which, paradoxically, I cannot remember the name of. We were the only whites there. Despite the abolition of segregation in the sixties, it is natural that the reality of integration would take many years to manifest itself, but our fears that we may be the innocent objects of diehtrapa – apartheid in reverse – were quickly dispelled by the welcome we received and by the warmth and friendliness of our extrovert playing partners, Clyde and Leroy. We were taken aback by their total lack of inhibition. Everything was said in a loud hip-hop style language. Greetings were yelled across adjoining fairways to their friends. "Howsa Wilhemena and those tots?" I recall Leroy yelling as I was about to take a shot and when Brian's approach shot on the seventeenth found the green Clyde slapped him on the back and with genuine enthusiasm said,"You'se on de dance floor man!" followed by, as the ball rolled close to the hole, a bear hug and "I can hear de music playin' for you!" So far removed from our reserved English reaction: "Jolly good shot sir. I believe you may be quite close."

Leroy and Clyde did not have a monopoly on flamboyancy, however. Not when it came to clothing. Brian was wearing his favourite golf gear – red trousers and a dazzling yellow shirt which later that year turned black when he wore it on Strensall golf course during the harvest fly season and millions of the little creatures mistook him for a giant buttercup. Sartorially our tastes are quite different. I wouldn't be seen dead in some things Brian wears and neither it seems would the criminal fraternity. Brian's car was broken into outside our house one night. Out of the two items visible on the back seat – a plastic Asda bag with a cabbage in it and his overcoat – the thief left the coat and stole the cabbage!

We again chose the popular holiday island of Ibiza for our first kid-less holiday together and it was nice for Chris and me to revisit Figueretes where we had spent our very first sunshine holiday with Liz. I have some good memories of Ibiza – the one-legged maid, the three-legged race, the nudists, chips – and chops.

When, on a previous Ibizan holiday, one of Jacob's sandals couldn't be found, Chris immediately suspected the hotel chambermaid, the look of whom she hadn't liked. The poor girl was reluctantly forgiven and vindicated when we pointed out that she actually had two feet and a single sandal would be of no use to her – and later when Chris found the missing sandal under the bed.

I really must make a big effort and try to find the photograph of an embarrassed Chris and Lynne struggling to reach the shore sharing Lynne's Bikini bottom after we had been frolicking in the sea and I had removed and confiscated Chris's. I never expected them to expose themselves, hoping to enjoy teasing Chris by leaving her stranded in the ocean for a while. But they too had flair in those days. It was a sight to behold. Emerging from the water like a couple of nymphs, fluffy ducks exposed and stumbling in their haste to reach the modesty of their beach towels, they provided much amusement to the dozens of onlookers, attracted at first by the commotion and then by the peep show. They were given a well-earned round of applause by the audience.

That same day, Brian and I decided to investigate the nearby nudist beach but our path was barred by a menacing well-endowed young male – they always are, aren't they? My hitherto interest in naturism diminished from that moment. I suppose if we had been starkers too he may have let us in. I wondered, since they don't have a problem exposing themselves, what they would make of it if I did join the colony and walked round naked except for a pair of trousers or shorts with my willy sticking out of the fly. Why should this be considered obscene whilst exposing yourself completely naked isn't? There go my weird thought processes at work again.

When the four of us are together we never ever speak the word *chips*. In those days there were only a few beaches where topless sunbathing was allowed and though Chris, the hussy, had bared her boobs before, Lynne was coy in that area and rather more reticent. She was eventually persuaded to get them out and, having done so, it didn't take the pair of them (Chris and Lynne, not her boobs) to become cocky and make an exhibition of themselves. Discreet topless sunbathing was one thing, but brazenly going into the beach bar and ordering chips was too much for the owner. He served them their chips but insisted that they must be eaten there and then and not taken away as they had intended. They were too embarrassed to enjoy their chips but the owner and the rest of his customers enjoyed watching their discomfort. The owner was making a point, too. When inside Spanish establishments it is protocol that tops must be worn always, not just by females but by men too – a custom often disregarded by ignorant tourists. You know the ones I mean – the tattooed, ear-ringed, pink, beer-bellied brigade – the ones who make you feel ashamed to be British. After that incident, whenever we are in a restaurant, instead of saying chips we always wiggle our breasts, a gesture which has evoked some quizzical glances from nearby tables and puzzled expressions from waiters.

For a little lass Lynne had a prodigious appetite. On a visit to Ibiza town we had lunch in a pretty little Plaza. Well, three of us had lunch and Lynne had *two*. Having devoured a starter and one plate of lamb chops, she ordered a second – and they were by no means small portions. She got through sixteen chops in all and then found room for a massive "postre". Pound for pound when it came to gluttony, Lynne must be up there with the best. Or is it the worst? We acknowledged her achievement by crowning her glutton of the week and carried her across the Plaza on our shoulders. Houlder Shy High, as Chris called it. Now, whenever one of us relates something we have done well it is always greeted with "Houlder Shy High eh?" Another entry in our private dictionary.

We had a few holidays in the Greek islands where, on one, at the upmarket flotilla resort of Fiskardo in Kefelonia, we found ourselves on a boat with TV presenter Juliet Morris taking part in an episode of the BBC holiday series 'The Travel Show'. We then went in search of winter sun to the Canary Islands. First to Gran Canaria and then, very reluctantly on my part, to Tenerife which I associated with lager louts and a Blackpool in the sun image. On Keith McGuinness' recommendation we stayed at the Victoria Court Apartments near the lively resort of Playa de Las Americas.

The females of the Sutherland family have very good singing voices, Kirsten in particular who I have no doubt could have made a very good living singing professionally. But one night in Churchill's Karaoke Bar it was her mother who was stealing the show and Brian didn't like it, especially when she was joined in a duet at the microphone by a handsome young man. Brian dealt with the situation, as you do, by ordering more drink in addition to the several gallons already on board. When the duet was encouraged by the audience to do an encore and then another, Brian joined in with his own encores of large local brandies and his mood became darker and darker. When Lynne was finally ready to leave, Brian wasn't, so the girls disappeared leaving me to eventually coax him away from his brandies. As we crossed some waste ground some dogs in a campervan started to bark. Brian went across and banged on the window and told them to shut up. They didn't take a lot of notice of him and their barking became more frenzied. They were evil black creatures, Rottweilers I think, and I was pretty scared. Not so Brian. The next thing I knew we were confronted by two big Nottingham lads, one of whom got hold of Brian and asked him if he wanted the dogs to be let loose. I was panicking in case he said yes but he didn't get the chance. Still unrepentant, Brian found himself on the deck. I joined him seconds later as I tried to jump to his defence. Brian was in a worse state than me. Boozed up and battered, I managed to get him back to his front door. Lynne did not respond to my hammering and I assumed she must be at ours. She wasn't. I had left Brian slumped on the doorstep with instructions not to move until I came back. When I did return he was nowhere to be seen. This time I got a response when I knocked at their apartment door, but when I received a bleary eyed confirmation from Lynne that Brian wasn't inside and tucked up in bed, my first thought was, *"Oh no, he's gone back to settle a score with the Nottingham lads!"* In his state he was capable of all manner of foolhardiness. I was left with little choice and trembling with fear I set off to rescue him. I can't describe the relief I felt when the bar from which our assailants had emerged before thumping us, was in darkness. On my way back I almost tripped over a body lying on the pavement. Had he been beaten up and dumped there? No. Brian was sleeping like a baby! Mohamed Ali had his Rumble in the Jungle and his Thriller in Manilla. We had our Fracas in Las Americas!

Lynne had been a big support during Chris' major operations. Her frequent hospital visits meant a great deal to Chris – and to me. Understandably Chris wanted me to be with her when she was poorly but I found it difficult to visit as often and stay as long as she would have liked me to and she couldn't understand why. But I had a lot on my mind and there was the small matter of a house to run and children to feed and look after. I visited every day, sometimes twice, but it was never enough. Being cared for in a private hospital may be good for patients but with unrestricted visiting times it can put a strain on their partners. I would find a way to repay Lynne for her solicitude.

Chester is a lovely historic city. We had stayed in a really nice hotel there once and I knew that Lynne would love it. With her fiftieth birthday coming up I arranged for her and Chris to have a few days break there as a birthday treat and thank you present for Lynne, who had her hair dyed red for the occasion. I booked the same hotel – four poster bed and all. The edge was knocked off the treat somewhat since Chris had not fully recovered from her hip operation and needed assistance with her mobility, so Lynne assumed the role of carer, pushing Chris around in a wheelchair. I composed a song for her which, as a surprise, everyone sang to her at her birthday party in the Tapas Bar in Norton.

THE GINGER MAID OF MIDDLESBROUGH
To the tune of Cockles and Mussels (Traditional)

In Boro's fair town – where the yobs get you down
There lived a fair maid by the name of Lynno
And though now retired, her help's still required
Pushing her friend round, streets far and wide.
In her task she is thorough, and not just in Boro
But also in Barney – and places beyond.

Chorus
Through streets here and there
She'd wheel her wheel chair
Surely- But slowly
Now that she's Five 'O'
Now that she's Five 'O' – Now that she's Five 'O'
She can't go no faster – Now that she's Five 'O'

She's now going to Chester, but not just to rest her
The kerbs will still test her, as she wheels her wheel chair.

Chorus
Through streets here and there
She'd wheel her wheel chair
Surely- But slowly
Now that she's Five 'O'
Now that she's Five 'O' – Now that she's Five 'O'

She can't go no faster – Now that she's Five 'O'

Up kerbstones she tussles. No cockles – but muscles
That ache as she bustles, her friend up and down
She continues to shove her, but she knows we all love her
And wish her good fortune, in this special year.
She's Five, Five 'O'
She's Five, Five 'O'
The Ginger Maid's Fifty
She's Five, Five 'O'

Gathering material for BBC's The Travel Show.
Juliet Morris and Chris sailing from Falaraki, Kefelonia.

Twenty-Nine

DISCO DAVE

Oh what a tangled web we weave
When first we practice to deceive.
Sir Walter Scott.

THE IDEA OF BIRTHDAY SURPRISES was introduced on Chris' fortieth when, as a 'special treat', I took her on a cheap package holiday to Falaraki on the Greek island of Rhodes. I don't think she was too thrilled that such a landmark in her life was to be marked only by a cheap holiday for the two of us. When we arrived at the airport, instead of waiting for the coach to transfer us to our resort, I organised a taxi, which she thought was a bit odd. "You're only forty once," I said magnanimously. "I know how to give a girl a good time." She didn't exactly say "big deal" but I didn't have to be a mind reader to get the message. Instead of the taxi driver taking us to our 'digs', a small apartment, I got him to stop at the road junction just a short walk away, explaining that I was hungry and we might as well eat then. Chris rarely needs persuading when it comes to food and we went into the local taverna. Halfway through the meal she felt a tap on the shoulder and heard a voice say, "Nice, is it?" She turned round and was amazed and delighted to see Lynne and Brian standing there. They had travelled on the same flight and how they had not been detected by Inspector Clueso remains a mystery. We call Chris Clueso because she is probably the most suspicious and observant (another word for nosey) person in the world. They had only been a few rows behind us on the aeroplane and I was on tenterhooks the entire journey. Surely Brian's persistent and very distinctive smoker's cough would be recognised! But it wasn't, and the surprise was very successfully accomplished. "Nice, is it?" became a part of our special vocabulary.

There was one particular incident during this holiday which I later recalled in a poem I wrote and which the four of us often have a laugh about when we reminisce together. Brian and I had gone off to play golf and the girls went into Rhodes Town for the day. Lynne was particularly keen to visit some old ruins. She's keen on that sort of thing. In fact, she's married to one. Whilst sight-seeing they heard a man's cough and looked up to find that the cougher was also a flasher and was playing with his exposed todger. As they fled, Chris shouted at Lynne to look back to see if he was coming. Lynne was furious. "I'm not going to give the dirty sod the satisfaction," she said angrily. Chris' request was quite innocent of course.

I sensed the air of subterfuge and mystery before my fiftieth but I was nevertheless taken aback when the doorbell rang and instead of the postman with a parcel as I had expected I was confronted by Brian, Peter Peyton and Mike Cherry in golf attire and carrying golf clubs. A surprise golf trip in the sun had been arranged for me. We flew to Majorca on 14th April 1986. This Balearic Island boasts some wonderful courses but as well as golf, Brian and I decided to challenge Mike and Peter to a tennis match. We knew that Peter didn't play but we should have checked Mike out. We lost five hundred pesetas and our status as reigning Valparaiso champions. Mike, it was later revealed to us, had been a County player.

Apart from a brief bout of Spanish tummy, the nocturnal beasts and an atmosphere for a while after Brian and Peter fell out, we had a great trip. I didn't know then and I can't recall now, what the spat between Brian and Peter was about but they kissed and made up. Brian and I had often shared a room together but this was the first time we had to share a bed. Lynne has my deepest sympathy. Brian doesn't snore. He does a variety of impersonations of wild animals. We visited Cellar Sa Prensa twice. On the first visit I did a Lynne and ordered a second helping of cochinillo but my bout of Spanish tummy allowed me only a bowl of soup on the second visit and I had to content myself with being a spectator while the others had gastronomic orgasms.

Following our Falaraki accomplishments in the art of deception, Lynne and I became comrades in conspiracy. Her assistance was enlisted to solve my annual Christmas crisis, until our cunning plan backfired one year. Some people are gifted gift shoppers – usually women who are much better at it than men. Chris always came up trumps and Christmas was always an exciting time, particularly for the children whose 'big' present was always kept as a surprise, hidden away until after Christmas lunch. The trouble was that Chris loved surprise presents too and I felt obliged to gratify her expectations in that area but I was always so busy at that time of the year and in any case I was useless. Perhaps they should have been, but presents were not top of my list of priorities. I remember one year Christmas shopping at Marks and Spencer in Glasgow. After an unproductive hour or so I pointed randomly in exasperation at three dresses on the rail and said to the assistant, "I'll have these." They were different sizes as the assistant helpfully pointed out. "No matter," I said, "my wife won't like them anyway so she can just change them for something she does like." I have to say that years later with more time on my hands I did improve and was able to put more thought into my choices. I can however boast one success story from those difficult days but it did turn out to be a bit of a pyrrhic achievement. Chris had accompanied me on a business trip to London and we had gone for lunch to Selfridges in Oxford Street where the salt beef sandwiches are to die for. After lunch Chris had tried on an outfit which was perfect on her. I told her I didn't like it, intending to return on my own later and buy it as a surprise Christmas present. I would get this one right! She couldn't hide her disappointment when I said she couldn't buy it. A strained atmosphere followed and spoiled what had been up to that point a nice day out together. I couldn't do right for doing wrong, as my mother used to say. Her attitude annoyed me. I thought about telling her what I had in mind. This would clear the air – but spoil the surprise, and I would be left with the task of finding another one. Or should I just not bother and tell her on Christmas Day what I had intended to buy her but didn't because of her attitude? That would just serve her right. I bit my tongue, endured the bad mood, swallowed my pride and secretly and resentfully bought it. Soft bugger.

Lynne came to the rescue the following year and a few Christmases after that. She was often out shopping with Chris and knew what kind of things she liked – or at least she thought she did. I gave her money and she would do my Christmas shopping for me which proved to be a perfect arrangement until Chris unwrapped the slippers. She said they were nice – as you do – and thanked me. I was pleased until I got the feedback from Lynne. Chris later showed her the slippers and said to her, "Can you believe he's chosen these horrible things for me! He hasn't got a clue!" Lynne replied tactfully, "Well, that's fellers for you."

Our deceit was much more effective when it came to organising Brian's fiftieth. He got wind of the romantic holiday for the two of them which was clearly not what he had in mind and he barely disguised his churlishness. His spirits sank further when only a handful of our pals joined us in the Cons Club for a lunchtime drink before he flew off to his romantic tropical paradise later that day. John Shaw was the last to leave "to get back to work" after staying for only one drink. Brian was struggling to hide his disappointment. "Come on," I said when there were only the two of us, "we mustn't keep Lynne waiting. You know what she's like about time keeping." I just caught a mumbled, "Who's bloody birthday is it?" from Brian as we got into my car. We had to drive past Acklam Park Club on the way home and I said, "Tell you what, Brian. Let's have a quick drink here and see if any of the lads are in." As he got out of the car his ears pricked up as he discerned the faint strains of 'Scotland the Brave'. His face beamed as he was piped into the club by the Scottish piper we had hired for the occasion, to loud cheers and applause from the dozens of family and friends, including John Shaw, assembled there to greet him. I felt so sorry for Lynne who had put in so much effort to make it a special occasion and was waiting in the doorway to greet him. Completely ignoring her, Brian swept past and joined his pals at the bar.

Instead of spending *her* fiftieth birthday at El Mirador on the island of La Gomera, Chris celebrated it at thirty thousand feet, having been summoned by

Brooks to sign a very important document on 3rd May 1997[1]. To make up for this, ten years later for her sixtieth, I planned another surprise for her and made arrangements secretly to tour Europe by rail. This had been an ambition of ours for many years. The original intention was to do the tour by car which was one of the reasons we had bought a new Ford Galaxy, but Chris then inexplicably lost her bottle and became the world's worst passenger. Before that surprise holiday we planned to visit son James in South America and Chris had hinted huffily that it would have been nice to celebrate her birthday there. This gave me an idea and I suggested that there was no reason why we couldn't have a party in Iquitos and invite all our Peruvian children. (I will explain this later.) It didn't have to necessarily be on the day of her birthday. At this point the exasperating suspicious side of Chris' nature manifested itself. "I know why we can't go in April," she said in that supercilious tone of voice which irritates me so much. "No you don't," I replied. Basically this was all about her not being suited because she had assumed that I wanted to spend the Spring and Summer in the UK playing golf and in her mind I would allow nothing to interfere with this. Yet I had just made plans right in the middle of the golf season for a three-week surprise tour of Europe and I bristled at her quite unfair insinuations. Instead of leaving it there she continued to goad me by putting me on the spot so that I would have to admit that I was a selfish sod and the reason for not having her birthday in Peru was that I wanted to be at home playing golf. I couldn't tell her the real reason of course because that would spoil the surprise. I tried to change the subject. I tried to evasively hint that there were other good reasons. She wouldn't believe me and persisted with the inquisition. Why is it when I tell her lies she believes me, and when I don't she doesn't? Eventually, unable to contain my frustration and righteous anger any longer and to shut her up, I told her the reason I was keeping her bloody birthday free was that I had planned a surprise for her. I didn't tell her what it was. I cancelled the arrangements and re-arranged the South America trip. So we both missed out on what would have been a really interesting European holiday.

By the time the four of us had all reached our three score we had mellowed somewhat and so had the intensity of our celebrations. Liz had produced our lovely granddaughter Daisy and Kirsten a grandson Harrison and later Findlay for the Suthies. Little Harry has probably added ten years to Brian's life expectancy. His visits to the club became less frequent and he started to go home early. He even attempted to cut down his prodigious cigarette intake after our very good friend and by then ex-butcher Chris Manson was taken into hospital for heart surgery. Being something of an expert on the subject, I was well qualified to help Brian to pack in smoking having done it myself five times!

---

[1] See Volume II

Lynne did have a sixtieth birthday party at which I was able to renew acquaintance with some of the old Arnott staff and their partners, including Jayne and "Mad Dog" Grant whose son James, a promising young billiards player, I met a few weeks later at my dad's annual billiards event. In keeping with tradition I wrote a poem for Lynne which I read out at her party:

A senior citizen.
Who would have thought.
Lynne an old lady? ... Nowt of the sort

Although you've reached sixty
...and got the bus pass
Don't regret it
Forget it... You're just a young lass

Yes it's time to look back
Now you've reached the three score
But look forward too... There's plenty in store
...and plenty of memories stored in the bank
Good times together
The vinos we've drank

The flasher in Rhodes
Unbuttoning his fly
The lunch in Ibiza... houlder shy high
Lots to amuse us
Down Memory Lane
But lots in the future
Will surely remain

And one thing's for sure
You'll never get bored
With the grandsons produced ....by Kirsten, our Ward
There's plenty to live for –
Your villa in Spain
Just a short journey
...and bingo, no rain

There are still many years.
Before life's journey ends
So Lynne – Happy Birthday – From us, your best friends

Derrick & Chris
26th May 2006

Her churlishness over my European surprise forgiven, Chris and I did fly to Peru to celebrate with eldest son James, accompanied by second son Tim.

Chris on a previous visit had befriended one of the families from Belen, a suburb of Iquitos, which is a conglomeration of rickety wooden houses on stilts – a bit like Venice except for the architecture, the filth and the abject poverty which has to be seen to be believed. Julio, the second son of the family, was a particular favourite of Chris' and, though somewhat apprehensive, she was delighted to accept Julio's invitation to his house, which consisted of one room in which all the family of twelve lived, ate and slept. James had faithfully promised to accompany his mother on this perilous excursion, for protection, to assist with the language and to help her to negotiate the precarious access to the house which was reached by a series of narrow wooden planks, below which were the murky waters of the River Nanay, in which the inhabitants both bathed and emptied their waste. Julio turned up at the hotel at the appointed time but James didn't. After half an hour or so Chris became agitated. She was so much looking forward to her adventure and didn't want to let Julio down. As the time dragged on she began to get angry and then absolutely furious when a telephone call was received from James to say that he had promised to pick up from the airport an old friend, Disco Dave, and the aeroplane had been delayed. Chris made her apologies to Julio and, still seething, she went with me to our room. She was so disappointed that her son considered it more important not to let down some casual acquaintance than keep his promise to her. James and Tim eventually put in an appearance, and James was greeted with the mother of all lambastings and his attempt to explain that his friend's flight was delayed only made matters worse. I had never before seen her so upset. After letting off steam she disappeared to the toilet and James took the opportunity to invite inside Disco Dave who had been waiting outside. Tired from his long journey he climbed into her bed and pulled the sheets over his head. Noticing the hump in the bed on her return from the toilet she demanded to know who the hell was in her bed and again blew a fuse when James told her it was no other than Disco Dave, the complete stranger whose arrival had caused such disruption to all her arrangements. As the sheet was pulled back she turned away in disgust at the sight of this unshaven intruder, then with a look of astonishment and disbelief on her face her head spun round and her eyes nearly popped out of her head at the sight of Disco Dave (aka youngest son Jacob who had also flown out to surprise his mam). The expression on her face had been unforgettable. It was a little while before Chris' emotions calmed down sufficiently for her to go over and give Jacob a long and tearful hug.

Her earlier disappointment was forgotten and Disco Dave's arrival made it a very special occasion. She got to meet the Belen family a few days later.

**Jim, Jacob and Tim with our favourite jungle family
from Belen Village, Iquitos.**

Thirty

INTERMITTENTLY BRILLIANT

Golf and sex are about the only things
you can enjoy without being good at.
Jimmy Demaret.

I LOVE SPORT. It's a wonderful substitute for fighting each other and I've never been much good at fighting – not physically anyway.

Football was my first love back in the good old days when football grounds, before all this sexist nonsense, had boys ends in which, for sixpence, youngsters could enjoy watching football matches without having their view obstructed by adults. I nevertheless chose to watch, as best I could, most of my football from the bob end, not the boy's end. That was because there was always someone willing to give me a 'squeeze' through the turnstiles. They were good old days too because there was no need for segregation of supporters. In those days there was banter. Today there is bother. In those days football was sport. Most of your team were local lads.

Fired up by the match, in the park afterwards there would be hordes of youngsters eager to emulate their heroes. These matches were contested often with more intensity than the real thing we had just been watching. I didn't always get picked for one of the teams. It depended on who it was who turned up with the casey. If he was a mate of mine then I'd be OK. It was a case of who you know, not what you know, even then. A casey (short for case ball) was a thick hard leather ball with an inflatable inner tube inside and fastened with a shoe lace which left a nasty bruise on your forehead if you were unfortunate enough to head that part of the surface. I also played a few times for the Wesley Methodist Youth Club but my physical frailty was a bit of a handicap. Ability, at that age, was no substitute for bulk. After my demob from the army I missed playing football and when I moved to Newcastle with RT&G I got to play in the Insurance Institute inter-company tournaments, but I wasn't in training and my performances were not enhanced by drinking a couple of pints at the pre-match briefings which took place in the Kenton Bar across the road from the sports field. I played on the left wing because I was quick but after a bright start I would be knackered and I would hide. To make sure no-one passed the ball to me I would stick to my defender like glue. I marked many a right back out of the game. I decided to hang up my boots in 1957.

My tennis career also came abruptly to an end in 1986 at the Tennis World Sports Centre in Middlesbrough when at seven o'clock in the morning (that's how keen I was) playing against Paul Adams, some fifteen years my junior, in my determination to beat him, I stretched for a low back hand and let out a scream of agony as a tendon in my wrist snapped causing me to lose the point, retire and concede the match. I don't like losing. The pain was excruciating – and my wrist was quite sore too! I should never have attempted the shot at my age but I was determined to beat my young opponent. A case of willing mind but weak flesh. I had played a bit when I was younger but looking back it wasn't really sensible to take up the game again in my fifties. Not if I insisted on playing with the pace and enthusiasm of a teenager. Fortunately tennis is a game which can be watched with something approaching the enjoyment of playing and has given me and my wife, who is even keener on the game, much enjoyment as spectators.

My motor-racing exploits have already been mentioned. Channelling my aggression in this sport achieved for me a fair amount of success and as I have said earlier my sports car lap record still stands at Cadwell Park. I drove always at ten tenths and was lucky to escape with only one serious crash in which all I suffered was concussion, bruises, and a dent in my pride.

I would be guilty of self-deception if I classed myself as a mountaineer. I did get involved with ropes and crampons a few times in the Cheviot Hills and of course the Pyrenees in 1956 when I climbed Los Encantats (The Enchanted Mountains). When I was young I did a lot of hill climbing, though it's more hill walking than climbing these days.

Anyone who knows me will realise that of all the sporting activities in the world, the one I would be least likely to excel in is arm wrestling. Yet in 1995 I became the Teesside arm wrestling champion. One night after a heavy drinking session a crowd of us, including solicitor Trevor Hirst, had gone back to our house. Trevor was generally acknowledged as the area's number one arm wrestler and in a flippant moment of bravado I challenged him. He took the challenge seriously and laid on the floor with his arm poised for action. "Bloody hell," I thought, "he'll break my bloody wrist!" His arms were thicker than my legs. How could I back out without losing face – and the use of my right arm during my period of convalescence? As I hesitated, desperately trying to think of a way to back out of my predicament, Trevor was distracted for a moment and when he turned his head to talk to someone behind him – I think it was Brian – I pounced and pinned his unprepared flaccid arm to the carpet. He claimed a void contest and foul play. I claimed that it counted because he was in the 'ready' position. He claimed a re-match. I refused, claiming the title, unofficially of course, and I am still undefeated to this day. That night I retired from the sport of arm wrestling.

Trevor is one of those larger than life characters you meet in serious drinking circles but Trevor was anything but serious. A serial practical joker, he reminded me of someone from Billy Bunter's Schooldays. His office was in Albert Road where most of Middlesbrough's professional firms were located. One Christmas Eve morning he telephoned each one pretending to be an official from the Water Board, saying that the area was subject to a serious loss of water pressure and would the office mind if it co-operated in carrying out a simple test. The scenario went something like this:

"Would you mind flushing your toilets for me?"

A few minutes later: "OK, I've done as you requested."

"Oh dear, we haven't noticed any significant change in pressure. Would you mind flushing repeatedly for the next hour or so?"

At that time professional people in the area met regularly for a drink in Henry's Bar after work. Trevor was waiting for them. Each one commented on the bizarre request they had received from the Water Board and a debate raged over the incompetence and unprofessionalism of that particular utility. Trevor enjoyed every minute of it.

Henry's was particularly busy on a Friday night and popular with young girls out on the town. A feature of the bar was a collection of potted plants. One particular Friday there was pandemonium as girls left their drinks behind and fled screaming into the street. Don't ask me where Trevor got the dead mice from, but he had carefully arranged them in every plant pot with their front feet on the rims and heads peeping over them. It took just one girl to spot them and lead the hysterical exodus.

Another of Trevor's escapades resulted in the temporary closing down of the Abbey National Building Society office. Trevor was a keen fisherman and was one of the few people in the world who had a degree of expertise in the incubation cycle of maggots. He needed to know when they were at their prime and most active and therefore attractive to hungry fish. He had gathered together hundreds of them in their final stage of incubation and somehow managed to introduce them into the central heating system of the Abbey office. The heat had, as planned, hatched them and a plague of flies pervaded the building which had to be evacuated, ensuring that after work Henry's would again be the scene of merriment induced by another Trevor triumph of outrageous pranks, of which there were many more. Typical of the man was the time he spilled beer over his trousers so he took them off and asked the barmaid to hang them over the radiator and carried on drinking in his underpants as if nothing had happened.

Athletics. Now there's a sport you are either good at or you quickly lose interest in. It's an almost impossible task for a games master to motivate the nine out of ten kids who range from average to useless. I suppose we had to be there to encourage the faster lads by making them feel good when they beat us. Why did they make us run when, left to our own devices, we could have found some alternative which would at least stop us from developing inferiority complexes? It wasn't until many years after leaving school that I thought I had my best opportunity for success in the field of athletics. I was invited to run in a charity race which at first I declined until they told me it was for blind and disabled people. I changed my mind. Surely I would be able to beat *them*. I came last. They had conned me. Not one of my competitors was blind or disabled.

Being a good billiards or snooker player demands a higher level of concentration than I have been endowed with and it doesn't help because these games are always played in social environments and invariably with various degrees of alcohol in the system. I had to make a decision. Did I want to be good or did I want to enjoy it? It's that sort of game. How often did you see Steve Davis or Stephen Hendry smile? The maximum break you can achieve at snooker is 147 by potting all the reds followed by blacks then all the colours. In only my second game I made a break of 121. I potted a red (one point) a yellow (2 points) and another red. On the few occasions I played billiards these were with Paul Radigan and we both enjoyed our encounters because, like me, Paul is competitive and likes to win. On the other hand my games of snooker were usually played in fours which can be frustrating. I enjoy the banter but prefer head to head contests. To do anything justice I must give it my undivided and individual attention and so far as snooker is concerned, the better the banter the poorer the performance. I did reach a few semi-finals in the Cons Club and of course I must be the only player to hold a winner's trophy without playing in a final. I refer of course to the Butlin Cup in 1967.

Inevitably, associated as it is with pubs, I played darts in my younger days but only for fun. The first TV programme to feature darts was called Double Top and it was televised from different venues throughout the country. On the occasion when the cameras visited Teesside the event was hosted by the Coatham Bowl in Redcar. Quite a severe disturbance broke out among the spectators and when Eric a dedicated local cop who was watching on TV saw this, even though he was off duty, he contacted the station and several squad cars and a dog unit were mobilised to deal with the trouble. When they burst into the hall there was nobody there. Eric had been watching a programme which had been recorded the previous night!

Forty years after nicking off school to play bowls in Albert Park, I was again to experience that feeling of satisfaction as my wood nestled on the jack when, In 1988, I joined the Conservative Club in Orchard Road, Middlesbrough. Not because it had a bowling green but because it was my nearest watering hole when I moved back to Middlesbrough. Even then it was several years before I took advantage of the bowling facility and then only very occasionally. My participation was limited to the bi-annual bowls and snooker matches against Great Ayton Cons Club which were inaugurated when our club steward Stuart Payne left to take charge there. Apart from these events and a few friendly roll ups the only other competitive event I then played in was the Benny Ralston Cup which my partner Gordon Walker and I won in 2003. We might have won it again in 2006 but our match was claimed by default by one of our opponents because I was unavoidably delayed by a mere half an hour – the same opponent who had, some years earlier, tried to claim by default a snooker tie against me. In an effort to persuade the sports secretary to award him the tie, he had written on the entry sheet that he had tried to phone me several times to arrange the match. How strange that there were no messages on my answer machine. I later turned out whenever I could for the Cons Club team in their Walker Cup matches against other local bowling clubs.

Although, except for a couple of trial matches in first year at school, I didn't play rugby, I did and still do enjoy the sport from the safety of the touchline or grandstand. I used to sponsor some West Hartlepool RUFC matches and I was of course a member of Middlesbrough RUFC based at Acklam Park, the scene of many a lengthy drinking session. I've been on a few memorable rugby trips with the club too, but only the one day ones to Twickenham and once to Murrayfield. I don't think even *my* liver could have coped with the weekend ones to London, which were later to include "Monopoly Crawls" which involved having a drink in every place featured on a monopoly board.. The trips were always superbly organised by Richard Ward who later became Secretary of the Cons Club and rescued it from its financial plight. The day trips themselves were mini marathons. The well-stocked coach would leave Acklam Park at seven am and I would try to pace myself and resist having a pint until we got to Northallerton (about twenty miles down the A19) by which time animals like John Westwood would be on their third! On arrival at Twickenham the coach would park in its allocated spot – one of the bays in the Twickenham Council refuse disposal site, pressed into service to cope with the huge influx of people on International day. Richard would then open the luggage compartment and remove and erect collapsible chairs and tables, on which would appear huge quantities of excellent food and wine. A triumph of good organisation by Richard and those who assisted. Surprisingly I never once was troubled by smells, either because of the favourable wind direction or oblivion due to the amount I'd had to drink. Or maybe the households in TW1 didn't get their bins emptied that week.

After a short walk past Harlequins ground and club house we would continue drinking in the Twickenham car park courtesy of old rugby acquaintances who had managed to qualify for a car parking space where they were able to enjoy their picnics in relatively fresh air. Apparently there is a twenty year waiting list to pay a small fortune just to park your car there for one day a year. Inside the ground the atmosphere was always brilliant. No crowd segregation – just like soccer in the good old days. Everyone had flasks and when England scored we would pass our flasks to nearby French, Scottish or Welsh supporters and they would reciprocate when their team scored. The greater the score the ghastlier your hangover the next day.

The return journeys were always broken at the same Northampton pub for a game of skittles, more beer of course, and a meal accompanied by raucous rugby songs. A John Westwood solo, 'Men of Harlech' was my favourite, delivered by John strutting round the restaurant slapping the heads of the diners, complete strangers, who always took it in good spirit. After the singing subsided on the long journey back up north, those who hadn't fallen asleep joined in the inevitable card schools. On one trip John Hodgson and I were the only two left in the school, the others having cashed in or crashed out. During the last few miles of the journey I had an amazing run of luck and playing double or quits I had, by the time we reached the gates of Acklam Park, won in excess of two million pounds! He still hasn't paid me even though I let him off with one million, and he's now left the country. I did manage to track him down. Not for the money, that wasn't really serious, but as an excuse to visit the Turk & Caicos Islands in the Caribbean, where he became a deep sea diving instructor after his engineering business and his relationship with girlfriend Katy collapsed.

I wasn't sure whether to include something about horse racing in this chapter which I intended to devote to sport, although they do say that it is the "Sport of Kings". I do believe that sport in its truest form should involve some degree of physical effort from human sportsmen or women. Jockeys just sit in a saddle and let the horses do all the work. Their success depends almost entirely on their mount's ability to run and jump quicker and better than the other horses in the race, but I'm sure the jockeys would not agree with me. At least they haven't included horse racing as an Olympic event. Not yet, at least. Probably because they wouldn't know whether to give the medals to the horses or the jockeys. Nevertheless, the so-called Sport of Kings does provide an excuse for us to indulge one of our basic instincts – greed. Three of my friends have owned horses, either individually or as part of a syndicate. Ron Evans (Pink Sensation), Adrian Tate (De Jordaan) and Iain Ferguson (Greylock). This helped to sustain in me a casual interest in the pastime. I only saw Iain's horse once. We paid a lad from Acklam Park to drive my new Rover car up to Kelso so that Iain, Brian and I could have a good drink. The meeting was "over the sticks" and despite jumping more fences than the other horses in the race Greylock finished last. For some reason it imagined fences that weren't there and jumped into the air between fences. Fortunately we didn't lose money. Iain had warned us that his horse wasn't ready yet. I think he was more than ready – for the knackers' yard. It was a ridiculous sight and Fergie who was so keen to show off his new pet was mortified. Never mind we had a good day out rubbing shoulders with the gentry in the owner's enclosure.

I haven't been to many horse race meetings but those I have been to I've thoroughly enjoyed. There were the occasional hospitality tent trips as a guest of insurance companies and trips to York races from the club, always relying on my dad's third best in the *Daily Mirror* betting forecast system to make me a bob or two Not very scientific but it rarely failed to throw up a couple of winners for me. Less haphazard was Ron Evans' "system" which was to bet on the horse which had travelled the furthest distance to get to the meeting. The horse's owner, reasoned Ron, would not send it a long way if it didn't have a chance. The secret to amateur gambling though is never to think how much you can win but rather how much you want to or can afford to lose. If it's £100 then that's all you take with you and if you pick an early winner then by all means have a punt with the bookies' money – otherwise stick to your ten or twenty quid a race. The possible exception to this is if you get a really good tip or if there is a good omen or two. I know this from experience because twice I've had good omens and twice, to my cost, I've failed to recognise them. One was on a golf trip in 1987 which I'll tell you about later and the other was on my one and only trip to the Cheltenham Festival, organised superbly by Adrian Tate.

I pride myself on being a good 'susser'. Putting a little effort into research can make such a difference. Why pay £100 when you can find something better and more interesting for £50? On the occasion of the Cheltenham trip I awarded Adrian the accolade of 'Susser Supreme'. He had found in the *Daily Telegraph* an ad for accommodation in a wealthy Cheltenham suburb – a large private house with tennis court and snooker room. Bed, breakfast and evening meal was made available to us for a fraction of hotel prices, with the bonus of being allowed to bring our own drinks, which would save us even more money – a lot more. Eight of us made the trip. Adrian of course, his brother John, Ian Sanderson, Paul Adams, Declan Davies, John Hodgson, Brian and me. The journey down was pretty scary. John Hodgson's new Jag suffered from severe under steer which we soon realised was due to the enormous amount of booze crammed into the boot. I didn't think we would get through it all. But we did. Sue, the owner of the house, was very amenable and very attractive too. She was going through a divorce and until all the mess was sorted out she had decided to rent out the house for a bit of pocket money and a bit of company. If it was attention she was seeking then she certainly got plenty. There would be arguments amongst us about who would take her dog for a walk and we generally vied for her favours. Except me, of course, who was happily married! We were joined at the races by Sue and some of her friends, one of whom was the wife of an England cricketer. An enjoyable day was had by all. Most of it was spent in the Champagne Bar. Not because we were flush with winnings, but because the Guinness Bars were heaving and you couldn't move. We hadn't intended to spend all day in the champagne bar but after a few bottles we couldn't be bothered to move on. The house champagne was 'only' £27 a bottle but they soon ran out of that and we had to go on to the medium quality stuff at £37. When there was none of that left we finished up drinking the Moet at £57. Well, you only live once!

Why on earth didn't I put my shirt on the big winner? Sue's children were away, presumably with their dad, and I slept in Toby's room. The name of the big winner? Toby Tobias.

Probably because of its association with the royal and the rich, there's something about the horse racing scene that has a hypnotic and delusory effect on your senses. You live for a while in a Walter Mitty world of self-deception. You recklessly splash money around as if it was unimportant and trivial. You show off. You spend £57 on a bottle of champagne – and you don't even like the stuff. Then after five losing bets you back a winner. What do you do? Say thank heavens for that and with a sigh of relief replenish your now empty wallet? Oh no. You give your winning ticket to the attractive barmaid who has already made a small fortune out of you in bonuses and tips. That's exactly what I did. Bloody fool!

Adrian Tate was a very good golfer and he and his friend and golf partner Declan Davies were a formidable two-ball team. Much better, it has to be said, than Brian and I. Whenever I meet Declan he always mentions the match we played at Fulford, a lovely but challenging championship course near York. In what we later believed to be a rash moment we had thrown down a challenge and played them for £10 a man which was equivalent to the green fee and in those days a lot of money. Brian and I gelled well as a team and at three holes up after sixteen, won the match. Over lunch in the club house, Brian and I gloated over our victory – as you do – and we were challenged to play another match in the afternoon, this time for £20. Thanks to a little gamesmanship we again triumphed. From something overheard by Brian it became clear that Declan was becoming exasperated by what he considered to be our slow play. After hitting my tee shot out of bounds on the next hole, instead of carrying on playing, I went in search of my ball knowing that I had little chance of finding it and knowing that this would irritate Declan. It did. His play was affected and we won this second match when we went four up on the sixteenth hole. By then we had them on our hooks and went on to record a third victory on the snooker table, this time for even higher stakes. Losers were to pay for a meal on the way home at the prestigious Cleveland Tontine restaurant. Magnanimous in victory Brian and I paid for the meal out of our winnings to end a wonderful day out.

I could have been a scratch golfer. Perhaps if my father had been a stockbroker and not a steelworker. Perhaps if he had been a member of a golf club instead of a working man's club. Perhaps if he had introduced me to the game when I was three, like Tiger Woods' dad did for him. Perhaps, if I hadn't allowed things to intrude on the development of my golfing skills. Things like getting married (twice), divorced (once – so far), raising children (four), working (forty-three years), holidays (as often as I could) and drinking (every night). But proficiency at golf only comes with practice and dedication. Since I didn't start to play until I was in my forties I had a lot of catching up to do. Without Tiger's early good fortune, it wasn't going to be easy. It needed commitment and dedication. It needed frequent practice and regular rounds and I think where I went wrong was substituting rounds of drinks for rounds of golf. Proposal forms took precedence over putting. Boozing over bunker practice. Children over chipping. Parenting over pitching. Don't get me wrong, I love my kids and would do anything for them but I don't get from them the same feeling of exhilaration as I do from a well struck seven iron to the heart of the green – not half a dozen times a week anyway! I hope they appreciate the sacrifice I made for them.

Fortunately I do have a big advantage over Tiger. He's handicapped. I could never figure out why, when I joined my very first golf club, they told me that they had given me a handicap when, in fact, they did precisely the opposite. They allowed me to make twenty-one mistakes in my round of golf and still return a scratch score, whereas poor Tiger isn't allowed to make any mistakes at all. So surely it is he who has the handicap and not me! So Tiger, if you ever get round to reading this, I'm throwing out a challenge to you – eighteen holes match play for a pound, a pound and a pound, with 20p birdies and ouslems – and I'll buy you a few pints of John Smiths in the bar afterwards. Tiger Woods may well replace the great Jack Nicklaus as the greatest golfer of all time. But he isn't perfect. His opening tee shot at the 1997 Open Championship at Troon was sliced into some pretty severe rough followed by a wonderful comment from one craggy Scottish spectator: "Aye laddie. Ye'll nae turn this intae a pitch and putt."

When it came to dedication and attention to detail, there was none to compare with the great Seve Ballesteros. On practice day at Troon in 1989 Brian, John Shaw and I walked round with the Spaniard, Lee Trevino, Tom Watson and Greg Norman. On each green Seve practised his putting but missed the hole by a very big margin. "You'll have to putt better than that tomorrow, Seve," said John. "Ah," replied the great man, "but the hole won't be there tomorrow!" – following which he proceeded to putt from every corner of the green and in every direction, committing to his memory for the following big day, every undulation. The importance of practice is encapsulated in another wonderful story about the great Arnold Palmer. "You got lucky there," said a spectator after Arnie had holed out from an almost impossible lie. "Yeah," was the reply, "The harder I practice the luckier I get." Sadly, on the 7th

May 2011, Seve passed away at the tender age of fifty four. *The light which burns twice as bright only burns half as long.*

There is a special camaraderie within the game and great rapport between the players themselves, the players and spectators and between fellow spectators. At the Canary Islands Open at Costa Adeje, Tenerife in 2004, won by local North East lad Kenneth Ferrie, I was seated in a perfect vantage spot between the sixteenth green, the seventeenth tee and the eighteenth green. The temperature was in the eighties and I had just bought a pint of cool lager and settled down to enjoy the closing stages of the tournament. The Scot, Ray Roberts, was in contention but needed at worst to par the final three holes. He bogied the sixteenth and as he trudged sweating towards the seventeenth tee he came over to me, offered me his driver and looking wistfully at my cool lager, said, "I'll swap you."

Another camaraderie story I love involved Brian who was on holiday in Spain when the Spanish Open was being held at Valderama. Like Brian, lots of other tourists took the opportunity to go along. The Spaniard Canizares with a difficult blind shot to the green had spent ages before deciding how he would play it and when he did, his ball finished only a few inches from the hole. "Excuse me," said one of the tourists who was standing next to Brian, "What do you call this game that they're playing?" Taken aback by what appeared to be such a strange question, Brian hesitated before replying, "It's called golf." The tourist thanked him for the information before muttering, "I wonder what they call the game that I play then."

Thanks to the handicap system mediocre golfers like me can still be competitive. In what other sport could I play against the World Champion and hope to compete? This is one reason why golf is such a wonderful game, a game for everybody. If you can walk you can play – from three to one hundred and three, which is how old Arthur Thomson was when at Uplands Golf Club, Victoria, British Columbia in 1972, he shot his age in a round which included a hole in one.

There are so many other things too that make golf the King of Sports. It can be played individually or as part of a team. There are several different formats designed to suit different occasions and different abilities, including stroke play, stableford, texas scramble, fourballs and foursomes (mixed or otherwise) and match play. You can compete against other players or you can play alone and compete against the course and the weather. It is a social game played over nineteen holes, the final one of course being the club house where the events of the previous eighteen are analysed over a drink or three! I always play the nineteenth well. But then I've practiced more at that one. The game is played in the open air often among stunning surroundings and is good exercise. Some say it is a good walk spoiled. They either haven't played or have tried and failed. Above all else, however, it is the game's etiquette and sportsmanship which makes it exceptional. It must be the only sport played professionally in which players not only don't cheat but actually penalise themselves. An example of the true spirit of golf that sticks in my mind occurred at the end of the Ryder Cup match between the late Payne Stewart and Colin Montgomerie in 1999. Monty had been heckled unmercifully by the Brookline gallery. Fortunately the disgraceful behaviour of American fans is not shared or condoned by their players. "We don't hate you, Monty!" yelled one fan, "We just want you to lose." This is probably the nicest comment the Scot had heard throughout the entire round. On the final green Monty had a tricky putt to win the match. Payne Stewart said to his caddy, "After what he (Monty) has been through he doesn't deserve to make that putt." In conceding the putt he lost his match but restored some US dignity and salvaged something from the wreckage that was to mark the occasion of that particular Ryder Cup match.

Unfortunately ungentlemanly conduct is not confined to the Americans. Etiquette requires that slow players do not hold up following games, which should be allowed to "play through". In 1982 Brian and I were playing behind a German five ball – four golfers and their dog with a football, which would be kicked around from time to time to keep him occupied. For several holes we had been held up at every shot and our body language failed to impress them. Finally, with two holes left to play, they waved us through after spending a good ten minutes looking for a lost ball only fifty metres or so from the tee. As we walked through to play our second shot I spotted the German's lost ball and pointed it out to him. Instead of thanking me and waiting for us to play our second shots, he actually played his ball through us! Etiquette or no etiquette, the next German ball I find will be firmly stood on!

There are referees at top pro golf events but they are there simply to interpret the rules. Unlike other sports they are not there to stop cheating and gamesmanship. They do not scrutinize every incident like they do in other sports. They don't, or shouldn't, need to and in most amateur or friendly games referees don't exist at all. The players themselves are their own referees. Only they decide whether to impose etiquette, discipline and rules on themselves. On one of the Unicorn Golf Society's annual Scottish trips my yellow ball was plagued by insects and in attempting to dislodge one I accidentally moved my ball. I penalised myself. My playing partner when marking my card after playing out the hole, queried my score and I told him about the penalty incident which he had not seen. He told me that he would overlook it but I insisted he put down the correct score including my penalty. That told me a lot about him and perhaps why he often came in with good scores off a bandit's handicap of twenty-four. Since Durham City I always play with a yellow ball and the reason is that I can easily identify it. I was playing there in a competition in a three ball with Graeme Craggs and Lol Davison. Our three drives were close but just off the fairway. Lol, without looking closely at it, identified my ball and instead of checking as I am required to do under the rules, I played it. In holing out I discovered

I had in fact played the wrong ball. I added two penalty strokes to my score – and lost the competition by one stroke.

The Unicorn is a pub in Norton and has a thriving golf society ably run by Tim Stephenson and pub owner Alan Franklin. I was invited to join the society by a good friend Ron Evans who I first met during the construction of our new Middlesbrough offices. Ron was an ex-cricketer turned golfer – and a very good one at that. On one of the Unicorn Scottish tours I had my handicap slashed to twelve, the lowest I have ever achieved although there was one occasion in Tenerife when son Tim and I played with a couple of lads from Oldham, Martin and Neil, both low handicappers, and following our victory in the first match in which I played well below my handicap, Martin grumbled (as golfers do when they lose) and was surprised when, instead of the usual dispute, I immediately offered to play off 9 for our return match. We lost. But it was worth it so that I could boast later that I once played off single figures! My present club is the Brass Castle Middlesbrough Golf Club, not to be confused with the Middlesbrough Municipal Club. I say this not for snobby reasons, it's just that I would prefer not to be associated with the "Muni" even though I had a lot of time for Alan Hope the Pro and knew many sound members there. Armed with false handicap certificates a team from the Muni won the West of Ireland Classic two years running and may have won a third had their disgraceful dishonesty not been discovered. They have given the Muni a stigma and I hope they are thoroughly ashamed of themselves. What possible satisfaction could they have got from those hollow victories? They had somehow managed to obtain certificates from their club which stated handicaps several shots higher than their correct ones.

The problem of false handicaps is unfortunately evident, if not rife, within the amateur game, but fortunately only among those who are not yet a part of the real inner game of golf and needless to say it is not a problem at the higher levels of the game. My opinion is that unless and until players have been subjected to a proper assessment of their ability they should play off a maximum handicap of eighteen in competitions where prizes are at stake, so many of which are carried off by people who are not a member of a club, have no official handicap, claim to play off twenty-four or twenty-eight and come in with forty-four stableford points, i.e. eight shots better than their unofficial handicap. These pot hunters are not confined to non-club members and all too often include people who, having obtained a generous club handicap, don't enter the club competitions and risk having it reduced. At one of my old clubs, Chester-le-Street, members' handicaps were reduced if they didn't enter competitions. Other clubs should follow suit. In fact I would like to see golf's governing body, the Royal and Ancient Golf Club of St Andrews, do more by at least issuing guidelines and recommendations for the regulation of the game at its grass roots and to encourage those of us who are proud to play off a proper handicap even though this may not win us many trophies.

Before joining Middlesbrough Brass Castle, I had been a member at Teesside. After playing there one day Gary Dodsworth and I were enjoying a drink in the bar when all hell let loose. John Kelly one of the other members, after changing in the locker room, discovered that his wallet was missing from his trouser pocket. Convinced the culprit was in our midst, he ordered that no one must leave the room until they had been searched. Angry and insulted by John's accusation, some members objected. This served only to convince John that his suspicions were justified. Angry words were exchanged, culminating in John making a call to the police on his mobile phone. His conversation with them was interrupted by Patsy, in muddy golf trousers, who happened to walk into the bar at the height of the commotion but had said nothing because he was enjoying the fun. "It couldn't be possible that you may have put on the wrong trousers?" suggested Patsy who, on going into the locker room a few minutes earlier had found that his trousers were missing. Sure enough, John was wearing Patsy's trousers which were of a similar size and colour. Accompanied by cat calls and boos, John left the bar, went into the locker room, found his trousers – and his wallet – and fled. He didn't even have the decency, or the bottle, to return to the bar and apologise and let Patsy know that *his* mud-free trousers were now available.

My previous golf clubs were Wynyard, Brancepeth, Penrith and of course Chester-le-Street and also the Cons Club, Tenerife Amarilla and SPEED societies as well as NUGS (Norton Unicorn Golf Society) where I am affectionately (I hope) known as "Cocker" because I had to cock off so many of their outings when I was spinning plates. My good friend and Chester-le-Street member Peter Peyton used to warn me that I was only allowed fourteen clubs so I had better settle at Brass Castle. Peter was facetiously referring to the rule which permits a maximum of fourteen golf clubs to be carried during a round.

With everything that was going on in my life during my early golfing days, I had no time to practice or to get any consistency into my game. We club hackers expect to rush on to the first tee with the day's problems whirring around in our heads and hit drives down the middle of the fairway. My wife must have been tired of hearing my hard luck stories and reasons why I didn't win. I did occasionally hit some very good shots – the ones that make you come back. I could drive the ball straight and long. I could hit approach shots into the centre of the green. I could chip stone dead, play accurately out of bunkers and sink tricky putts. I even had a hole in one at Teesside's third hole playing with Adrian Tate in an invitation event, for which I was awarded a prestigious Sunday Post putter. Interspersed with these wonderful achievements however, there would be a series of slices, hooks, scuffs, duffs and lost balls. I even experienced an occasion when a ball was lost before a shot had even been played. At Chester-le-Street nine of us threw our balls in the air which is a practice adopted to determine playing partners. When the balls came to rest only eight were claimed by their owners and the whereabouts of the ninth remains to this day a complete mystery. In our matches between teams selected in this random way Patsy usually found himself on the winning team. He wasn't a particularly good golfer and never ever practised – not hitting golf balls, that is. He did spend hours in his back garden throwing balls up though.

So when someone asks me how my golf is or how well I have played, I say INTERMITTENTLY BRILLIANT. With equal, perhaps even more honesty, I could also say INTERMITTENTLY CRAP!

After struggling for many years to achieve success I did eventually win a medal competition at Chester-le-Street for which I was pulled three shots off my handicap. So delighted was I with my long-awaited victory that I just had to stay behind and celebrate. When I eventually arrived home it was quite late and the house was in darkness. I didn't switch on the lights, crept upstairs, undressed, quietly got into bed, and whispered to my wife:

"How would you like to make love to a golf champion?"

"OK," she replied, "but you'd better be quick. Derrick might be back soon."

Despite the abuse to which it had been subjected, my body retained sufficient suppleness to enable me to continue to swing a club after I retired. My game improved with age although the improvement may have had something to do with my state of mind, the absence of stress, a reduction in my alcohol intake and the fact that I could then devote some time to practice and an occasional lesson from the Club Pro. I must also give a lot of credit for my improvement to "Penina" Pete Hardisty who, during a round we were playing together, adjusted my alignment. "You look like a golfer now," he said, "not just someone who plays golf." That made me feel good. I started to win competitions and even achieved a second hole in one, again at Teesside, but this time on the 178 yard seventh hole with a sweetly struck four iron.

I have been privileged to be just a tiny part of this wonderful game of golf which has given me so much enjoyment over so many years. I owe to it some of the best times of my life, notably during golfing trips away with the lads – and Patsy. I have been fortunate enough to play some magnificent courses all over the world, including the K Club Dublin, Valderama in Spain and also Torrequebrada when I was holidaying in Dave Smith's apartment with daughter Liz, and later on a SPEED tour. I've played Laguna Quays in Queensland, Australia, Penina and the lovely San Lorenzo in Portugal, Reims in France and North Berwick in Scotland. Hopefully I may get to play some of them again especially San Lorenzo. But before I do, I will let Brian know this time. I have also played the world's most remote golf course – the Amazon GC at Putamayo near Iquitos, Peru, where my son James is a founder member. I played there with the Club Pro, Sergio, one of Peru's top golfers. On that occasion we both played off scratch. As we approached the final hole, a par five, I held a slender lead of one stroke. Sergio found the green in regulation and made his par. I had pushed my third shot a few yards to the right of the green which left me with a difficult lob shot over a mound. I was playing with only a half set of clubs and with my most lofted club, a nine iron, I tried to bump the ball into the mound to take some pace off it, succeeding only in leaving the ball embedded in the mound. The best I could do was a double bogie and I lost the match by one stroke. Not bad you might say, against a top pro and with only a half set of clubs. What I haven't told you is that the course was under construction and only three holes were open!

As I have mentioned earlier golf can be an exasperating game. The right clubs and equipment can help of course, but only marginally. In Tenerife I used to play golf with Scouser Steve Springer who ran a bar there. He told me a story about his pal Eddie, a talented natural sportsman who decided to take up the game of golf. Eddie, who excelled in several other sports, expected to easily master the game and invested heavily in the latest equipment. He strode confidently on to the first tee but after slicing three balls into a lake could no longer contain his frustration. He hurled his golf bag and clubs into the water and stormed off the course. Steve and his other playing partners were stunned. A few minutes later when putting out on the third green they saw Eddie walking back towards the lake and when he waded into the water and retrieved his bag of clubs, assumed that they were to be given a reprieve until, to Steve's astonishment, they were once again thrown into the lake. Eddie, they later learned, had returned only to retrieve his car keys which were in one of the bag's pockets!

There is a lovely poem which sums it all up.

An Ode to the Dimpled Ball

In my hand I hold a ball
Dimpled, white and rather small
Oh how benign it does appear
This harmless looking little sphere

By its size no one could guess
What awesome power it does possess
But since I fell beneath its spell
I've wandered through the fires of Hell

My life has not been quite the same
Since I chose to play this stupid game

My mind's consumed for hours on end
A fortune it has made me spend

It's made me yell and curse and cry
To hate myself and want to die
It promises me a thing called Par
If I can hit it straight and far

To master such a tiny ball
Should surely not be hard at all
But my desires the ball refuses
And does exactly what it chooses

It hooks and slices, dribbles and dies
It can disappear before my very eyes
And often on a truculent whim
Will hit a tree or take a swim

With miles of grass on which to land
It finds a tiny patch of sand
I would offer up my heart and soul
For it to find its elusive hole

It makes me whimper like a pup
And swear that I will give it up
And take to drink to ease my sorrow
But knows full well I'll be back tomorrow

Anon

Thirty-One

DA versus FA

He doesn't swallow fools gladly.
Chrissarism.

I N AN EARLIER CHAPTER I said that the only thing I could not tolerate was intolerance. That's not quite true. Hypocrisy and arrogance must be added to the list. Particularly the kind of arrogance displayed by people in important and responsible positions who consider themselves to be a protected species answerable to none but themselves, accountable to no-one and shielded from the discipline and authority of natural justice. Firmly into this category I would put the Football Association and their bedfellow the FA Premier League (FAPL) who deducted three points from Middlesbrough FC in 1996/97 season.

Just before Christmas 1996 a virus swept through the club, whose first team were due to play an away fixture against Blackburn Rovers on the 21st December. On the eve of the fixture twenty-three of the playing staff were unavailable and of those who were available three were goalkeepers, five were juniors and two were not in training. Theoretically a team of eleven could at that point have been fielded but fearing that on the day of the match more players may be struck down by the virus, as indeed was the case with Roberts and Hignett, the club's Chief Executive Keith Lamb sought guidance from the FAPL following consultation with Brian Robson, the manager, and the club medical adviser, Doctor Dunn, who said, "I am uncertain how many of the remaining fit players will be fit tomorrow due to the virus."

Conscious of the inconvenience which would be caused to both sets of fans and others were the match to be called off at the last minute, Mr Lamb telephoned the FAPL on Friday at 11 a.m. and asked to speak to the FA supremo Rick Parry, who was, or so he was told, not available. Nor was his deputy Mike Foster. Eventually Mr Lamb was able to speak to a Mr Adrian Cooke who told him that the league did not have the power to postpone a match under the existing rules but asked Mr Lamb to send by fax a list of the unavailable players and then send the medical evidence by post. Before sending the fax Mr Lamb checked with Mr Cooke to make sure the wording and content was sufficient for the Premier League's requirements. In the absence of a response to the fax Mr Lamb telephoned Mr Cooke at 12.50 p.m. to say that the club considered that it had little choice other than to call off the match. Mr Cooke undertook to notify Blackburn Rovers. He failed to do so. This fixture was quite significant not only to both clubs but to several other clubs who were in the relegation zone at that time. The foot of the League Table on 21.12.96 read as follows:

	Played	Won	Drawn	Lost	F.	A.	Points
Sunderland	18	5	5	8	17	26	20
West Ham	18	4	6	8	18	26	18
Southampton	18	4	4	10	27	33	16
Coventry	18	3	7	8	14	24	16
Blackburn R	17	2	7	8	16	22	13
Notts Forest	18	2	7	9	16	30	13

Had the match been played – and I'm sure this was the dilemma faced by the club – Blackburn Rovers would have undoubtedly inflicted a heavy defeat on Boro and been gifted three valuable points as well as a valuable boost to their goal difference which could have proved vital to them at the end of the season when the relegation candidates were decided. It could have also undoubtedly proved vital to the other clubs involved and there would have been an outcry by them, followed by recriminations. And what about the entertainment factor? Remember the criticism levelled at Manchester United when they fielded weakened teams? Much of this criticism came from the direction of the FA! No question of points deduction of course. This was the mighty Manchester United.

Rovers' fans, I'm sure, would have been delighted to see their team pick up an easy three points in a 10-0 victory but would the travelling Boro fans consider they had got value for money? So, FA, what do you believe this game of football is all about? Is it a sport? Is it a business? Not about entertainment obviously otherwise why penalise Boro for not fielding a side capable of producing a fair sporting contest between two evenly matched sides?

Had the fixture gone ahead and three points virtually gifted to Rovers, I wonder in whose direction the anger of the other affected teams would have been unleashed? The Boro's? The FA's perhaps? We can only speculate on the many ramifications resulting from this scenario, but the FAPL got themselves nicely out of having to face up to these uncomfortable hypotheses by opting out of the decision making at the time, then blaming Boro and deducting three points from them..

There have since been umpteen occasions of specific rule breaking by clubs. Chelsea's illegal approach to Ashley Cole in 2006 prompted the FA to warn the club that if they were caught doing it again they could face a points deduction. Naughty boys. According to a report in Private Eye (issue 1168) a VAT tribunal revealed that Newcastle United over a period of years had routinely lied to the FA about their use of agents in clear breach of FA rules. Either that or the FA had failed to check their papers or had turned a blind eye – neither of which inspires much confidence in the FA officials who had earlier vowed to clean up the game. When approached by Private Eye the FA, as we will see later, did do something they are good at – refused to comment!

Unaware of the events of that fateful Friday morning, thirty thousand fans, including me, were dismayed when the FA made their announcement. We were angry too but at first our anger was directed largely at the club who many thought had cocked things up again following their earlier cup tie ticket allocation debacles. Nevertheless, because of the severity of the punishment, feelings against the FA were running high too. Other clubs had broken rules and escaped draconian punishment – Spurs for example – and speculation was rife that had this happened at a more fashionable club or one from London, then the old boys' network would have kicked in. From what little information we were fed by the press it seemed that the FA may have acted unreasonably. Indeed the club was considering an appeal.

On 15th January 1997 I wrote to the FA on behalf of the fans, asking a number of questions to find out for myself the reasons for justifying their decision to deduct the three points. Mr Foster replied a week later (to Mr Arnold – they couldn't even get that right). He apologised for failing to address all my questions explaining that he didn't want to go into detail because of the impending appeal. The two highly significant points he made in his letter, and I quote, were:

"Premier League rules… state… 'upon finding a breach of the rules to be proved a commission may: impose such penalties by way of reprimand, fine, suspension, deduction of points… as it thinks fit.'

The Club was warned that if they did not fulfil the fixture they could face a points deduction."

Again, my instinct was to blame the club, putting it down to incompetence on their part if they had in fact called off the match knowing full well they could be docked three points, which is what Mr Foster's letter to me more than implied. If this were true then the club was bang out of order. The club after all had a bit of form when it came to incompetence, unprofessionalism and even (allegedly) dishonesty. Private Eye was provided with plenty of material at the time, although to be fair much of this was pre 1983 and before Steve Gibson and Keith Lamb took charge. Let me give you an example, first hand, of what I am talking about. When we lived in Wolviston we had a nanny for the kids called Barbara Davis, a Boro fanatic, who in 1978 emigrated to New Zealand. She was a great help to us in those difficult days and we thought of her as one of the family. So for a Christmas and thank you present we decided to send her a Boro scarf and various other merchandise. I went along to the Boro shop next to Ayresome Park and emblazoned across the scarf I was offered were the words, "Up the Borough." Now every Boro supporter and I guess every other football fan in the country know Middlesbrough Football Club as the 'Boro' – everyone, that is, except whoever it was within the club itself responsible for ordering its merchandise and sending it back if it was incorrect. When I pointed the error out to the dozy girl behind the counter all she said was, "Oh yeah, I never noticed." Thankfully the club these days is a bit more switched on commercially.

There was a mood of anger and a sense of injustice in Middlesbrough after the summary jurisdiction handed out by the FA, fuelled by an earlier decision by them to deduct points from another club which for no apparent reason (other than it was one of the big London clubs) was reversed and the points reinstated. The services of top barrister George Carmen had been secured by the club and there was much optimism in the town that the FA's decision would be overturned on appeal. It wasn't. Although I wasn't privy to all the detail it was clear that Mr Gibson the club's chairman was incensed, not only by the FA's appeal decision but also by the fact that he felt that the hearing had not been conducted in a fair and judicial manner. I was curious to find out just what had really happened on that Friday morning. Surely there was more to it than we had been told or than I had been able to find out for myself. Never mind, I thought, there were still a few matches left to play. Maybe relegation could still be avoided and not too much harm done. Then on 23rd March an article appeared in a Sunday newspaper which cast further doubts in my mind about the FA's assertion that the club was aware that it would have points deducted, so again I wrote to the FAPL saying that if their decision resulted in Boro's relegation, then the fans would demand a full explanation of the events leading up to the decision.

The season of 1996-1997 was surely the most eventful in the long history of Middlesbrough Football Club. The original club was formed in 1897, went into liquidation and was on the verge of disappearing into obscurity, when in 1983 it was resurrected by its new owners Middlesbrough FC (1983) Ltd. In the 96-97 season the club reached two cup finals losing 2-0 to Chelsea at Wembley in the FA Cup Final and to Leicester City in the Coca Cola Cup Final replay at Hillsborough after a last minute equaliser denied them victory at Wembley. Because of a back log of fixtures they were forced by the FA to play four of their last five matches in the space of eight days and the task proved just too much for them. Despite winning more points than Coventry, Sunderland, Nottingham Forest and Southampton, Boro were relegated. But it wasn't the men in the blue shirts of Chelsea and Leicester who ruined what should have been a memorable season – it was the men in grey suits at the FA Headquarters in London.

The bottom of the league table in season 1996 - 1997 finished like this:

	Played	Won	Drawn	Lost	F.	A.	Points
Blackburn	38	9	15	14	42	43	42
West Ham	38	10	12	16	39	48	42
Everton	38	10	12	16	44	57	42
Southampton	38	10	11	17	50	56	41
Coventry	38	9	14	15	38	54	41
Sunderland	38	10	10	18	35	53	40
Boro *	38	10	12	16	51	60	39
Notts Forest	38	6	16	16	31	59	34

* 3 points deducted

As well as the thirty-eight league games that season, Boro were involved in sixteen cup ties, a total of fifty four games in all, and had given their fans some tremendous entertainment. My son Tim composed a couple of songs which the crowd enthusiastically adopted. To the tune of 'Que Sera Sera', they go:

> "Tell yer mam yer mam
> We're going to Wemberly
> We're going to Wemberly
> Tell yer mam yer mam."

…and after the second semi-final victory:

> "Tell yer mam yer mam
> To put the champagne on ice
> We're going to Wembley twice
> Tell yer mam yer mam."

The whole town was buzzing, but we were soon to be brought down to earth. Relegation was followed by the inevitable inquest. Questions were being asked. Had the club deliberately and knowingly forfeited the three points? Surely not. Why was there no senior officer available at FA HQ capable of giving the club proper guidance? Why wasn't Adrian Cooke required to attend either of the hearings? After all he was the FA officer directly involved in the dialogue with the club that Friday.

Just what do the FA rules say about such situations? What exactly is this Ouster Clause which had been mentioned in the press?

It was now being suggested that Adrian Cooke, whilst not exactly encouraging Mr Lamb to postpone the fixture, had not discouraged him either. It was being suggested too that FA Chief Executive Rick Parry was in fact in the building at the crucial time. Couldn't he be bothered to speak to Mr Lamb then? Was he afraid he may have to commit himself to making a positive decision? I did find out what the Ouster Clause was. Apparently, in return for the privilege of playing in the Premier League, clubs must agree to a clause in their contracts that prevents them from taking legal action against the FAPL. In other words it removes the fundamental right enjoyed by everyone – except it seems football clubs – in a civilised and so called democratic country, to seek and obtain natural justice. With the club's co-operation I was able to obtain a copy of the relevant rules. This was an eye opener. The FA in their letter to "Mr Arnold" had quoted Rule 7 dealing with the punishment aspect but what they had, in my view quite deliberately, failed to do in order to keep me quiet, was to mention Rule 19. Now Rule 19 was, or should have been, the epicentre of the dispute. I quote:

> 19.1 No club shall WITHOUT JUST CAUSE fail to fulfil its fixture obligations in respect of any league match on the appointed date or dates.

> 19.2 The club failing to fulfil its fixture obligations shall be liable to pay compensation for any expenses necessarily incurred by the opposing club as a direct result of the failure. The amount of compensation shall be at discretion of the Board who will consider every such case on its merits.

No mention here of the possible deduction of points.

With the route to the Country's constitutional right to natural justice being denied to the club by the Ouster Clause, were the FA therefore to be allowed to arrogantly ignore legitimate questions put to them? Not if I had anything to do with it. They hadn't got me to sign an Ouster Clause! On the 16th May I again wrote to them to explain certain inconsistencies which were puzzling me. I told them that there was a widely held view that had it been possible to challenge their decision through the proper courts and not their own version of the kangaroo type, then there was every possibility that it would be overturned. I inferred that if I didn't receive a satisfactory reply to my questions then legal action would be considered by the fans from whom at that time I was receiving considerable encouragement. The FA ignored my letter and the reminder I sent a month later. Clearly I was not going to get the information I was seeking by asking for it nicely. I couldn't force them to reply to my letters so was I just going to have to let them get away with their arrogant indifference? No. I would issue a summons through the small claims court for a nominal amount – £342 – the price of my season ticket. They would be obliged to respond to that.

I duly received another letter from the FA which merely repeated what they had told me in their earlier letter except the bit about the warning had been somewhat modified, the words "the club WAS WARNED they could face a points deduction" being replaced by "the club was STRONGLY ADVISED against calling off the fixture". So had they lied to me in the first letter? Or were they lying in their second letter? Pertinent questions remained unanswered.

By this time more and more information was emerging and the more I found out the more convinced I was becoming of the FA's culpability in the matter. I was able to obtain copies of letters to the FA from the club's Chairman, Steve Gibson, detailing the events of the 20th December and seeking answers from the FA to nine questions concerning these events and a further sixteen questions following the first hearing on the 14th January 1997. As far as I am aware he did not receive the courtesy of a reply. The local *Evening Gazette* also wrote to the FA on the 20th June. The involvement of the press must have stirred the FA out of their apathy and arrogance because they did issue a brief press statement which failed to address any of the ten questions raised by the newspaper and was characteristically unsatisfactory and dismissive. The FA's intransigence made me all the more determined to put the FA in a position where they would be obliged to answer the questions and justify their actions and it seemed the only way they could be forced to do this was to get them into court.

I had studied law in my CII exams and my understanding of contract law then, and is still, that any ambiguity or lack of clarity in a contract is construed by the courts in favour of the contesting party and against the party, in this case the FA, who had drawn it up and decided on its wording. There was no doubt in my mind that the dominant rule governing postponement of fixtures was Rule 19 which clearly specified the penalties involved for failing to fulfil a fixture *without just cause,* i.e. fines, compensation etc. and nowhere mentions the deduction of points. I remain quite convinced that no legitimate court in the land would have upheld the FA's decision to ignore Rule 19 and invoke Rule 7 instead, and that an irrefutable argument could have been put forward that the FA must take responsibility for the lack of clarity and the ambiguity in their own rules. But as we have seen, the club was not able to rely on the proper process of the law of the land.

Let me ignore for a moment the legal aspects of the matter and consider the scenario on the morning of December 20th. Mr Lamb, for reasons already mentioned, found himself in a quandary. Did he allow a weakened team to be trounced by a fellow relegation struggler and the possibility of being accused by other clubs threatened by relegation of 'throwing' the match? Or should he seek to postpone the fixture? He did, I believe, what any reasonable man faced with the situation would do. He sought advice from the controlling body. Surely he was entitled to expect some positive direction and advice instead of the wishy-washy response he got – "Er, well, I don't really know, so you'll have to decide for yourself but we might decide later to penalise you, but we are not telling you what that means." Heaven knows, the FA have substantial resources and should surely have been able to produce a comprehensive and clear contract or alternatively to appoint officers capable of making a positive decision. Instead they remain quite impervious to the consequences of their vacillation and obstinacy.

So what about Mr Lamb's actions on that black Friday? My guess is that he looked at Rule 19 and like me and everyone else outside Lancaster Gate, assumed that either:

The club could successfully argue just cause, or, even if they failed, then the worst that could happen would be payment of compensation and a fine.

In hindsight, I bet Mr Lamb wishes he had phoned Ladbrokes instead, put his life savings on Blackburn to win, and fulfilled the fixture with a no hope team. I don't think the insider trading regulations governing the stock market could be invoked in these circumstances. This is an interesting point to ponder. If the FA had been positive in their response to Mr Lamb's request for guidance and insisted on the fixture being played and if Mr Lamb had won a lot of money on his bet, would Ladbrokes have sued the FA?

Once word was out that the FA were being taken to court by a mere football fan, the news was manna from heaven for the media who just love this sort of David and Goliath type of story. It made front page headlines in the Evening Gazette and was prominently featured in many other local and national newspapers over a period of several months. I was interviewed on BBC and ITV, local radio and even on Radio Blackburn. I wasn't seeking celebrity status, just answers to a few simple questions. People from all over the region and beyond were willing to pledge money to support my action and even Keith Lamb telephoned with an offer to help. I was swept along on a tide of righteous outrage like the Crusaders of old. The Middlesbrough born MP Alan Keen briefly got in on the act, slamming the FA for the distress they had caused to the people of Middlesbrough all because, as the FA's counsel at the appeal conceded, "*of an honest error of judgement made in good faith.*"

We are told that Premier League status, in money terms, is worth £60 million. So, in effect, Boro, for acting "honestly and in good faith" were fined this enormous sum – quite a draconian punishment. What on earth, I wondered, would happen to a club if it were to act *dishonestly* and *knowingly* in total *bad faith*? During the following ten years the FA either ignored or were not competent to deal with the corruption and illegal payments (bungs) which were blatantly evident within the "beautiful" game. Then something happened which even the FA couldn't ignore.

With only a handful of fixtures remaining of the 2006 – 2007 season, West Ham United were ten points adrift at the foot of the Premier League and seemed doomed to relegation. In desperation they knowingly fielded a player who they had signed illegally. Argentinian Carlos Tevez's goals undoubtedly saved them from relegation. Honest but luckless Sheffield United were relegated instead.

Now everyone involved at the grass roots level of the game knows and accepts that automatic deduction of points is the standard punishment throughout the lower FA leagues for clubs fielding unregistered or illegal players. Surely the FAPL would throw the book at West Ham. What did they do? Give them a £55 million reward (the value of Premier League survival less the paltry £5 million fine which they imposed). I must be careful what I say, but do you think I am being excessively cynical by suspecting that favouritism may have been shown to West Ham? The reasons for the FA's leniency will, I suppose, never be revealed. West Ham is a London club and their ex-captain Trevor Brooking is, I believe, on the FA Committee. Could there have been a bit of the old pals network in action? Surely not! There is much evidence to support the accusation that the FA's inconsistency in dealing with breaches of regulations is biased in favour of the bigger influential clubs. No less than sixty four points have subsequently been deducted from relative minnows like Luton, Rotherham and Bournemouth for breaching FA Regulations.

Despite advice from John Tate, a lawyer friend of mine, that my case, whilst having much moral justification, lacked legal credibility, I persevered. Even if I lost I would, or so I thought, have an opportunity to ask some awkward questions. The FA tried to have the case transferred to London. I challenged this and won. The usual exchange of information and arguments took place between Plaintiff and Defendants and the case was listed for an informal hearing in Middlesbrough County Court before District Judge J. Mainwaring Taylor on 2nd January 1998 – my wedding anniversary. My intention was to subpoena as witnesses Adrian Cooke and Keith Lamb and I contacted the Court to say that this may not be possible at such short notice. I was told not to worry and since this was to be purely a preliminary hearing witnesses need not be called. Naively I assumed that this hearing wasn't the main match and I was not legally represented. In contrast the FA were represented by their London lawyers Denton Hall and local barrister Stuart Lightwing, who had been a neighbour for several years and whom I knew quite well. He was able to produce an obscure case law precedent which enabled him to persuade the judge that since I had no direct contractual relationship with the Defendants they were not obliged to answer my case. Not only that, but costs were awarded against me. There were however a few positives I could take away from the experience. I had found something very interesting and useful to do during a period of time following my retirement when I needed something to get my teeth into and to stimulate my grey matter. I found out that the small claims court system which was originally set up to enable individuals to access legal redress cheaply and which I have used occasionally, didn't always work like that. And finally I had proof of what I suspected all along. That for all their posturing, bodies like the FA don't exist for the benefit of the fans who ultimately provide the money which allows them to exist and that they are undemocratic and unaccountable.

When confronted afterwards by the TV cameras and the press outside the court I was able to get these points across, quite eloquently I am told. But will someone, I wonder, ever do anything to remove from the FA the unfettered power they enjoy and which is not tolerated in any other aspect of the Country's establishment? I suggested to the Chairman of Sheffield United in a letter I wrote to him, that a protest by their fans should be organised, calling on football fans everywhere to withhold their votes for the Government at the next general election. Only by direct and positive action like this will something be done to change the FA's privileged position which, in the opinion of many, many football fans they have abused by failing to act with responsibility and consideration towards them. At the time of writing Sheffield United are preparing a civil action against West Ham United. I wish them success.

To be fair to the FA they did write to me and waive the costs awarded against me. This gesture probably prevented me from enlisting the promised support of hundreds of Boro fans who would certainly have provided the financial backing to mount a serious appeal which may have at least elicited the answers to some of the still unanswered questions.

I think we are entitled to draw our own conclusions from the FA's coyness. I suppose we'll never get to the bottom of it – unless perhaps Adrian Cook writes his autobiography too!

Thirty-Two

............& OTHERS

Getting a bit wet under the collar are we?
Chrissarism.

PEOPLE WILL ONLY STOP doing wrong and those with bad attitudes will only change, if there is a good chance that they will be caught or challenged, that there are consequences to face when they are and that deterrents are commensurate with the wrongdoing. Punishments should ideally be implemented firmly against the *individual* responsible so that there is a personal and not a corporate accountability. I'm not necessarily talking about criminals here. I include those who abuse power and act unreasonably, selfishly, incompetently or pompously. We will only put an end to such behaviour if people instead of whingeing about these people, actually do something. Apathy and cowardice are the breeding grounds for corruption and complacency.

I am the kind of person to whom arrogance, pretentiousness and injustice are an anathema. Whenever I see evidence of these I feel a need to do something about it. My principles are often prosecuted at personal cost and inconvenience. Nothing is achieved easily, particularly when one's adversary is stubborn, cunning, powerful, or occasionally all three. Once the decision to act is made, it takes courage and tenacity to stay the course. But I will not enter the arena unless I am up for the fight and have a reasonable chance of winning. If not I simply accept that there is nothing I can do about it – or I bide my time and wait for my opportunity to strike, which usually presents itself at some point. I can be very patient and if necessary quite vindictive. As I have said earlier there may be peace in acceptance but it can be very satisfying to challenge injustice and win. My actions against the Hopkinsons and the FA were only two examples of the resolute and crusading characteristics in my makeup.

I didn't reach the summons stage in my dispute with Red House School. I don't think I would have won and I didn't have the time then to devote to this particular matter of principle at stake. It's a pity because I would have enjoyed challenging and

237

exposing some of the 'enlightened' platitudes in their prospectus, like "...all those aspects of pastoral care which are part of the fabric of our school which enjoys (?) a firm but kindly (!) discipline. This can lead a child happily... and with a sense of security through a confused society, caring for all facets of his growth and progress" and... "offences... bring minor corrective actions commensurate with the offence." *Like two weeks suspension for nicking a twenty pence chocolate egg?* This is typical of the longwinded bullshit produced by academics. It sounds wonderful but is exposed for what it is when put to the test.

My summons against Skydeals/Thomson Holidays did however do the trick. I got a reluctant £130 compensation – but no apology. Despite arriving in good time at Reina Sofia Airport in Tenerife, and having valid tickets on Flight HOA552 to Newcastle, we were told that we must get a later flight. The reason given – two people from the later flight must have got on ours by mistake! This was either a blatant lie or an even more blatant breach of security.

The threat of summonses was enough to ensure a climb down in disputes with Sky TV and with HSBC Bank who had debited my credit card twice with £142.58 for a meal in the Victoria at Sheen S.W.12. Every time I wrote and queried this they simply sent me a copy of the voucher I had signed claiming that it was correct, ignoring completely the point of my complaint. *"I know it's bloody correct,"* I finally wrote in exasperation, *"but I only signed one voucher; you have sent me a copy of one voucher, but I've paid you twice!"* Then they said they would try to persuade the Victoria to co-operate but I wasn't prepared to wait or to rely on the co-operation of the restaurant. I had paid HSBC twice, not the Victoria. HSBC had done that and I held them and not the Victoria responsible. They eventually issued a refund plus £53.70 interest.

Although I did my little bit to help, there was one particularly unpleasant practice which was widespread and which needed to be exposed nationally. This involved the placing of bonds by students who rent accommodation through unscrupulous letting agents. I've only heard of one student who has actually had his bond fully refunded on vacating the property – my youngest son. When he was at university in Leeds he rented a flat through Mayfair Properties (not real name) and placed a refundable bond of £400. His requests for a refund at the end of the tenancy were ignored. Eventually and after many phone calls I was able to establish a reason for the non-refund. There were unpaid bills, I was told. This, I established, was not the case. What *was* the case, I began to suspect, was that this was simply a part of a deliberate process to delay making the refund and perhaps result in us giving up because it wasn't worth the hassle. I can imagine such tactics having a good success rate with students who have left the area and who don't have the tenacity or the experience to fight their corner. Dean, the son of Bill McDougall, a friend of mine, had a similar problem and his attempts to have his bond refunded by his unscrupulous landlord were unfairly rejected. The agents in this case claimed that it was necessary to employ cleaning contractors despite Dean and his flatmates doing a thorough cleaning job themselves. I suspect there may have been some incestuous relationship between the alleged cleaning contractor and the letting agent.

Mayfair Properties picked on the wrong student in my son's case. He too had a dad who wouldn't be deterred by procrastination. In cases which I think may end up in court I always write letters and keep copies. I always write in long hand because psychologically these are more likely to be ignored or not taken seriously and it always looks bad in court if the defendant is seen to be contemptuous by not responding. My final letter is always sent by recorded delivery and encloses copies of the previous ones so that they cannot claim to have not received them. The summons against Mayfair for £400 and £50 court fee, was issued on the 22nd October 2001. A cheque for £400 dated 21st October wondrously landed on our doormat on the 23rd October. What a coincidence. Our attempts over a period of fifteen months to get the refund had been ignored, yet they had decided to cough up then – the day before the summons. The court obviously considered the possibility which I had put to them that the cheque may have been backdated and judgement was passed for the full amount – including the £50 court fee which they were obviously trying to avoid having to pay. Numerous telephone calls were received, presumably made by the owner of Mayfair Properties hoping that I would withdraw the summons to avoid a CCJ against them. Chris pretended to be the cleaner and I didn't return the calls. They only had themselves to blame. Hopefully this kind of unscrupulous behaviour is now a thing of the past since the recent introduction of government backed deposit protection schemes removing control and power from private agents.

I don't seek confrontation but nor do I shirk it. I won't be fobbed off and I'm not afraid to take on the powerful and the mighty. In fact I rather enjoy the David and Goliath challenge and there aren't many bigger giants than the British Government.

The European Parliament had issued a Directive, No 73/239, requiring all member states to implement certain steps to regulate financial organisations for the protection of investors. The UK Government chose to exclude Lloyds from these regulations and continued, contrary to European Law, to allow Lloyds to self-regulate, the scandalous consequences of which are described in Volume II. Some years later a group of ex-Lloyds Names, including me and led by Christopher Stockwell, decided to explore the possibility of holding the UK Government to account for our losses, which were due largely to Lloyds' failure to properly audit their accountancy procedures, particularly in the area of reserves. Our case is strong but even if we win it will be appealed and we are only too well aware of the fact that the Government has an almost unlimited budget of taxpayers' money and other resources to fight their case. As court cases go they don't come much bigger than this one. It may not be settled in my lifetime but I will have to wait and see – or my estate will.

As well as my personal battles there was of course corporate litigation. It was I suppose inevitable that the sale of my shares in the companies would not be straightforward. I was one of the few successfully to sue Brooks Mileson before he died, went into posthumous bankruptcy and took others with him – including Gretna FC. But that's another story.[2]

---

[2] Related in Volume II – Accidental Millionaire.

Thirty-Three

CROCODILE SHOES

I don't like him, he puts the willies up me.
Chrissarism.

WHILST ON MUCH LESS FAVOURABLE TERMS than I could have achieved ten years earlier, I managed, in 1997, to sell my shares in the Arnott and Albany companies for a seven-figure sum at around the same time as "Reconstruction and Renewal", a solution to the Lloyds of London debacle occurred. To my immense relief and unmitigated joy I became a man of leisure with my future and that of my family secured.

Most of us, I believe, harbour a smug sense of wellbeing about the things we are good at. If those things have enabled us to be successful in our business, professional or commercial lives, we can easily become a little anxious as retirement approaches. What are we to do now that the things we are good at are no longer needed by anyone? For this reason many people who have enjoyed their roles or positions of importance hang on to them as long as they can. They would prefer to ignore or postpone the challenge of the unfamiliar territory of retirement. This is a pity. If we open our eyes and minds there is an exciting world of new opportunities out there just waiting to fulfil us and eager to replace our old skills with new ones, or perhaps to use our old skills in a new and exciting way. The beauty of it is that this time we needn't be so good at what we choose to do because it doesn't matter. We don't *have* to do it. We do it because we *want* to do it – and we don't *need* to do it to pay the mortgage etc. A survey was carried out to find out what people would really like to do if they didn't have to rely on their existing jobs for money. Entertaining and acting were, surprisingly, the most popular choices. They may not be yours but it is a very good example of the scope of what you can do when you retire. It is but one option of many thousands. Charities are crying out for volunteers. Sports teams need helpers. Few will turn down the offer of free help. Alas to those people in the survey, their choices will probably remain pipe dreams. Few, if any, will get off their backsides and join the local amateur drama group. It is a great pity therefore that so many people don't find a completely new and different activity with which to replace the void created by retirement. And you must do it without delay. If you don't quickly find something which gives you an excuse to (metaphorically) "leave the house" you may find yourself at everyone's beck and call and the opportunity to fulfil your own dreams is lost. Take time out to record a little of your life. It needn't be a lengthy narrative. Something is better than nothing. This is a simple legacy which future generations will be interested in and probably cherish – even if you disclose some darker sides of your life. Especially if you do, perhaps. Maybe use it as a written confessional and if there are reasons for keeping the door of the skeleton cupboard locked during your lifetime, arrange for it to be made available posthumously.

My wife had rejected any suggestion that we do some wholesale buying and selling of goods which we had enjoyed so much during our Centrepeace days and for which she had shown considerable flair. People will buy something if it is different and on our travels we had come across so many new ideas which were available only in their country of origin and which could easily have been imported into the UK and sold here, often at big mark ups. The situation was similar in reverse. It would have been very satisfying exporting UK goods too. Being an international buyer has got to be one of the best jobs in the world if, like me, you enjoy travelling, staying in nice hotels (on expenses!) and meeting people from other countries and cultures. Having led a busy business life I suppose I was on the lookout for something to get my teeth into, something which would keep the grey matter active but would not consume my time too much. I enjoy reading and watching TV occasionally but I am essentially a doer, not a reader or a watcher. Plenty of time for that when I am in my dotage. I couldn't take up golf or bowls because I already had years before. You can only spend so much time on the golf course and on the bowling green. There is only so much you can do with a garden, rewarding as it might be. I was already drinking and with more time on my hands and a Gamma GT level of 109 instead of 85 I needed to find ways of spending less and not more time indulging in that particular pastime, enjoyable as it is. To get the most out of retirement you've got to think about it. Sit down alone with a drink, some unintrusive classical music and allow your mind to wander and think about what you really would have liked to do if you hadn't been a schoolteacher, a brain surgeon, a plumber, a clerk – or an insurance man. Then recognise that you now have an opportunity to do it. Then do it.

That's what I did. That's how I came to write this book. That's why I sued the FA, stood for Parliament and got involved in children's charities. There is so much to life beyond the little worlds we live in when our noses are firmly to the grindstone, if we take the trouble to look up from it. So many things we can do, and the beauty of it is that because we are not doing them for a living it doesn't matter a jot if we do them badly as long as we enjoy it. With more time on your hands you can have lots of fun on the internet – and do your bit to stamp out fraud. We are advised to ignore spam e mails but you can beat them at their own game. I delight in responding to them and supplying all the information requested which appears genuine to the fraudster but are fictitious of course. If we all did this their illicit operations would be made almost impractical. Banks for example could be alerted and they could notify the police who may be able to ensnare the perpetrators of this pernicious practice.

After a few brief holidays in Tenerife I became rather partial to wearing a T-shirt, shorts and sandals, swimming in the sea and eating tapas and *pescado a la plancha* on sunny terraces in the middle of winter, and whilst it may not be the prettiest island on the planet it does enjoy three hundred and fifty nine days of warm sunshine every year, boasts a fine selection of restaurants, golf courses and some good sandy beaches. The Canary Islands are the only European destination with guaranteed winter sun to which you can fly frequently from all local airports – and at cheap fares, especially if you can be flexible. For these reasons we decided to buy a property there, or, to be more accurate, Chris bought it, to keep Lloyds' hands off my assets. Our first apartment was modest by many people's standards but well maintained. The spacious gardens and swimming pool were never crowded and with the sandy Las Vistas beach an easy fifteen minute walk away it suited us very well. Situated on the top floor with south and west facing balconies and total privacy made for free and easy al fresco living. No bikini lines for us. I finally joined a nudist colony – even if it only had two members!

I can't describe the excitement we both felt as the day for moving into our new place abroad approached. We would walk past the building every day and gaze longingly up to the top floor where we could see "our" balcony. "That will be ours in seven days' time," we would say to each other. Then "six days" then "five" then "four, three, two" and finally "tomorrow!" After officially moving in we went out on the town – Los Cristianos – to celebrate. After copious *copas de vinos* we returned "home" quite late and continued our celebrations. After watching the TV series 'Auf Weidersen Pet' we had just read Jimmy Naill's autobiography *Crocodile Shoes* in which he recalled his exploits as a young man in the North East of England which included his proud accounts of playing pool without a cue, using instead his manhood, which obviously wasn't pinched for size. He had recently recorded an album by the same title and we were playing this rather loudly while we danced naked to the music. Chris climbed on to the breakfast bar which presented me with an opportunity to consummate our new apartment. At a height of ninety centimetres Spanish breakfast bars are not particularly convenient for copulation. For Jimmy Naill, perhaps, but not for me, even on tiptoe. I frantically tried to find a solution to the problem but before I could do so the doorbell rang. We hadn't made a particularly good first impression with the security guard or our new neighbours who had complained to him about the noise. We quietened down after that and I bought a pair of stepladders which have been used regularly since that night – for cleaning the windows! If you don't strike while the iron's hot...

My decision to set up a Spanish company was greeted with dismay by both my mother and my wife who, I think, both hoped that I had retired in order to devote all my time to them. But all I had done, for heaven's sake, was to end one chapter of my business life. I hadn't suddenly reached my dotage and, besides, the enterprise in which I was to become involved was relatively stress-free and an excellent investment vehicle for some of my share sale proceeds. The idea was put into my head one day during a conversation with Keith McGuinness who worked with my friend Brian. Keith and Paul Frost, a local media celebrity, had formed a company called My Place Abroad (MPA) to identify or acquire properties abroad, mainly in Tenerife, which could be purchased from home equity release and rented out to produce an income sufficient to repay the borrowings, thus providing the client with both a holiday home and an appreciating asset in effect, at no cost. The idea appealed to me and I shared it with my old and wealthy friend Joe Laidler. Having decided against an involvement in the Arnott companies we were interested in doing something, business wise, together, so we bought a fifty per cent share in MPA. The plan was for Joe and I to buy or build properties in Tenerife for MPA to sell and rent. A neat arrangement. Feelers were put out and some land in the province of San Miguel close to the airport was identified as a possible acquisition. The land comprised eight plots in prime front line location, totalling around thirty thousand square metres, ideally located on the Atlantic coast and flanked by the challenging Amarilla Golf Course. They were offered to us in 1997 for 339,932,000 pesetas by an agent who claimed that planning permission and building licenses were readily available. What he failed to mention was that in fact, three years earlier, the Tenerife Cabildo (government) had placed an embargo on the land preventing any further development because the original developer had failed to put in place the necessary infrastructure and was now in liquidation. We discovered too that the land had been repossessed by Lloyds Bank and that the agent had no authority to sell it. Despite its problems, however, we recognised the ultimate potential of the land and Joe and I flew to Madrid and after haggling over lunch with the Bank's Spanish Director, we agreed a price of 232,500,000 pesetas – some 107,432,000 pesetas less than the price asked by the agent, who was clearly trying to stitch us up. He had picked on the wrong people. The agent then had the nerve to ask us for a finder's fee which Joe and I rejected out of hand. Keith and Paul disagreed and a meeting of the partners was held to discuss the matter at which it was agreed that we paid the agent £2000, which is all that MPA had left in the bank. Joe and I were certainly not going to dip into our pockets as I suspect Keith and Paul were hoping. MPA offered to pay more when construction was completed and they had some money. Unfortunately for Keith and Paul and for the agent, Keith disappeared to Lanzarote, Paul had a heart attack and MPA folded. The land had nothing to do with MPA. Joe and I had personally financed its purchase and it was bought in the name of our new Spanish Company. Eight years later the embargo was lifted and we sold three of the plots, around *eleven* thousand square metres, to a developer for a price well in excess of what we had originally paid for the *thirty* thousand square metres. We wanted to retain some of the prime front land but the developer wouldn't agree. Tongue in cheek I suggested that he built for us two villas there at a price equivalent to the cost of construction. He agreed and an agreement was drawn up by the agent. We were able to take out our original investment and leave sufficient money in the company towards the development of the three remaining plots – one as a retirement home, another as four apartment blocks and the third a shopping plaza. It turned out to be a profitable enterprise. The prunes may be working at last! When I had prunes as a young boy I always ate exactly five. Do people still count the stones? One for tinker, two for tailor, then soldier, sailor, rich man, poor man, beggar man, thief.

In Joe I finally found a business partner who was straightforward, competent and reliable – whose mind was firmly focussed on the fundamental objective of business which is not to build empires or become important, but to make money.

I used to quite like Frank Sinatra's "I did it my way" but I grew to hate it so we sold our apartment to get out of earshot of the karaoke bar on the next block from which we had to put up with regular renditions by tone deaf Frank impersonators late at night. Our new house which is in a quieter and more prestigious area of town overlooking Las Vistas beach has become our winter home in the sun. We joined the colony of "Swallows" from northern Europe who migrate to Tenerife every year.

Thirty-Four

JUDGE JOE

Our criminal justice system is like an old banger. Out of date, rusty, no longer roadworthy and needs to be replaced by a new model.
D.A.

W HEN JOE LAIDLER and I gave each other Power of Attorney to represent our affairs in Tenerife, it took the Notary about sixty seconds to sign the documents. Yet this exercise robbed us of the best part of two days out of our lives.

Just about everything you do in Spain has to be notarised and three hours after our appointed meeting with the Notary we gave up and left, returning the following day when, after another long wait, Senor Cutillas eventually dealt with us. He had earlier swept past us a couple of times stopping once briefly to shake hands. On another occasion we were told to follow him and the young man who had drawn up the documents but after a few paces they split up, disappeared into different offices and closed the doors behind them. Bewildered, we rejoined the equally bemused mêlée in the waiting area until eventually we were ushered up some stairs where at the third attempt Sr Cutillas found an empty office, signed the document, shook hands and left. Our Santa Cruz lawyer, Enrique Robayna, a good friend of the Notary, had telephoned him earlier to make the appointment and was assured that we would receive priority attention. All I can say is that if ours was priority attention, then the other poor buggers must still be there now. I think Joe began to appreciate how difficult it had been for me to administer the affairs of our Spanish Company having to cope with SMS – Spanish Manana Syndrome. Joe and his wife Dorothy were visiting the island to try and make some progress with the development of the land we had bought in 1997. But it wasn't all work. Whenever the Laidlers come to Tenerife we have a couple of lunches together with our wives, usually on the terrace of our favourite fish restaurant in the bay of La Caleta. On this occasion lunch only lasted six hours, some three and a half hours short of our record marathon lunch in 2004. We can't stand the pace like we used to! I always enjoy lunching with Joe.

There is always much to talk about. His court room experiences, some of which are chronicled later, I find particularly interesting.

Our wives are not the most socially adventurous women in the world, preferring their own tight-knit handful of close friends. They also have in common with each other husbands whose priorities in life have not always been to their liking. This however hasn't prevented the Laidlers from reaching their golden wedding anniversary in 2009. Joe and I were surprised and delighted when our wives agreed to join us for a game of golf at the Las Americas Club. They were complete rabbits. Neither of them had played before so we played mixed foursomes, a game played with one ball per couple, each taking alternate shots. The girls were given "Mulligans"[3] for fresh air shots, i.e. when they completely missed the ball, which is just as well when I think about Dorothy's approach shot on the seventeenth – well, six shots, actually, each one removing a larger chunk of fairway than its predecessor. I can't call them divots – they were too big for that. The ball stubbornly refused to budge until her sixth attempt sent it scurrying off at right angles in the direction of the nearby lake. I apologise, Dorothy, for failing to contain my laughter, but it was pretty hilarious. Despite a number of similar agricultural moments the girls admitted they would like to play again. They had both enjoyed it, especially Dorothy. The earth moved for her that day!

While we sat on the balcony overlooking the eighteenth green having a beer afterwards, Joe received two calls on his mobile. One was from Boro manager Gareth Southgate accepting his offer to buy Gareth's villa on the Algarve in Portugal – a golfer's paradise. The other call was from Government Cabinet Minister Harriett Harman. When you are in Joe's company you can be sure there is never a dull moment.

Joe and I go back a long way, to 1959 in fact, when he came into our office to insure his first Austin A35 van. Like me, he had taken the plunge and gone into business on his own, shaking off the shackles of his working class background. Unlike me, however, he comes from a large family, being the eldest of eight children. His father Joe was clearly luckier in the leg over department with his mother Reana than Tommy was with Beatrice! From mending washing machines Joe diversified and developed a very successful group of international companies which included suspended ceilings, contract cleaning, TV repair, printing, property development and banking. We have much in common including unfortunately the fact that we were both Lloyds Names, but Joe has never ever resented me for introducing him to the idea. He stands and falls by his own decisions. We happen to share too a deep concern for the plight of children and young people who have been let down by adults in society – people from whom they should be entitled to expect love, care and understanding. We each have our reasons for our special interest in

---

[3] A "Mulligan" is when a player need not count his or her shot.

children's welfare. Reasons which, to avoid embarrassment, will have to sit this dance out and remain as skeletons in our cupboards. We each try to do something to help – me through the charities I support and Joe more directly in his hands-on day-to-day role as a Magistrate and Chairman of a local Youth Court, which in my day would have been called a Juvenile Court until someone with nothing better to do decided to change the name and in consequence all the stationery, documents, signs, publicity, etc., etc., all at a massive cost to public funds, the biggest waste being that particular person's salary. These people with institutionalised authority are very good at tinkering with peripheral things like this but quite incapable of even recognising let alone addressing the glaring inadequacies within the Criminal Justice System in which they work, a system which causes so much unnecessary distress to young people whilst at the same time disgracefully squandering public funds. It is because there is no accountability that these people get away with their mediocrity. They enjoy high salaries and early retirement on full guaranteed pensions and don't want to see past their noses. It takes people with public consciences who are not paid a penny to do something about it. With that off my chest, let me now recall some accounts of a few court cases and situations as related to me by Joe from time to time. I haven't used real names.

Fourteen-year-old Amy appeared before Joe accused of criminal damage. The prosecution described her as an unruly girl. On this occasion when she couldn't get her own way she had smashed a calculator and a telephone in anger. She was in the care of the local Authority. Joe asked her whether she had in fact done what she was accused of and she owned up. Most magistrates would have left it at that, accepted what was in fact a plea of guilty and passed sentence. Not Joe.

Amy was accompanied in court by a probation officer. This was a practice which Joe had already gone on record as condemning as unsatisfactory. For young persons appearing in court, probably for the first time, the experience can be a terrifying ordeal. They need the support of someone they know and can trust – someone who will stick up for them and who knows some of the background, not a probation officer appointed to the task who they have met for the first time perhaps only half an hour before the hearing. In more fortunate circumstances a young person's parents may be in court. They may have appointed a solicitor to represent their son or daughter. Why should a youngster less privileged be denied similar support?

Looking at this pitiful waif before him, Joe instinctively felt uneasy. He called for some background which of course the probation officer was unable to supply. He adjourned the case insisting that the Crown Prosecution Service provide a comprehensive report on Amy's history and of the facts leading up to the incident. He needed to hear Amy's side of the story too.

At the second hearing it was revealed that Amy had been taken into care because her mother was dead and her father was in gaol. Further probing revealed that Amy's father had a history of violence of which she herself had often been a victim. She had regularly witnessed her mother being beaten by her father. In fact, it was one of these beatings, a particularly severe one, which had caused her mother's death and her father's imprisonment for murder. Amy had been present at the time. Her mother had been brutally killed before her young eyes and this one tragic incident had resulted in the loss to her of both parents. Little wonder that Amy's behaviour was disturbed with that kind of background. By demanding from the CPS some more specific detail of the calculator incident and by trying to put Amy at ease and gently questioning her, Joe was able to piece together a picture of the events leading up to the 'criminal damage'. It appeared that Amy was still attending her old school where she had some good friends. The caring parents of one of them had suggested to their daughter that she should invite Amy to have lunch and spend the Saturday afternoon at home with them and enjoy a little bit of family life. Amy had been thrilled. She woke early in the morning. She was excited at the prospect of tasting a little bit of family life. She wanted to look her very best for the occasion and washed out her favourite outfit. The ironing room was locked so she had asked for the key. She was told she would have to wait. She tried later, explaining that she was going out and received the same response. With time ticking away she was becoming anxious so after being frustrated for a third time she confronted the Senior Care Officer in his office, who was on the telephone. She was going to be late. Her friend's parents had very kindly invited her for lunch and she was going to be late – despite her early start. During the officer's lengthy telephone conversation Amy's agitation mounted. When the telephone was finally replaced Amy told the Officer that she needed to iron her clothes urgently but she had been told to wait. When the officer said, "Well, if you have been told to wait, then you'll just have to wait," her agitation turned to anger. She had picked up the telephone and slammed it down on the desk and in doing so she had damaged the calculator. The police were called.

Joe looked round at the people assembled in the court. The court officers, the probation officer, the policeman, and the prosecuting officer. He asked them if like him they too were parents. They were. "If in similar circumstances your daughter did what Amy did," he asked them, "would you call the police?" His question was acknowledged with a few shaking of heads. "Of course you wouldn't," he went on. "It wouldn't cross my mind. I wouldn't want my daughter to be branded with a criminal record at fourteen-years-old. That wouldn't be in her best interests, would it? I believe that a parent should always act in the best interests of his children. Nobody, I believe, will dispute that." There was silence in court! "The local authority is charged with the duty of being Amy's parent," continued Joe. "From what I have heard today they have failed spectacularly in that duty. I am adjourning this case again and I expect the care officer involved to be present at the next hearing." The officer refused to attend and

Amy was given an absolute discharge. There is nevertheless a record of her appearance in court which could be prejudicial to her in the future.

Several weeks later, as if directed by providence, an invitation arrived at the court for Joe and a colleague to attend the opening of a recently refurbished section of a local authority hostel and it happened to be the one at which Amy stayed. Joe welcomed the opportunity to meet the heartless public servant who had declined his request to be present at Amy's trial. Obviously sensing that he may be in for an uncomfortable confrontation, Mr X took the day off. Joe did however get an opportunity to speak to one of his colleagues to whom he expressed the view that those responsible for the welfare of children in care should be required to attend court when one of their charges was in trouble. A perfectly reasonable requirement, you may think. The officer's reaction was to polarise, withdraw into defensive mode and say, "You won't get me into court without my solicitor being present." How sad is that?

In another case a fifteen-year-old boy appeared before Joe on a charge of arson. Justin's case highlights the all too prevalent attitude in the CPS and the police force that prima facie evidence will be sufficient to obtain convictions and a reliance on the people charged to plead guilty rather than face the trauma of a court appearance. The consequence of this is often to create a resentment against the police among those who feel they have been unfairly charged.

Justin admitted he had been one of four boys present when a fire was started in an old disused and dilapidated bothy on Lord Lambton's estate. Joe was pleased to see that Justin's mother and father and his gran had taken the trouble to attend court and overruled court procedure which permitted only two members of the family access, after querying the gran's presence and finding that Justin was very close to her and spent most weekends with her. Justin was also represented by a solicitor who was hoping that Justin's previous good behaviour coupled with a good character plea and the presence of his family in court would persuade Joe to be lenient in his sentencing. Joe did better than that. He did the solicitor's job for him and acquitted Justin of the charge. He did this because he first took the trouble to dig a bit deeper than the prima facie evidence and to unearth certain factors with which that evidence could be challenged. Apparently Justin and his friends used the old bothy as a den. The door had long ago fallen from its hinges and there was no question of forcible entry. They decided one day to light a fire in the grate of the old fireplace. The flue had disintegrated and smoke had been spotted coming through the roof. Someone had called the fire brigade and when they arrived on the scene followed shortly by a police car Justin was still there. His friends had fled but Justin had delayed his escape trying to put out the fire and had been caught, as it were, red handed. His friends were later apprehended, charged, pleaded guilty and were convicted. Now arson is a very serious offence and carries with it severe penalties and Joe could not easily in his mind reconcile the facts of the case with the severity of the charge.

"What constitutes arson?" he asked the police witness. He didn't know. "Did you see the defendant light the fire?" was his next question. He hadn't. "And did you go into the building?" He didn't. "And were you aware that the fire was confined to the fireplace?" He wasn't. "Was it," continued Joe, "the intention of this young man to burn down the building?" The policeman didn't know. Joe concluded as follows: "To secure a conviction for arson the prosecution must prove and this court must be convinced, that there was a deliberate attempt to cause damage. You have failed to do this and I therefore consider that there is no case to answer." I suspect that most other magistrates in the absence of an effective defence and an admission by the accused, would have simply passed sentence but Joe's long experience on the bench has made him all too well aware of the degree of incompetence and apathy that exists in our Criminal Justice System on the part of solicitors, the police and the CPS itself. But for Joe's intervention Justin would now have an undeserved criminal record and his three friends would not have been able to appeal against their wrongful convictions, which is exactly what they did, successfully.

Michael's is a case which reveals just how remote the system is from accountability and how the cost factor never, it seems, ever enters into the heads of those involved in it. It tells us more than that. Michael had mugged an old lady. The case seemed fairly straightforward.

"Why then," enquired Joe when it appeared before him for the first time after no fewer than ten previous adjournments by other magistrates over a period of eighteen months, "had the case not already been heard?"

The police explained that a key witness had not turned up. Because the matter had dragged on for so long, Joe was conscious of the distress this must have caused Michael's family and was anxious to conclude the case that day.

"Are there any other witnesses?" Joe enquired.

"Two Sir," was the reply.

"Well then, let's get on with it. This family has been put through enough stress."

"Sorry Sir," said the policeman, looking sheepishly at Joe, "we've sent them home."

A not very happy Joe wanted to know why and discovered that the police were relying on their key witness, the victim, to secure a conviction.

"Can you explain to me please," said Joe, "why the key witness has not turned up? Not just today, but on ten previous occasions?"

The reason it appeared was that she was an eighty-one-year-old lady and was terrified at the prospect of appearing in court. Joe put it to the police that if he were to agree to another adjournment, would they be able to guarantee that she would attend next time? They couldn't, but they would try their best to persuade her. "If you couldn't persuade her when she was eighty-one, I think it is highly unlikely that you'll be able to do so now that she's a year older," was Joe's observation, and fearing that in the absence of a conclusion under his jurisdiction the case may drag on indefinitely or until the old lady died or the system ran out of cash, he dismissed the case. So, because of the stupidity of our Criminal Justice System and after dozens of police man hours lost and at great cost in terms of court time and public funds, a mugger is freed to walk unpunished on our streets. No wonder there aren't enough bobbies on the beat when so much of their time is wasted on lost causes like this.

Joe couldn't believe his eyes when sixteen-year-old Yvonne appeared before him in the dock at one o'clock in the afternoon – dressed only in her pyjamas. She had been arrested the previous evening for fighting with another girl over a slice of toast in the communal kitchen of the Local Authority hostel where she lived. The probation officer of course was unable to give Joe an explanation but he managed to listen sympathetically to Yvonne's story by putting her as much at ease as it is possible for a sixteen-year-old girl in court dressed only in pyjamas to feel. He was again able to make the point that no caring parent would allow his or her daughter to face such an embarrassing ordeal. He instructed that Yvonne should be taken back to the hostel and allowed to have a bath and get dressed. He ordered that the senior person at the hostel should appear before him at the next hearing. They withdrew the charge against Yvonne. There's a surprise.

I am assured that not all Local Authority hostels are as insensitive as the examples cited. I sincerely hope not, but the fact that there are such examples makes a massive statement and is an indictment of the supervisory Social Services Department watchdog which exists for this purpose – if indeed one does exist. There has got to be a big question mark over the selection process for the lucrative posts in Social Services. Is too much emphasis placed on administrative and bureaucratic ability and not enough on the basic human qualities of love and care, or indeed plain common sense? You don't need to pass exams for these.

With a wealth of stories like the few I have related, Joe should write his own book. I may offer to be his biographer – if I can pin him down long enough.

He is not alone in condemning a system which has been also branded as "chaotic" by another senior youth court judge. District Judge David Simpson has described the system as "crappy" and "bankrupt" claiming that the courts, struggling to keep up with record numbers of cases, were "slow and inefficient". Since 1997 there has been a rise of twenty-five per cent in juvenile offenders behind bars. He is reported as saying that eight out of ten cases brought before him had to be adjourned after failure by the legal teams to collect or present the correct evidence. I was particularly impressed with his criticism of the fundamental nature of the system which, he observed, "revolves around proof not truth" and "discourages the accused from accepting responsibility for his actions unless there is incontrovertible evidence against them". But this sort of radical thinking strikes at the very core of our judicial system which is stoutly and powerfully defended by our legal profession against which our government in its present form is unwilling to make a stand, even if it had the will to do so. There will, I fear, be no meaningful changes to the establishment unless there is a complete change to our parliamentary political system to one which would prevent individual MPs being defensive when faced with uncomfortable issues like these.

Joe's campaign to give power to magistrates to call as witness the protected species in the form of local authority and social services officers, had it seems caused panic in the corridors of power – hence Harriet Harman's call. She told Joe that a delegation of her senior ministry colleagues would be sent to meet him. In the end only one turned up, listened to what Joe had to say, assured Joe that a full report would be prepared for the Minister and that was the last he has heard on the matter. Certainly not one thing in the system has changed so far and nor are we expecting it to, such is the power and influence vested in the Establishment coupled with the ineptitude and the unwillingness of members of the government to grasp the fiercest nettles which choke our national garden, in case they sting, preferring instead to concentrate on the lesser weeds.

Just in case an impression has been formed that Joe is a lenient magistrate, let me cite a couple of instances which may dispel such thoughts. He can be quite severe when necessary and, on occasions, devious, when for example, after passing sentence he is threatened, which happens often. Such behaviour is not tolerated. He has the culprit immediately arrested for contempt. In such cases it is expected that the case is brought before him on the same day. It is rare that contempt on this scale is serious enough to warrant a custodial sentence so instead of staying behind, as required, to hear the case, Joe pretends that he has forgotten about it, sneaks out through a side door and hears the case the following day – after the culprit has had time to ponder on the advisability of his outburst in a cell overnight. On another occasion Joe had just returned from a skiing holiday during which he had taken a particularly nasty tumble. He went to see his doctor suffering from concussion and temporary amnesia. He was prescribed complete rest for two weeks and strongly advised to make no important decisions during that period. The next day in court Joe sent one defendant to prison and deported another. They should give more judges a bang on the head.

Judge Joe in court.
"Honi soit qui mal y pense"

Thirty Five

SPEED

*The place of a father in modern suburban family life
is a small one, particularly if he plays golf.*
Bertrand Russell.

MANY OF THE INSURANCE COMPANIES we dealt with had annual golf outings and I was fortunate enough to receive invitations to most of these – and very well organised and enjoyable they were too. Some involved overnight stays in hotels and some, notably the Holman Lloyds Brokers and Berger Paints outings, were abroad, the latter being perhaps the only benefit and perk I received from my involvement with Wheatsheaf Coachworks.[4] By far the most memorable however were the golf trips we organised ourselves with people who knew each other well and who were totally relaxed in each other's company.

One of my earliest 'lads' trips was in 1984 when Hello Dandy won the Grand National. The reason why I remember this is because we were staying only a few miles away from Greystoke in the Lake District where he was trained by Gordon Richards. There were six of us all crammed into my static caravan at Whitbarrow Hall (pre-Hopkinson); me, Brian, Solicitor Gary Johnson, Ron Evans and the two Shaws – Sandy and John (JR). Hello Dandy's owner Richard Shaw shared his name with two of our party and like John and I, was an insurance broker. The jockey Neale Doughty was the boyfriend of the barmaid at the nearby Sportsman's Arms where, each night, we would spend our post-golf hours drinking. Again I ignored all the signs and failed to back the bloody thing. God has since washed his hands of me and stopped sending me signs to try and win me some money. John Shaw did have a flutter on Hello Dandy which romped home at thirteen to one. Poor lad. He was, a few years later, found dishevelled and neglected in a field and was rescued to spend

---

[4] See Volume II.

his retirement at the Thoroughbred Training Centre in Lancashire. I'm not talking about John Shaw by the way. He wasn't so lucky.

The National takes place in March and the Lake District can be pretty bleak at that time of the year. It was so cold the Calor Gas bottles froze and the caravan was without heating. Just as well it was well stocked with whisky and we were able to keep warm with wee goldies as Sandy called them. After hours of lively conversation and debate, most of which was the kind of trivial nonsense you thoroughly enjoy when you're pissed, I got dressed (i.e. put on some extra layers of clothing) and went to bed at 2 a.m., having picked my all-time great football team to represent Planet Earth should we ever get round to playing against Mars or some other cosmic soccer planet. Caravan walls are thin of course and from my bedroom I was able to hear clearly Sandy's selection in which there was no place in the starting line-up for great players like Franz Beckenbauer, Bobby Moore, Ferenc Puscas or Bobby Charlton. Even the great Pele was required to play out of position to accommodate Johnny McKenzie. Sandy was deadly serious and Johnny was among no fewer than four Scots in his team, the others being Jim Baxter, Denis Law and, unbelievably, goalkeeper Alan Rough. "Who the hell is Johnny McKenzie?" was the chorus which greeted Sandy's selection. Apparently Mr McKenzie played at half back for Partick Thistle in the sixties when Sandy, an avid Thistle supporter, never missed a Saturday at Firhill.

Despite our late night we were all up, not so bright but early, the following morning. It was too cold to sleep. Ron Evans actually had an icicle hanging from his nose. Our game at Carlisle was interrupted by snow and the conditions didn't lend themselves to scintillating golf. As was often the case on these trips the crack was often better than the golf.

After brother-in-law Paul gave up his caravan at Whitbarrow Hall he bought a cottage at Threlkeld near Keswick and he very kindly allowed us to stay there when we repeated the Lake District golf trip three years later, this time with Brian, Mike Cherry and Peter Peyton, our Majorcan four ball. On our trips we try to organise ourselves loosely by, for example, each taking responsibility for certain duties. One of mine was car packing and security, a role for which I considered myself suitable and for which I had volunteered my services. When we stopped on the way up to the Lakes at Hexham Golf Club for a round of golf there the other three went into the club house to order lunch and left me in the car park to carefully hide our clubs and belongings from view, a job which I felt I had accomplished competently enough. Until, that is, I was later tapped on the shoulder by someone who told me I had left the door of the car wide open. I was given a second chance but was relieved of my appointment a few years later when on another golf trip I left the Stan the Man Trophy on a window ledge at our hotel in Brampton and had to drive back twenty miles to retrieve it. The trophy was donated by Stan Johnstone, a dear friend from Chester-le-Street whom I hadn't seen for years and who I was eagerly looking forward to meeting again at Jonathan Peyton's fortieth birthday bash at the golf club. Unfortunately it wasn't to be. Sadly Stan, who was in the advanced stages of multiple sclerosis, passed away only a few weeks earlier. Peter Peyton, the last winner and holder of the Trophy, told me that right up to the end Stan was as cheerful and optimistic as he had been in his golfing days. It would be nice to resurrect the tournament in Stan's memory.

Our second trip to the Lake District again took place in March though, fortunately, the weather was kinder this time. It was during the weekend when the clocks were turned forward by one hour. I could never remember which was which until somebody recently told me of a great aide memoir – Spring forward, Fall back. Good, isn't it? Peter, Mike and I decided to play a prank on Brian and during the night when he was asleep we would put his watch on an extra hour. We were due to tee off at 10.30 at Penrith Golf Club where at that time I was a member, and we somehow got Brian to accept that our tee time had been put forward one hour. Brian's observation that we therefore had ten minutes to get to the course puzzled us and when he went to the toilet Mike, Peter and I got our heads together and discovered that each of us had at some point during the night added an hour on to Brian's watch, assuming that this had not been done by the others. The outcome was that it was actually 8.20 a.m. Brian's watch showed 11.20 a.m. and in fact we had two hours and ten minutes before tee off time. We duly teed off at 10.30 (1.30 p.m. BST – Brian Summer Time). I had been able to convince Brian that my influence as a member of the club would enable us to obtain a later tee time. We finished our round about 2 p.m. (5 p.m. BST) and had a few drinks in the clubhouse by which time it was nearly 4 p.m. (7 p.m. BST). Brian commented on how light it was and I waffled on about the Lake District being peculiar in that respect which, amazingly, he didn't seriously query. We arrived at the Gloucester Arms in Penrith just before 6 p.m. (9 p.m. BST), managing somehow to divert Brian's attention until they opened the doors, by which time we were famished. Brian urged us to order the bar meals in case they closed the kitchen. It hadn't even opened! We managed to delay ordering for a further hour and ours was the first order placed. When the pub started filling up around 8 p.m. (11 p.m. BST) my explanation that the Gloucester Arms was renowned for its stoppy backs and lock ins was a bridge too far. It didn't wash. Brian became suspicious and we had to reveal to him the full and intriguing details of our deception. He took it in very good part of course.

We played Penrith the following day too, where I received some disapproving glances from some lady members. I realised why when I took out my three wood and found a condom stretched over the head. This was Brian's revenge. But it hadn't been achieved without embarrassment. When buying his packet of three from the chemist's (these were pre-machine days) he too had to endure some disapproving looks and raised eyebrows from the lady assistant when he demanded the cheapest possible item. Noticing her raised eyebrows, Peter burst out laughing and said,

"That's how much he respects his girlfriend." Then, realising the reason for her disapproval, Brian was quick to explain the true purpose of his purchase. I don't know whether the lady believed him. On the following and final day of our trip, after three holes, we abandoned our attempt to play the Carlisle Municipal Course which was a quagmire. We had our green fees reimbursed and Mike suggested that we should drive back across the Pennines and play at Westerhope which was on the way home and where he was a member. Brian and I were level with Mike and Peter on matches played over the weekend and a decider was required. So close was the final match that we actually putted out on the eighteenth green in total darkness.

In 1985 John Shaw, courtesy of General Accident Insurance, had managed to get hold of four hospitality tickets for The Open at Sandwich in Kent and he very kindly invited Brian and I to accompany him with Tom Suffle, another local insurance broker. John is a very loveable but a very laid back character and when he said to leave all the arrangements to him we had misgivings which, two months later, and still with no accommodation booked, turned to grave doubts. We offered to relieve him of the responsibility but he would hear nothing of it. We were only too well aware that such a big event in such a remote location would mean that all the decent accommodation would be snapped up and if there were any rooms to be had they would be either cheap and grotty, hugely expensive or involve a long drive to the venue. John assured us that the matter would receive his urgent attention but we knew that his definition of urgent was not consistent with that contained in the Oxford Dictionary and as understood by the rest of us. We didn't like to pester him too much in case he felt that we were being ungrateful but when, with only a few days left, he had done nothing and my thoughts were beginning to include tents and sleeping bags, he called to say that his quest for lodgings had succeeded. We would be staying at the Delbridge Gentlemen's Club in Faversham. He then proceeded to describe the facilities there which included two snooker tables and full breakfast. My thoughts immediately switched from canvas to cost. This was going to be an arm and a leg job. Surprisingly it was very reasonable. The establishment was run by Guy and Julian, two very nice boys indeed. "Breakfast from seven thirty. Lots of hot water. Just ask and we will do anything for you boys," was the greeting we received on our arrival. What we were not told was that breakfast was cooked at seven thirty but if you didn't come down then it would be completely shrivelled up and quite inedible. What they also didn't tell us, as Tom was to find out because he couldn't sleep for Brian's snoring and got up at six a.m. to have a bath, was that yes, there was plenty of hot water, but no cold. Before he realised this Tom had half-filled the bath and had to spend the next two hours walking round a desolate Faversham until it had cooled down sufficiently for him to get into it. By then however it was filthy. Thinking that someone had very kindly run the bath for him, John Shaw had availed himself of this solicitous gesture and bathed in Tom's water.

That night we had stocked up with drinks to allow mein hosts to close the bar, leaving us to watch the day's highlights on BBC2. We soon realised that there had been a miscalculation in quantity and when we ran out of drinks Brian and I decided to raid the bar, intending to settle the bill the following day. Grills had been pulled down denying us access from that approach so we both crawled under the bar flap seeking access via that route. Two voices were then heard. Brian's ("The bastard's put a padlock on the door") followed immediately by Julian's ("Can I help you boys?"). Our embarrassed explanations were received with coolness and a less than friendly, "We told you boys we would do anything for you. All you had to do was ask." So we asked him to open the bar which, after his remark, he could hardly refuse to do. This second helping of drinks was considerably more expensive than the first.

I can only describe the food provided by our hosts at Sandwich as sumptuous, the wine excellent and plentiful and they themselves generous and charming. This hospitality was repaid by John annoying the wife of their Managing Director. Seated behind her in the grandstand at the eighteenth green John opened a can of fizzy drink which spurted its contents over her expensive hairdo. In a tight finish with Bernhard Langer, Sandy Lyle's was a popular but narrow victory. After missing the final green with his approach shot and finding a nasty lie he fluffed his chip shot but recovered to win by one stroke.

These early golf trips whetted my appetite for more. I was among the first to put my name down when the opportunity arose. There were several outings to the Scottish Borders, Slaley Hall in Northumberland, Ireland, France, Portugal and Spain. The Scottish Tourist Board's Freedom of the Fairways packages were and probably still are very popular and deservedly so. I've played some very nice courses in that part of the world. My first trip there was with some fellow Chester-le-Street members, Brian of course, Peter Peyton, Stan 'the man' Johnstone, Bob Roxburgh and Peter Hoyle. We stayed in Melrose which boasts a fine nine-hole course and an excellent French restaurant.

Paul Woods, an occasional 'square tabler' in the Cons Club, invited me to several Slaley Hall days. This beautiful championship course nestles in some lovely countryside near the village of Slaley in Northumberland. Paul's Company was a main sponsor there and we were able to enjoy a number of 'freebies'. Several years later Paul and I were invited to join a group there on a trip organised by Patsy and his friends, most of whom, like Patsy's dad, swore like troopers – very loudly too. *They* were surprised when they received VIP treatment from the management who invited us to dine in the private banquet room. *We* weren't. The reason was quite obvious to Paul and me. They didn't want us in the public dining room because their bad language and rowdy behaviour would have upset the other guests. A novel, if unwitting way of receiving VIP treatment!

Although I have been many times since, my first visit to Ireland was with the Unicorn Society which gave me the opportunity to play both the K Club and Druid's Glen. Other visits to the Scottish Borders included two with the Unicorn and, not counting the BABITTS in 1995, two with the Cons Club and Acklam Park lads. On both of these occasions we were accompanied by Ron Evans who was presented with the winner's trophy by John Tate during the coach journey – on the way there! It didn't seem to matter what handicap we gave Ron, he always managed to raise his game and win. Even an attempt at sabotage on one of the trips could not prevent the inevitable victory. One of the lads had taken with him some laxative chewing gum for a joke and during their round offered some to Ron. He also gave some to Ron's playing partner who happened to be Patsy. They were both later offered more. Ron declined. Patsy didn't. Back at the hotel both Ron and Patsy's tummies were churning. Ron's first beer made matters worse and sensibly he stayed on soft drinks, ate a light meal and went up early to his room which he was sharing with Patsy, who of course ignored his intestinal turmoil, drank several pints of beer and had the full works for dinner. The following morning he couldn't wait to check out of the hotel. He brought his suitcase down and skipped breakfast. A strange smell permeated the foyer and the culprit was Patsy's case. He had shit the bed and had been too embarrassed to leave the sheets on the bed. They were included among the contents of his case, as were also the contents of his bowels! And whilst on the subject of smell I must mention Ron's Revenge. On most Unicorn day trips we took turns using our cars and we travelled in convoy. Ron was unfortunate enough one day to be a passenger in Patsy's car. Not many people share Patsy's sense of humour on the subject of farting but he seems to find it very amusing to let rip and the worse it smells the funnier he seems to find it. He was on particularly good form on this occasion and the more Ron and his fellow passengers objected the more he did it. Eventually, in retaliation, Ron opened the valve on his colostomy bag. Patsy's was no match for the stench which this released. Ron unfortunately suffered from Chrone's disease. His lovely wife Angela was confined to a wheelchair in the advanced stages of MS but I've never heard Ron complain and rarely have I seen him less than cheery and without a smile on his face. He makes us all count our blessings.

The local opticians formed a golf society and I was fortunate enough to be invited to two of their trips to France where we stayed in the Ibis Hotel in Reims and played some delightful courses built around old chateaux. The fellow Cons members on the trip instead of eating in the hotel preferred to go out on the town and Graham Duffield, John Tate, Peter Hardisty, Mick Coppinger and I soon gained ourselves a reputation. We were known as the piss heads. I think the others were surprised at our ability to drink so much and stay the pace. They were particularly astonished when I even had cans of John Smiths ale for breakfast. I had brought with me in my golf bag seven cans, one for each day, which I drank when I got back to the hotel after golf. I didn't want to destroy our reputation by confessing that my empty cans were actually filled with water when I brought them into breakfast!

Golf trips were usually thinly disguised excuses to get away from home and let our hair down. I wouldn't say that the golf was incidental, not for me anyway, but it only accounted for about five hours of our day which, even with nine hours sleep, left us with ten hours in which to find mischief. Mind you, having served our apprenticeships in the Club at home we would easily sustain lengthy drinking sessions when we were playing away and these would take up most of our spare time.

I suppose it was inevitable, given the camaraderie around our table at the Cons Club, that we should form a golf society of our own. The proposal was accepted enthusiastically, even by those among us, notably Hodgy, who didn't even play golf but knew that the après golf would afford plenty of scope for enjoyment. An inaugural trip was organised to Portugal and another member of the Club, Alan Watson, who I don't think always approved of our behaviour, accidentally provided a name for the new Society when he referred to us as a Set of Pathetic Early Evening Drunkards. Thus, SPEED was born.

The year before the Portugal trip we had a dummy run when in 1995 Tatey organised BABITTS – The Boys Are Back In Town Tour of Scotland. We were joined on this occasion by Rainbow and his Irish pal Tommy the hairdresser. En route for North Berwick and the Marine Hotel we stayed in Melrose, which gave me an opportunity to play the lovely little course there again. However the format had been changed since my previous visit and we were told that even though we only wanted to play nine holes we must pay the full green fee for eighteen holes, which was no use to us since we had planned an early afternoon arrival at North Berwick in time to play a full round there. Having recommended Melrose I volunteered to have a word with the starter to see if I could negotiate a discount for nine holes only. After some explanation of our situation and some haggling he finally agreed a price with me at which point Irish Tommy, who had been impatiently itching to get involved, strode across to us, pushed me out of the way and said to the starter, "We'll give you £12 each and no more. Take it or leave it." He was stunned by the starter's reply. "I'll take it," he said. "I've just agreed £10 with your pal."

It was quite late when we came off the eighteenth at North Berwick that evening so we decided to eat in the hotel where Irish Tommy, having tasted three different wines and complained that none were sweet enough, was given a spoon and a sugar bowl by the head waiter. Although it was a hotel of very high standard it was run by long serving manager Alistair in an unstuffy friendly way. Alistair came to the rescue the following night when we all decided we would eat out but couldn't agree among ourselves where to go. I went to reception and enquired about good local restaurants, explaining the problem we were having because Hodgy fancied Indian, Rainbow preferred Chinese, Brian Italian and so on. Overhearing this, Alistair came over and said, "I'll sort it out. Tell them all to be here in twenty minutes." A mini-coach was soon waiting to take us to the Riverside Bistro in Haddington where a great night was had by all, culminating in us each having to sing a song. Instead of 'High Noon' I chose my other party piece 'Mama's Little Baby Loves Shortenin' Bread', to which everyone can join in the chorus. Tatey's rendition of 'Brian Robson's Red and White Army' however brought the house down and nearly the table too when he hammered on it for emphasis. Most of us had a nightcap in the resident's bar when we were returned to the hotel. Tatey had several, crashed out on a settee in the lounge and woke up in the morning surrounded by a coach load of ladies from the WI having a coffee morning. The blue rinse and pearl brigade, he called them. He was diplomatically requested by Alistair to vacate his random resting place as his snoring was upsetting the ladies and when asked why he hadn't gone to bed in his room, replied that he wanted to see the sunrise. "Don't they have sunrises in Middlesbrough?" Alistair enquired with just a hint of disapproval. He had seen it all before. Ron Evans was the winner the following day – but it had cost him £20. That was the amount we all put into the kitty for nightcaps. Before he was allowed to escape, Ron paid his money, skipped the drinks and went to bed.

Living up to my "cocker" reputation I had to cry off the Portugal trip and listened with envy later as the adventures were recalled by the ten pioneers, Brian, Tatey, The Duff, Penina Pete, Coppy, Stevie Joe, Hodgy, Westy (Basher), John (JR) Shaw and Patsy, whose face and head resembled a Maris Piper with potato blight, in consequence of him having fallen asleep round the swimming pool without sun protection. He couldn't understand it afterwards as everyone fell about laughing when, referring to his latest sexual partner, he said, "Mind you, she's no oil painting!"

The first sort of serious committee meeting was conducted round that particular pool and concerned mainly the appointment of officers. Stevie Joe accepted the office of Life President but, he said, "Only for one year!" Nobody was keen to hold the hot potato of Events Organiser after Patsy, who had arranged the golf at Islantilla the previous day, had been slagged off by the others. He had booked the tee for 10 a.m. but when they arrived at the course he was told they had missed their slot. A heated confrontation followed, with Patsy insisting that the starter was mistaken and the club house clock was an hour fast. This golf course happened to be just over the border in Spain which of course is one hour ahead of GMT and Portuguese time, a fact which the others insisted that Patsy, whose responsibility it was, should have taken into account – even though they themselves had been fooled too. The fact is that these trips wouldn't have been such fun if it hadn't been for these unpredictable incidents and subsequent recriminations, like the time on a subsequent tour when Penina Pete and Riki Birch had booked single rooms but after a few days decided to share Riki's twin-bedded room and use the other one purely for their more unpleasant bodily functions. During the course of one of these visits Pete thought he heard a noise. It sounded like people talking in German. Surely he must be mistaken. On his way out he glanced into the bedroom and was shocked to find a couple in his bed. Obviously the hotel staff, having found the bed unslept in, had assumed that the room had been vacated and rented it to the Germans. I wonder what Herr and Damen made of it when they realised that some complete strangers were using their en suite for their daily bowel movements!

The lads had obviously had a great time on that first trip and nothing short of bereavement would cause me to miss the next one. I was thereafter an ever present until the Society's membership criteria was relaxed, which I wasn't when I found myself, for an entire week, in the company of people I didn't know. They were, I'm sure, sound lads but it wasn't the same as sharing my time with people I already had an easy relationship with after numerous drinking sessions together and who had become my brothers in booze.

Following two visits to the Costa del Sol the second Portugal SPEED trip, "The Final Frontier", took place three years later in 1999. It was there that Peter Hardisty earned his nickname by playing perhaps the best round of his life at the tough Penina Portuguese Championship course where he shot a gross 76 (nett 62) following which I wrote a song for him to the tune of 'Maria' from Rogers and Hammerstein's musical *West Side Story*:

> *Penina... I've just played a course called Penina*
> *... And suddenly I found*
> *I'd played a perfect round*
> *...At Penina.*
>
> *Penina, Penina... I hit a purple patch*
> *... at Penina*
> *... and with my purple patch*
> *I easy won my match*
> *... at Penina.*
>
> *Penina... Penina, Penina, Penina...*
> *Played the front like I'm almost in heaven*
> *Played the back... in a gross thirty seven*
> *... at Penina.*
>
> *Penina, Penina, Penina*
> *Forty six points round Penina*
> *A feat I won't repeat*
> *I'm now Penina Pete*
> *... at Penina.*

Fired up by his performance, Peter was regaling The Duff, Tatey and I with a stroke by stroke account of his round later, much later, that evening. He was keen to play again the following 'free' day for which no golf had been arranged. The lovely San Lorenzo course had been mentioned earlier but everybody had rejected it because of the green fee which was the equivalent of £100. But at that time of night £100 wasn't a problem. £1000 wouldn't have been – drinks in, wits out and all that. We decided to go for it and arranged to meet in the foyer of the hotel at 8 am. Amazingly I was awake before my alarm went off and I got dressed quietly to avoid disturbing Brian, who I was sharing with. Mick Coppinger is the uncrowned king of wind up and as soon as I returned from San Lorenzo to the hotel he came over to tell me that Brian was furious because I hadn't told him I was going to play golf. I'm sure Brian wasn't furious to begin with but under Coppy's skilful manipulation fuelled by a day on the drink our innocent four ball had become in Brian's mind a conspiracy and my thoughtful silence that morning had become a deceitful act of stealth in order to sneak off and play golf without him. It all blew over of course and the phrase "cosy four ball" which is how Brian had scathingly described our "deception" was to become a part of the Speedsters vocabulary, as was another, which I plagiarised from *Fawlty Towers* – "Don't mention the war".

It was at San Lorenzo that I first experienced the thrill of walking on to the eighteenth green to applause from a "gallery" as golf spectators are called. There wasn't a big crowd, only a few who obviously hadn't realised that the important mixed fourball competition we were following had finished and thought we were the final pairing. Tatey was my partner that day and we still speculate as to which one of us they thought was the *lady* golfer!

It had rained during the night before we were due to play Villamoura and buggies were not allowed on the course. This presented a problem to Stevie who suffered from the bone disease spondilitis. We pleaded his case hoping that they would give him dispensation from the ban and the starter agreed to send Stevie to the Course Marshall for assessment. He returned with a grin on his face and the news that "He had failed with flying colours" and was therefore allowed to hire a buggy. This phrase too was to be adopted by us and used whenever one of us under achieved. To make up for Stevie's "handicap" Brian, who was our Handicap Secretary, allowed him to play off fifty four so he had an extra three shots at each hole. I played with him a couple of days later at La Quinta where he broke Manuel Pinero's course record – nett of his handicap of course! I had simply suggested during our round together that with three shots a hole there was no need to fly four irons over the lakes when he could play three wedges round them. On the same trip however he was thrown off the Santa Maria course when he fell over and was spotted by one of the Marshalls who approached him and asked him what his handicap was. "Thirty six," replied Stevie proudly. "I was fifty four but I won yesterday." Any hopes he had of persuading the Marshall to allow him to continue were dashed when, in response to the Marshall's next question, "Who gave you that handicap?" he naively said, "Brian." Since then many courses insist on the production of an official golf club handicap certificate. This however did not present Tatey, our organiser, with a problem. He had some "Berwick Hills Golf and Country Club" certificates printed. Berwick Hills is a council housing estate in Middlesbrough.

Cala Honda on the Costa del Sol was again chosen for the SPEED tour in 2000 where again I became the subject of Brian's wrath, again unfairly. We had been drinking in a Karaoke bar and some of us decided to move on. I must have been crashed out back at the hotel for quite a while when I was woken up by Brian muttering something about English t-ts. I pretended to be asleep while Brian continued to lambast the Sassenachs and also the Spanish bar owner who apparently had been a disgrace for not ordering him a taxi and who, apparently, wouldn't have lasted five minutes as a barman in Glasgow. When the others had decided to leave the bar Brian had insisted on staying put and the bar owner's un-Glasgow like behaviour meant that he had to walk back to the hotel. Unfortunately the route he chose was several kilometres longer than the five hundred metres one chosen by the rest of us and he had spent hours walking round in circles.

With so many of us with opinions and preferences, the decision of where to eat was always the subject of much dispute. On another occasion at Cala Honda, Brian, who by then considered himself something of an expert on Spanish culture and culinary matters, decided one night to make a decision for us and booked a table at a restaurant at which he had pre ordered a traditional Spanish meal. It was awful. Only Brian could choose to eat that nation's traditional dish in an establishment run by two nice boys from Huddersfield. Tatey, who could sleep anywhere, anytime, used his plateful of paella as a cushion when, without warning, he slumped forward and in seconds was in the land of nod.

We stayed at the same resort, Cala Honda, for the third tour and given the frantic lifestyle we were leading it came as no surprise that we suffered our first casualty when JR was hospitalised suffering from exhaustion, dehydration – and amnesia. He had forgotten to pack his medication!

We also went to the Costa del Sol the following year but this time at a new venue Puerto Banus, the playground of the rich with its harbour full of multi million pound yachts and its restaurants full of their owners and with prices to match. This didn't deter us. We had a kitty. We chose one of the top restaurants on our first night and with the kitty in mind ordered our meals modestly – or so we thought. The bill for The Duff's meal alone took care of half the money in the kitty. He insisted that he had ordered the lobster because it was cheap and in the face of severe heckling from the rest of us produced a menu to prove he wasn't taking advantage. Sure enough, the price on the menu was cheap but what he hadn't realised was that the price quoted was per gram!

For some of its members golf was only a part of the SPEED Society's *raison d'etre*. Another of the region's delights which we were told was a 'must' was the topless night club La Stark, or more specifically its topless hostesses, so we piled into taxis and paid it a visit. It was my turn to get the drinks in and I was staggered when I got the bill. A small beer cost one thousand pesetas! Now when you pay that kind of money for a drink you want to enjoy it in peace. The last thing you need while you are drinking is some lecherous scantily clad female fondling your private parts – no matter how young and beautiful she might be. So most of us drank up and left. Patsy stayed behind of course and later told us that he had fallen in love with one of the hostesses, a particularly stunning young Columbian girl, had gone upstairs with her and paid her five thousand pesetas for "extras" but in his fumbling haste to get undressed had knotted the lace in his trainers and when he had eventually managed to unravel the knot and take them off his time had run out. The next day he went to the big department store El Corte Ingles and bought a pair of slip-ons.

We did get around to playing some golf but one of the courses, Lauro, must rank as the worst I have played in Spain. It was a bad day all round, starting off with a visit to the local hospital to see JR who had again taken ill and was recovering in what then became known as the John Shaw Wing of the local hospital. We were severely hung-over. The course was a three hour drive from the hotel – at least it was using our itinerary - and we were not into long drives, on or off the course. By the time I had got ready there was only one buggy left and it wouldn't start. While I was pumping the accelerator pedal and fiddling around with the key Brian was checking the electrics. The buggy suddenly leapt forward, almost decapitated Brian and crashed into a wall. All this before a ball had been struck. No wonder I played lousy golf.

However we were scheduled the next day to play one of my favourite courses, Torrequebrada, which I had played previously when daughter Liz and I had holidayed in nearby Benalmadena several years earlier. With a crowd of irresponsible lads away from home things cannot be expected to run smoothly. This is all part of the fun. Our visit to Torrequebrada was no exception. The tee had been reserved and we had pre-paid the green fees but we didn't have the vouchers. Patsy had them for safe keeping. The problem was that there was no sign of Patsy when we gathered at breakfast and his bed hadn't been slept in. We drove to the course hoping to persuade the office to allow us to play without the vouchers. We were not too hopeful. Imagine our relief when we drove into the car park and found a dishevelled Patsy sitting on a low wall with his head in his hands. With time running out we got him into the office where he joined the queue. I stood beside him because he was a little unsteady on his feet and was swaying slightly from side to side – a condition which had not gone unnoticed by the reception staff. It came as no surprise when they refused to allow us to play, thinking presumably that we were all in the same state as Patsy. The official reason given for their refusal was that we were late for our tee off time which was not strictly true since though it was going to be tight, we did have a couple of minutes to spare. I thought it prudent at this stage however to interrupt Patsy's protestations and take control of the situation. They reluctantly agreed to allow us to start on the tenth tee but we would have a three hour wait before we could resume our round on the first tee. This was a welcome and necessary break for Patsy who after scoring only one point on the first nine holes we played, after his customary power nap as he called it, scored twenty four on the second and helped his team to tie for first place. The procedure in these circumstances is for the result to be decided by a count back on the back nine holes. Patsy's team had a better score on holes one to nine but the other team had easily won the holes which were played first, ie ten to eighteen. Naturally this led to a dispute. Did holes ten to eighteen constitute the back nine if they are played first or only if they were played after the front nine? A call was made to golf's governing body the Royal & Ancient Golf Society of St Andrews. Michael Bonalleck the president was not available but we did manage to speak to Carol who couldn't give us a definite ruling but her opinion was that "back nine" meant the holes that were played last rather than the back nine on the scorecard. This decision was not accepted by Brian who would then have been on the losing team. He demanded to know what authority Carol had in the R&A. He could hear what sounded like a Hoover in the background and she may have been one of the cleaners for all he knew. The result was inconclusive. But whenever there is a rule query in our friendly matches we always threaten to phone Carol. Patsy refused to tell us where he had spent the night – but I noticed he was wearing his slip-ons!

More and more people were keen to become SPEED tourers attracted, I suspect, more by tales of the Puerto Banus night life than the golf. "Don't mention the war," I found myself having to constantly say to Patsy as he talked in the club, often indiscreetly, of his exploits and occasionally those of others. With the increase in numbers, logistics, which had never been our strong point, became a nightmare. I had to squeeze John Shaw into our car one day when his team car left without him. Brian had his customary contrary moment one evening when, with John his roommate, he turned up pissed at the restaurant we had chosen to eat in. Annoyed that we hadn't waited for him, Brian loudly expressed his feelings in true Glaswegian fashion. It was Paul Radigan's first SPEED tour and he wasn't yet used to the routine. I explained later, after he had taken a swing at Brian, that these incidents shouldn't be taken to heart. It was all part of the SPEED tradition and the tour wouldn't be the same without them. Paul again got himself upset about something on the flight on the way home, so much so that he would write a letter of complaint to the airline. He asked Tatey, who had booked the flights, whether he would have any objection to him sending a strong letter to Monarch Airlines. "Of course not, why should I?" said Tatey. Paul, a few weeks later, then complained to John that Monarch had not had the courtesy to reply to his letter. "I'm not surprised," said Tatey,"We flew out with Monarch but the return flight was with Air 2000."

The SPEED tours are still going strong minus me, Brian, Tatey, Hodgy, JR, Rainbow and Westy. Patsy is still an ever present though. I was one of the first to drop out. After that last Puerto Banus trip I finally came to terms with the reality that I could no longer keep up with the younger lads – and I didn't want to be the first one to come home in a plastic bag as one of them surely will one of these years.

The 1999 Tour at Los Arqueros.
Top row L to R: "Penina" Pete Hardisty, Stuart Wilkinson, John Shaw, Brian Sutherland, Mick Coppinger, Graham Duffield, Derrick Arnott, John Westwood, Simon Cruikshank, Paul Radigan, Graham Craggs, Stevie Lowe.

Front Row – L to R: Denny McGiven, Ray "Rainbow" King-Lane, Peter Horsefield, John Tate.

Thirty-Six

GOODBYE GREATIE

The supreme happiness in life is the conviction that we are loved –
loved for ourselves, or rather, loved in spite of ourselves.
Victor Hugo.

MY **MOTHER WAS EIGHTY-THREE** when I retired and being an only child the burden of caring for her fell to me. Oh, if only my sister had been born. Not just because she could have shared the responsibility, though this undoubtedly would have been welcomed, but more importantly she would have been a great comfort to my mother. Females tend to be much closer to their mothers and are generally more competent in this area. A daughter's a daughter all her life and a son's a son till he takes a wife.

There had been a change in my mother since my father died. At around the same time she had also lost her sister, Auntie Peggy, and soon afterwards, just a few months before her one hundredth birthday, Auntie Ginny, her half-sister, had died. Living to a ripe old age can be a mixed blessing because you outlive all your friends and same generation family and are left to deal with the loneliness and void which this leaves in your life. As we grow older we do in some of our characteristics become younger. A young child relies entirely on others for all its needs and its demands are entirely selfish and unrelenting. So it is with old people. As children grow older, however, they become more independent and rely less on their parents. On the other hand, as *they* grow older, elderly people become less capable and seek and demand more attention. We can impose our wills on youngsters to influence their behaviour but this often is not possible with older people. Certainly it wasn't in my case. I found myself in a situation where I was expected to help but not allowed to do so in the manner I felt was most effective. Although my mother was lonely, she refused to consider giving up her house and moving into something smaller and more suitable where perhaps she could find new friends. Instead, she chose to rely on me for companionship, nurturing, I suspect, the hope that I would ask her to move in

269

with us – something I was determined to avoid, particularly as having just retired and divested myself of one massive area of responsibility, I was looking forward to finding some enjoyable use for the time and the energy this would release, not being tied down with *more* responsibility. My mother could be difficult at times. She wasn't perfect. I was aware that it would be my wife on whom the demands would be made and whilst, had I asked her to, Chris would, as a caring person, have made a good job of it, I felt it wouldn't be fair on her. I had already expected her to assume the responsibility of raising someone else's child. I would not give her the thankless task of looking after someone else's mother. She too needed a break. My mother *did* manage to get to live with us for a few months when she broke her leg walking round to visit us one evening. She had spent the day with us and after tea I took her home in treacherous conditions barely fit for driving let alone walking and especially so at eighty-five years old. She suffered from claustrophobia and panic attacks and often the urge to escape from her lonely surroundings became irresistible. Later that evening the doorbell rang and I opened the door to find a stranger standing there with my mother virtually in his arms. He had found her lying where she had fallen at the roadside in the snow. So concerned was I for my mother that I didn't get the chance to properly thank that Good Samaritan.

I was grateful to my wife who did a wonderful job of nursing my mother during her stay with us, an exercise which, due to the lifting involved while she was still recovering from a hip operation, contributed I'm sure, to her needing to have a second one just a year later. My mother of course, poor thing, revelled in the fuss and attention she was receiving and though it's an awful thing to say, there may just have been a little bit of attention seeking involved on my mother's part. I'm not saying that she deliberately broke her leg of course but perhaps she wasn't too upset that she had. Old people can be quite guileful and manipulative, something we have just got to accept as a symptom of growing old and deal with sympathetically. "At least they won't be able to go on holiday now," she had said to my mother-in-law Vera during one of her visits to us to lend a hand. My mother would become distressed and panicky when I mentioned going on holiday and this made it very difficult for me so, with a couple of exceptions, I could get away for no more than seven days at a time and then I couldn't properly relax. In an effort to ease my conscience I would telephone her every day, which in itself was stressful because she was hard of hearing – mutton deaf, as my wife would say – although half the problem was that she didn't concentrate and wouldn't listen. I was lucky to get more than two words into a sentence without being interrupted with "Eh?" I found myself beginning to hate that word.

In many ways it was easier having my mother under our roof. At least I didn't have to worry about her being alone and vulnerable. But when she was well enough I made the difficult decision to insist that she went back home. Her plight fortunately had provided me with some ammunition with which to persuade her to move and she finally agreed to give up her house and her garden which she loved but which by then was becoming a burden since she insisted on tending it herself. The sheltered accommodation I found for her only a short distance away in Moray Close was in my opinion ideal for her and though she wouldn't admit it, I'm sure it was a relief to her not to be like a pea in a drum in her three bedroom semi.

We had countless confrontations on the issue of hearing aids. If I hadn't telephoned her by ten o'clock in the morning she would call me and ask me where I was even though since she called me at home and I was speaking to her from there, it was obvious where I was. She would call several times a day and if I wasn't in she would panic. I installed an answerphone machine so that she could leave messages when I was out, but technology wasn't exactly her strong point. "Who's that woman who answers the phone now?" she would ask me accusingly. She came to hate the answerphone woman with an intensity she normally reserved for the upper classes and Tory politicians. It took a long time and umpteen inconclusive attempts at explaining its function before she could leave a cohesive message. She still couldn't fully grasp the concept and still assumed that "that woman" was living with us. I gave up trying to explain to her the wonders of modern telecommunication technology.

Still a staunch leftie at heart she resented, refused to wear, and eventually rejected the top of the range hearing aids I got for her privately and when she lost one, probably deliberately, I took her to get some new NHS ones which again proved to be a futile exercise since she rarely wore them anyway unless I insisted and physically inserted them myself. Her attitude towards anything involving private wealth or privilege is one shared irrationally by many in this country, the only country in the world to think like this and an attitude which inhibits our development as a nation. Our culture has earned the respect of the world and whilst not perfect we should be careful before we set about dismantling it in favour of something else.

My mother had never been good with pans and taps and it was her deficiency in these areas which eventually led at the age of eighty-seven to her move from sheltered accommodation at Moray Close to Roseleigh Care Home. There were only so many fire alerts and floods the warden at Moray Close could take. I was then able to relax, knowing she was under constant but discreet surveillance by trained carers. Understandably she wasn't keen on the move. The nomad in her had been finally laid to rest. There were fewer things she disliked about Roseleigh than the umpteen other care homes I had shown her and she finally accepted the inevitable. As care homes go, I have to say that Roseleigh must be up there with the best. She had her own small room and, very important to her, her own bathroom and toilet. The only real difference was that she ate her meals communally. To help make her feel at home she was able to take her own favourite pieces of furniture and of course her personal belongings. The staff were lovely with her and I think that was what influenced her final decision. Beatrice had always been a stylish dresser and took great care with her appearance. She could always, in her own words, "rise to the occasion". So despite space being at a premium she insisted on keeping her entire, and substantial, wardrobe of clothes, most of which had to stay in boxes which she promised to sort out "when I get round to it." She never did.

The telephone was her lifeline, her contact with the outside world. I had a line put directly into her room. This and her hearing aids were the bane of my life. She continued to call me several times a day on the slightest pretext, then started to complain that I never called her, which was not true of course. I confess that at first I was quite pleased that she wasn't answering my calls because, or so I thought, it meant that she was out of her room socialising with the other residents. I should have known better. When I suggested that this may be the reason why she rarely answered my calls she was quick to seize on the opportunity to get a bit of sympathy by insisting she never saw anybody and was always in her room. The second part of her reply may have had something to do with the first part but I didn't labour the point. Instead I suggested that there may be something wrong with her phone, a claim she strongly denied, pointing out that she was always able to get through to me – or "that woman" – the answerphone voice, which of course wasn't the point since it was my calls to her which was the issue. She again rejected my suggestion that her phone may be the problem and supported her stance by telephoning my home number and triumphantly passing me the receiver to listen to "that woman". It was pointless pursuing my theory verbally so, whilst sat beside her, I called her number from my mobile phone and she was oblivious to it ringing. I duly replaced her telephone with a higher decibel one recommended by the hard of hearing centre she attended every Friday.

"They send someone round to test your eyes here," she announced one day, showing me her new glasses. "They should send someone round to test your bloody ears," I replied after a particularly gruelling conversation conducted at the top of my voice. For some reason hearing aids were to her an anathema and sadly, her inexplicable aversion even hostility towards them was diminishing her quality of life since there was nothing more she enjoyed than a good conversation.

I suppose we must just accept that when we get old, we become stubborn, irrational and unable to come to terms with certain changes even if they are for our own good. It can be very frustrating for those who care for us. We can always do more of course but I think I made a decent effort to be a good son and I tried to make my mother's time at Roseleigh as tolerable as she would allow it to be, though I suspect she was more comfortable there than she would admit to me. Whenever I had to go somewhere in the car I took her with me. I visited her regularly and had her round for tea often. I took her to her hard of hearing group every Friday and to Morrisons supermarket every Saturday where we would do the family shopping and have lunch together. This wasn't always as straightforward as it sounds since she would constantly wander off. I've lost count of the number of times my name has been called over supermarket tannoy systems to collect my 'lost' mother. We were once apprehended by the security guard when she quite innocently slipped some bananas into her handbag. Her spirits would visibly sink when it was time to take her back to Roseleigh. She summed up her feelings about it in a remark she once made to my son Tim when he was dropping her off after spending the day with us. "Home sweet home Granma," said Tim brightly. Her quite sagacious response was, "Aye, without the fire on." She had some quite descriptive turns of phrase.

When I started to write this book I decided that nothing was to be taboo and because it is such a painful subject, death is something we avoid talking about. I think this is sad, because the more we air the subject the more capable we will be of dealing with it when it happens to us or to those close to us. The end of course was as inevitable for my mother as it is to us all. She was tough and came from a family with a history of longevity but she was in her ninetieth year and over the Christmas period of 2003 the signs of her bowel cancer were evident, and embarrassingly so, at the Royal Hotel Scarborough, where we had celebrated the last several Hogmanays with her. Perhaps it hadn't been such a sensible decision to go there that year but she had so much enjoyed the previous occasions we decided to risk it. Her incontinence, bless her, caused some embarrassment. Back 'home' she was becoming more and more depressed. Her faculties were failing. In particular her mobility was causing her concern, even with the help of a contraption I had acquired from the local disability centre which we had called her Ferrari. Her new legs. It was finally replaced with a wheelchair. She wasn't eating, couldn't be bothered to watch TV or read which latterly she had been able to do only with the aid of a magnifying glass. She weighed under six stones and was clearly failing. "Why does it take so long to die?" she would ask. What on earth do you say in reply to that? She stayed in her room and couldn't be bothered with anything. We thought she had given up. Then on the first of April something amazing happened – and she wasn't doing it to April Fool us. When I called to see her she was sitting up in her chair as bright as a button. I couldn't believe it. She had eaten a hearty breakfast and seemed up for anything, so I got her into her wheelchair and took her out. It turned out to be a quite sentimental journey for her. Our first stop was the Highfield Hotel where she had worked for many years. We had a drink on the patio. Then to Park Lane where she was born and had lived as a child, and then through Albert Park, "to feed the ducks," I told her, "like you used to do with me when I was little" – which brought a bright smile to her face. Was this the same person who the day before had lost hope? I pushed her all the way to our house where she sat in her favourite chair in the sun room from which she was able to look out over the garden which, to her delight, was a mass of Spring colour. Daffodils were her favourite flower. Unaided she read the Evening Gazette, something she hadn't done for months. We chatted easily without her hearing aids with not an "eh?" in sight! She talked about her childhood and her first taste of ice cream from a "penny lick", and about the songs she used to sing. Chris picked up a guitar, which had been left by a friend of Tim and as she began to strum my mother burst into song about the first Italian immigrant who had introduced ice cream to Middlesbrough.

> *Umberto Pannico*
> *He sells ice creamio*
> *Where does he sell it oh*
> *Down by the parkio*

We ended the day with her favourite Chinese takeaway meal – followed by an ice cream of course. It was almost as if God had given us that wonderful day to cherish and to soften the pain that would follow.

Two days later she was taken into hospital. The tests carried out and the scan proved to be inconclusive and the surgeon was not able to pronounce a definite diagnosis. She had stomach or bowel cancer or both. We agreed that a second scan may cause her further discomfort and wouldn't help anyway and she was taken back to Roseleigh for the only treatment that could then be effective – TLC – tender loving care. The absence of a precise clinical prognosis meant that she was denied the care of MacMillan Nurses but it is hard to imagine how they could have possibly matched the sincere and loving care she received from Sue, Denise, Emma, Jackie, Lorraine, Tracy, Chris and the rest of the angels at Roseleigh. I will never forget them and will be for ever indebted to them.

These final few weeks were the most harrowing I have experienced, sitting at my mother's bedside waiting for her to die, watching her suffer, with her beseeching me to answer her pleas "Why won't the good Lord take me?" to which I was powerless to offer any adequate consolation. Her attempts to speak were so feeble we found it hard to understand what she wanted and what we were so anxious to give her. We could just barely discern the word 'bread' which she had repeated on a number of occasions. Yet she shook her head in feeble frustration when bread was brought for her. It was Chris, I believe, who finally realised that she was trying to say the Lord's Prayer – "Give us this day our daily bread." We and the carers join hands with her and said the Lord's Prayer together. What a highly charged emotional moment that was – rewarded by the aura of peace and serenity it evoked in my mother.

Exactly seven years from the date I had retired, she was granted her wish on the 3rd May 2004 when the Good Lord finally took her. It had been a long and agonising ordeal for her and for us all. I will resist the temptation to be too sentimental. Instead I have chosen to include at the end of this chapter one of the cards I received, from Denise at the care home, and an extract from the tribute produced for her funeral service depicting her granddaughter Daisy's interpretation of Heaven. Daisy always called her great grandmother Greatie and had asked her one day when they were talking, what Heaven was like. "It's like a big beautiful garden in the sky," was the reply.

Exhausted from my bedside vigil I had gone home to rest and wasn't with her when she died. That experience again fell to Chris. We can send men to the moon but we are still without an answer to the unnecessary suffering experienced by terminally ill human beings. I watched on TV an episode in the Animal Park series from Longleat in which Babes the rhino was humanely put to sleep. She had been on the park for many years and her parting was a sad occasion, but the gentle and humane nature and timing of her death made it possible for all the staff there to come along and share her final moments. This seems a much more satisfactory and humane arrangement than we humans have for ourselves.

As I mentioned earlier, Beat and Tommy are remembered in the "Walk of Art" at Wakefield Sculpture Park and also in the hearts of all those people who were privileged to be a part of their lives.

Beatrice Arnott 1914 – 2004

We all hope Beattie has found her beautiful garden in the sky.
Night, night and God Bless to a very special person.

To,

CHRISTINE , DERRICK , LIZ & THE
3 LADS.

May your many
cherished memories
help bring you peace
and comfort through
all the days ahead.

I AM THINKING OF EACH AND
EVERY ONE OF YOU AT THIS
SAD MOMENT IN YOUR LIVES
I AM SO SORRY
FROM
DENISE
(CARER)

I AM NOT VERY GOOD AT WRITING BUT TO HELL WITH IT. AS YOU ALL KNOW BETTIE WAS ALSO VERY VERY SPECIAL IN ALL OUR LIVE'S WHOM LOOKED AFTER HER, AS FAR I AM CONCERNED I WILL NEVER MEET SUCH A LOVELY LADY AS YOUR MAM, BETTIE WAS ALWAY'S ASKING ME TO STOP SMOKEING I DID FOR 6 WEEK'S SHE WAS VERY PROUD, BUT NEAR THE END SHE SMELT SMOKE ON ME AND SAID TO ME YOU HAVE BEEN SMOKING WITH A SMILE ON HER FACE I KNOW ALL OF YOU & BETTIE WENT TO HELL AND BACK OVER THE LAST FEW WEEK'S, THANK GOD SHE IS NOW IN NO PAIN AND IN HEAVEN WHERE SHE WANTING TO BE. ALL YOUR MEMERIES WITH YOUR MAM ARE GOOD ONES AND SHE WILL BE WITH YOU ALL FOREVER, I KNOW I WILL ALWAYS FEEL AS THOUGH SHE IS STILL WITH US ALL AT THE HOME.

WE ALL MISS HER ALREADY.

THANKS FOR THE FLOWERS AND CARD.

Thirty Seven

GRAND SLAM

*When you travel remember that a foreign country is not designed
to make you comfortable. It is designed to make its
own people comfortable.*
Clifton Fadiman.

I USED TO THINK that fan clubs were things that star-struck teenagers joined. Until, that is, just after I became an OAP, when I joined tennis champion Greg Rusedski's fan club.

Chris had always been passionate about tennis. Wimbledon fortnight meant the kids and I lived on pre-packed meals left in the kitchen with our names on so that she wouldn't miss a single shot or interview on BBC TV. 1982 was an exception. Adrian Tate's sister Mary was an official for the LTA during that particular fortnight and Adrian had been able to get hold of some Centre Court tickets for the Ladies' semi-finals. It was Chris Evert Lloyd's last match at Wimbledon. She lost to the great Martina Navratilova. As the late Jack Atkin, the Acklam Park steward, had once observed about TV sport, "You can see it – but you can't smell it!" We loved every minute "smelling" our live Wimbledon experience. We wanted more.

Good tickets for Wimbledon are like gold dust but there are alternatives. The Stella Artois tournament took place at Queens Club in London just before Wimbledon and most of the big name players use it as a competitive warm-up on grass before the big one. We bought a couple of weekly ground tickets. This enabled Chris to continue to glue herself to the box for Wimbledon and experience some real live action too. Centre Court tickets at Queens were much easier to come by then and after a couple of years supporting the event we qualified for our own personal and permanent seats in a prime position. For ten years from 1993 we never missed Queens week and were privileged to see close up such all-time greats as Stefan Edberg, Ivan Lendl, Pete Sampras, Andre Agassi, Boris Becker, Goran Ivanisovic and many more, including a seventeen-year-old Leyton Hewitt, in England for his first ever Wimbledon and who we first saw at Queens on one of the outside courts and immediately tipped for stardom. We always stayed for the week in an apartment in lovely Richmond from which every day, laden with a mouth-watering selection from our favourite delis and bottles of nice wine, we would take the District Line to Barons Court, next to which there is a splendid little French patisserie selling freshly baked crunchy French baguettes. Complemented by a bowl of crispy salad from the buffet inside the ground our picnics were perfect.

One day a group of people wearing G-Force tee shirts joined our table. We discovered they were members of Greg's fan club, who travelled all over the globe to support him. Special deals and events tickets were arranged by Paul, Val and Sandy, the officers of the fan club and we were soon persuaded to join. After all, we were Greg fans already. Apart from being Britain's number two he was simply a very nice guy. Very handsome with a broad engaging smile, it came as no surprise that most of the fan club members were female. We had encountered Greg at Queens some years earlier when he was relatively unknown. He was surrounded by a horde of autograph hunters, one of whom said to him, "But who *are* you?" He smiled and continued until he had signed every autograph. A few years later everyone knew who he was. We took advantage of the special arrangements made by the fan club to see some Davis Cup matches and to visit Devonshire Park in Eastbourne where the ladies equivalent of the Stella Artois is held.

We were keen to explore further afield in pursuit of the pleasure we had experienced in England and after visits to the Paribas ATP tournaments at Bercy and the French Open at Roland Garros in Paris I began to dream of a possible Grand Slam but I was tied with my mother and since I could only get away for one week at a time, visits to the US and Australian Opens would have to be put on hold. However, middle son Tim had temporarily emigrated to Australia and this gave me an opportunity. Whilst mother found it difficult to accept that I should want to leave her and go somewhere just for selfish enjoyment she accepted the fact that I may want to do so to see family, so in 2002 I grabbed the opportunity and made the most of it, flying club class to Melbourne via Bangkok where we broke the journey both ways and stayed at the five star Royal Orchid Sheraton. That in itself was a wonderful experience. I was fascinated by the Buddhist inspired Thai culture. The Oz experience however was up there among the best in my life. Had I gone there forty years earlier I would have been sorely tempted to uproot, emigrate and bring up the kids there. It helped of course that Tim was there to show us the ropes. We had of course timed our visit to take in the Australian Open at Melbourne Park and we based ourselves at the Grand Chancellor Hotel in Melbourne which is great value for money and well recommended. After the tennis and a visit to the Royal Melbourne Club for the Heineken Open Golf we moved on. First to Sydney where we ate fish at Doyles overlooking the Opera House, pie and peas at the famous Harry's Bar on

Wheels, had the customary swim on Bondi Beach which we had entirely to ourselves because it was pouring down, and generally did all the touristy things there. Then further north to Queensland and Airlie Beach which we used as a base to take in the Whitsunday Islands, Whitehaven Beach and the magnificent Barrier Reef. Tim and I got a wonderful deal for a day's golf at one of Australia's finest courses, Laguna Quays, which boasts the biggest driving range in the Southern Hemisphere. Including car hire for the day (an old Ford Capri convertible), clubs, shoes and buggy hire and lunch for three we got change out of a hundred dollars, (about forty pounds). The mosquitoes were thrown in for free. Back in Melbourne Tim and I enjoyed more golf at the Yarra Valley Club and at Ivanhoe where at the eleventh hole Tim got his first hole in one. At Yarra Valley we played with a lad from Oxford, his Aussie friend and Cosmo. Cosmo, on a signal from his master, had been trained to bark on the opponent's back swing! Normally I wouldn't have been too happy playing with a dog but over there everything is so laid back and fun. Course etiquette is strictly observed but they don't have a yob culture like the UK and don't need a dress code. Jeans and trainers are fine. No-one there is discouraged from playing sport. That's why for such a small country they and New Zealand produce perhaps more successful sports people per capita than anywhere else in the world. The Pro at Ivanhoe was genuinely delighted that we had enjoyed playing his course and wouldn't accept payment for the extra nine holes we decided to play. Can you imagine that happening on the money mad Costas?

As I said earlier, having offspring domiciled abroad did afford an excuse for getting away for a decent stretch. My visit to South America via New York and the US Open in 2005 to complete our "Grand Slam" was my third to this vibrant continent. James was based in the jungle town of Iquitos in Peru and it was not without some trepidation and umpteen jabs that I first went there in 2001. What an amazing experience it proved to be (notice I've avoided using the Amazon pun!). With more than five Nuevo Soles to the pound the cost of living there is so cheap so we again flew business class, this time with Iberia, the Spanish airline, which made the trip even more memorable, particularly for Chris. I had experienced the Iberia club class before with Brian. We had no choice. After the SPEED tour of 1997 we had arranged to join our wives in Tenerife and, being a seasoned traveller who knew the ropes, I persuaded Brian that by leaving the booking until the last minute we would get cheap flights. I was wrong. We nearly didn't get a flight at all. The economy class seats were sold out and we had to travel business class at more than three times the price. We made the most of it though and kept the wine steward busy. Chris and I made the most of our Iberia flight too, stopping off at Madrid for a few days to celebrate our wedding anniversary en route to Lima where we were met by Jim in an emotional reunion. After a few nights at Hotel La Castellana in Mira Flores, Lima's posh end, we took the short ninety minute Aero Continente flight to

Iquitos, which is actually an island surrounded by the Amazon and Nanay Rivers and accessible only by air or an arduous five day coach and river journey from Lima.

What a culture shock our first jungle holiday turned out to be. I could easily fill another book relating our experiences during my several subsequent trips there. The Rio Amazona is quite breathtaking. A mile wide, it was, on our first visit just after the rainy season, a raging torrent of red muddy water and jungle debris. The tributaries fortunately were calmer and we spent one day rafting, a popular pastime for the few wealthy people there. The rafts are actually large floating platforms, some with BBQs and their own bars. We visited a tribe of Quechua Indians who needed little persuasion from Jim, who knew them well, to perform a tribal dance for us. We were taken on another day by puk puk moto taxi to Belen Village, built on stilts, where you can buy anything from boa constrictor juice for arthritis to a monkey's penis for luck. I've held snakes and sloths, seen colonies of monkeys, drank sap from special trees, eaten giant grubs and cuy (guinea pig), hunted at night and caught cayman (crocodiles) and piranha fish and swam with pink dolphins in the Amazon in which I was just about to have a pee when someone yelled from the boat, "Whatever you do don't have a pee!" The reason, as I was told later, is that there are tiny creatures which swim against your urine flow in search of a warm breeding ground inside your penis, vagina or bladder. Urgh!

On our second eventful visit to Peru we were accompanied by our three sons and Chris's niece Leigh. En route, flying KLM, we took the opportunity to visit the lovely island of Bonaire in the Dutch West Indies.

My visits to Peru have given me an insight into third world culture and have left a lasting and humbling impression on me. None more so than the street kids.

We flew to South America in 2005 from Tenerife with Air Madrid because their business class fare was relatively cheap, due, we discovered, to their business class being little better than Thai, Iberia, BA or KLM economy class. The airline is now out of business. For our first week in New York on our way to Peru we stayed in a hotel near the amazing Grand Central Station where we discovered that there are such things as healthy American breakfasts and where I developed a taste for granola, yoghurt and fruit from one of the many food bars there, before taking the train to Flushing Meadows. I do believe the US is ahead of the UK in tackling the obesity problem. Certainly I saw fewer fatties in New York than I had seventeen years earlier in Florida where at first I was puzzled by the number of disabled people in wheelchairs. Until I realised they were not disabled at all, merely grossly overweight. It had proved quite easy to get tickets for the Arthur Ashe Court at Flushing Meadows on which most of the top games were played. Naturally being the US they have the biggest capacity court in the world (23,157) but though we were well back from the action it was nevertheless quite a spectacle, with the typical

American razzmatazz entertainment before the matches. Roger Federer and Kim Clijsters were that year's champions.

On the way back from Peru we again stayed in New York for a few days, this time near Central Park. The weather at that time of the year (September) is perfect and we picnicked in the Park a couple of times while we watched the friendly games of baseball. We barely scratched the surface of the Big Apple as it is called (but nobody could tell us why) and Chris is now a regular visitor since her niece Leigh went to live there. I am looking forward very much to my next visit.

With the Grand Slam finally under my belt I'm running out of ambitions, or at least realistically achievable ones, but there is still much to keep my grey matter ticking over. There is still much of the world to explore to satisfy my wanderlust and of course this bloody book to finish.

Queensland, Australia 2002.

Thirty-Eight

05.05.05

*British democracy is a system by which the country is governed
by a political party which around 80% of the people
don't want and don't vote for.*
DA.

UNITED BRITISH INSURANCE COMPANY specialised in motor traders' insurance and in my days as a young insurance inspector with UB covering the County Durham area it was my job to service the garages we insured and who acted as agents for us. My favourite call was to a small petrol station in one of the pit villages. It was inactive in a business producing sense but it counted as one of the twenty calls I was expected to make each day by my old slave driver of a boss, Dick Geddes. I called regularly and often went out of my way to do so. The reason? I just enjoyed talking to Arthur Patterson, the forecourt attendant. Before being forced to take early retirement due to ill health Arthur had spent all his life down the pit, as had his father and his father before him. They had all endured hardship and deprivation and Arthur had some fascinating tales to tell. Like me he had seen the Labour movement as a means of emancipation for the working man led by public spirited philanthropists, as indeed the movement probably was in its early days. Arthur was such a man. Salt of the earth. A Socialist in its truest sense. Determined to seek justice for the workers but intelligent enough to appreciate the broader picture, his was a well-balanced blend of passion, compassion and reason, with which I totally identified. He had joined the Labour Party and had been elected to serve on the local Council. To Arthur that meant putting the interests of the people first. He gradually came to realise that not all his fellow Councillors shared his altruism. They were there for their own aggrandizement, for gain financially or for both. Certain activities disturbed Arthur, particularly as these involved the influential leaders of the Council. He tried to discover the truth but his efforts to do so were obstructed. His life was made difficult but he persisted, determined to expose what, by then, he was convinced was at best dishonesty and possibly corruption, involving some Council Members. He had the support of some who shared his concerns but fearing for their own positions they left it to Arthur to make the waves. To be the renegade. Before his investigations were complete he was due for re-election. His principles would not allow him to climb down, countenance the dubious goings on and to support the Party line. The Party deselected him as a candidate. Without the endorsement of the Party, Arthur's chances of regaining his seat were worse than slim. This was a typical Labour stronghold where voters ignored the merits of the individual and voted for the Party. His political career was at an end. He became disenchanted. "Politics stink," he said, "and vermin thrive in sewers." At the tender age of twenty-three I was having doubts too.

I believe it was Denis Healey, the old Labour Party Foreign Secretary, who said, "If you are not a communist when you are twenty then there's something wrong with your heart. If you are still one when you are thirty then there's something wrong with your head."

The trouble with such ideologies is that they are motivated not entirely by altruistic desire for wealth redistribution but largely by simple jealousy. The "have nots" who would overthrow the "haves" want to become "haves" themselves and find it more exciting and a damn sight easier than hard work and personal risk taking, to achieve this by having a revolution. The ordinary people are no better off because the leaders of the revolution having seized and spent the wealth are not as good as the old "haves" at creating new wealth and the system collapses leaving a few of the opportunist leaders to capitalise and become the new super-rich as happened in the Soviet Union. When I was a boy Russia was held up to me as an example of true Socialism. I believed that the upper classes were all evil creatures hell bent on keeping me down and that the workers were all down trodden, good, salt of the earth folk. The fact is, as I came to realise for myself later, that there are goodies and baddies among all levels of society in equal proportions and that eliminating the upper classes will not change this, though it is convenient and often expedient for left wing politicians to have us believe otherwise.

It takes a long time for childhood indoctrination to filter through and out of the system. For many it never does. At that time I still voted Labour but did so with less conviction. The aims of the movement had largely been achieved. Dire poverty had been eliminated and workers enjoyed decent pay and conditions. Old fashioned us and them attitudes had been replaced with modern management. Unfortunately bitterness and an irrational, emotional, hatred of management which they still associated with upper class privilege still persisted and influenced the judgement of many within the Labour movement. Trade Union power forced pay rises and restrictive practices on employers which were unsustainable and the country's major industries were priced out of world markets. Steel making, shipbuilding, motor manufacturing and coal mining all went into decline and all but disappeared, resulting in the widespread loss of jobs which it should have been the Trade Unions' duty to prevent. The Labour governments of 1964-1970 under Harold Wilson and 1974-1979 under James Callaghan were reluctant to curb the excesses of the Unions who were their paymasters and it took the Conservative government of Margaret Thatcher to do so. The confrontation was bitterly unpopular but necessary. But to finance its election campaigns her Party too relied on donations from sources with vested interests and as we all know, he who pays the piper calls the tune. Governments should not be the puppets of external paymasters. As such they are obliged to consider the interests of those who bankroll them before those who vote for them.

Fortunately in the world of business and commerce today positions of management and power have generally been achieved by hard work but there are still those on whom privilege has been bestowed (e.g. our politicians) or inherited (e.g. our upper classes) – a situation which is resented by most ordinary people. The Royal Family, in addition to its constitutional function, in fact symbolises Britain's upper class which, unlike anywhere else in the world, identifies itself by speaking in an affected "posh" way which gets up many peoples' noses. The Conservatives are seen to represent this upper class and Labour, the workers. This simplistic (and generally inaccurate) assumption perpetrates our confrontational style of government. Thus we find ourselves a nation disrupted by dialect and divisiveness. Do we really need a monarchy and its hangers on? Do we need to change our political system?

Ironically the success of the Socialist movement in the redistribution of wealth would be the cause of its demise. Having achieved many of its goals, the party found itself without an ideological purpose. Its right wing successor called itself New Labour and cleverly usurped the Conservative position. Some diehard left wingers in the party resisted the move to the right but didn't have the courage to break away and form their own party. When it came to the crunch they decided that keeping their jobs and their salaries and their perks was more important than principles. These spineless creatures no doubt were influenced by two other considerations. Fear that they may not get enough votes to be re-elected and no longer enjoy their privileged status as MP's and secondly that by splitting the Labour vote this would allow the hated Tories to gain power. This was probably true but in the long run the existence of a left of centre party would have been better for the Country. The left of politics needs to be properly represented in its own right and not as an ineffective group within a party which does not share its ideology, even if it pretends to do so. Today only about ten per cent of Labour MPs could be described as working class, even in its broadest interpretation. The existence of a genuine Socialist party may well have been effective in curbing the excesses within the unregulated free market economy in which greedy individuals later amassed obscene fortunes without an eyebrow being raised. The few individuals who raised concerns that their disregard for prudence would have serious consequences were sacked and the voices of those few politicians who should have spoken out against the unscrupulous activities of big business were effectively gagged by their party whips. Hedge and Equity fund managers have been allowed, *no, encouraged*, to manipulate the UK's financial and fiscal systems to create enormous personal wealth without any productive benefit, and with minimal fiscal contribution to the nation, since many of them are allowed to assume non domiciled status by our government. This means that the money they and others make out of us is removed from the UK economy and our pension funds. To add insult to injury this new super-rich class don't even pay taxes, because the government has given them tax concessions not available to small businesses. The UK is seen as a "soft touch" and has become a tax haven for these "foreign" billionaires. So how are they allowed to get away with this abuse of our country's wealth and hospitality? A glance at the list of donors to political party funds will give you a clue! Let me quote from Robert Peston's[5] excellent book *Who Runs Britain*: **"Gordon Brown has become the economic prisoner of the super-rich class, whose ranks he swells through providing them with tax breaks."** What a curious epitaph for a Labour chancellor and Prime Minister.

Several years down the line Socialism could have re-emerged as an alternative to the right wing parties that vie for power today. Alas this did not happen and Socialism died. Many Socialist voters still think with their hearts and not their heads, refuse to recognise this fact and continue to vote for the Socialist Party's right wing successor New Labour, which undeservedly benefits from their support on polling day. I can only hope that as these traditional voters die off the new generation of voters will become more circumspect.

Uneasy with political parties generally, with the way in which decisions were made in local and national government and with Arthur Patterson in mind, I did not bother to vote at all for thirty years. How could I endorse and encourage a system of voting which, in the name of democracy, enables power to be controlled by a handful of MPs and local councillors and denies an effective voice to dissenters like Arthur and his supporters? That couldn't be right. Nor could it be right that I was required to cast my vote in secret but not Councillors and MPs. Having always been interested in politics I decided that, when I had some time on my hands, I would examine the subject in greater detail and become better informed before voting again.

Probably every ordinary man and woman knows that the way we are governed is unsatisfactory. How can it be otherwise when the main objective of the party in power is to stay in power and it knows that the best way to do that is to feed us with lies, quick fixes and promises they have no intention of keeping. How can it be otherwise when candidates are selected, not on their ability to run a country, but on their political skills? These include the ability to be devious, deceitful and downright

---

[5] Robert Peston is the BBC's award winning business editor.

dishonest and a Machiavellian proficiency to make us believe they are none of these. How can we hope to be governed efficiently when the two main parties spend more time bickering with each other than doing the job they were elected to do – running the Country. What hope have we got when somebody comes up with a great idea to benefit the country and irrespective of its merits, the members of the party which didn't have the idea are instructed to vote against it! When one party rejoices in the failure of measures to improve things which were introduced by the other party. Let me quote H.L. Mencken, the most prominent American newspaper man and political commentator of his day:

> *"Under our form of democracy one party always devotes its chief energies to trying to prove that the other party is unfit to rule – and both commonly succeed and are right."*

We know too that politicians are hypocrites. Sending their children to private schools whilst publicly condemning private education is but one of many, many examples of this. Banning smoking everywhere except the members' bar in the House of Commons is another. We know or should by now know, that above all else, politicians represent not us, but themselves and their parties. They do not seek the Nations good, but wish only to save their own majorities. How do they get away with it? How on earth do we, in this enlightened age, continue to tolerate this state of affairs? Why do we allow ourselves to be led like sheep to the polling booths to register our endorsement of lies dishonesty and corruption? Why do we allow people who cannot be trusted to be in charge of our destiny?

"90% of politicians get the other 10% a bad name," said Henry Kissinger – and I think he was being generous.

Running a country is about as big a job as you can find but if we look at the background of our MPs few of them have ever before run *anything* in their lives. Surely we should have our best brains and skills at the helm of Great Britain plc and not naïve inexperienced career politicians who are slaves of the Party. As it is they are nothing more than good blaggers and con merchants, selected not because of their ability or integrity but simply on the basis that they could be counted on to toe the Party line. Even those few with some integrity must be prepared to compromise this by sacrificing their souls to one of the main political parties. There is no other way into office. The candidate subrogates his or her individuality – and his or her conscience – to the party and its leader, who instructs his or her puppet on how to think and vote. So we end up with two leaders, three if you count the Liberal Democrats, and six hundred and fifty six zombies. No wonder we lurch from crisis to crisis. The whole set up is frighteningly sycophantic. Our government has more in common with dictatorship than democracy. Any MP who questions the party line has his card marked, just like Arthur Patterson. To enforce discipline in Westminster the Party employs an equivalent to the Nazi SS – Party Whips – whose main function it seems is to force members to vote *for* what they are against and *against* what they are for and since most of them crave power above all else and that power is bestowed upon them by their leader, they timidly and ingratiatingly follow instructions when it comes to division time in the House of Commons.

Our parliamentary system is quite frankly, a farce. An important issue can be debated in the House and MPs don't bother to listen. They either don't turn up at all or they go for a drink in the members' bar until the division bell rings and then go and vote the way the Party Whips tell them. What is the point of having six hundred and fifty nine MPs at the expense of tax payers when they take no active part in government? In 2001 when Tony Blair made his statement on the war against terrorism, only eighty MPs were there to hear him. This when four thousand British troops were packing their kits to put their lives on the line. They were all present a few weeks later to vote themselves pay rises and privileged pension provisions while at the same time supporting the Government to deprive everybody else of both.

So if all the important decisions are made by one person assisted by twenty two cabinet ministers, how do the other six hundred and thirty seven zombies fill in their time, other than voting themselves pay rises and filling in lavish expenses claims? The answer is very little. Their attendance record at "work" would have got the rest of us the sack after our first few weeks. To justify their existence back benchers are allowed to indulge themselves by imposing upon us their own personal brand of morality in the form of politically correct laws and regulations, aided and abetted by their counterparts at local government level. They are invested with this power by their party leaders in return for being yes men and women when their vote is needed in the House of Commons at division time. Like political Gods, they tell us how we must think and behave, yet they fail with flying colours when it comes to setting us an example. They are selective in what they consider is right or wrong. For example many of them were against the invasion of Iraq, but did they have the moral fibre and courage to vote against it, or even abstain? Oh no, they toed the party line and voted *for* the invasion. As a result they must shoulder the blame with their leaders for the tens of thousands of deaths to innocent Iraqis and the British servicemen who lost their limbs and lives in the conflict. They do nothing about the immorality within their own party, or the corruption, because they are fearful of upsetting their leaders. Yet these hypocrites have the audacity to preach to us how we should behave.

When dishonesty, inefficiency and incompetence exist at the top, whether it be within a family, a business, or the government of the country, this inevitably manifests itself further down the line. Hence the bungling ineptitude within our government departments and social services.

Apart from those involved and who are enjoying the power and the perks that go with it, I think it is fair to say the rest of us are fed up with politics and the ethics of politicians. Our opinions of them range from disinterest, disillusionment to downright disgust. Yet we feel powerless to change things. All we can do is to register our discontent by voting for the party that is not in power even though we know it will not make a scrap of difference because most politicians, even if they were inclined to do so, do not possess the vision or the courage to make the radical and unpopular changes necessary to deflate the bubble before it bursts and destroys our welfare and our planet.

All modern governments are committed to a "pro-growth" economic policy – one that perceives its voters as consumers who must want to consume more and more. Ever increasing consumption is the breath that inflates the world's economic balloon: as soon as you stop buying, it shrivels up into a pathetic wrinkle. You have to keep on buying until the balloon bursts and we are left with grubby scraps of rubber on a wasted planet. How did we come to fall for such a ridiculous way of running our world? Anuradha Vittachi.

"Politics is too important to be left to politicians," said Charles de Gualle, and he is right. Government should be made up of, or at least include, independent people chosen to provide a cross section of skills necessary to run Great Britain plc. People who want to earn their salaries and take some responsibility instead of spending even more taxpayer's money delegating everything to committees and consultants as they do at present to the tune of a billion pounds every year. People whose concern is for the long term future of the Country and the planet not their own and their party's short term popularity achieved by promising the voters more and more material possessions. This alternative form of government will not happen without fundamental electoral reform, but the first past the post system suits the existing political establishment even though they know how unfair and unrepresentative this is, a fact that even *they* occasionally acknowledge, if it suits them to do so. I wonder how many votes were secured for the Labour Party when Tony Blair, in his 1997 Manifesto on the back of which he gained power, said, "We are committed to a referendum on the voting system. An independent commission on voting will... recommend a proportional alternative to the first past the post system..." The inclusion of this "promise" in the Labour Party's election manifesto was a clear acknowledgement that our electoral system is both unfair and undemocratic but there was no way of course that the promise would be kept. No political party is ever going to change a system which enables it to grab complete power with the support of just a small minority of the voters. Blair's "promise" is just one of many, many examples of the flagrant and contemptuous hypocrisy which four out of ten people condone by voting for one of the two main political parties.

"Ours is the mother of parliaments," we are told by those who seek to preserve the status quo and who would have us believe that this is something to be proud of, the inference being that, *per se,* it must be the best. This is complete eyewash. This particular mother is senile, out of date and "Not fit for purpose" as one Cabinet Minister once dared to say about his department – a remark which earned him the sack.   Britain's electoral system of first past the post is both illogical and unrepresentative and we are one of the few nations in the world, and the only one in Europe, to cling on to it.   We do so because it enables our political parties to maintain their undemocratic grip on absolute power – a dangerous state of affairs which universal suffrage has failed to alter.

In the 19th Century only the rich and powerful land owners were entitled to vote. It took a group of people called the Chartists forty years of petitions and demonstrations to achieve the franchise for the common man.   With its power threatened the establishment fought long and hard to resist reform.   Eventually in 1832, certain selected common men were grudgingly given the right to vote, only to be subjected to further intimidation by their masters. Voting at general elections was conducted in public. The voter was required to stand before the election officer and announce his choice for all to hear. Accordingly both employers and landlords had full knowledge of the way in which a particular person voted and were able to control the voting. If the voter did not cast his vote in the way that his master demanded then he could lose his job and his home.   This effectively sabotaged electoral reform. Finally, in 1872 after more demonstrations, The Reform Act, better known as The Secret Ballot Act, was passed and the franchise widened to include more common men, who could then vote without fear or favour. It took another fifty six years of struggle for women over the age of thirty to get the vote in 1918. Again this logical progress was delayed by the resistance of men, whose power was threatened. Only with the passing of the Equal Franchise Act in 1928 did all men and women get the right to a secret ballot. At this point democratic evolution ceased.

If we compare the way in which the Country was run in the 19th Century before the Secret Ballot Acts and how it is run and controlled today, we find some startling similarities.   In the House of Commons the MPs we elect to represent us are no different to the common man then. They too must vote in public by walking through a division lobby for all to see. Accordingly the Party leaders are able to control the voting by intimidation or bribery, just as the landlords did a hundred and fifty years ago. If the Member does not vote in the way his or her master demands then he risks being deselected as a candidate at the next general election and effectively loses his job just like the 19th Century common man. At best he ruins his political career by blowing any chance he may have of being promoted to higher office.   This is intimidation. There is no question about it. Yet political parties consider they have the right to use such methods whilst at the same time condemning them in others. Many will remember the way in which Trade Union leaders intimidated their members by the kangaroo court methods they used to deal with dissenters identified by their show of hands method of balloting. By banning Trade Unions from conducting their voting in the same way as parliament votes, the government clearly acknowledged that the practice was undemocratic. The 1984 Trade Union Act which imposed secret balloting was legislative hypocrisy of the most brazen kind. If intimidation was unacceptable in 1872 and in 1984, then it surely has no place in our 21ˢᵗ Century British parliament. It makes no difference surely whether those who practice intimidation to get their own way are 19ᵗʰ Century land owners, Trade Unions or Prime Ministers and their henchmen the party whips.

My idea of democracy is when a country is governed according to the will of the majority of its citizens represented by a government elected by the *majority* of the people and made up of intelligent individuals chosen by the people for their proven ability and integrity to serve *them* and not their political party. By individuals who are expected to debate matters of national and international importance with dignity and impartiality and then reach decisions based on their judgement and conscience which, first and foremost, are in the best interests of the country and the majority of its citizens. To ensure that this happens without fear or favour, their vote in the House of Commons should be in secret and permitted only when they have taken the trouble to attend the debate and be in a position to consider all the issues. Is this too much to expect?

In "our form of democracy" referred to by Mencken none of these criteria exist. The process by which our politicians are selected ensures that they are merely party puppets and not of the quality we deserve. The division method of voting in the House ensures that our MP s, having sworn their allegiance and sold their souls to their Party, cannot cast their votes without fear or favour and according to their consciences. The electoral first past the post system ensures that the will of the majority of the people cannot be truly represented and our two party political system ensures that reason and impartiality are replaced with conflict, confrontation, distrust and even hatred. Even the Chamber itself is logistically divided into two "ends" like a gladiatorial arena or a football ground where the opposing factions hurl insults and derisive catcalls at each other like a bunch of overgrown schoolchildren. Little wonder that people see government as a game and not a serious attempt to run the country with efficiency. Isn't it about time parliament grew up, slimmed down and modernised itself? The chamber itself can only accommodate about four hundred members. How ridiculous is that? Tradition is fine, but only when it serves some useful purpose and the House of Commons would make a very good tourist attraction after government was moved to more suitable premises elsewhere with modern up to date facilities.

In nearby Hartlepool 'Angus the Monkey was elected as Mayor on the promise of free bananas for all schoolchildren. Perhaps it will take something like this to capture the imagination of the electorate and stir them out of their apathy by providing an opportunity to register their disapproval of politics and an alternative option for their votes.

For those unfamiliar with the tale let me explain. Local folklore has it that during the Great War of 1914-1918 a monkey was found on the beach at Seaton Carew near Hartlepool. Such had been the power of the propaganda by the government depicting Germans in cartoons as animals that the good citizens of Hartlepool caught and hung the monkey thinking it was a Hun.

Stuart Drummond, dressed in a monkey suit became the mascot of Hartlepool FC and "came out" in 2002, borrowed his £500 deposit from the club chairman Ken Hodcroft and secured enough votes to be elected. He was re-elected in 2005, doubling his vote and is doing a much better job for the people than his political counterparts.

The level of disdain in which our contemporary politicians are held is confirmed by the level of turnouts at general elections, down from 83.6% in 1950 to 59.4% in 2001. The successful party will get about 40% of the vote which is about 20% of the electorate which means that we get a government which four out of five of us don't vote for and don't want. Thus the will of the people is replaced by that of one person, the Prime Minister, aided by twenty two Cabinet Ministers appointed by and therefore controlled by him. The situation at local government level is even more alarming. A party can gain power when fewer than one person out of ten vote for it.

Before we can truly claim to be a democracy three things need to happen. Firstly the absolute power vested in the Prime Minister and his Party needs to be diluted. This can be achieved by a free vote or secret ballot in parliament which would allow back bench MP s some degree of influence in the decision making process of government. Secondly the first past the post election process needs to be replaced by a fairer and more representative method and thirdly, before being allowed to vote, MP s must actually be present when issues are being debated so they know something about them and not, as at present, "pair up" or turn up afterwards and vote as instructed.

If turnouts at general (and local) elections continue to fall we can only hope that government will get the message. But with the present unsatisfactory state of affairs so firmly entrenched and government unwilling to introduce a fairer and more representative system which will inevitably threaten their power, it is difficult to imagine how things will improve. Difficult – but not impossible. The Electoral Reform Society has been campaigning for some time for reform but nobody had taken the matter into the political arena.

Quite unprepared, inexperienced and naïve I decided that on the 5th May I would stand as an Independent candidate for Middlesbrough in the 2005 General Election. Without a powerful political party to hang my hat on and therefore with little in the way of resources I knew that my chances of election were zero. This was another Labour stronghold and made the act of voting at all quite pointless since the result was a foregone conclusion. It was for this and other reasons I hadn't hitherto exercised my franchise. But life is about new experiences and I believe that unless you are prepared to do something you shouldn't waste time complaining about it as so many do. All I could do was to attempt to expose the inadequacies in a system which enables arrogance, dishonesty and corruption to flourish. Nobody before had encouraged people NOT to vote. We have been browbeaten into thinking that we must exercise our right to vote. Yet turning out on polling day merely endorses the scam by politicians to make us believe we are being democratic. I know that people say that having fought so hard to earn the vote then we should use it, but I would argue that the franchise first given to the common man in 1832 was meaningless. Only when the right to vote in *secret* was achieved was he empowered to influence the destiny of his country. But the first past the post method of appointing a government coupled with the absence of free voting in parliament has failed to remove the ultimate power from the privileged few and until our political leaders are themselves willing to submit to a similar discipline as the Trade Unions and the rest of us then *our* secret vote is pointless. A boycott on polling day may be the only way in which we can communicate our disenchantment to government. If I could convince enough people to stay at home on polling day or register a protest vote, then a strong message would be sent for electoral reform. It would be the first step towards honest and efficient government. This would be the main thrust of my campaign. I would try to get across to the voters that we are not a true democracy. Try to make them realise that a secret ballot in our Houses of Parliament would effectively weaken and eventually destroy the stranglehold in which our MPs were held by their leaders by virtue of the undemocratic power vested in them - a dangerous state of affairs with some historical precedents. That was how Hitler and the Nazi Party managed to achieve what it did without popular support. I am not suggesting that this could happen in the UK but there is no safeguard in our system to prevent it. The voters of Middlesbrough were given an opportunity to register their disapproval of party politics either by voting for me or staying at home. I would persuade the voters of Middlesbrough that we could change the face of British politics. I had fifty thousand leaflets printed which contained my message, enhanced by some excellent graphics. These were delivered by the Royal Mail to every household within the constituency of Middlesbrough.

In the hope of drumming up some positive protest votes I decided to target young (non) voters in my election campaign but this wasn't as easy as I thought. I prepared an election manifesto speech for the students of Teesside University. I wasn't to know that the Students' Union was itself politically correct and would not permit the promotion of my views within the University because they may then be obliged to provide similar facilities to the British Nationalist Party. Why not for heaven's sake? What right have *they* to censor what students should or should not look at or listen to? They sanctimoniously condemn discrimination yet are flagrantly guilty themselves of the same narrow minded bigotry. Why can't they see that only when malevolence is exposed by open scrutiny will it be crushed? Surely if the BNP is bad then students are not so thick that they cannot judge this for themselves and need a nanny students' union to make their minds up for them. Free speech is free speech and the BNP's views are entitled to be and should be heard, even represented in Parliament – as should the Green Party and others who can demonstrate sufficient support among the people. It is particularly unfortunate that with the very serious threat of global warming facing the planet, we have no specific voice in Parliament on this issue. Given its vital contemporary relevance and support surely the Greens should be represented in Parliament instead of some of the six hundred and thirty seven MP s, who have no useful role in Government and just make a nuisance of themselves or simply exist to make up the numbers. Broad representation is what efficient democracy should be about so that if, for example, 5% of the people in the country vote for the Green Party, then they should have 5% of the total MPs.

I encountered similar frustrations when I tried to get some air time and was told by the local radio stations that this was permitted only for the main parties who again got the lion's share of the vote. I lost my deposit of course but I knew that was inevitable. At least I had got my message *out* to, if not *across* to, fifty thousand people – and one thousand five hundred and seventy seven fewer of them voted this time.

What a fascinating experience it was though! I can understand how easy it must be for certain people to be seduced by the patrician prestige and glamour of politics and once devoured by it, lose sight of what should be its purpose - to reflect and represent the wishes of the people, not to impose their own version of what they think those wishes should be. Standing on the platform at the Town Hall in the early hours of 06.05.05, I said in my post declaration speech that I would be back better prepared to fight the next election. Out of courtesy I congratulated the elected candidate Sir Stuart Bell, but what I wanted to say but didn't in case it sounded like sour grapes, was that Bell's victory had nothing to do with his personal qualities or suitability for the job, but relied on a powerful party machine funded by big business and the fees paid by Trade Union members coupled with an electoral system which was decadent and undemocratic and which produces a government which four out of five people did not vote for.

I determined that, with the campaigning experience gained from my adventure, I could get across my message much more effectively next time. I would start campaigning well before the announcement of the election date when, quite unfairly, restrictions come into force for minor parties. I would form a forceful but moderate political party - The Reform Party - with which the silent majority could identify. I would involve the Electoral Reform Society, CAPC (The Campaign Against Political Correctness) and the students from the departments of politics at our universities, whose imagination would, I'm sure, be captured by my radical ideas.

If only I had become involved when I was younger! If only I could find a younger version of me to sponsor. If only Arthur Patterson was still alive to see that his integrity had influenced at least one young mind. I'm sure that he would have been proud that his honourable resignation was not in vain.

UPDATE 06.05.2010

Alas, by 2010 I was in my seventy-fifth year and too busy enjoying my retirement to get involved again. I was invited by Sir Paul Judge, the former Director General of the Conservative Party, to attend a meeting in his London apartment, one of the objects of which was to persuade me to stand again as an Independent candidate, supported this time by his Party machine The Jury Team and a coalition of Independents known as The Alliance for Democracy. The plan was for only one Independent to contest each constituency and hopefully to take advantage of the mood of anger and disillusionment among the people in the wake of revelations about the fiddled expenses and abuse of parliamentary privilege by members taking bribes from commercial organisations to influence government decisions in their favour. I wished Sir Paul well but declined

On the 6th May 2010 I voted Liberal Democrat because they were the only party which seriously advocated electoral reform and, more importantly, had a vested interest in achieving it. My hope was that a hung parliament would be the outcome of this general election in which the Lib Dems would hold the balance of power. I hoped that they and other minority parties would hold out for a reform of the voting system which would enable them to have a greater say in future governments more representative of the wishes of the people and not just the 20% or so who elect one party. I feared however that they might be seduced into a pact with one of the main parties in which they would enjoy a temporary taste of power and the opportunity for reform would be lost. However a coalition with the Conservatives was formed and a glimmer of hope emerged. Their leader Nick Clegg stood firm and made reform a condition of his support. Good for him. Would we now, like other European countries, get full proportional representation which could herald the demise of rule by one party "mandated" by only 20% of the people? Or would we see the introduction of a watered down AV (Alternative Vote) system which is the lesser of the two evils for the Tories – and for Labour for that matter – who would prefer to cling on to the old system? In the end reform was rejected by the people and the status quo was preserved. George Bernard Shaw was right when he said "Democracy is a device that ensures that we shall be governed no better than we deserve."

Thirty-Nine

FIGHTING COCKS

When children are good you know they're up to something.
Chrissarism.

WHEN OUR KIDS were young we used to love singing, usually in the car –
one of the many stratagems I devised to divert their minds from territorial
disputes in the back seat where they would be packed like sardines. Oh, why hadn't
they invented multi-seater vehicles like Ford Galaxies in those days? To be honest, I
think I probably enjoyed the singing more than the kids did. I would compose my
own ditties and adapt versions of existing ones. One in particular became a sort of
family anthem with which to instil some clan-like pride, which probably had its roots
in my Scottish heritage. It was the regimental song of the Gordon Highlanders, "A
Gordon for Me." This was my version:

> "An Arnott for me
> An Arnott for me
> If you're no' an Arnott
> You're nae use tae me
> The Marshalls are braw
> The Sutherlands an' a'
> But a bonny wee Arnott's the
> Pride 'o 'em all."

The four benefactors of my will, (if I haven't spent it all by the time I go) have
given me much pleasure – and pain too when they were young fighting cocks, as my
mother called them, but with all the hard work now behind me I'm looking forward
to getting my own back by being grumpy and difficult in my dotage. Only joking
kids – I hope.

299

An alcoholic when only thirteen and rescued from the white slave trade at fifteen, Liz didn't have the best of starts in life but I think we can take some credit for her turning out to be an intelligent and balanced woman who is now the happy and contented wife of Andrew James. I doubt whether I could have found a better son-in-law, nor a better father for granddaughter Daisy. Liz and Andrew were married on 11th August 1992 and because of the awkward family logistics a decision was sensibly taken to do the deed in Las Vegas. An upgrade to first class on their flight and a splendidly enjoyable wedding party later at Morton House I hope made up for their disappointment. They bought a nice house near the duck pond back in Wolviston where Liz was brought up and close to Andrew's parents Steve and Jean. Daisy did very well at Teesside High School and loved every minute of it. When Andrew was promoted by his Company to their HQ in Cheshire they had to move there and though they missed the North East, they quickly settled into their posh new house just over the Welsh border and Daisy into her posh new school near the village of Holt in Cheshire. Abbey Gate School is a lovely converted old monastery on the Duke of Westminster's estate. I must drop in on him one day and renew our acquaintance!

Having the responsibility of three lively young boys and a teenage girl when we lived at Wolviston was never going to be easy and not without its moments of crisis. One day I had to go to London on business and needed to catch a train. Being an incurable optimist, I always think I've got more time than I have and taking advantage of the dry weather decided to mow the lawn. I found I was cutting it fine – the time not the grass – and asked Chris if she would drive me to Durham Station which was going to be extremely inconvenient for her. She couldn't leave the kids and would have to bring them with her. They were not exactly overjoyed, particularly Liz who was playing in her room with her two friends, Debra Lindsey and Joanne Watson. We took a chance. Chris would be away for no more than forty-five minutes or so and after extracting strict promises from the girls that they would not leave the house, open the door to strangers, all the usual things, Chris decided to leave them. There was one unforeseen contingency we omitted from the list of instructions under the heading "all the usual things". Feeling guilty Chris sped back from Durham and it was just as well that she did. She opened the door to find Liz lying in the hall frothing at the mouth. What on earth could have happened? She called out to Deb and Joanne to see if they could throw some light on the mystery, only to find that they too were in an incoherent and incapable state. Then noticing the door of the drinks cabinet ajar, the awful truth began to dawn on her. Had she not dashed back from Durham and quickly organised emergency assistance who knows what dreadful consequences we may have faced. Thankfully, their systems purged by stomach pumps and none the worse for wear, save for severe hangovers, the girls survived their booze up and were released from hospital the following day. Liz later explained that they had been playing Charley's Angels, a TV series featuring three glamorous female detectives who it seems rarely had a cigarette out of their mouths or a drink out of their hands. But, unlike their three wannabes, the real Angels were only acting. Who says TV doesn't have a bad influence on children?

On holiday in Tunisia we were convinced that Liz had been abducted. This was in the early days of that country's development as a tourist destination and we stayed on one of the first holiday complexes to be built there. It was huge, with its own stretch of beach and was designed to provide all the facilities necessary for a family holiday and to encourage people to stay within the complex where they were less vulnerable. The fact that they deemed it necessary to restrict our movements in this way made me feel uncomfortable. I found it a little scary being isolated, ghetto like, in what was obviously a dangerous and hostile locality. Liz was suffering from sunburn so I took her to the medical centre for treatment. When, an hour later, she hadn't returned, we began to worry and when a visit to the medical centre revealed that she had left half an hour earlier our anxiety deepened. A search of the complex proved fruitless and having been warned of the potential dangers lurking outside our confines we began to panic. After another fruitless search by the hotel staff we insisted that the police were informed, at which point one of the younger members of the reception staff spoke to the manager, whereupon his face broke into a broad smile which we took to mean that all was well, until he brightly reassured us that Liz had been seen riding off on a motorbike with Nikos. I think we were expected to react by saying "Oh that's all right then!" but it was far from all right. We didn't know who the hell Nikos was and all I could think about was my little girl at large in a third-world environment of opium dens, bazaars and belly dancers. I can't describe the relief we felt when Liz eventually turned up on the back of Nikos' motorbike. We had no idea that Liz had been seeing this young Tunisian waiter who had fallen in love with her and had taken her to meet his parents before proposing marriage. His father, he announced proudly, was the Chef of Police. Whether that meant he held some high office in the Tunisian Constabulary or he worked in the police canteen didn't matter. We had our Liz back safe and sound. That's all that mattered.

Anyone who has brought up a teenage girl, or boy for that matter, in this fashion-driven age, will know what a fierce battlefield exists in the matter of clothes. Your daughter's friends and everybody else at school always have the latest expensive designer gear, or so you are led to believe. Nothing but the best is good enough when somebody else is picking up the tab of course. In an effort to reduce confrontation on this issue I sat down with Liz one day to see if we could reach an understanding. A deal was thrashed out. A monthly clothing allowance was agreed so that she could buy her own. Having concluded the deal she decided it was time for a change of image. No more designer gear. Only a small fraction of her allowance was subsequently spent on clothes – all from second hand shops. We didn't mind. Unlike Chamberlain in 1939 we had achieved peace in our time!

Of course Liz, as the eldest, was able to control and manipulate her brothers and, as in all normal families, started the chain of power which would gradually evolve into outright bullying by the time it reached the youngest.

All those educational hours spent with Liz on my knee reading *Twinkle for Girls* eventually paid off. She got good GCSE 'O' and 'A' grades and secured a place at the University of East Anglia at Norwich. She was into books and films and chose UEA because it had a good Department of English and Media Studies. It was a strange feeling suddenly finding my little girl hundreds of miles away where I wasn't on hand to help and support her. Norwich is not the most accessible of places, especially from the North East. Our first journey down was tortuous. The Volvo estate we used was full to the gills and my mother and I just managed to squeeze ourselves into the front seats with Liz buried beneath her chattels somewhere in the back. It is a massive emotional moment in the life of a parent (at least it certainly was in mine) when one's child is abandoned hundreds of miles from home, to face the vagaries of the big wide world. As we waved goodbye I said a prayer that she would settle and be happy there. It worked. I was informed one day, shortly afterwards, that Liz had made a good friend, Mairaed, with whom she had just spent a long weekend in Paris. I was staggered. Had she blown all her money on one extravagant spree? "Don't worry dad," she reassured me. "I paid for it with my credit card." This threw me. How could she possibly qualify for a credit card with no means of income? The banks who set themselves up on University campuses (or is it campii?) were, I discovered, quite persuasive and totally irresponsible. The crunch of course came. It took a great deal of willpower on my part not to step in immediately to pay off my daughter's debts, but I could only take so much of her working night shifts in the local potato crisp factory before, having acknowledged that she was making a big effort, I paid off the then much reduced balance by sending a cheque to Visa with a not too complimentary letter. The discipline of credit card restraint is rarely an attribute of youth and often of many adults. After a taste of *la dolce vita* Liz found it difficult to return to planet Earth and live within her means and after a number of confrontations between Liz and her friendly bank manager, his patience eventually ran out. In a grand gesture one day and in front of a distraught Liz, he cut her card in half. In an effort, by way of revenge, to make him feel bad, Liz angrily and tearfully accused him of leaving her destitute to face the long journey on foot back to the campus. In another grand gesture he took some coins from his own pocket and gave Liz her bus fare. She did finally forgive him. But it took a few years.

I was glad when the last of those awful journeys to Norwich were over. The final one, for Liz's graduation, was worth it. She came out with a very good degree and chose as a career, journalism. Like most talented young people she wanted to start at the top and several weeks of pasting up pages for magazines with not a single cocktail party meeting famous authors in sight, was followed by disillusionment. Her skills at CV distortion and misrepresentation, however, secured well paid employment for her in London where she lived for a while with her friend Mairaed and then on a house boat on the Thames at Chelsea, until she came back home and met up again with Andrew, an old friend from schooldays. They were married the following year. Liz came back to her roots. I doubt whether the boys will.

Six thousand miles now separates me from number one son James. Who could have imagined such a dramatic change in the child who wouldn't stay with anyone other than his mam or his gran Marshall, wouldn't join the cubs or scouts and to whom even the thought of school trips filled him with dread. Two hours were all it took on his first day at school for him to decide that this wasn't for him. He climbed out of a window and came home. Fortunately Josephine was in the house that day but his mam, who was expecting son number three, was due to attend antenatal clinic the next day and she made it clear that he must stay at school because there would be no-one in at home. "Just leave the key under the mat then," was James' answer to the problem.

My reluctance to move back to Middlesbrough, one of the most aggressive towns in England, had a lot to do with my fear that this might not be the best environment in which to raise teenage boys, all of whom had a tendency to gravitate towards the rough and ready types of which there was no shortage in the Boro. James in particular suffered from the stigma of his earlier private education. With his aggressive tendencies – inherited from the Marshall side of the family of course – it didn't take him long to find himself in trouble and we found ourselves in court defending a breach of the peace charge after he had punched a neighbour's boy whose father reported the incident to the police. This is the same father, I discovered later, who used to go into town looking for fights when he was younger. I was and still am grateful to my lawyer friend Trevor Hirst who happened to be in court that day and offered to represent James. Franz Wheldon, James's adversary, was a year older than him and, as Trevor sensibly pointed out to the court, most teenage boys fight, no injuries were sustained and if every schoolboy scuffle was to end up the subject of proceedings then the courts couldn't cope. If Franz's father, the hypocrite, had kept his nose out, I'm sure the whole incident would have blown over, as indeed it did. The case was dismissed

If bad attitudes are abundant in Middlesbrough, then so too is humour. In Wards the old established fishmongers in Parliament Road one day, Dave the proprietor was serving a customer when he was rudely interrupted.

"Ow, Jack, where's Finsbury Street?" demanded a passer-by in a loud voice, without an "Excuse me" in sight...

"How did you know my name was Jack?" asked Dave.

"I guessed," said the ignoramus.

Clearly irritated by this ill-mannered intrusion, Dave's reply was a classic:

"Well, you can guess where Finsbury Street is then."

I encouraged James to channel his aggression into boxing which, as a member of Joe Walton's Boys Club, he did enthusiastically and with some success. Unfortunately he suffered from nose bleeds so his pugilistic career was short lived. Many people believe that boxing should be banned. I don't agree. Boys are aggressive. They are competitive. Removing these elements from a controlled situation like sport, as the do-gooders advocate, can only lead to frustrations building up and being released in other damaging ways – and as Roger Black our medal winning Olympic sprinter says, the removal of competition limits our chances of producing medal winning Olympic athletes and other sporting heroes and heroines. To make up for his early enforced retirement from the ring I took James down to Wembley in 1987 to see Frank Bruno fight for the World Heavyweight Championship. He absolutely loved it until the American Tim Witherspoon dumped our hero on the canvas in round eleven.

If you have a good open relationship with your kids they reveal all sorts of secrets later in life like when James, having promised me he was finished with scrapping, had to be rescued from humiliation in a Newcastle bar by his younger brother when he found himself second best to a Geordie hard lad. Tim, who was half his size, jumped on the lad's back and hissed, "Don't mess with the gypsies." It did the trick. Tim, thanks to his quick thinking, saved his brother from being on the receiving end of a beating.

In Middlesbrough and in many big cities, teenage years are there to be survived and James managed to leave school with decent grades too, got a place in the University of Northumbria and in his final year, instead of a degree, he opted for the more appropriate HND Course in Construction, his interest in which had been stimulated while working for Edwin Davis Ltd at weekends and during school holidays. He had earlier spent two years studying Finance and Accounts which he was also to find useful. It was during his university years that James developed his wanderlust, taking every opportunity during vacations to get away to places as far away and remote as possible. No safe destinations for him. Wherever he went it would be to the most uncivilised and dangerous region of each country. His warmth and almost naïve friendliness towards everyone ensured his survival. The world was his oyster. A European tour in 1996 which included the Hungarian Grand Prix followed a trip to Mexico, Guatamalo and Belize the previous year. 1997 took him to Kenya, Tanzania, Malawi, Mozambique and South Africa followed by Brazil and several other South American countries. 1998 was dedicated to working hard to fund his next trip which was to explore the jungle regions of South America the following year ending up in Cuba for the millennium. With no more than half his 1999 adventure accomplished he found himself in Peru. Not in Lima, Cusco, Arequipa or similar relatively safe and therefore popular traveller's destinations, but in Iquitos, the main town in the jungle province of Loreto where few gringos ventured. This bustling third-world town is inaccessible by road and James had made the tortuous five-day journey there by coach and boat down the Rios Amazona and Nanay. There James' travels came to an abrupt and painful end when he sprained his ankle playing football with some local lads on one of the beautiful sandy beaches which appear in the dry season in certain parts of the Amazon and its tributaries as the water level drops by several metres. Stuck in Iquitos and unable to move on James became bored. He noticed across the road from the house of his new and very good friend Robinson Valasquez, constant and long queues winding out of the local college. Curious, he decided to investigate and found that the students were waiting to use the only photocopy machine in the building and to pay two Nuevo Soles for the privilege. When he was able, James went to Lima, brought back a photocopy machine, installed it in Robinson's front room directly opposite the college and erected a large sign: *"Fotocopias Uno Sole."* Business boomed and two further shops were opened in town. A few years later James – or Jimmy as he is known there – acquired some property on the Iquitos Boulevard with stunning views across the river. The site consisted of a concrete house (for many years the secret hideaway of a Nazi war criminal), a courtyard and an enormous verandah with thatched roof once used as a brothel in the set for the film *Pantaleon y Las Visitadores.* The house has been caringly restored by Jimi and converted into apartments, the top penthouse of which he occupies himself. Additional chalets have been constructed on the land and the balcony serves as a five-star residents' lounge in which they can relax in comfort on sofas and in hammocks and enjoy the *"bella vista".* Rolando the janitor, his wife Beysi and children Evila, Tania, Elibeth and Junior were given one of the apartments to live in but the family, which had moved to Iquitos from the jungle, couldn't get used to luxury living, were frightened by the shower and moved out to live in a shack in a corner of the land, where they felt more comfortable and able to wash as they had always done by pouring water over their bodies using a tin can!

Jimmy of course speaks the language fluently and is a respected member of the community. He was invited to apply for the post of British Consulate to Loreta, the largest of the Peruvian provinces but on this occasion declined! He preferred what he was doing to running around after tourists who had lost their passports. Perhaps we might see him spending more time in Europe as things develop in my Tenerife enterprise.

With Tommy's genes in the family there had to be one Jack the Lad. On the 3rd March 1974 I plucked up the courage and attended the birth of son number two – our balcony baby. We call him that because he was conceived on an Ibiza hotel balcony. I think women quite enjoy seeing us males floundering and completely out of our depth in these very female of female situations. Desperate for something to do instead of sitting at Chris' bedside feeling totally useless, I asked the nurse if I could help in any way. "Measure the time between the contractions," she offered. With much relief I applied myself diligently to my task. Some time later the nurse came back, held Chris' hand and enquired, "How long between the contractions now then?" Helpfully I responded, "Three minutes twenty seven point five seconds." Ignoring me and without taking her eyes off Chris, the bitch said to her, "And how long between yours, Mrs Arnott?"

By playing it low key and not letting on that these were their names, I had got away with calling my daughter Elizabeth and first son James after their paternal great grandparents. But Chris' residual Baptist influence meant that we called our second son Timothy and not Thomas as I would have preferred. Quite unfairly I think, George was given to him as a second name after Chris' father. But what's in a name? It was clear from an early age that Tim was my dad's favourite. Tommy made no bones about it. Tim was the only one of the boys he would regularly take out in the pushchair to see the fire engines and to feed the ducks in Albert Park. The only time I ever saw Tommy distressed was when, whilst in his care, Tim was run over by a car, which I am pleased to say, for both their sakes, he survived.

Tim was too busy larking about and having fun to take school seriously. He wasn't exactly top of the pops with his teachers, especially after breaking the thumb of the teacher's pet in a fight. This particularly obnoxious child was a bully and had caused Tim's younger brother Jacob much distress. The teacher would not concede that such a model pupil who played in the school orchestra and was himself the son of a school headmaster could be capable of such behaviour towards a younger boy.

"I'll get him," offered James when we were finally able to get to the bottom of the cause of Jacob's distressed state.

"No you won't," said his mother, "you are older than him."

"Well," said Tim, "I'm younger. I'll get him."

Without thinking about the possible consequences, "That's different," said his mam.

Of course I was again away on business when, after the attack and after the bully had grassed by complaining to his teacher, Chris was summoned to the school to explain whether what Tim had said ("My mam told me to get him") was true. It was, more or less, and Chris didn't or couldn't explain fully the background. Not that they would have believed her if she had. I wish I had been there to tell them that the attack wouldn't have been necessary if the school had been doing its job properly and realised that they had a sneaky bully in their midst who was particularly clever at conning them into thinking butter wouldn't melt in his mouth. I think it is the case that schoolteachers are not well qualified to deal with the problem of bullying. They need to be streetwise and few of them are. They haven't experienced the real world. They've gone from school to teachers' training school and back to school. I know this is a generalisation but I think teachers would command more respect from the kids if they had done something different in their lives. I don't think people who want to be politicians should be allowed to be politicians – and I don't think teachers under thirty should be allowed to teach.

In a strange twist of fate the bully boy's father called at our house, again when I was away, of course, to complain about the incident. He was quite pompous and rude and made Chris feel quite uncomfortable. But she recognised him from an incident which had occurred a couple of years earlier. On my return I went round to confront him. "So you don't believe in physical violence between kids then?" I asked him. Before he had finished spluttering his reply I interrupted: "I think fights between kids of the same age can be excused." Then, looking him directly in the eyes, "Wife beating is something different and the opinion of a wife beater on the subject of violence is not worth a toss in my book." He knew what I was talking about. He and his wife had called in at one of our New Year's Eve parties a couple of years earlier. He had been annoyed that his wife was enjoying herself a little bit too much for his liking and he had hit her and dragged her outside by her hair. With my parting shot of "You may be able to do it in your headmaster's study with children, but don't ever speak to my wife like that again" I left him standing on his doorstep, hopefully feeling pretty uncomfortable. But knowing what this type of people are like, maybe not.

There was one particular teacher at secondary school, a Mrs Langabeer, who for some reason disliked Tim and, despite his repeated requests to be called Tim as he was known by everyone else, she persisted in embarrassing him by calling him Timothy. One day she suddenly started to call him Tim and then, straight after her lesson, ordered him outside where, with two of her crony colleagues, he was given a stern lecture on the authority of schoolteachers. He hadn't a clue what they were talking about. Without Tim's knowledge I had written to the headmaster asking him whether he believed that in order to teach effectively, teachers should make an effort to win the confidence and respect of their pupils, rather than deliberately humiliate and alienate them as Mrs Langabeer had done with Tim. I give the headmaster credit for dealing with Mrs L. It had clearly infuriated her. Sad bitch. Regrettably there are still many people who abuse their positions of authority thinking that merely holding such positions is in itself sufficient to earn respect. Fortunately there were some decent staff at the school, like Mrs Owen, Tim's drama teacher, and Mr Porter, his English teacher, who supported and encouraged him and got the best out of him.

Guess where I was when the police arrived at the house and took Tim down to the Station for questioning in connection with the murder of Dr Birkett, the Middlesbrough coroner, who lived nearby? Tim's friend Mickey Marr was a suspect though completely innocent. Some weirdo from Whinney Banks Estate was eventually convicted but it was another traumatic situation which Chris had to deal with while I was away on business.

Tim didn't stay on at Sixth Form of course and for a while tried his hand at the insurance business in our Middlesbrough Office where he was extremely popular despite being the boss's son, but because he was, it didn't feel right for him and he moved on. At only seventeen he hitch-hiked to Northern Spain and got a job in Lloret "propping" – short for propositioning. Without warning we decided to drive down to see what he was up to. Most sons would have resented such an intrusion but Tim was different. We have no secrets. We talk normally and openly with complete frankness. No subject or personal matter is taboo. We enjoy a healthy uninhibited dialogue which many families may not be comfortable with. We knew Tim would be pleased to see us. He knew he could expect a few treats too, like slap-up meals and good wine in The House of Garlic which only served food which was smothered in the stuff. We found him on a busy street corner working with a multinational team of young people whose job it was to persuade holidaymakers to patronise the particular bars and restaurants which paid them a small fee and fed them. He was good. Especially with the females, who, if they showed any hesitancy, would be swept into his arms and carried into his particular establishment, a heavy metal bar. They loved it. He lived in a pokey little room above a restaurant called the House of Roast Beef where he helped out at busy times. How easy it is to con holidaymakers. None of that busy restaurant's customers ever ate roast beef. They got flattened and coloured pork which was cheaper.

On his return to England at the end of the season Tim did a diploma course at the Newcastle College of Performing Arts which was right up his street. His performance as Jesus in the College nativity play was, for his proud Christian Gran Marshall, one of the most moving things she had ever experienced. Afterwards he got a few parts in episodes of local TV's long running serial *Byker Grove*, but his restless spirit was urging him on once more. Two of his illustrious fellow students at drama school went on to become TV stars Ant and Dec.

Tim is nothing if not an opportunist, just like his Granda. Taking advantage of my open offer to all my family to provide funds for anything which will benefit their education he moved to Brighton. Travel was, I recognised, the growth industry of the future and with Tim's Lloret de Mar experience I saw this as a possible career path for him. A period at Hove Travel College in Sussex and another diploma, a distinction, for his bedroom wall was followed by three years in Folkestone working for a sea freight company before trying his luck in Sydney, Australia, as a roller blind fitter.

Whilst earlier travelling around France with a touring circus (not as a clown, though it has to be said, he would have made a good one!) Tim had picked up a little of the language and this was very useful in his job at Folkestone where he frequently supplemented his salary with a "baccy run" to Le Havre. On one such trip he enlisted the help of his mother during one of her visits. Laden with carrier bags full of duty frees she disembarked from the ferry to be confronted by an army of HM Customs officials. Seeing other "baccy runners" just dump their contraband and leg it, she panicked. Among the turmoil of emotions she experienced were dismay at the thought of being arrested and fury at being so stupid to allow herself to be persuaded to become involved in such a dubious enterprise. She was about to jettison her booty and flee with the rest of the smugglers when she felt a tap on her shoulder and heard a man's voice. "Come this way madam," she was ordered by the peak capped "official" who turned out to be Tim who had borrowed the cap and saved his mother from further embarrassment.

Tim took on board wholeheartedly and perhaps a little too literally the advice I constantly gave to all my family. KEEP YOUR OPTIONS OPEN. The epitaph they have planned for my tombstone will read, "THIS IS ONE OPTION HE COULDN'T KEEP OPEN."

After his return from the Southern Hemisphere Tim spent a couple of years planting trees for the Forestry Commission in Scotland. Just like his granda he never allowed work to get in the way of his busy social life. He kept summers free for the many music festivals which took place then. His exploits at these events with his many friends and occasionally his younger brother will I am sure, provide enough material for his own book but I must mention his success at what may have been his final festival appearance which took place at the Green Gathering in Somerset and where he became the BBB champion. Completely starkers and conceding height and weight (but not length) he had floored his opponent in the first round. Bare bottom boxing was one of the many unorthodox activities which take place at these gatherings.

From Scotland he moved across the Irish Sea into the Euro Zone, Eire, where he worked at tree felling and later renovating derelict crofters' cottages. His girlfriend at that time was quite a talented poet. Here is a sample of her work which she scribbled up in just a few minutes when we were over in Ireland on a visit. It was written during a drive round a beautiful part of Ireland known as the Conemara Loop as a comment on the failure of the Irish Country Planning Authorities to preserve the landscape.

BUNGALOWS... by Claire O'Byrne

"There's something vulgar happening round Donegal's vast bay
It's Happening in Dingle, Letterkenny and Galway
On Kerry's wild peninsula, the hills around Kenmare
All over Sligo county and the Curragh at Kildare
In Connemara's mountains and the fields of Athenrey
Ten thousand tasteless bungalows have fallen from the sky

Cushioned by a tarmac pat, enclosed by ugly walls
There seems to be no mercy to the places that they fall –
Round a rugged mountain corner that is too nice to be true
Five hundred bastard bungalows obliterate your view
In nightmarish magnolia, in lime and mint and peach
The ghastly dwellings cluster thick round hill and glen and beach
In strangely garish pastel shades they squat upon the ground
– Of their supposed inhabitants there's neither sight nor sound
We must presume these tasteless few have other homes elsewhere
Too far away from Ireland to know or even care."

Tim eventually bought, renovated and extended his own cottage near Drumkeeran in beautiful County Leitrim. It commands striking views across the valley to Lough Belhaven and will provide a fine home for him, our grandchildren and wife Catriona of the Irish protestant Langrell family descended from the French Huguenots, a number of whom (about 10,000) fled to Ireland around 1685 to escape persecution. Tim and Catriona have exciting plans for the future which include the cultivation of the extensive land attached to the cottage, keeping pigs, poultry and a pony and trap for transport.

I don't suppose Tim will ever achieve his ambition of having a pint in every county in the British Isles, though having achieved this in England and most of Wales and Scotland, you never know.

With my new grandchildren I will try to resist the temptation to "talk". This is a sort of game we played originally with Liz and then with our first grandchild Daisy who regularly stayed with us when she was younger. Every morning I would bring her and her granny a drink in bed and would get in beside them and pretend my hands were mice – a good one and a naughty one. This charade developed into a full scale theatrical production involving dozens of her small dolls, her dolls house and various other props and went on for ages with me and Chris doing the voices. It required a great deal of imagination since a new or modified script would be expected for each performance. "Talk, talk," Daisy demanded as soon as she woke up. Good fun, but it became very hard work. Once you start something with kids they won't let you stop.

Another one to keep his options open is son number three, our tinsel tot. He even has the option of several names – John, Jacob, Edward, Bena, Jake, Jigs (changed to JIIGGS when we had a car with that registration), Jigsaroony, Riiggs and Rigsby. The first three he was christened with. The origins of the others are vague, except for Bena. When he was very young his hero was David Banner who played the Incredible Hulk in the TV series of that name. His pronunciation of the actor's name stuck and that's what his siblings called him. He was later known as Dick Whittington, Compound John and, because of his interest in astronomy and technology, The Professor.   Perhaps some of the Stephenson genes have finally filtered through. We had all his names printed on a T- shirt for him.

Let me first explain the tinsel tag. One night during the Christmas of 1975 when the kids were in bed Chris and I opened a bottle of wine and relaxed, so much so that we ended up dancing with only pieces of tinsel to cover our nakedness. My piece was hanging round the only part of the male body suitable for such adornment. Instead of the tinsel I should have worn a condom. But I didn't and on the eleventh of September 1976 our family increased to four. The new arrival was greeted with joy of course but also with some anxiety on my part, reflected in the announcement I placed in the newspapers.

> *"ARNOTT. On the 11th September at North Tees Hospital, John Jacob Edward. A third son for Derrick and Chris. A grandson for Tommy, Beatrice, Clifford and Vera and an accomplice for Liz, James and Tim."*

Again my attempts to influence the choice of name, despite resorting to subterfuge, were not entirely successful. My first choice was John. Chris, again with Biblical influence, preferred Jacob. To resolve the stalemate we decided to put all the suggested names into a hat. The first name drawn out was John but Chris was suspicious and before I was able to destroy the evidence she grabbed the hat and discovered that I had written John on every piece of paper. I had to concede defeat but Chris, magnanimous in victory, decided on John Jacob Edward (after my uncle who died on his birthday) but she insisted that he should be known as Jacob. In the end it didn't matter at all. In fact they called him John when he went to school and he didn't object. Parents make such a big issue out of choosing names, few of which survive beyond primary school when nick names take over. We should all be allowed to choose our own names at the age of twelve or thirteen.

My anxiety at the time of Jacob's birth was due to the extra responsibility of another dependent which would fall on my shoulders should anything happen to Chris – and it did. A hernia operation during her pregnancy was followed after the birth with a period during which she was out of action with post natal depression and Jacob was bundled off to South Shields to be looked after for lengthy spells by his Gran. During one of these visits he lost his dummy. After searching high and low, his Gran, in desperation suggested that they should pray and ask Jesus to help Jacob to do without it. "Why don't you just ask him to find it," was Jacob's helpful suggestion – an early demonstration of his logical thought processes. Jesus' failure to oblige did nothing to shake his Gran's faith but must have led Jacob to conclude that The Almighty wasn't so smart after all!

After an accident involving a full glass door while playing with Lance the dog, Gran had all the glass removed and they would all access the kitchen by stepping through the empty door frame. All except the stupid dog who used to stand and bark until someone opened the frame! I mention Lance because he was indirectly involved in making Jacob's life a misery when his brothers caught him pee-ing on the dog and threatened to tell unless he obeyed their every command. Can't kids be cruel? So not only was he exiled from home and denied the love and attention of his parents, he was then subjected to a particularly nasty type of blackmail and bullying by his siblings which went on for many years. No wonder the poor lad had made out a will at the tender age of eight, as we learned some years later when we found it in a drawer. How sad is that? Fortunately Liz never got to inherit the fish tank.

I had put a lot of effort into Liz and to a lesser extent into the older boys but with so many distractions and responsibilities in other directions there wasn't much left in the paternal input tank for Jacob, at a time when it was most needed. I found myself being uncharacteristically impatient and irritated by his normal boy-like exuberance. Mind you I would not allow anyone else to be. One day I looked out of the window to see him being frogmarched towards the house. I was furious and dashed out to confront the elderly man who had hold of him. "Get your hands off him and stay right there," I barked at Jacob's captor and before he could utter more than a few words of explanation I took my distressed son inside to comfort him until he had calmed down sufficiently for me to return my attention to the man waiting outside. Apparently Jacob, I learned, had committed the horrendous atrocity of throwing a piece of clay at the gable end of the man's house. "And that justifies you manhandling and terrifying a five-year-old, child does it?" I interrupted his bleating protestations with, followed by, "I have a distressed child who now needs my comfort. That is the only thing that is important to me right now. Tell me where you live and I'll deal with you later." Having obtained this information I turned my back on him and went back inside. I don't think the man was quite expecting this reaction. I wonder what he was expecting? For me to meekly apologise and give the lad a good thrashing? I did call round later to see him but he wouldn't open the door further than his security chain would allow. He was clearly terrified and I will always remember him calling for his wife's support. "Darling, darling, it's that man," he whimpered. He then said something about trespassing. I told him that he had trespassed on my son and nobody does that except me. I think he got the message. At least I was home this time when there was trouble.

Jacob seemed happy and settled at Red House Private Prep School but Tim's kinder egg incident, related in an earlier chapter, meant that unfortunately he was uprooted and sent to Green Lane, Liz's old school when, in 1983, we returned to Middlesbrough. Jacob's teacher Mrs Andrews was really nice and the school was a good one despite the headmaster, Mr Caswell, about whom we had some doubts. My "casual acquaintance" in the Club, John 'Hodgy' Hodgson, had told me that he had occasion to complain to him about the school's inefficiency when his son, on a school swimming trip, had been left behind in the baths when the coach departed without him. We too found cause to complain of Caswell's negligence – or should I say that Chris did because at the time of the incident I was "you know where". Jacob complained of a pain in his knee after PE one day but was told by Mr Caswell that there was nothing wrong with him and to stop fussing. His teacher however was concerned and, I suspect behind Caswell's back, telephoned Chris who collected Jacob from school and took him down to A&E where they discovered, lodged completely inside his knee, a pin left over from the Christmas decorations which had been attached to the gymnasium ropes. Had it been ignored the consequences, she was told, could have been quite serious as the pin moved around and perhaps could have punctured an artery.

To deal with disputes among the kids I would hold kangaroo courts, allowing each party no more than one minute to explain their grievance. Interruptions would be penalised. I suspected all was not well when Jacob, obviously fearful that his dog peeing incident would be revealed, always seemed reluctant to implicate his brothers, who treated him quite contemptuously as an inferior. It gave me great satisfaction therefore when on holiday one year in Ibiza the three boys entered a go kart race which Jacob won in a canter. Even an exchange of karts which James insisted would reverse his fortune failed to prevent another crushing defeat by his young brother. A few years later at a corporate day we organised at a local kart track, Jacob comfortably reached the final and was only narrowly beaten into runner's up spot in a big field of experienced drivers – this before he had even passed his driving test. Keen to have a son follow in my footsteps on the motor race track I helped him to buy a kart in which he put in some extremely fast lap times. His lack of confidence prevented him from taking part in competitive racing which was a great pity because he was clearly very talented. It took only a few lessons from Fred Bell for him to pass his driving test. He didn't even tell us he was taking it. He later easily qualified for a Heavy Goods Vehicle license. Fred Bell, who had taught the others, came out of retirement to teach Jacob. We still use some of Fred's sayings today, like "Watching that mirrow now" which we adapt to all kind of situations and which has become a bit of a family joke. "Watching that speed now/temper now/language now…etc. etc. etc."

Because of his alternative thinking, his interests and his technological proficiency (he achieved 'A' grades at both GCSE levels) we often referred to Jacob as The Professor. He was constantly involved in some project or another. We were under strict instructions not to disturb the labyrinth of wires which constantly covered the floor of his bedroom and much of the top floor landing, spreading like tentacles from an array of electric sockets and extension plugs. When we moved from Westlands to No 68 Roman Road, a smaller house, I looked forward to a reduction in the electricity bills. Instead they soared. This puzzled me until one day, noticing a particularly complex set of wires leading into a large cupboard. I was curious and decided to investigate. There, inside the cupboard which was clad entirely in aluminium foil and heated by an array of arc lights were probably the most healthy and robust marijuana plants outside Afghanistan. This discovery also explained why Chris was always running out of kitchen foil. Jacob wasn't the only one into the illegal cultivation of the weed. One of the boys' pals, Simon Gibb, or Big Nomis as he was known, told us some years later about the time his dad questioned him about the strange looking plant which had appeared in the sunniest spot in the garden. "It's a kind of mint," was Nomis' lame and unconvincing explanation, to which his dad responded, much to Nomis' relief, "Your mam loves mint on her tatties." I'm not surprised if it was Nomis' "mint" she put on them!

Unlike his siblings who spent theirs on transient pleasures, the thousand pounds he was given by his Grandma one year, acquired for Jacob a sophisticated telescope with which he indulged his hobby of astronomy. I don't know whether he still has the lovely letter of encouragement he received from Patrick Moore, the famous astronomer whose BBC TV series 'The Sky at Night' we both keenly enjoyed. When it comes to deep thinking, Jacob and I are *ad idem*. Like me, he is fascinated by space and infinity and our inquisitive minds have resulted in some interesting discussions on a range of strange topics. For example, can plants feel pain? Vegetarians wouldn't want to consider that possibility of course and would choose to reject it. But how do they know? Why do they deny themselves carnal nutrition? Is it because they believe it is cruel to kill cows and pigs? How much more cruel would it be if they were not born at all? Just ask any cow that question and I know what she would say! And what's so special about cows and pigs that we should not kill them? Rats and mice and wasps and flies and even germs and bacteria are God's creatures too, yet nobody cares when we slaughter *them*! We must kill to survive whether it be by slaughtering animals or fish or chopping a cabbage's head off. We in the well fed developed world are very fortunate to be able to indulge ourselves in the choice.

But the dialogue between my youngest son and I was not all heavy stuff. There now exists between us a close relationship of love and respect. When he was a young man I purged myself of guilt for my negligent treatment of Jacob when he was a child, by apologising to him and explaining the circumstances.

As if it were not enough for him to be bullied by his siblings Jacob had to suffer at Boynton Senior School too and instead of going to Sixth Form College locally, chose to travel every day to Billingham where at Bede College he made some new and lasting friendships, as indeed he did at Appleby during the caravan season which must have afforded a welcome escape for him during the worst of his torment.

Tim didn't go to university so Jacob made up for that by going to two – first Liverpool and then Leeds, both of which he dropped out of. Looking back it is hardly surprising that our youngest son became a bit of a drop out, attending hippy music festivals up and down the country with brother Tim. He worked only spasmodically, made money building computers for people and because of his insomnia led a nocturnal life during which he became very knowledgeable on a wide range of subjects courtesy of the night time educational channels on TV. It took him a long time to kick the spliff habit but he finally came out of his shell and gained the confidence to travel and live the green dream on his converted lifeboat on the English canals with partner Rachel and daughter Sarah. They bought a house in Sowerby Bridge close to the boat and are very happy together. He finally emerged from the shadow of his brothers from whom he now commands respect and admiration. I am so happy that they and sister Liz are now very good pals.

Before I close this chapter let me try to explain the origin of his other two names, "Dick Whittington" and "Compound John". Polly was our household pet cat and he and Jacob became inseparable even after he left home and moved to Leeds. Note that I refer to Polly as 'he'. This is because we were informed when we bought him that he was a she and it wasn't until the vet had shaved his belly and was about to insert the neutering scalpel that the error was spotted. Jacob was broken hearted when Polly died of old age whilst cradled in his arms as the vet inserted the needle that was to terminate his life and his suffering.

While saving money to buy his boat, Jacob lived in a tiny caravan which he had brought down from Scotland where he and Tim had been planting trees for the Forestry Commission. We went down to visit him one day at the caravan site but they hadn't heard of Bena or Jacob or Riggs or Jiiggs Arnott. We left, but having no luck at any of the other sites nearby, returned to the original one where the penny finally dropped and the site manager said, "Oh, you mean Compound John", so-called because to save money Jacob had elected to stay in the compound rather than on the main site. The name stuck.

His brothers were eventually punished for giving Jacob a hard time. To encourage the kids to brush their teeth we would squeeze a line of toothpaste on to each of their brushes and check them before we went to bed. There was one occasion when we found toothpaste on the brushes of James and Tim. We asked them the following morning why they had not brushed their teeth before going to bed and they both insisted that they had. Telling lies was one of the misdemeanours for which the wooden spoon would be administered and both of them received a whack. Jacob had achieved vicarious revenge. Many years later we learned that it was he who, during the night, had put the toothpaste on their brushes to get them into trouble. Justice was done though. Ten out of ten for ingenuity Jacob.

Bringing up four kids is no picnic and it didn't help that Chris and I didn't always see eye to eye on the subject. Her approach to parenthood was one of organised routine which was disrupted by my involvement. She was right of course and knowing that my young kids were in capable hands I justified my failure to be a hands on dad and devoted much of my time to other things, like winning the bread – a role to which I was eminently more suited. I regret missing out on much of their early childhood and I was determined that this would not be the case with my grandchildren.

Fighting Cocks 1984.

L to R: Jacob, Tim and James.

Forty

THE PRODIGAL PARENT

You could have knocked me down with a hammer.
Chrissarism.

Now it came to pass that in the land of Sunder there lived a man and his wife and their baby daughter.

The wife left the marital home and forsaking her sacred vows went to live with another man, leaving her husband to raise the daughter.

The man divorced his wife and remarried. He and his new wife loved and cared for the daughter until she was a young woman and found a husband.

The mother became jealous of her daughter's affection for her stepmother and one day she spoke to her daughter who was then five years old, saying that it was wrong that she had to live with a stepmother and that children should live with their real mothers and fathers, even though she herself had made this impossible.

After the mother had poisoned her daughter's mind against her stepmother she left and took no further part in her daughter's life even though she lived nearby.

Many years later the daughter became curious about her real mother and arranged a reunion. The mother was invited to the daughter's house. A fatted calf was killed and there was much rejoicing.

IT IS HUMAN INSTINCT to ignore unpleasant truths. Blood is thicker than water. The mother's irresponsibility and hitherto disinterest in her daughter's childhood, her adolescence, her education and young womanhood were forgotten and forgiven. Unlike the brother of the Prodigal Son, the father and his new wife

317

were genuinely pleased for the daughter when she and her mother became reconciled. It was unfortunate that in the process of her reconciliation with her mother, the daughter's relationship with her stepmother suffered. The seeds of discontent sown in her mind as a child and which had caused much unhappiness and insecurity lay dormant for thirty years. Once reconciled with her mother however, the daughter's attention was once again focused on the issue of her disadvantaged childhood and the resentment she felt at not being brought up by both her real parents – a quite normal and understandable reaction. This resentment against the stepmother had manifested itself in a number of ways. Instead of chastising his daughter as he should have done, the father comforted her instead of his wife – an example of the over-protectiveness which occurs in mixed families and which must be so frustrating for the stepparent. The stepmother was deeply hurt and took it badly. She was devastated to find herself spoken to in such a vitriolic manner by the stepdaughter to whom she had devoted so much love and care. Perhaps she had given too much of her love. Perhaps this is what made it so painful.

It is human instinct also to find someone to blame for problems in our lives and we don't always choose the person responsible. In the daughter's case there were three candidates for her recriminations – her father, her mother and the man who took advantage of a young married mother whose marriage was in difficulties. The three of them were spared reprisals and instead the stepmother became a convenient scapegoat. Stepparents are like immigrants. They are brought in to do a job others don't want and are resented by those who benefit from their labours. The stepmother's pain may one day soften and perhaps she may understand that the daughter's anger is forgivable in the light of her mother's spiteful influence. Perhaps the daughter one day may understand that her stepmother too had a disadvantaged marriage. Perhaps they may one day become close again. The mother, as a result of this turn of events, perhaps felt that she had achieved her revenge on the person who she perhaps quite irrationally blamed for usurping her place in the life of her daughter. She did so however at the cost of her daughter's childhood contentment. It was she who chose, well before the stepmother was on the scene, to abandon her daughter. It was she who chose to miss out on her childhood. It was she who filled her mind with disillusionment and doubt, a despicable and unforgivable thing to do.

"Heaven has no rage like love to hatred turned," said William Congreve, *"Nor hell a fury like a woman scorned."* The mother's conduct may have been, if not acceptable, then perhaps understandable if this were the case. But it wasn't. It was she who did the scorning.

At the root of many of the problems within our modern Western society is without doubt the breakdown of traditional family units. Despite all the protection and love and care her father, stepmother and grandmother put into raising the daughter she may have felt that this wasn't enough. Children are entitled to expect the full devotion of both parents within a normal family environment. If they are denied this then they are entitled to feel angry. Fortunately, despite the mother's conduct the daughter survived. Not all products of broken homes and single parent families are so fortunate. You don't have to look far to find what is probably the main reason for crime and anti-social behaviour. The anger bottled up by these kids is often directed against the society they feel has let them down and can manifest itself in various anti-social ways. Don't blame the kids. It's not their fault. But before something can be done about a problem, the causes must be recognised and for some reason there seems to be a reluctance to acknowledge that kids with no dads (or mams) are disadvantaged and therefore more likely to be rebellious. It isn't politically correct to be seen to criticise minority groups like single parents. But whilst many do deserve sympathy and support there are many too who deliberately become pregnant because they are bored or they want a council flat and other perceived benefits. Instead of discouraging irresponsible parenting recent governments have done the opposite, fearful of losing votes by taking a hard line on promiscuity, discipline and parental responsibility. A by-product of this irresponsible attitude is a reduction in the number of traditional family units and a corresponding increase in insecure children and young people with problems.

This is not to say that people shouldn't divorce but when children are involved, this should not be an easy option and it should not be allowed at all without both parties making a legally binding commitment to their responsibilities. There is no longer a stigma attached to unmarried mothers, rightly so in many cases. But to encourage the production of fatherless offspring by financial incentive only produces more disadvantaged children and irresponsible parents relying on the nanny state to look after them. And what about the suggestion that homosexual couples be allowed to adopt – another example of over the top liberal thinking and "votes for favours". Indulging people for these reasons takes no account of the feelings of the children involved and what they will go through at school. Adoptive parents and stepparents can of course give children their love and this is very important. However, we spend much of our adolescent schooldays striving to be one of the herd. Adopted kids can escape presenting to their peers a bullying opportunity by pretending that their adoptive parents are real mam and dad. This is not possible when they are both dads or both mams. Given the slightest excuse bullies will make a disadvantaged child's life a misery, which is compounded by the absence of the support of two normal parents. Without such support we should recognise just how seriously we disadvantage children. Why condemn kids to a childhood of misery and torment to appease a handful of deviants? This may not be the politically correct way to describe people who in many peoples' opinion are unsuitable for parenting. It is not meant to be offensive. Merely honest. The desire for homosexual couples to gratify themselves by adopting a child is perfectly understandable and who can blame them for doing so? The blame rests with those people who make it legally possible for this to happen.

The emphasis today is on material and selfish needs. Previous generations couldn't have what they wanted. Either it wasn't allowed or their parents couldn't afford it. But unlike today's generation they all had, with few exceptions, the most precious gift a child can have – their mothers *and* fathers.

Our country, like many in the West, is like a dysfunctional family in which the parents (the politicians) concerned only for their own self interest and short term popularity, try to buy the favour of their kids (the electorate) by giving in to their selfish demands and by giving them toys (cars, luxury goods, houses and mortgages they can't afford and for which they have to go into debt) hoping that this will get them off their backs and love them (vote for them). But this doesn't earn respect. It just makes kids (voters) demand more and more. By giving them everything except discipline, these kids turn out to be spoiled brats. We have become a country of spoiled Brits. When the toys are taken away there will be tantrums.

The Clandestine Christening 1965.

Forty-One

EXTENDED FAMILY

I was angered for I had no shoes. Then I met a man with no feet.
Chinese Proverb.

AS WELL AS OUR OWN LOT we seem to have accumulated quite a large extended family too. There's Julio, Miguel, Jose, Marjorie, Suli, Thaila, Rudolfo, Choclo, Rueben, Irvine, Roy, Elena, Lorenzo, Marcos and many more – all Iquitos street kids who have been taken under our wings during our visits to Peru. These poor kids are considered pests by many of the visitors to this primitive jungle town and are shunned. Jim, I discovered, is idolised by them and to me this says a lot about him. I was and still am impressed by the way he treats them – with kindness yet with authority and discipline, always encouraging them to earn and appreciate whatever generosity is bestowed on them. It is so easy in such circumstances for us to simply give. Jim will not condone this although when he was not looking, I've noticed his mother sneaking many a Sole coin into many a grubby little palm. When I am there I have my shoes polished, several times a day, and because I once repaired Roy's shoe shine box I became a sort of patron to the dozens of boys plying their simple trade. At every opportunity they would discover and, I suspect even create, some slight damage to their boxes so they could bring them to me for repair and for them to be decorated with one of the hundreds of stickers we bring from the UK and which are such a novelty there. I also find myself buying lots of bon bons and chiclets which I don't even like but which helps the street economy. Despite their abject poverty I do really believe that these poor skinny kids are happier than many in the so called developed world. Interestingly during the many weeks I have now spent there I have never seen a fat child or witnessed a tantrum and have yet to hear a baby cry. Is this, I wonder, because even when mothers work they have their babies constantly strapped to them instead of being dumped in a nursery? Affluence doesn't come without consequences. Western kids by comparison seem generally a discontented bunch.

Chris was in her element with hordes of kids around. They loved her. Julio who was one of her favourites became her business partner. With beads plentiful and cheap she was able to indulge in her hobby and made necklaces for him to sell on the street. They shared the takings and Julio learned a little about the world of business.

On one of her visits Chris took a particular liking to a young boy called Lorenzo who always seemed to be on his own. The reason was that he didn't know any of the other boys because he lived in the jungle and only came into town occasionally when his father was on tribal business. We later discovered that his father was the chieftain of the Shipibo Indians. Because of the kindness shown by Chris to his son, the next girl to be born in the jungle village was named Christina in her honour. And she has been invited to be the chieftain's guest at a ceremony to be held for her in the village – an invitation she is unlikely to be sufficiently intrepid to accept since the village is accessible only by an arduous three-day journey by boat and foot deep into the jungle.

Whether it is down to my experience on the train to Saltburn all those years ago or for other reasons, I am acutely aware of the vulnerability of children and of the deviousness of those who prey on them. I wish I had been able to help by becoming more involved in the problem but with the demands of business, family, the club and other selfish interests I have had to content myself with helping financially. My two favourite charities are NSPCC and RTU – Reaching the Unreached – to which I was introduced by Ian Fletcher. RTU is a Catholic charity set up many years ago by Brother James Kimpton, the nearest thing to a modern day Saint, who has devoted his entire life to helping underprivileged and neglected children in the Theni region of Southern India. Initially Br James' main concern was for children discarded by their families either because they were ill or disabled and therefore a burden, or were simply female and considered worthless in Indian culture. A small village, which has since mushroomed into several, was established in which to create a caring family style environment with a 'family' of orphans of different ages, each living in its own small house. I confess that I stopped reading the periodic RTU Newsletters because the harrowing accounts of neglect and suffering disturbed me too much. Wallowing in the luxury of Western comfort they also made me feel quite guilty. In recent years the charity has focused on orphans of the AIDS epidemic sweeping the Indian and other continents. RTU is a registered charity No 1091295. Visit www.rtu.co.uk. I used some of the money I was able to recover from Brooks Mileson through the courts[6] to pay for the lifetime education of some children in the village. In return I was 'offered' an addition to my extended family, a lovely little six-year-old girl called Sathya who lives in the village of Siru Malar (Little Flower). Both Sathya's parents died of AIDS and she herself is HIV positive. Before coming under the care of Br James and his team of dedicated helpers Sathya was in another orphanage who

---

[6] See Volume II.

rejected her when they discovered she was infected. She is now on the correct drugs and hopefully will be able to live a fairly normal life in the village. I don't suppose we shall ever meet but I suppose it is a comfort to her to know that there is someone out there in the big wide world who is interested in her welfare. We send presents on her birthday (or what Brother James estimates it to be) and at Christmas. She writes occasionally to let me know how she is.

What a small world it is. During my third visit to Iquitos I met Father Joseph Plumb who is a younger version of Br James and who has set up a similar operation in the Nanay area to help the poor children there. A native of County Durham, Joseph and I have mutual friends, Peter and Angela Peyton, whose daughters went to school with him and who confessed to being disappointed when he entered the priesthood because they both rather fancied him. He decided to leave the priesthood so here's your chance, girls! The church, I believe, still supports his work with the poor children in Iquitos.

I chose as my main children's charity, the NSPCC, because as the largest I felt that, apart from all the excellent work it does on the ground, it may have the capability to influence government thinking on certain issues. Another reason was that I was impressed with the sincerity and dedication of their officers. Many years ago through St Aiden's Christian Fellowship I became friendly with Harry Brown who was at that time the Society's Regional Manager. Harry invited me in 1983 to sponsor a local Centenary Reception for the charity's supporters at the Crathorne Hall near Yarm, which my Company was more than happy to do. I was privileged there to meet the Society's Patron, the Duke of Westminster. What a nice man. A clever, subtle and successful businessman capable of making a tremendous contribution to sensible unbiased debate, he was subsequently booted out of the House of Lords to make room for one of the Prime Minister's 'cash for Peerage' appointments who knows which way to vote and can be trusted not to have one single idea of his own. That's what happens to Dukes who give money to charity instead of political party funds!

As one of its main supporters I received regular invitations to attend NSPCC functions all of which took place in London and all of which, because I was always busy, I had to decline, but with more time on my hands after I retired I tried to become more actively involved in the affairs of the Society. My first attempt was a visit with Joe Laidler to New Scotland Yard to meet the team of police officers who had recently smashed a worldwide paedophile ring. Talking to the officers I found it most interesting to hear of the difficulties they faced and how they overcame the obstacles put in their path, often by our own legal system which, frankly, has surely gone too far in protecting the interests of criminals. Before finally getting the breakthrough they needed, the officers had to spend many months of surveillance before an opportunity afforded itself to legally enter the ring leader's premises which were heavily protected with substantial iron grilles. They knew full well what was going on within this fortress but were denied access, not just by the individual suspect, who used to delight in taunting them, but by our upside down legal system which refused to authorise a search warrant without sufficient proof of guilt which was of course only possible to obtain by searching the premises! It was clear too from what we were told, that there was a feeling of frustration among some of the officers and that they would welcome more positive support for what they were trying to achieve. It must do little to encourage them or give them a degree of job satisfaction when they see convicted and dangerous paedophiles and other criminals being given quite inadequate and inappropriate sentences then released to re-offend. This is surely one of the many areas in which government either doesn't care, is ineffective or is totally out of touch with the wishes of the people – and we call ourselves a democracy!

I hesitate to criticise the NSPCC which, as I said earlier, does tremendous work to help children who have suffered abuse. I believe however that the Society needs to be a little more realistic in its aims and to become more pro-active politically. It does an excellent job of fire fighting but I do feel that given its influential status it could do much more to tackle the root cause of the problem of child abuse. A massive amount of the Society's funds is spent on TV advertising and whilst I agree that awareness is important and accept that its FULL STOP campaign may have raised welcome funds, it will not achieve its stated aim, which is to eliminate abuse. This, I believe, will only be done by making the consequences of abuse unacceptable to the abuser. Yes, many of the abusers have a history of abuse themselves and, yes, they deserve some understanding and sympathetic help, but this can be only minimally effective and only with a minority of abusers. Abusers seem to broadly fall into two categories; those who abuse within the family and those who do so at large within the community. The former present a more complex and difficult problem to the latter and I will therefore concentrate for the moment on the professional abuser who goes out of his way, often at great lengths, to gratify his sick indulgences and whose activities I find more inexcusable. Many of these people manage to infiltrate into jobs involving children. It is in this area that I feel that the NSPCC and other children's charities could be more positive. It seems pretty obvious to me that if a paedophile gets a job with children then the employer's selection process must be flawed and if he remains in the job then its monitoring process has failed too. So what happens to the person, department or organisation (usually a local authority) which is guilty of the failure? Invariably the answer, apart from a lot of buck passing, is not a lot. Indeed people within the system who actively try to identify abuse are often made scapegoats and become victims themselves because nobody wants to accept responsibility or invite hassle and would prefer to turn a blind eye. One example very close to home involved Marietta Higgs, who bought our house in Roman Road and for a while was our neighbour. Dr Higgs was a senior local paediatrician specialising in children and she became concerned when she identified evidence of anal abuse among an alarming number of children she examined. The authorities, true to form, were reluctant and then unwilling to accept that child abuse was so widespread in the area and instead of taking the doctor's diagnosis seriously chose to question it and then subjected her to a campaign of vilification. Even local MP Sir Stuart Bell, my opponent on 05.05.05, though he knew little about it since he rarely strayed outside London, chose to make political capital out of it and joined in the chorus of baying hounds, which finally succeeded in removing Dr Higgs from her post. What a travesty. Those who stuck their heads in the sand and preferred to believe that the extent of child abuse was not consistent with Dr Higgs's findings may care to reconsider their opinions in the light of facts revealed several years later. It takes a lot of courage for a child to seek help and my guess is that only a small minority of them do. Yet every day four thousand five hundred children call NSPCC's Childline for help. Is this the tip of an enormous ice berg? What to me during this period was significant was the fact that not one of the fathers or stepfathers or uncles who were in danger of being rumbled ever publicly protested or denied abuse. It was their indignant wives or partners, encouraged by a defensive Social Services, who reacted angrily and openly. I suspect that the reaction of many of the suspects' partners was perhaps a little too emotional and may have been influenced by an unwillingness to accept that they may be living with an abuser. The problem was solved, as often happens, by everyone, except the doctor and her colleague Dr Wyatt, pretending it wasn't happening. Not a thought was spared for the poor kids. With no meaningful accountability in place within local authorities and other organisations the situation is unlikely to improve.

I put forward a proposal to the NSPCC that they should lobby government to change the rules and permit sufferers of abuse to hold Local Authorities responsible for the suffering they have endured. I explained that the due processes of the legal profession and commercial world would lose no time in identifying victims to come forward and sue for damages. Insurance companies would seize the opportunity and the authorities would be encouraged to take out insurance protection. This would give the insurers an opportunity to look at existing recruitment and monitoring procedures and recommend stricter ones which if not implemented would result in penal premiums. Ideally government would make such insurance compulsory. Accountability would be introduced externally and greater protection for children would be the result. Frankly many local authorities are too incompetent, reluctant or indifferent to be relied upon to self-regulate. Similar changes to the ones I suggested were introduced into industry many years ago. The Workmen's Compensation Act and the Factories Acts have resulted in work places being much safer places and employers much more accountable. If it works in industry, why not in the public sector?

My proposals, which were carefully drafted and sent to the Society, were not seriously considered. I don't think they were even acknowledged. People who attain high office in organisations like NSPCC are very nice people. Their hearts are in the right place and they do a great job of patching up casualties. But nice people are not always capable of taking the extreme, bold and often unpopular, steps needed to reduce the number of casualties or of standing their ground in the face of criticism and opposition.

A few years after my visit to New Scotland Yard I attended a forum held at the Unicorn Theatre in London organised by the NSPCC and chaired by Jeremy Vine, the BBC personality and interviewer. It was entitled "Question Time" and designed to seek the views of supporters. The distinguished panel comprised Giles Pegram, NSPCC's Director of Fund Raising, Baroness Walmsley the Liberal Democrat spokesperson in the House of Lords on Education and the NSPCC's Parliamentary Ambassador, Deidre Sanders the agony aunt for the Sun Newspaper, Wes Cuell, NSPCC's Director of Services and Claire Phillips, Director of Policy and Research at the Office of the Children's Commissioner for England.

I took the opportunity to raise the question of castration for habitual offenders. I had some years earlier seen a convicted serial paedophile interviewed on TV in which he acknowledged that he had an uncontrollable urge to molest children which various measures including lengthy spells in prison had failed to curb. He didn't like what he was doing and had tried hard to stop. He had repeatedly requested those responsible for his treatment and rehabilitation to allow him to be castrated. They had denied him this solution to his problem saying it couldn't be done. For God's sake why not? Who made that decision? Who is to be held responsible for the paedophile's next victim? Is it the paedophile or is it the people in whose hands lay the means to prevent the abuse but who, for some inexplicable reason, shirked their responsibility? They surely are the ones with blood on their hands. Here is the official response to my question:

"The whole idea of castration needs to be thoroughly researched but just to reinforce that sexual abuse isn't always about sex. Sexual abuse of children is often more about control than sex. So you could chemically castrate somebody, but they would still want to go to the same pattern of behaviour. At the end of the road castration would not be the same as a committed and very motivated change. If they volunteered for it, if they believed it was the right thing to do, as the only alternative to spending a life in prison, I don't have any moral objection to it. I just doubt that it would be used effectively."

In other words don't let us even explore the possibility – and until we find a way to stamp out every aspect of abuse – do nothing about those aspects we *can* do something about in the meantime. I was disappointed, frustrated and irritated by the response.

Does the NSPCC seriously intend to put a FULL STOP to child abuse? Do they believe that realistically this will happen if no new approach is taken? The evidence so far would suggest not. Unbelievably these people, the so called experts, are saying that compulsory castration would not be a deterrent. That it would not reduce paedophilic activity. Do they live in the real world? His sexual capability is probably the most coveted in the male psyche. Are they suggesting that its removal would not be an effective punishment and an even more effective deterrent? Come on!

The panel of important people may have had little appetite for my question and I received little encouragement from them or from the senior NSPCC personnel present, but during the drinks and nibbles session afterwards some of the young helpers made a point of telling me how much they admired me for saying what I did and how much they agreed with my views – and therefore, by implication, how much they were disappointed that they had not been taken seriously. These were kids who themselves had been abuse victims, who had been helped by the Society and who had volunteered their services freely on the night. I was encouraged by their support and I believe that they as victims are much better qualified to know what the real score is than all those "experts" in their ivory towers.

Sathya (2nd left) and her "family".

Forty-Two

MEIN KAMPF

The punishment of criminals should serve a purpose.
When a man is hanged he is useless.
Voltaire.

66**T**HAT'S A BIT BRUTAL, ISN'T IT?"** remarked John Hodgson in the club one evening when we were discussing the merits or otherwise of capital punishment. This is the same John Hodgson who only a few moments earlier was advocating a reintroduction of hanging. His remark was made in response to my suggestion that consideration should be given to amputation in certain circumstances. "You don't see many one-armed Arabs," once observed a neighbour of ours who had spent several years in Saudi Arabia where, unlike in Britain, he never felt threatened by its people, who he found to be honest law-abiding citizens. I don't believe for a moment that the Saudis are intrinsically better people than we are so, I wondered, could it have something to do with the way in which criminals are dealt with there?

I am sad when I see places of sanctuary and worship with their doors locked and windows protected by security bars. In my lifetime I have seen respect for authority all but disappear and standards of behaviour deteriorate enormously, though this is hardly surprising when our political leaders set such a bad example. Consequently dishonesty, anti-social behaviour and crime flourish, a state of affairs to which we have become almost desensitised. We are conditioned to accept this as normal – in schools, in the streets, in the workplace, in the City and in government. Instead of doing something about it governments just tell us they have spent more money than the previous government. All too often government's response to a problem or to criticism is to create a new law. This quick fix policy is designed to delude us into thinking they have "done something about it" so as to win our votes. But introducing legislation without thinking it through first and without proper consultation at street level is ineffective and often creates more problems than it solves. Surely one day we will see through the scam and there will be a backlash from the silent majority – if they haven't all left the country to live somewhere abroad where old fashioned respect and behaviour still prevail.

Governments talk about crime with persuasive political rhetoric and platitudes like Tony Blair's "Tough on crime. Tough on the causes of crime". Ten years down the line only one crime in ten ends up in court. The police no longer it seems take minor crime seriously. If people get away with petty crime what's to stop them becoming bolder and pushing boundaries further? Nothing.

The only two ultimate punishment options at present available to our courts are fines and imprisonment, neither of which now hold any fears for our criminals. However, the reintroduction of the death penalty is unacceptable for two reasons. It is too final and given the less than perfect nature of our legal system, irreversible, but more importantly it is not a deterrent. Amputation on the other hand would, without a doubt, be a very powerful and graphically visual deterrent. A few hard lads walking round the streets with no hands would certainly make the wannabes think twice.

Prison sentences where the offender presents a danger to society should be much longer but this need not necessarily mean an increase in the prison population if, as an alternative, prisoners were offered their freedom by agreeing to amputation. Faced with twenty or thirty years behind bars I'm sure many would go for this option. Being the hard man with no hands is not an option. The risk of violent offenders re-offending would thus be virtually eliminated. These harsh measures would undoubtedly reduce crime (and the number of active criminals) as the message quickly got across to would be offenders and, as in Saudi Arabia, would need to be resorted to less and less. Billions of pounds would be released into the economy. Social conditions could be improved and so could the quality of life for us all, including those who otherwise would have drifted into crime.

I can just hear the hysterical cries of anguish from the do-gooders and the civil liberties people whose methods I would point out, have already been given a more than fair trial and have failed. When are they going to realise that you can't make people good – but you can stop them from being bad? By all means devote resources to the rehabilitation of offenders but only to those who cooperate and are genuinely prepared to respond and not just pay lip service to con their gullible probation officers.

I do share the concerns of those who find the idea of capital punishment abhorrent. I wish there was another way. But unlike them, I am not deluded into thinking that there are alternative deterrents, ones that are both effective *and* affordable. They are quick to reject positive ideas yet are incapable of having any of their own. If there is an alternative to a physical deterrent, please let us hear what it is and let us implement it to see if it works because the existing measures are failing spectacularly. To all those dreamers and misguided optimists – those unrealistic people who are responsible for wasting billions of pounds of tax payers' money on lost causes – I would say, consider also for a moment the plight of the many, many thousands of innocent citizens who find themselves ill or old and who, for lack of funds, cannot get proper care for themselves and their families. Some are themselves victims of violent crime which has deprived them of their independence. The NHS is in a mess financially. This is down partly of course to incompetence but more funding would undoubtedly improve the lot of those poor folk, who are denied help and support on financial grounds. So on the one hand we spend many billions of pounds imprisoning and trying, usually unsuccessfully, to rehabilitate anti-social citizens while at the same time denying funds to those who behave themselves. It doesn't make sense.

"Let's put our old age pensioners in jail and the criminals in nursing homes," suggested one disgruntled cynic. "This way the OAPs would have access to hobbies and supervised walks, would receive free haircuts, prescriptions, dental and medical treatment and wheelchairs. They would receive money instead of paying it in fees. They would have constant video monitoring so they could get instant help if they fell or needed assistance. A member of staff would check on them every 20 minutes and if necessary would bring drinks, snacks and meals to their rooms. They could have family visits in a special suite built for that purpose and regular visits from members of the clergy, rehabilitation officers and volunteers from charity organisations. They would have access to well stocked libraries, fitness rooms, games rooms, outdoor exercise areas and gardens. Their rooms would be comfortable and secure and a PC, TV and radio could be supplied free on request. Their loved ones need not worry about the quality of their care since a zealous and efficient government inspectorate would regularly monitor their guardians should they fail to adhere to the strict code of conduct laid down. The criminals on the other hand would enjoy few of these amenities, pay £900 a month and have no hope of ever getting out!"

Our legal system is responsible for much of the problem. It functions primarily, not for the people it is supposed to protect, but for the benefit of the influential and powerful legal profession. When crime and litigation flourish, then so do the lawyers who will of course resist any change which will affect their pockets. Criminals should not be allowed to escape justice on technical points of law or procedure. Why should the taxpayer fund a system which permits this to happen? And isn't it about time the burden of proof of guilt be adjusted so that more emphasis is placed on proof of innocence? The Crown Prosecution Service is not exactly brilliant when it comes to presenting evidence and securing convictions so, heaven knows, they could do with a bit of help from the system. Let's make it easier to convict criminals and when they are convicted let us punish them in a way that will make sure they and others think twice before offending again.

There are of course risks, but surely it is preferable for a few to suffer the occasional miscarriage of justice in order to protect the many who would otherwise become victims. OK, the amputation idea may compromise genuine innocent amputees and be a little too much for a lot of people to stomach. I have always believed that putting forward ideas which are unlikely to be implemented isn't sensible. The time has got to be right. Mind you I would like to see the result of a public referendum on the matter.

So is there a gentler way forward? One which is nevertheless effective? Let us look at the case of our paedophile friend from the last Chapter who begged for castration. He is now banged up in prison costing us £1000 every week. Let us also look at the case of Miriam Foster who suffers from dementia and needs full time care which has been denied to her because it is too costly and because she has a husband who has sacrificed his own life to look after her. If the paedophile was castrated and released then £1000 a week would be freed up to provide care for Mrs Foster and respite for Mr Foster – two people who have been good law abiding tax paying citizens for many, many years. Let us now multiply this situation by our prison population of eighty thousand. How many Mrs Fosters and others suffering from lack of NHS funds would have their quality and expectation of life improved? Would it not be better too for the families of prisoners to have their castrated husbands and fathers back home? Why should they suffer? Would it not be better for the prisoners themselves to be free instead of spending years behind bars? But, as well as saving billions of pounds, the two big pluses would be that they would be incapable of fathering another generation of criminals and that others would not see them as heroes to be held in awe or feared for their glorified ex-con status, as is the case at present among the criminal fraternity. Instead they would be seen as sad eunuchs not to be emulated. That's what I call a deterrent – and there was another very important person who agreed with me. This is what he said:

If your right hand causes you to sin, cut it off and throw it away. It is better to lose one of your body parts than have your whole body go to hell.

Jesus Christ (Matthew 5:30)

Since my visit to the Unicorn Theatre in 2006, it has been shown in the United States that castration is in fact an effective way of stopping paedophiles from continuing to abuse. In fact it is suggested that it may be the *only* way, since people with such tendencies are no different to homosexuals and like them, cannot be "cured". Unnatural behaviour of this sort can be tolerated between consenting adults, but not when it harms innocent children. So, off with their balls I say!

Until the silent majority is provided with a voice none of these things will happen of course. One day surely they will wake up to the reality that no political party has the guts or the incentive to tackle the problems we face. There must be people out there with integrity who have not sold their souls to a political party and who are prepared to make a stand against the decadence we are slowly but surely witnessing. Roll on the revolution.

For holding such extreme views on the subject of punishment I have been branded an animal, an accusation I am happy to acknowledge and accept as a compliment. Unlike so-called civilised Homo Sapiens, we animals do not kidnap and exploit each other's' young for sexual gratification. Animals don't indulge in gratuitous violence or rape each other. And they don't have do-gooders to prevent them from protecting their young if some other creature threatens them.

We improve the behaviour of male horses by gelding them, so why not humans? To quote from an encyclopaedia: "**Geld** *vi. The elimination of hormonally-driven behaviour... allows a male horse to be calmer and better behaved, making the animal quieter, gentler and more suitable as an everyday working animal."* Isn't that precisely what we try to achieve through our prison rehabilitation service which costs the taxpayer billions of pounds and has only a marginal success rate?

Forty-Three

THE PATH

Opinions are like arseholes. We all have them,
but nobody wants to hear them.
D.A.

As I approach my three score years and ten
And gaze across the landscape of my life
I do not see one single rutted road
Cut stark and straight across its valleys wide
Nor many footprints trampled into mine

Instead I see a little trodden track
That winds with care along the banks of streams
That pauses in the evenings in the woods
And dances lightly through this Autumn scene
Led only by things I have done and seen

For I have always trod the lesser paths
That wind with care among the roots of trees
Then boldly step on mossy rocks
Which led me to the hilltop where I now see
Mine is a path worn true by only me

T HIS IS ANOTHER POEM given to me by Claire O'Byrne which I adapted for my seventieth birthday, on which occasion I think I was entitled to a bit of sentimentality.

It was on this birthday that I aged fifty years. It was the fairy's fault – the one who appeared at the foot of the bed and granted us a wish. My wife, who is ten years younger than me, wished for a luxury trip around the world with her husband and in a flash two tickets appeared on the bed. "What about *my* wish?" I shouted after the fairy before she flew out of the window. "I'd like to go around the world too, but I want to go with a younger woman, someone half my age." With a wave of her magic wand I became one hundred and twenty years old. The bitch. Fairies are female, of course. I should have realised that before trying to be so smart. Fortunately the spell only lasted a couple of hours and I was able to enjoy my big day. Neighbours and friends came round in the morning and I had a small family dinner party later in the day. As a surprise, Jim had flown back from South America and Tim had come over from Ireland. I received some nice presents that year including one from Liz, Andrew and Daisy which was quite unusual – a goat! I don't suppose I will ever get to see my pet unless I visit the Himalayas though. This apparently is the new trendy line in gifts. You give the money to Oxfam and they pay some third world peasant to buy and feed the beast. What a great idea. I hope this is the first step in reversing the ever snowballing materialistically competitive hell that Christmas has become, where we are expected to somehow buy bigger, better and more imaginative presents than the year before. Mind you, I can see this new innovative ecological trend in gifts getting out of hand too. It wouldn't surprise me if in a few years' time, perhaps for my eightieth, Liz buys me a herd of Wildebeest! Seriously though, I do hope this very practical and worthwhile idea catches on. I don't want to sound like an old scrooge, or one of those weirdoes who want to ban Christmas because it may offend non-Christians, but I would do away with Christmas cards. Multi-texts and e-mail messages are so much easier and environmentally friendly too. In 2006 I put a note in all the cards we sent, saying that we would be sending no more and that we would send the money to charity whilst at the same time doing our small bit to save the rain forests, a cause close to my heart following my visits to the Amazon jungle. As the poet Cesar Calvo wrote:

> *When the last tree has been cut down.*
> *When the last river has been contaminated.*
> *When the last fish has been caught.*
> *Only then will mankind learn that it cannot eat money.*

It was really nice to have all my family around me for this milestone birthday and the thought crossed my mind that perhaps the next time that happens I may not be taking an active part – unless they drop the coffin!

Funerals are things we don't like to talk about but for the sake of your family it is irresponsible not to make your wishes known before it is too late. I don't know how this topic cropped up at our "electric lunch" around the time of privatisation of the utilities, when lots of my friends and I had bought shares in the new private electricity companies and a few weeks later sold them and made a quick killing. We celebrated our good fortune with a long and splendid lunch at McCoy's prestigious

Cleveland Tontine Bistro near Northallerton. We each decided to choose a tune or song to be played at our funerals. The conversation started off on a serious note with good Catholics, Mick and Anne Coppinger, choosing *'Sweet Sacrament Divine'* and *'Bring Flowers of the Forest'*. Chris was undecided about her selection except that she definitely did *not* want *'The Old Rugged Cross'* because it would remind her of her dad and make her sad! She couldn't understand why we all laughed. From there it degenerated. Stevie Lowe's *'We'll Meet Again'* and Chris Manson's *'I'm in Heaven'* were among some of the corkers which followed. I chose from the musical Oklahoma *'Oh What a Beautiful Morning, Oh What a Beautiful Day. I've Got a Beautiful Feeling Everything's Going My Way'*. That should give the mourners a laugh. Patsy of course had to go one better. He wants his funeral service at the Crematorium and he wants them to play *'Come on Baby Light My Fire'*.

I don't want my family to be sad but I know they'll probably choose something from Goran Bergovic's *Music for Weddings and Funerals* like we did for my mam's funeral, or perhaps that very moving and appropriate Kathryn Jenkins song 'Time to Say Goodbye' – a real tear jerker if ever there was one! Plenty of time to think about that, though. There's still lots of life in the old dog and I reckon I'm fitter than many guys younger than me, though I realise this won't always be the case and that eventually I will have to slow down and lead a less active life if I want to reach a hundred, at which age, according to George Burns, you've made it, because not many people over that age die. Only wine improves with age but then only if it is made with good grapes. *"They"* say that wisdom comes with age. I hope so, but the only thing that for certain comes, is wrinkles.

Although I really enjoyed my big day I wasn't too dismayed when it was all over and I could get on with forgetting how old I was and getting on with my life – a life of new experiences. *"Yesterday is history. Tomorrow is a mystery. Today is a gift to enjoy."* There is a sure-fire way to recognise when old age catches up with you. You make a point of telling people how old you are, hoping they will be surprised and tell you that you don't look it. I'm not there yet.

Having lived through seventy years of history you are bound to draw some conclusions from events which have occurred during your lifetime, and to accumulate quite a few opinions on a wide range of matters. The beauty of writing a book is that you can express your thoughts and opinions without being interrupted or contradicted. Your readers unfortunately must hear them if they want to read your book.

During my lifetime I have seen much progress, particularly in the fields of medicine, communication, travel and technology. In the developed world a huge choice of consumer goods now exists but this has resulted in a craving for quite unnecessary and useless material possessions fed by persuasive and often wildly misleading advertising. Multi-million pound businesses have sprung up selling us things we didn't need before and are now persuaded we can't live without. Great wealth has been created in stark contrast to world poverty which still exists on a huge scale. The gap between rich and poor is wider than at any time in history. This gap is wider in Britain than in any other European country despite years of so called Socialist rule. I don't suppose it would have been any different under the Conservatives – just a little less hypocritical. Failure to tackle world poverty will be the historians ultimate indictment of the twentieth century – and probably the twenty first.

The inevitable consequence of a "must have" consumer society like ours is an increase in crime. The more things there are to steal the more thefts there will be. The poorest people on the planet, those living in remote regions, don't steal from each other. Sadly we seem to have created a "civilisation" which tolerates a state of affairs in which its old people (and many not so old) are frightened to walk our streets. In broad daylight in a busy shopping area my own eighty five year old mother was mugged and hospitalised. Why don't we get angry enough to force government to act? Why don't we take to the streets and demonstrate our anger? There are plenty of demos from minority interest groups yet we meekly accept the unacceptable, thereby allowing our politicians to escape their responsibility on major issues. Instead they indulge themselves in relatively trivial matters. Matters about which few of us give a damn. For example, a mere seven hours was devoted to debating whether we should go to war and kill tens of thousands of innocent human beings, including our brave servicemen, yet *seven hundred hours* of parliament's time were wasted in deciding how a handful of farmers should be allowed to kill a few foxes!

Have our politicians nothing better to do? It infuriates me that with so much poverty in the world and so much crime on our streets politicians are allowed to indulge their tiny minds with frivolities like this. They must be ousted from their privileged status and replaced by people who have their priorities right and with the intelligence and capability to take meaningful action. They have enjoyed their cosy zones for too long.

On the subject of cosy zones, my financial adviser Nick Matthews was fined £75 by a Council official for dropping a cigarette in Peterborough railway station. A stranger to the town, he was unaware of the Council's zero tolerance policy towards litter. An easy target, you might say. I wonder whether the same zealous official had ever been on duty on a Friday or Saturday night in Peterborough town centre and been zealous enough to confront the local yobs and binge drinkers who disdainfully discard *their* fag ends, empty packets, cans, food cartons, snack wrappers and occasionally the contents of their stomachs!

Much about the two World Wars has already been written by historians but I believe they may, in years to come, record also another significant feature of the twentieth century and that is the progress made in eliminating racial discrimination – progress which is in danger of being disrupted by over zealousness. Attempts to enforce integration too quickly however will only hinder and delay the natural process. Passing laws to make us love each other do not work, especially if they are passed by people who command no respect from the overwhelming majority of the people. Such laws draw attention to and emphasise the differences in culture, colour and creed. They create more problems than they solve. I wish they would leave the development of intercultural and international entente cordiale to us, to our children and to our grandchildren. Presumably the object of the legislation is to ultimately bring about racial harmony. Yet at the same time government, anxious not to offend, authorises new separatist faith schools subsidised by taxpayers.

The purpose of education should be to impart knowledge, not the beliefs and opinions of narrow minded religious teachers.

Racist laws as existed in the USA and South Africa have no place in a civilised world. But nor do ill-conceived and hastily enacted anti-racist and similar laws, designed to make us think as the lawmakers want us to think. Opinions should be heard. Even those which may offend. No – *especially* those which may offend. Making them illegal is a dangerous path to tread. A free society is willing to accept new laws and regulations imposed upon it if they make sense, if they are fair and if people understand why they are necessary. Those who wish to impose them should surely be required to explain and justify their purpose. The politically correct brigade steadfastly and arrogantly refuse to do so. Nobody knows who they are. They are not prepared to stand up and be counted, preferring to introduce their ideology by stealth and anonymity knowing full well that it would not stand up to reasonable scrutiny and democratic debate and would be rejected by the overwhelming majority of the people. A million laws will not stop me disliking a person whatever his colour, class, culture, political persuasion or religion. Nor will they force me to like him. Quite the opposite, probably. I will choose to like who I like and so will everyone else. So, you interfering busybodies stop trying to justify your existence, concentrate on sorting yourselves out before you tell us how we should think and behave. You are a threat to Britain's culture and to its tradition of freedom of speech and thought. We must all resolutely ignore rules and if necessary, break laws which are introduced against the will of the people and designed to restrict our freedom of thought and expression. "If you go to the zoo, always take something to feed the animals," said Forrest Gump, "even if there is a sign saying don't feed the animals. Remember that the animals didn't put up the sign."

Most reasonable people will accept that immigration can be desirable and even necessary. Most immigrants, their children and future generations settle into their new country, accept its values and respect its laws and beliefs. They enrich its culture and, with their enterprise and skills, its economy. The women, or most of them, bring colour to our streets with their bright traditional saris, etc. Others however do the opposite, dressed entirely in sombre black burkas which I find a bit creepy. I think they are trying to make a statement, but whether this is to say they are holier or uglier than their sisters we will never know. Alas, their contribution has been somewhat devalued by those ethnic British citizens whose allegiance continues to lie elsewhere. The existence of many thousands who fall into this category places an enormous burden on the country's resources. The sheer number of Al Qaeda sympathisers among the UK Muslim population, for example, makes the task of our security forces both difficult and costly.

In the nineteen-sixties, instead of a sensible policy of selective and controlled immigration, a few powerful and influential politicians, contrary to the wishes of the vast majority of its indigenous citizens, indiscriminately opened Britain's doors to all and sundry. This, we were led to believe at the time, was inspired by philanthropic principles. The concept of racial and cultural integration is indeed a noble one, but many years later reports emerged which suggested that the influx of three million immigrants may have been motivated by political rather than humanitarian considerations. The Labour Party, which had offered a new life to these people, felt pretty certain that they would show their gratitude through the ballot box as Labour voters and thereby enable the party to cling on to power. What a disgraceful state of affairs! Historians may well say that this changed the face of Britain, its culture, its tradition and maybe its greatness. I hope not.

Societies should be allowed to evolve and not be re-engineered for selfish political expediency. If integration had been the purpose of wholesale immigration, particularly if it were predominantly from one particular culture, then surely those responsible must have considered the likelihood that this actually delays and possibly defeats the objective. Instead of adapting to a host country, alien cultures, if present in sufficient numbers, will choose to establish themselves as separate and segregated communities with no desire and little need to integrate, without which tension and mistrust is inevitable. I am pretty certain that the minds of the politicians involved at the time were so excited by the prospect of perpetual power, that they chose to ignore such considerations.

On the 20th April 1968 Conservative MP Enoch Powell, rather melodramatically but in hindsight not without some justification, made his famous speech on immigration in which he said, "As I look ahead I am filled with foreboding. Like the Roman I seem to see the River Tiber flowing with blood."

On the 7th July 2001 in Bradford, despite a demonstration planned by far right groups being called off, an almost exclusively Muslim crowd of hundreds of young men went on a twelve-hour orgy of destruction, robbery, looting, assault and arson on a scale never seen before in England. This carnage was directed against white owned businesses, property and people, causing £25 million damage and resulting in three hundred and twenty six police officers being injured and the arrest of two hundred and ninety seven mainly Asian men.

On the 7th July 2005 our neighbour and friend Sylvia Groves was in a corner shop in one of the ethnic areas of Middlesbrough. She was hidden from view behind some shelves and could not be seen from the door. A jubilant British citizen burst into the shop to tell his friend the shopkeeper that fifty-six of his fellow citizens had been killed in suicide bomb attacks on the streets of London. Then, noticing Sylvia's presence, they continued their rejoicing in Hindu – a rejoicing which was doubtless shared by many thousands of fellow British citizens. Not a very nice way to treat a country which opened its doors and welcomed you. Having said that, surely our stupid government should have known, like Enoch Powell, that if they invite millions of Muslims to live in Britain and then a few years later invade a Muslim country, then reprisals and blood on our streets was inevitable. Much of the blame for those deaths therefore, must lie at the door of our government.

The obdurate minds of those doctrinaire fanatical politicians and their supporters who were the architects of this divisive state of affairs are in denial and still stubbornly refuse to even contemplate the possibility that they may just have got it slightly wrong. Instead they insist that we must exercise tolerance towards those who would destroy us. They pass laws to suppress any demonstration of the anger and injustice felt by the indigenous population. They then react with furious perplexity when support increases for the BNP who would seek to rid Britain of people like the shopkeeper and his friend

I do not share the views of the BNP but I can understand why they are shared by an increasing number. What alarms me is that the vehemently anti-BNP people are in complete denial of the causes of the party's support. If anyone should be kicked out of Britain it should be the narrow-minded decision-makers who have created the kind of divisive Britain in which suspicion and resentment thrive and whose traditional values are being systematically eroded by people supported and encouraged by undemocratic government. These people accuse people who disagree with their views of racism. They fail to understand that the anger and resentment against immigrants is due not to their race, colour or religion, but to the do gooders' own determination to over-protect them and often to give them preferential treatment because they feel sorry for them.

My old friend Brian Sutherland owns a number of street houses which are rented out. There was a need for immigrant accommodation and the Local Authority offered to guarantee the rents if Brian agreed to house some of these unemployed immigrants, which he was happy to do. Until, that is, he was required to get rid of the perfectly adequate furniture and household goods which had been good enough for everybody else, but not it seems, for the immigrants who had to be supplied with brand new replacements.

I am told that a certain Town Council, anxious no doubt to cultivate the Muslim vote, instructed its traffic wardens not to issue tickets to motorists who parked their cars on double yellow lines in streets close to a mosque on Holy days.

More recently I read that in May 2010 Tohseef Shah spray painted a British War Memorial with "Islam will dominate. Osama is coming" He was fined £50 and walked free from court.

In November 2010 Emadur Choudhury burned a poppy during a two minute silence. He too was fined £50 and walked free from court.

In 2011 two men were sentenced to 12 months imprisonment for spray painting a poppy on a mosque.

It is not the fault of the immigrants that because of this inconsistent and clearly preferential treatment they find themselves the subject of hostility and resentment. The blame lies squarely on the shoulders of those, who in their eagerness to demonstrate how "good" they are, go overboard with their excessive "goodness" whether or not the recipients of their benevolence deserve it, need it or want it.

Here is an example of how desperate Local Authority do-gooders are to do good and the lengths they will go to to identify their "victims" on whom to practice their goodness. It is also a reason why our council taxes are so high. Ms Chow received a letter from her local council written only in Chinese, a language she doesn't speak. She had it translated and discovered that it was an invitation to some sort of Chinese women's support group. I quote from her e-mail to CAPC (The Campaign Against Political Correctness):

> *"I wondered how impaired they imagined Chinese women to be, if we needed to be herded together in a pigeon hole and 'helped'. It doesn't make sense. True equality will only come when we are allowed to be different and those differences no longer matter. Not when we are being treated as being the same as everyone else in our sub group and the differences to the 'majority' constantly emphasised. For those of us who have pursued equality for so many years, it is disheartening to see how little has been achieved. Equality is not political correctness. In a truly equal country, the best candidate gets the job even if it is the Anglo-Saxon chap. There is still a long way to go."*

Christmas has never been my favourite time of the year but almost everyone else in the country seems to enjoy it. Yet the PC brigade want to ban it or modify it on the grounds that it may offend other religions. No question of banning Ramadan in case it upsets Christians of course. Why? Do they know of any Christians who object to Ramadan? Do they know of any Sikhs or Muslims who object to Christmas? And if they do, is this tiny handful of bigots going to be allowed to spoil it for everyone else? The answer sadly is yes – unless we can somehow curb the power of those responsible. The Muslims I have spoken to actually look forward eagerly to Christmas, especially the taxi drivers who take advantage of the opportunity to charge higher fares!

"What are they going to ban next, snow?" was the resigned comment of a young mother in a south coast town when, probably in a fit of pique because they couldn't manage to ban Christmas, the Local Authority insisted that Santa Claus should dress in what they described as "authentic green" instead of red. Next we'll have the animal rights people joining in because Christmas is cruel to reindeers! And these fun-prevention officers are not just a phenomenon of the UK. In Germany a dog became another victim of political correctness when, following the arrest of its owner, it was taken into kennels – the canine equivalent of death row. The poor creature's crime? He was a Nazi sympathiser. His owner, who had what the authorities were completely devoid of – a sense of humour – had taught his pet to raise its paw to the command of Zeig Heil!

And once the zealots got their hands on Health and Safety they had a field day. The coffee ordered by my friend Judge Joe in Costa Coffee at Liverpool Street Station was served lukewarm. He sent it back and asked for a hot one. He got another warm one and was told by the waitress that this was the standard temperature for their drinks. Joe demanded to see the manager who explained that they were not allowed to use hot water for Health and Safety reasons. Yet their menus throughout the country advertise *hot* chocolate drinks which presumably can now be challenged under the Trades Description regulations. The UK is the only country in the world that puts up with this nonsense.

I used to think that the PC brigade were just a few harmless, well-meaning but stupid cranks who nobody would take seriously. But far from being harmless their power has grown alarmingly and they now pose a very serious and invidious threat to our freedom. If you are worried too, why not support CAPC. I joined and apart from doing my bit to eradicate PC, the campaign's website is a fertile source of (amusing? disturbing?) examples, information and views on the subject. Visit www.capc.co.uk

And just how far off from becoming a totalitarian state are we? This message should set our alarm bells ringing. It worried me.

> *"I discovered PC during my studies in the UK,"* wrote Peter Mosoriak a Slovakian student. *"At first I heard it I laughed at it. It reminded me of our own PC from iron curtain times. That time to be PC meant to be Party Correct. We could say or write whatever we wanted as long as it expressed the views of the Communist Party. What is going on in the UK is sad and scary at the same time. I hope it never comes to Slovakia. We don't want to lose our right to free speech again."*

We don't either Peter.

♣

I have a confession to make.

The story about the fairy wasn't true. If a real fairy offered me a wish, I would have asked to be a judge at a tribunal involving the paedophile from Chapter 41, the parents of the little girl he abused after being refused his request for castration and the people who were responsible for that decision. Would they be able to look those parents in the eye and justify it? If not, then the anger of those parents would be at least partly assuaged by the sentence I would pass on them, which would not be very pleasant! The sentence I would pass would be that the children of the do-gooders be taken away from them and given to a bunch of un- castrated paedophiles. I wouldn't enforce it of course but it would be nice to make them sweat for a while and give them a taste of what it feels like to be on the receiving end of their own apparent indifference towards the feelings of those who live in the real world and not the ivory tower one they inhabit, cocooned as they are in their ideological existence so remote from reality and public opinion.

Perhaps I may be able to impose such judgements of Solomon when I am a ruler in the Kingdom of God, which according to the Jehovah's Witnesses, because of my "born again" experience, is what I am going to be!

70th birthday group.
L to R: Liz, Jacob, the birthday boy, Daisy, Jim, Chris,
Andrew and Tim.

Forty-Four

RANDOM RECOLLECTIONS

It's a pleasure to share one's memories. Everything remembered is
precious. At least the past is safe – though we didn't know it at the time.
We know it now. Because it's in the past. Because we have survived.
Susan Sontag.

T O RECORD A LIFETIME of experiences in just a few chapters is an
impossible task, so as this literary journey reaches its conclusion, selected at
random from the memory bank are a few experiences I found particularly enjoyable,
amusing, embarrassing and scary.

I have been a big football fan all my life so let's start with my favourite match for
which there were quite a few contenders, including Sunderland's FA Cup run in 1973
and Boro's fantastic year in Europe and their victory over Bolton Wanderers at the
Millennium Stadium in 2004 to win their first bit of silverware, The Carling Cup. My
choice may surprise you but for all sorts of reasons I have selected a match which Boro
lost 0 – 1. It was at Stamford Bridge, Chelsea, a play off at the end of the 1987/88
season for promotion to the old First Division. Daughter Liz was living in Chelsea at
the time on a houseboat on the Thames and being able to visit her was one of the
reasons why the occasion was so special. Fourteen-year-old Tim and I drove down full
of eager anticipation and met up with Liz on her boat. I had taken the precaution of
getting three tickets for us in the family enclosure. The season was at an end and we
had been warned that there could be trouble, not only from the Chelsea fans but also
the hooligan element of other London clubs, notably Millwall, to whom the match
presented their last opportunity for three months to satisfy their craving for violence.
This was before all-seater stadiums, when football hooliganism was at its worst.
Twenty minutes or so into the match when a cross from the left shaved the Chelsea bar
we couldn't contain our disappointment and were instantly surrounded by a mob of
Chelsea meatballs. After what seemed like an age a policeman eventually appeared and
I demanded that he protected us. He didn't seem too interested in that idea and

suggested that for our own safety we should vacate our expensive reserved seats and transfer to the caged enclosure behind the goal which housed the main contingent of travelling Boro fans. The situation was pretty menacing and fearing for our safety I didn't argue with him. We tried to find our way there and in doing so ran the gauntlet through hundreds of hostile Chelsea fans who were attacking Boro fans as they too fled the stand trying to find their way into the enclosure with no guidance, help or protection from the police or stewards. It was chaos. Although crammed together and with poor viewing we were finally able to relax and enjoy the rest of the match with Joe and Dan Gilgan who we had literally bumped into. After the final whistle we had to survive another half hour or so of intimidation as somehow, hordes of baying cockneys (are we allowed to say that?) were allowed on to the field and confronted us. The police and the Chelsea stewards had absconded and only the effectiveness of the wire barrier prevented carnage. Our would-be attackers eventually tired of hurling and receiving verbal abuse and dispersed, leaving the coast clear for the players to come back out and enjoy the adulation of their rapturous fans. Yes, Boro had lost the match 0 – 1 but a 2 – 0 victory in the first leg at Ayresome Park meant promotion. The players did a strip tease and Tim caught one of Paul Kerr's socks which he treasured and still has to this day, sweat and all. It has never been washed.

The entertainment continued after the players went back to their dressing room. One Boro fan had somehow managed to scale the high barrier and was standing precariously on top of the fence waving his scarf and conducting the Red Choir which was still in high spirits and good voice. Quite harmless really, until a Chelsea steward put in an appearance and instead of trying to calm the situation down or keeping out of the way altogether, invited the Boro lad to jump down and fight. He duly obliged. Would this drunken Boro fan be a match for the bulky Chelsea steward? We did fear for him as the steward began to throw punches, each one of which was cleverly parried or avoided, causing the steward, who was now being jeered by thousands of hostile fans, to become more and more furious and reckless, still failing to connect with any of his punches. After what seemed like several minutes of humiliation the Boro lad coolly went on the offensive with a series of skilful left jabs. This lad could obviously box. He prolonged the steward's agony before flattening him with a perfect right hook to the noisy encouragement of us all. Before he could make his escape back into the bosom of his new admirers several other stewards arrived on the scene and marched him off. Heaven knows what happened to him at their hands once he disappeared from our sight. We had been treated to a double bill of sporting action. I wonder if anyone knows where I can contact our boxing hero. I would love to meet him and shake his hand. I later wrote a letter of complaint to the then Chelsea Chairman Ken Bates. I did get the courtesy of a reply even though it wasn't particularly helpful.

After the match we had a meal with Liz, made our farewells and drove back up north arriving home in the early hours. During the last few miles of the journey we listened to local radio. I'm sure many people in the area will remember Megamouth Stannich who hosted a late night programme in which people were invited to phone in and be insulted. Can you believe that the show was taken off the air because one listener complained that she had been insulted! Mind you, just like our Stamford Bridge hero, The Mouth didn't pull any punches. Anyway Tim decided to phone him and tell him about his day's experiences, suggesting that in future, before football matches, all those people who wanted to fight should be allowed on the field as part of the pre-match entertainment. The Mouth had never heard such a stupid and irresponsible suggestion since serious injury could be sustained – by the players slipping on the blood and tripping over the torn off limbs etc. A memorable trip indeed.

I did eventually lose much of my enthusiasm for what, quite unjustifiably, is called "the beautiful game." When oh when will they update some of the archaic rules and procedures – starting with sin bins?

There was an embarrassing moment, also involving Tim, in Brighton, where he was doing his Tourism and Travel course at Hove College. We had taken the opportunity, one of several, to visit him and sample the delights of this famous south coast resort. We were to subsequently stay in a nice apartment above the Metropole Hotel but on our first visit we opted for a guest house. We parked the car outside one with a Vacancies sign in the window but Chris – all dog as usual – wanted to stay in the car and left Tim and me to book in. Now Brighton is generally regarded as a gay friendly city – but not, as we were about to discover, by everybody. My request for a double room was met with a cool stare and "I'm sorry we have no vacancies". Irritated I said accusingly, "But your sign says you have." The man stood his ground and glanced from me to Tim and back again. The penny dropped. Hastily I appealed to him, explaining that the room was for my wife and me and that Tim was our son. He fixed my eyes with one of those "That's what they all say" stares. I couldn't get out of there quick enough.

Our garden is completely secluded and I liked nothing better on a warm summer evening than to sit on the veranda and enjoy the tranquillity of the garden in full bloom. One afternoon with the demands of young mouths to satisfy there was more than normal activity round the bird feeder hanging from one of the Rowan trees from which the feeder became dislodged and crashed to the ground breaking in half the protective terracotta weather cover. It looked like a fairly straightforward repair job but the superglue hadn't been used for some time and stubbornly refused to be squeezed through its nozzle, so I poked a hole in the tube. This time the contents were only too eager to surrender themselves and spurted out onto my exposed todger. In the warm weather I often sat out in the garden FKK, as the Germans say. The spontaneous reaction when you spill something is to wipe it away which is what

I tried to do. Now superglue is pretty powerful stuff and very efficient and it had other ideas. My finger, in fact two fingers, and my todger then became firmly and I feared permanently attached to each other. What a predicament. What would I say when I got to A&E? How would I drive the car? How would I get my trousers on? What would people think about an old bloke walking around with his hand inside his flies? Might I be arrested for indecency? I had on my hands not only an intractable penis but a seriously critical dilemma. After liberal applications of Cussins Imperial Leather soap and WD40 I did manage to retrieve one finger and an hour later the remaining hairy finger plus a bit of scrotal skin was eventually prised away and what could have been the mother of all embarrassing moments was averted.

I'm a fairly pragmatic kind of guy but there have been a few occasions when I've been really scared. Once, when the door slammed behind me, I was locked in a dark room at my golf club and failing to find a light switch or open the door I panicked and hammered on the door thinking that someone would be on hand. After several minutes and in a state of some agitation, I was rescued by the assistant pro Jonathan Lupton. It was quite embarrassing too. My playing partner had hired a buggy and Paul Radigan who had a key to the trolley store had suggested I leave my trolley inside instead of taking it back to the car. There was a stupid TV programme "I'm a Celebrity Get Me Out of Here" running at the time and that's what I said to Jonathan when, puzzled by the noise, he eventually opened the door for me. It gave him a laugh and the rest of the lads too.

I should have been scared when my Lotus X1 Sports Car crashed into a concrete ditch at Wallsend Sprint in 1963 but adrenalin takes over at times like that. I was more scared afterwards thinking about what might have been. It didn't stop me from driving at ten tenths in subsequent events. There isn't much point in motor racing if you don't.

The woods and the grounds of Morton House were an ideal habitat for its colony of pheasants provided they were not disturbed. I had occasion one day to threaten two locals with trespass when I saw them approaching the woods with shotguns. The moral of the story I am about to tell is that circumstantial evidence can be unreliable. A few days after my confrontation with the gunmen I got up from my desk and as I passed the window which overlooks the grounds, it suddenly shattered. *As retribution for spoiling their sport, the bastards are trying to shoot me!* was the first and only thought that flashed through my mind. On all fours so as not to again present my would-be assassins with a target, I crawled back to my desk and still crouching down lifted the phone and dialled the police. When firearms are involved police response time is normally instant. On this occasion they took ages. I had gone down to reception and told them what had happened and asked them to call me when the police arrived. Back in my office I poured myself a brandy and slumped on the settee. Puzzled by a strange noise from behind a cabinet I investigated and discovered a badly shaken pheasant cowering against the wall. The reality dawned on me. The poor creature, obviously confused by the reflected image of the sky and trees in the window (it was a bright sunny day), had assumed it was flying into the woods and the force of the impact had propelled it through the glass. I had a lot of explaining to do. I felt a complete fool. The gunmen, who claimed that they only shot rabbits, were interviewed by the police and apologised. As a gesture, they made a contribution to ROSPB but I wasn't convinced. Something had disturbed and panicked the bird. I took it to the RSPCA and I'm told that it recovered fully.

That scary experience doesn't compare with the terror of Peruvian airline TANS Lima-Iquitos Flight 581 on 23rd January 2003. We had returned to Lima after visiting Arequipa, Cusco and Machu Picchu and were staying at Hotel El Castellano in Mira Flores. When I say *we*, I include Chris, her niece Leigh and three sons Jim, Tim and Jacob, who was suffering from severe toothache which needed urgent attention. Lima being the capital city, it made sense to find a dentist there, so the girls flew on to Iquitos and left me and my three sons behind. We had booked tickets on an Aero Continente flight for 22nd January. Our family dentist in the UK, John Lyne, is young, highly qualified and inspires confidence. His staff are professional and his surgery is pleasant and boasts the latest in dental equipment and technology. The first dentist we visited in Lima was John's antithesis on all counts. Jacob refused to sit in his chair which was reminiscent of World War One. The next dentist we saw had been recommended by Jim's then girlfriend Kati. His set up was an improvement in only one respect. He was young. Again Jacob declined treatment, preferring to put up with the pain and discomfort of his toothache rather than submit to third-world butchery. I don't quite know how it happened but we ended up having lunch with the young dentist and his fiancée at a nearby fish restaurant which he had recommended – and with justification. Apparently it was the seventh anniversary of their engagement and, he informed us, they always celebrated each one in style. They had been engaged, we learned, for seven months, not seven years as we had assumed. They held monthly celebrations. It was a great lunch. The spontaneous ones usually are the best.

On the eve of our planned departure to Iquitos I was dragged by the lads to a nightclub and didn't get to bed until two o'clock in the morning. They arrived back at the hotel two hours later, one with a girl in tow. I won't say which one. Our already crowded room had an extra guest for a few hours. With a struggle I roused them the following morning and stressed that we must leave no later than 10.30 to catch the plane. It was like organising schoolchildren. First one disappeared – to do some last minute shopping, he told me later. Then another left urgently to find a Farmacia. The reason for the urgency, I later discovered, was to buy some morning-after pills for the girl! The third son then left to look for the first one, leaving me completely stressed out standing in the hotel foyer with our taxi waiting outside. To put the tin hat on it, the taxi broke down on the way to the airport and we missed our flight. The only flight available the following day was with TANS Airline which operated with ancient ex-military planes and whose safety record left much to be desired. Their latest incident had occurred only a few weeks earlier when one of their fleet had crashed in the Andes killing forty-seven passengers and the crew.

Normally when boarding an aeroplane you don't take much notice of its condition but on this occasion because of the TANS reputation we couldn't help closely scrutinising the aircraft and we didn't like what we saw. Tim in particular, who isn't fond of flying at the best of times, was all for aborting the flight but with the girls anxious for us to return to Iquitos we reluctantly boarded. Our seats were directly over the starboard wing. Only a few minutes after take-off Tim noticed smoke streaming out of the starboard engine and immediately pressed the call bell. By the time the stewardess had responded the engine was on fire and we could feel the heat through our seats and the side of the plane. I cannot describe the feelings going through my mind at that moment. I don't think Chris could cope with losing one of us – but all four! It didn't bear thinking about. Yet I could think about nothing else. *"Fuego, fuego!"* one of the passengers was yelling hysterically. The stewardesses were floundering too. One of them, incredibly, started to distribute newspapers – probably to wipe our backsides it occurred to me later. We were certainly shitting ourselves at the time! I can't remember what we were saying to each other. Tim in particular was in quite an agitated state. There was no reassuring announcement from the flight deck which probably meant, I concluded, that the pilot was either concentrating all his efforts into achieving a crash landing – or he didn't want to tell us we were all about to die. Why the hell was he continuing to fly towards the Andes where the other TANS aircraft had crashed only a few weeks earlier? What chance would the survivors have, if there were to be any, if they were stuck thousands of feet up a mountain range? Why on earth didn't he turn back and try to land in the sea or at Lima which after all can't be that far away since we had only taken off a short while earlier. At least there would be a rescue team and a fire fighting crew there. These and dozens of other thoughts were spinning through my mind when, after what seemed an age, the pilot did turn back and started his descent into Lima. We took up brace positions for the landing. The tension and the complete silence gave the whole thing an eerie feel. I suppose we were all deep in our own thoughts, or saying our prayers.

All credit to the pilot who, in the circumstances, performed an exceptionally good landing. We descended the steps and walked quickly across the tarmac in silence. Jim was the first one to speak. "You must be bloody joking!" – or something like that – he yelled in Spanish at the TANS rep who was calmly attempting to hand out replacement tickets for their next flight!

With only a few days of the holiday left, I decided to stay in Lima. I wasn't ready to face another flight to Iquitos. The lads did return there but not by air. They took a coach to Tarapoto and a boat from there – an uncomfortable and lengthy, but considerably less traumatic journey.

I had a bit of a scare once in Menorca too when we hired a boat from our resort to visit Colin Johns, an ex-insurance broker from North Ormesby who sold his business to open a bar in Cala'n Porter. On the return trip the boat started to ship water and we were in grave danger of sinking completely when a dinghy came to our rescue. You don't enjoy life without taking a few risks along the way.

Do I have any regrets in my life? Well yes, of course I do, but what's been done can't be undone, and what hasn't been done cannot now be done. I suppose I shouldn't have got married in 1964. But then I wouldn't have had Liz. I suppose I could have been a better husband, a better father and a better son. I would have liked to have gone to university but I did OK anyway but I would have loved to have been able to communicate better in other languages to experience more fully the delights of other cultures on my travels. I would have liked to have lived in the country but my wife was scared of mice. I wish I'd listened to her when she warned me about certain people.[7] I wish I hadn't been so generous in giving away shares in my business to certain people, some of whom did little or nothing to deserve them and who later behaved disgracefully towards me. I wish I hadn't become a Name at Lloyds and having achieved all I really wanted to in the insurance business I wish I had sold out earlier instead of carrying on for the benefit of others. I would have enjoyed putting my business experience to use in other, new, directions. But on the whole life hasn't treated me too badly. I've had plenty of happy times. So what was the happiest day of my life? I really couldn't point to one single day that sticks out above all others, but I know someone who is in no doubt on that score and whose eloquent recollection of it I could not hope to match. I will let Patsy have the final say. This is how he described it to me:

> *"The occasion was blessed with a perfect Spring day. We decided to walk. The journey was only a short one and the exercise was welcome. David and I had been reminiscing over more than a few drinks until the early hours. We were friends from schooldays and before David had emigrated we had been business partners. He was my best man. He had flown all the way from Canada to be with me on this very special day. We took a short cut through the fields to the village green, where the daffodils in their prime and majestic splendour extended their friendly greetings, nodding it seemed, their approval and encouragement as they swayed in the breeze – a gentle zephyr with scarcely the energy to distort their images in the nearby duck pond. I think Spring as it emerges from the dark cloak of winter is truly the most magnificent season of the year, don't you?"*

---

[7] See Volume II.

Without waiting for me to vocalise my opinion on the subject Patsy pressed on. *"As we continued I was acutely aware too of those unmistakeable sounds of spring – the buzz and chatter of insects and birds as if they too were sharing with me an optimism for the future, boldly proclaiming their presence with calls of love. Perhaps, like me, excited with the delights of new partnerships in prospect. Save for a scattering of wispy intruders the sky was clear and the sun's warmth, though pleasant, when coupled with my exertions, did cause me a little discomfort. Why on these occasions are we expected to wear smart new leather shoes and suits? I would have preferred something casual. Something more cavalier. Something to reflect my buoyant mood. But protocol must be observed. Finally we stood before the imposing portals of Saint Cuthberts and as I passed through I made a conscious effort to subdue an inclination to manifest outwardly the elation which consumed my whole being. Jumping for joy is something you just don't do in churches. Such occasions demand a certain dignity. Plenty of time for celebration later. A new life beckoned. But formalities had first to be observed. As Doreen arrived at the altar the organ's final note faded softly, usurped by an ethereal aura of solemnity as the priest delivered his benedictions. I edged closer to Doreen and for the benefit of those present, leaned across and kissed her lightly on the cheek. **Then I closed the coffin lid.** "*

This story provides a fitting opportunity to finally close the lid also on this narrative, rather than conclude with an Epilogue as most books of this kind do. This must wait a few years. The title 'Epilogue' suggests finality, but how can one record the final moments of one's life, or the early ones for that matter? When does one choose to write the last word? If I am lucky there may well be many more noteworthy experiences to record, but on the other hand, for all I know, the onset of dementia may be imminent and the rest of my life dull, boring, even brief. Besides, memory is an unstable and degenerate entity, particularly during those periods close to the extremities of its cycle – periods immediately after the cradle and before the crematorium! The first because the cerebral computer hasn't yet been programmed, and the second when overcapacity diminishes its capacity.

On that depressing note I will conclude this manuscript, but first a word about my uncle.

One day my uncle's car phone rang.

It was my auntie urgently warning him to take care because there was a madman speeding down the A19 going the wrong way.

"It's not just one car," said my uncle, "It's hundreds!"

My uncle survived the accident and a few years later died peacefully in his sleep.

I want to die peacefully just like my uncle – *not screeching in terror like the passengers in his car!*

THE END

Forty-Five

THE ALBUM

Paternal grandfather Richard James Arnott (left) with his best man, who nobody had met or seen before and was never seen again! Believed to have been one of Richard's Masonic brethren. C.1905.

Maternal grandfather Joseph Gardner (left) with one of his six brothers, John, Thomas Stephenson and John Williams. C.1898.

Joseph Gardner (second right, seated) and fellow cycling club members. C. 1892.

Margaret Mulcaster (later Gardner). C.1919.

Tommy and Beatrice betrothed, 1935. L – R. Elizabeth Arnott (nee McLeod), George McLeod Arnott, Dad, Aunty Peggy, Mam, bridesmaids – cousins Evelyn Simpson and Mamie Mulcaster, Joseph Gardner and Margaret Gardner (nee Mulcaster).

Dad's eldest brother James. C.1942.

My grandmother. August 1928.

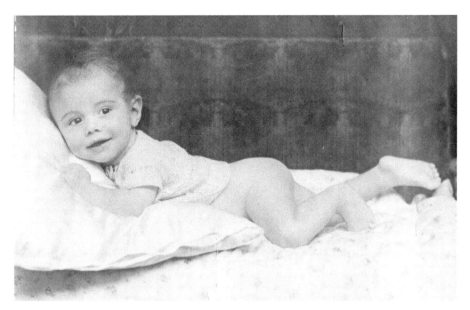

Me – in what my mother called my shirty willy!

Dad with cousin Neil and me outside the Bishop's House. C.1939.

**My parents in law, George Marshall and Vera Tennick on their wedding day.
24th April 1943.**

Captain George Marshall and Wolsingham FC. C.1950.

Bill Limbert and I at The Wainstones on the Cleveland Hills, with Madge Jackson, Pat Cronin and Jazz Howells. C.1954.

**The groom with wedding guests Beatrice, Tommy, Auntie Ginny, Uncle Edward
and Auntie Mary outside St Mary Magdelens Church, Seaham Harbour.
1st August 1964.**